Working Inside Out

WORKING INSIDE OUT

Tools for Change

Margo Adair

Illustrated by JOAN CAROL

WINGBOW PRESS

Wingbow Press books are published and distributed by Bookpeople, 2929 Fifth Street, Berkeley, California 94710

Library of Congress Cataloging in Publication Data

Adair, Margo, 1950–
    Working Inside Out.

    Bibliography: p.
    1. Meditation.   2. Spiritual life.   3. Success.
I. Title.
BL627.A3   1984   158'.12   84-22912
ISBN 0-914738-50-4

2nd printing, March, 1986

Book design by Janet Wood, Berkeley.
Typeset by *turnaround,* Berkeley.
Cover Design by Margo Adair, San Francisco.
Cover Illustration by Joan Carol, Oakland.
Printed by George Banta Co., Menasha, Wis.

To Casey

Contents

The beginning of the book addresses how the outside of all of us has affected the inside of each of us, and how we can participate in our own inner world to begin to solve our personal problems.

The end of the book addresses how the inside of each of us affects the outside of all of us, and how working on the outside changes us on the inside—each process necessary for resolving social problems—in other words, how the outside has moved in on all of us, and how to move our reawakened insides out.

Chapter One

Inner Consciousness: Reawakening

Everybody wants change nowadays—that's one thing we all have in common. No one likes the state of the world, and hardly anyone really feels good about the state of their lives either. People may point to different things as being the cause of their malaise, but no one anymore would say everything is okay the way it is. Our lives tend to be so harried we've lost access to the enormous potential to create change that lies within each of us. Instead, stress has become the number one killer. This book is not just for stress reduction, although that's one of its more important side effects. My purpose is to awaken the creative resources within each of us so we can take charge of our lives.

When you come to have a better understanding of the nature of consciousness, of the imagination, and creativity itself, and the relation they all have to the world around you then you won't feel so powerless—so buffeted about by all the turmoil. Instead you can tap the powers within you and fully employ your creativity to deal with the issues more effectively. When you are not at the will of all that's going on about you, you will be free to participate with clarity and vision—a very different feeling from that of being under pressure and constantly on the run just to keep up.

Intuition is fully neglected in our technological society, whereas it can actually provide the map for each of us to overcome the limitations in our lives whether they be discarding bad habits, healing health problems, enriching relationships, or even grappling with the massive political issues of our day. You need not hope to get only an occasional glimpse of what your intuition knows, instead you can learn to tap its power at will and you'll discover that it gives you invaluable guidance no matter what your concern is. This book will teach you how to do just that—how to use the intuitive and imaginative powers within you for whatever your particular problems.

Creativity, intuition and healing powers originate in our innerconsciousness. It is the home of the collective knowledge of the human race. It is our innerconsciousness that experiences wholeness, that feeling of being "at one," which is at the heart of all spirituality, the merging of the existential "I" into something greater.

DEVELOPMENT OF APPLIED MEDITATION

In 1972 I was catapulted into the realms of consciousness where my work has been focused ever since. Until then I had pretty much taken my mind for granted, and my attention was focused solely on the external world.

Twelve years ago a friend told me about his participation in a series of guided fantasy exercises developed by José Silva. What particularly caught my interest was his description of the last one, called "doing cases," which consisted of being given only the name, age, and address of someone you knew nothing about, with the expectation that you would describe this person in full detail. As I was brought up in an academic home where reason was paramount, I had always thought that if psychic powers existed at all, only strange characters born every few hundred years possessed them. Intrigued, I joined a women's group that was going to try this same set of exercises. We did them without any prior explanation. When it came time for me to do a case, though I felt I couldn't, I went ahead and tried. I relaxed, and a woman gave me the full name and address of a friend of hers named Martha. I proceeded to talk about Martha for forty-five minutes, feeling all the time as if I was simply making up a story. It felt as ordinary as anything that had ever gone on in my mind. When I was finished, I opened my eyes and the woman told me that everything I had said about Martha was true. I had accurately described her character and physical appearance, including a grey print dress that buttoned up the back, and black "old-lady" shoes with brown laces. I'd seen black spots on her stomach and a chalky substance at the base of her spine. It turned out that she had an ulcer and cancer of the spine, and that she did wear that particular dress all the time. My friend said that everything was correct except that she couldn't understand my description of the shoes because Martha had always loved to wear the latest style. Two weeks later I ran into my friend and she told me that the last time she'd seen Martha she was wearing "old-lady" shoes—black with brown laces!

I was awed by the experience: my mind had powers I had never dreamed of! What was so overwhelming was how *ordinary* it felt while I was describing the case. It was not as if a thunderbolt had come out of the sky illuminating the truth. To this day I view having successfully done that case as the most profound experience of my life. I knew I wasn't one of those weird people born every two-hundred years; I considered myself rather ordinary. Everybody else in the group was also successful at doing these readings.

Having done this case, I was *obliged* to pay attention to what went on in my mind, for all I had done that day was make up a story—simply used my imagination—and yet everything I had said matched the reality of Martha. As a result I realized that my imagination was real—as real as the ground we stand on. The techniques of Silva Mind Control teach that if you imagine something, you can create it; so I started to direct my imagination toward changes I wanted to make, and that worked too! For the first time I began to pay attention to my mind and direct my imagination. I found that I had powers, which, when applied, changed every aspect of my life. I moved from being acted upon to being an actor; my world view swung around 180 degrees.

I realized that if I could do it, anyone could. This lead to my beginning to develop a theory of consciousness, and starting to teach Applied Meditation. Ever since then, I have used a similar exercise in my teaching and have guided hundreds of people through the process of doing cases successfully—all of them, no doubt, ordinary people. I still don't understand why it works, but the point is, it does. Somehow our minds have access to information beyond our experience—the implication of this is awesome. Call it the collective unconscious, call it God, but whatever you call it, what is important to realize is that we all have access to it. We all have powers residing within us that go virtually untapped. This is why I say that our innerconsciousness is the home of the collective knowledge of the human race.

It is often more comfortable to avoid the truth, however it is well known that the condition of the world needs to be changed if we are going to secure our future. Repossessing our innerconsciousness will heal our alienation thus overcoming the fragmentation of our society. Living in supportive communities, we can then work creatively together to put the world into some kind of liveable order.

HOW TO USE THIS BOOK

This book provides safe structures to explore the vast realms within you. The training gives you a language to communicate with your deeper self as well as providing methods to employ it for problem solving. This will rekindle your intelligence. The guided meditations create a clear and simple navigational course through your inner dimensions so you can use the resources available within you to improve the quality of your life; this is Applied Meditation. The purpose of this book is to help you to be more effective in making the changes you want. Whether that be in your health, your behavior, your relationships, your work. Whatever it is, your inner-consciousness can help you.

The book discusses the subjective—what's going on inside each one of us—our consciousness—as well as the objective—what's going on in the world around us. And it clarifies the interplay between them, where the limits and the potential lie, both inside and outside. In gaining a deeper understanding of each, we come to know where to apply our energy to improve our lives. Because the book covers such a wide range, it could be used solely to shed light on understanding the *nature* of consciousness and the world around us. If this is your interest you may want to read only the text. On the other hand if your interest lies in gaining a framework for exploring your deeper powers to help you in your life, you might want to work only with the meditations.

REPOSSESSING OUR INNERCONSCIOUSNESS

Innerconsciousness—our deepest processes—has been fully mystified; our inner levels are contemptuously dismissed. We are taught to believe that everything is rational and logical, that whatever is "out of control" originates in our "subconscious," and that if psychic powers exist at all, at best they are bizarre, and at worst "evil." We are led to believe that the output of our imagination is, by definition, unreal, that "daydreaming is a waste of time," and that if you can't explain *why* you know something you don't really know it.

For all intents and purposes the very ground of our being has been ripped off. But just because we don't pay attention to our inner processes doesn't mean that they are inactive and have no effect on our lives. The very nature of innerconsciousness is that it is suggestible and programmable. It is predominant whenever we are relaxing. In consequence we are lulled by television, teachers, Madison Avenue, and all the everyday propaganda of our society. We think that we're consciously making choices but everyday, as long as we do not repossess our inner levels, we act more and more like robots. To be autonomous, not automatons, we must reclaim the levels that have been programmed and choose what we want to store there.

The content of your inner awareness regularly seeps into your daily experience; it resides just below your rational surface. However, most of us have never learned to recognize it or know its powers, much less be able to tap it at will. Instead we have been taught to be suspicious and discount it whenever it peeps its head above the surface. We have a rich language to enable us to use our rational consciousness, but virtually no language for tapping the creative and insightful powers of innerconsciouness.

As long as we do not repossess these parts of ourselves we will be increasingly relegated to leading non-creative lives. It is no coincidence that our inner realms have been denied—they tell us too much. We've been taught not to question the status quo, distrusting our own knowingness, our own intelligence, and instead we look to authorities to resolve our problems and tell us what is good for us. (Common sense ain't so common anymore.) We've come to believe that they certainly know better than we do: when we get sick we see a doctor, when we have disputes we see a lawyer, when our families are in turmoil we see a social worker. It is our deepest selves that experience our heartfelt connections with one another; when we are alienated from each other, it's because we are also alienated from our deepest selves. We often don't know our neighbors, much less how to work together to solve the problems that arise in our everyday lives. Suspicious of our inner experience, we find ourselves full of suspicion for one another. We are unable to live together with open hearts, enriching one another's lives; instead we find ourselves competing for our individual positions in the world. When we resurrect our innerconsciousness, we will have regained our own creative resources for solving our problems, relying on ourselves, our families and our communities, thereby depending less and less on the established, licensed professionals (planned obsolescence). The alienating effect of suspicion will be replaced by the connectedness of trust.

Instead, denying our own creativity, we have become a captive audience for the entertainment industry whose programming clogs the channels to our deeper experience. We're discouraged from daydreaming—instead we go to the movies or watch television. We get it coming and going. Not only have we lost access to our own creativity, but the very nature of popular entertainment is such that we relax, become passive, and it is done to us. Compounding this is the fact that this relaxed state of being is programmable, suggestible; so we uncritically accept the messages conveyed through the media. We find ourselves wanting and buying the latest gadget, the newest "improved" remedies, and impractical automobiles. We have been transformed into a consumer society where enjoyment comes from things rather than from each other. All this 'propaganda has been shoveled into our depths, blocking the channel to our inner processes and suffocating our creativity.

It is of paramount importance to understand that we *always* act out of the messages of our innerconsciousness. We move through our daily activities in terms of our past experiences which are the building blocks of our personal belief systems; our belief systems are the glasses through which we each view the world, and our behavior is always in accordance with our own beliefs. Everyone has had the experience of knowing something, but acting to the contrary—thinking one thing yet doing another—and then later hitting oneself over the head saying, "How could I? I know better than that." The cliché, "I just don't have it down yet" is literally true. Your knowledge is intellectual, rational, and does not yet reside in your inner levels where the mass of your memories are stored.

Beliefs are the way we organize our memories into our personal definitions of how the world ticks; they are the assumptions out of which we operate. They stem either from continual repetition of social messages (programming) or from traumatic incidents. For example, if you find yourself nervous every time you get in a car because you once had an automobile accident (belief: cars = danger), you may try to reassure yourself by reasoning, "It's okay, the brakes have been fixed." To no avail—this doesn't relieve your tension. Or if you are a woman who has learned that by being assertive you will avoid many problems, yet you find yourself responding passively (belief: "Nice girls aren't aggressive"). In each case you are acting out of your stored beliefs. These examples illustrate a dynamic operative in all of us when we find ourselves behaving in ways we know are inappropriate.

You needn't wait months or years before you get the new behavior down. Since you behave out of your inner messages all you need do is to insert the desired message in an inner level. (Much of Applied Meditation can be likened to the techniques of hypnosis, which work with these same dynamics.) There is no reason to be anxious about learning these techniques. It is a fact that no one's psyche can be coerced. Because your innerconsciousness is suggestible if you want to get some new knowledge down, you simply need to put it in at *that* level. Directing your imagination while in a meditative state will enable you to do so. You will find yourself able to act in accordance with your choices and no longer a victim of thinking one thing and doing another.

Your innerconsciousness is not by nature inaccessible or far away. It is always right there just under the surface. Whenever you are relaxing or doing something rhythmic or automatic—not using your rational mind to decide what to do next—your innerconsciousness has moved from its usual position below the surface to that part of you that is predominantly present. But the problem is that because of the prevailing attitudes it is at these very times that you ignore or discount your awareness. So that your innerconsiounsness has become, for all practical purposes, inaccessible and it is only natural for you to be a victim of unwanted behavior. Whether it is the result of a traumatic incident in your past (car accident) or from the programming by the propaganda of our society (women are passive), you will continue to be a victim as long as you do not repossess your own innerconscousness.

If you have never taken control and chosen what to keep in your innerconsciousness, then it has simply become the accumulation of *everything* you've ever experienced. Imagine what it would be like if you never threw out any of your trash. It wouldn't take long to accumulate more plastic packaging than furniture, and you'd find yourself virtually unable to move. *We need to clear the debris out of our minds.* Let me reassure you, the procedure for changing what you store in your inner levels of consciousness is simple. It boggles my mind to think of the enormous energy we can release if we rid ourselves of old and constricting beliefs.

There are two ways that you can work with your innerconsciousness. One is to reprogram yourself, enabling you to act the way you want to by *putting in* new information while meditating. The other is to gain creative insights which will help you move forward when you're stuck—*pulling out* new information. It is through your innerconsciousness that you have access to universal information, and it is at that level that you receive creative insights and inspiration. It is when you are relaxed, that the classic "Aha!" experience occurs. It is also through relaxed awareness that ESP takes place. Once you learn how to enter and use your inner levels of consciousness you will no longer need to hope that an answer to a gnawing problem will dawn on you at some later time. Instead you can enter the meditative state and simply ask for an answer. Knowledge becomes available to you when you direct your questions inward. *The question itself acts as a flashlight* directing a beam of light on the particular spot in the amorphous collective unconscious where the answer resides, some believe that God resides within everyone and for this reason they are able to get guidance by looking within through prayer. Whatever your belief the important thing is that clarity does come when one asks while in a receptive state. You will find yourself intuiting an insight that helps resolve the problem. The trick is to have a *clear* question.

THEORY OF CONSCIOUSNESS

The abrupt transformation in my life came about in the opposite way from what usually happens. Normally we're taught something and then learn to apply it—theory precedes practice. For me, it's been the other way around. Throughout the last twelve years I have always experienced the fact of directed consciousness working, and then later begun to piece together *why* it works. In other words, my rational understanding follows my experience. True, I suspect, for anyone who follows an intuition. I have found myself changing and developing techniques, seemingly out of the blue—intuitively. While teaching, changes pop into my mind, and without exception, they are always refinements—always improvements. Each time these changes happen without any planning on my part. There has always been a time lag between my teaching something and being able to explain why it is that it works. In retrospect, I am glad to have discovered that intuition does not work by trial and error.

I would like to emphasize that originally I had no understanding of how consciousness worked, and yet my life changed profoundly when I began to direct my own imagination. But now I want to elaborate my perspective on consciousness and its relation to experience and behavior. You don't need to agree with my explanation in order to explore your inner levels; the power of the experience will speak for itself. (If you prefer, you can skip this section for the time being, and move on to the next chapter.) But I share my ideas with you because they have given me a rational understanding of the phenomena of consciousness, providing a footing that enables me to navigate more easily through my inner dimensions.

I use electroencephalographic (EEG) measures as a language through which to view consciousness. Our brains continuously give off electromagnetic pulsations which can be measured by an electroencephalograph. EEG levels refer to the different rhythms of these emanations. There seems to be a correlation between what we're subjectively experiencing and the objective brain-wave emanations. The different levels, called beta, alpha, theta, and delta, are each part of a complete spectrum. The divisions are arbitrary — it's like the dividing lines between the colors white, grey, and black: where white stops, grey starts, grey stops, and black starts is arbitrary, yet there is a complete change from one end of the spectrum to the other.

In Western culture we are most familiar with beta consciousness because it is that level that is rational and therefore recognized as valuable, so it is only this aspect of our consciousness we have been taught how to use. Reading, writing, and arithmetic are all beta functions, as are cause-and-effect thinking, goal orientation, and our experience of clock time. This linear thinking of beta is particular and critical, computing lots of different data all at once, such as talking to a friend while you're cooking, and at the same time thinking of all the errands you need to do. In beta you're dealing with lots of particulars at the same time in a logical goal-oriented manner. It is a necessary state of consciousness for coping with contemporary urban living, where we have to be dealing with many issues at once.

Beta consciousness both promotes and maintains life in the fast lane. It is overused because at times it becomes defeating. Particular thinking, by definition, separates elements of the whole, ordering them in a linear manner. Its natural operating mode is therefore competitive; since it separates elements of the whole, it also isolates people from one another. It doesn't make sense to be forced into a competitive mode just because we only know how to function with a betà mentality. In a competitive atmosphere one is certainly not relaxed. In consequence, the most prevalent causes of death in our society are related to stress in one way or another. We need to have the choice of being able to relax and connect with others easily, moving out of our isolation and into mutual support. Working with innerconsciousness will do just that.

I think of beta consciousness as if it resides at the top of the brain, and of the innerconsciousness — alpha, theta, and delta — as residing in its deeper portions — alpha right below beta, moving down to theta, and below to delta in the depths. These deeper levels of consciousness experience reality holistically. They do not separate things; they make connections. They do not categorize; they make things whole. They are not critical, nor do they order things in a linear manner. Instead they experience reality in images, patterns and sensations.

To understand the term holistic, imagine that you can't figure out how to solve a mathematical formula; you are absolutely stuck so you give up and go for a walk (in a relaxing activity such as this you will be predominantly at the alpha level). As you walk, all of a sudden the solution dawns on you like the proverbial light bulb flashing on—not the specific answer but an unquestionable sense of the whole pattern. Everything becomes clear; you can go home to your work and your *beta* mind will easily figure out the missing parts of the equation. This is an example of the classic "Aha!" experience referred to earlier.

Any rhythmic activities such as running, weaving or working on an assembly line induce alpha because you don't need to use your mind to decide what step to take next; linear thinking is unnecessary. While dancing, you've probably had the experience of losing the beat if you begin to think about what your feet should do next. The alpha level feels much more flowing. It is so fluid that you find yourself thinking about something and you have no idea what led you to that thought. It is a familiar state for you are in it during large portions of your day, but since you are probably unaware of its uses it's likely you've always ignored it.

Theta and delta, unlike beta and alpha, are not so familiar. It is these levels of consciousness that are active when your focus is in *one* place. You may have heard the term "one-pointedness of consciousness"—being one with all that is—which refers to the satori experience that is strived for in Eastern religious tradition. It is a complete focus of awareness and occurs at these deep levels.

Whenever your survival is threatened, it is a given that all of your attention is needed to deal with the situation at hand, and anything else is simply not in your awareness. For instance, if you are in an automobile accident it lasts at most five seconds, yet in memory it feels as if it had lasted half an hour—like a slow-motion movie. All of your energy was focused on surviving, and rather than being spread out on lots of issues, as it is in the beta state, it was all funnelled into the exclusive awareness of the threatening situation, having the subjective effect of expanding time. You may have heard of people who thought they were about to die and whose entire life paraded before their eyes—this is complete focus of energy and subjective expansion of time.

Throughout this description of the EEG levels of consciousness I am referring to them in relation to the predominant rhythm of brain emanations present at any given moment. When you are in the beta level of consciousness, there are also emanations of a different rhythm present. However, the slower your predominant brain wave pattern is, the more synchronized all the emanations are. So at the other end of the spectrum, in the delta level of consciousness, the only patterns present are delta waves. The degree to which brain wave patterns are synchronized corresponds to the degree to which we feel in sync with what is going on around us.

Thus the spectrum from beta to delta is simply one of the focus and concentration of awareness—at beta it is spread out; at delta it is completely concentrated. At beta it is particular; at delta it is holistic. Let's say you are relaxed and daydreaming. At a time like this you're aware of your objective circumstances, e.g. you know that you are lying on the bed in your room, and that you need to get up at a certain time for an appointment or to take a cake out of your oven—all this is in your awareness while you are still daydreaming. This is the alpha state. On the other hand, if you suddenly realize that you have been dreaming, without being aware of where you are—or that you have already missed your appointment or burnt the cake—you were at the theta level (no longer goal-oriented). This is called the hypnogogic state, wherein the contents of the dream become reality and have a three dimensional quality—the dream itself is extremely vivid, and your objective circumstances have faded from awareness. This is the difference between alpha and theta. In alpha your daydreaming consciousness is more spread out, in theta more concentrated. In alpha, you are daydreaming in an off-hand manner; in theta your dream is as real as life. In fact your dream has replaced your objective reality.

The effects of mind-altering drugs further illustrate this spectrum. If you have ingested nicotine, caffeine, or cocaine, you will be at a very high level of beta consciousness, your brain waves will be emanating very quickly (speeding). On the other hand, if you've had a drink, some valium, or smoked some marijuana, you'll be predominantly at the alpha level (mellowed out). Lastly, if you've taken a psychedelic such as mescaline, psilocybin, or LSD, you'll be predominantly functioning at the theta level. This is why experiences under the influence of these psychedelics are more vivid and have a time-expanding effect (mind-expanding).

The theta level is an extremely receptive state of consciousness because one is *only* aware of what is happening at the moment and has no concept of anything else. It is therefore a suggestible state of consciousness because it is non-critical. It does not divide things up, nor categorize things; it simply *experiences*. Since theta is exclusively focused on what is occurring in the moment it is not linear or goal-oriented—whatever may happen next is completely irrelevant. Considering alternatives is not possible while at the theta level, so that thinking, "on the other hand . . . " would never occur.

Some developmental psychologists say that an individual's personality is essentially formed by age three. Although I don't think that our personalities are static, I think that the basis for this theory is the fact that up until this age everybody functions predominantly at the theta level. This explains why infants are totally engrossed in whatever is occurring at the moment, and why toddlers cannot grasp plans—the concept of what's happening next. For theta consciousness does not possess the critical capacities of beta or its ability to understand time. So anything that occurs during these years becomes a person's reality, because theta consciousness has no awareness of alternatives, i.e., that there could be another reality. Remember, you act in accordance with your beliefs. For example, if you lived next to a freeway with the constant noise of traffic during the first three years of your life, the chances are you wouldn't be fully comfortable in the quiet of the country—something would be missing—because your belief system defines the world as noisy. This discomfort may be something you're not fully conscious of, but only experience in a vague and ill-defined way.

This example illustrates how we act in terms of our past experience, our belief systems; our memories are stored deep in our consciousness at the theta level. We remember things holistically: if you smell the scent of a flower you're not going to remember what you learned about that flower in biology class; instead, a *whole* scene in which that scent was present will flood your awareness. Our memories function associatively, not logically. The beliefs we act out of stem either from childhood experiences or from life-threatening events, or from an accumulation of repetitive programming.

When children are of elementary school age they are predominantly at the alpha level (actively getting programmed). It is not until puberty that we have full access to our critical capacities and begin to function predominantly at the beta level (except when watching TV). So it's our deepest levels of consciousness that house the totality of our past experience and through which our behavior is directed.

Alpha residing between beta and theta, is composed of the characteristics of each and it is for this reason that it is so powerful because *it can be both active and receptive, simultaneously. It is the threshold between inner and outer consciousness.*

To sum up, when you meditate you will be predominantly in alpha. You can reprogram yourself, i.e. give yourself the messages you choose, by changing the beliefs you act out of; your deeper levels, being suggestible, will absorb the new information. Or you can call up information from these receptive states of awareness. In alpha you can choose what you want to work on (active) and then be effective in doing so (receptive).

With this map of your consciousness in your mind the next chapter will give you a vehicle for your travel.

Chapter Two

Bringing Meditation into Your Life

How can you apply all this? When you want to change your behavior you simply need to get the information in at the appropriate level. If the information that you want to put in doesn't have anything contradicting it deeper down, in other words, if there are no counter messages at the theta level, then putting in a new message is a simple straightforward process and one application is usually enough for it to sink in. For example, if you need to awaken at seven-fifteen, all you need do is enter the alpha level and tell yourself, "I will awaken at exactly seven-fifteen in the morning," (active). If there is nothing contradicting the suggestion at the theta level, such as a childhood message from your mother who always said, "You *never* get up on time," it will simply sink in (receptive). Your inner consciousness will have a new program out of which you will find yourself responding by awakening at exactly seven-fifteen. This works on the first try because you do not have a lot of energy focused on the issue.

Now if you want to change your response in an area that has some charge to it, such as a phobia or an allergy or a deeply implanted message ("I can't get up on time"), you do it the same way as the process above. It simply takes longer (more applications). You need more energy around the new message than around the old. You need to replace the pictures which reside in your theta level, but you need to work in the alpha level because theta is not goal-oriented and by the time you have gotten there you've forgotten what you were going to do (spacing out). Since there is less energy at alpha it takes longer to accumulate enough to replace the old message.

PUTTING THEORY INTO PRACTICE

To illustrate, if you have had an automobile accident and feel nervous every time you travel in a car—not a very convenient response in today's society—you can change this by replacing your old picture with a new one. You enter the alpha state and imagine feeling good riding in a car. This may be rather difficult, given your past experience, so you should think of something that *does* feel good—maybe for you it's listening to music. Then you imagine listening to music until you are feeling wonderful, then imagine yourself in a car listening to music on the radio. If you lose your good feelings at that point, go back to listening to music without the car, and keep doing this. Eventually you will be able to imagine yourself maintaining your good feelings while in the car. Then after more work you'll be able to imagine being comfortable in the car without music. It's at this point that you will have a message you can focus on (it is pleasant to ride in a car) and you will find yourself able to do so comfortably. It's a simple process—just a matter of taking the time to replace the old messages and accumulating new energy around fresh ones. The important distinction is that beta works with thoughts and our inner levels work with feelings, sounds, sensations, pictures. The difference is not in thinking the car is safe, but in *feeling* that it is.

To repeat: working with these energies falls into two categories. One is replacing old, inhibiting messages that have patterned your everyday behavior with new, liberating ones. The other way of working with inner awareness is, when you're stuck, to ask yourself for an insight to enable you to move on. Remember the example of the mathematical problem: instead of giving up, you simply need to go into the meditative state and ask a *clear* question at that level of awareness with the *expectation* of receiving an answer. In so doing, the solution inexplicably becomes apparent, for the information exists. The question itself acts as a spotlight illuminating the particular area of the collective unconscious where the answer resides (the clearer the question, the brighter and more steady the light). All your hunches, inspirations and creative insights originate at your inner levels where extrasensory perception occurs. So when you don't know—you ask a question, and when you do—you put in the information.

I make it sound so simple. The profound thing about it is that it *is* simple. We've allowed these parts of ourselves to atrophy; it's time to exercise them. Like everything else in the world these powers work only if we use them. If you decide to take this journey through your inner self, you will discover that the effects are extraordinary.

USING THE MEDITATIONS:
CREATING A CONTEXT

We expect spiritual work to be surrounded with lights, colors, and whispering voices. In short we expect to sit back and be entertained by the awesome. The important thing to understand is that the alpha state is nothing extraordinary, for you are frequently in that level of awareness. It's just under the surface and easy to enter at will. The common view that meditation, hypnosis, and the like are exotic is simply part of the mystification—our culture teaches us that these things are extraordinary and strange. Well, they're not. The knowingness of intuitive powers resides within each of us. You don't have to go far to discover answers to the daily problems that arise in your life. All you need do is pay attention to, and take seriously, a very familiar part of yourself that you've probably never before realized could be of use. Up until now it is likely that you felt slightly guilty whenever you were relaxed because you thought you were wasting your time and not accomplishing anything. It's time to refocus and pay attention to that very level that you've always ignored—to listen to the voices within.

Our society tells us we must always be productive (the Puritan Ethic)—that it's not okay to be in the clouds, to live in a fantasy world or to daydream. Now you get to bring the clouds down to earth, moistening the ground of your life for new growth. You can smooth and soften your edgy existence. You get to be productive in your daydreams; you'll be amazed at how wise this part of you really is. If you're skeptical, give it a try anyway because at least you'll have an excuse to relax, and we could all use a little respite from the turmoil of our daily activities. Although you'll discover your inner work isn't awesome, it is quite entertaining. The journeys through your inner dimension are very enjoyable, full of humor and the celebration of life.

The last portion of each of the rest of the chapters consists of guided fantasies which I call meditations; these are to help you tune into your innerconsciousness and learn to solve problems with it. They are best experienced in a group setting because the nature of the energy with which you will be working is such that the potency expands geometrically with the number of people sharing the experience. So it is my suggestion that you set a regular time aside and instead of watching television, bring some friends together, make some popcorn, and discover the movies of your minds—develop your *own* programming. Those of you who do not yet have a community to share this work can begin by reading the exercises first and then doing them on your own.

In every meditation in this book, all I'm doing is providing helpful guidelines for you to voyage through your inner landscape. If you have your own ways, for instance, to relax your body and mind, use them. The important thing is to work within yourself, not how you do it. There are no "shoulds;" there is no right way of doing this. (If anyone tells you there is, the chances are it costs a lot of money to learn their technique.) The correct approach is to pay careful attention to your own inclinations and use only those techniques you find helpful. Always feel free to make any necessary adjustments. I can't overstate that the only "should" is to pay attention to your own inclinations; they are subtle and it is often hard to catch them because we've been taught to distrust and squelch them and instead to follow the instructions of the experts. But *you're the expert of yourself.* I'm only providing guidelines for you to meet that expert within you; each time you meet that part of yourself that knows what's right for you, follow it and disregard the guidelines, for they will no longer be necessary.

This book is laid out as a training course. Each of the chapters and meditations builds on the preceding ones. To gain the optimum benefits from it I recommend you set aside a regular time and go through the book at your own pace from start to finish. Go through the meditations at whatever rate is comfortable. There is no set amount of practice necessary between one meditation and the next. Feel free to skip any which deal with issues you are not concerned with, or jump ahead if you feel the inclination. You are likely to find some you'll want to use over and over again. The meditations are meant to create a context, an atmosphere in which to explore— each word needn't be listened to (or read). For that matter you may prefer to use only portions of some of the meditations. Tune in and out at will. Each of the meditation sections of all the chapters following this one open with an Induction and close with a Count-out. These are meant to be used for each of the meditations included. Some of the meditations flow easily from one into another so feel free to combine them. On the other hand some are particularly long, so you may want to use only some of the passages while leaving out others.

If you are doing the exercises by yourself I recommend that you read them aloud, recording each meditation as you come to it.* It's easier to go through the meditations without having to think of what you need to do next, a linear process that will only activate your beta consciousness. Using a tape will solve this problem, but if you don't want to pre-record them, make yourself a cribsheet—a chronological list of one-liners that describe each phase of the meditation—or underline particular passages, so you don't clutter your mind by trying to remember what to do next. Instead you can keep the sheet right in front of you and open your eyes for each step (this won't disturb your meditation). Some find themselves meditating while simply reading them.

However, if you are working with a group, I suggest that someone lead the meditation when everyone is together, and that it be taped. The leader can then catch up with everyone else by listening to it later. Obviously this is a responsibility that can be rotated.

---

*I have produced tapes of each of the meditations. If you are interested in ordering any, see information at end of book.

This strategy is best, for anyone will be much more inspired leading the meditations when there are people right there experiencing them and responding, making it easier to intuit the best timing and tone for reading.

As all the meditations are written poetically you'll find yourself reading in a trance-inducing tone. An important thing to keep in mind, however, is to give people time for their inner work. Some sections of the meditations simply create an atmosphere to evoke particular experiences within, these sections can be read in one continuous flow. On the other hand, there is much in the meditations that asks people to do inner work on their own, for example, inner conversations, re-creations of memories, etc. When this is the case it's important to give people space for their inner work, and therefore some silence is necessary. For this purpose I have created marks for pauses: three dots indicate the time it would take for a deep breath. One dingbat indicates a short pause (approx. 15 seconds), three dingbats indicate a long pause (approx. 1 minute). On occasion there are lists of questions or affirmations; you'll want to give about 10 seconds to each.

For the meditations to be most effective, timing is vitally important. Trust your intuition. There are two common mistakes: on the one hand people read continually without giving time for inner work, and on the other hand people give too much time which results in losing the attention of the meditators who will space out or fall asleep.

You probably have the impression that you need total peace and quiet in order to meditate, so if you're trying to relax and you find yourself aware of your noisy neighbors, the traffic outside, or the ticking clock, you conclude that you're not relaxing properly so that you can't meditate because of all the distractions. To the contrary, the more you're relaxed the more you'll be aware of your surroundings and your inner state. For example, it's only when you're relaxing that you may realize how tense your neck is—that's okay—normally you're so tense you're unaware of your stiff neck; it's only when you relax that it becomes apparent. Hearing the neighbors outside doesn't mean that you need to listen to them, it just means you have noisy neighbors. Meditating is simply settling down a bit; your body/mind need not be *totally* relaxed.

The fact is that the contemporary world is not a tranquil place.

Should that mean that meditation is impossible? Absolutely not, but it means that your meditation won't always be tranquil either.

There are a few requirements, though, for your meditation practice. Arrange not to be disturbed and make yourself comfortable. Noisy neighbors don't interrupt you—they're not asking you for anything—but the phone does, so unplug it and put a note on your door. Then be sure that your clothing is comfortable and your breathing is not constricted. Have a blanket handy because when you meditate, just as when you take a nap, your metabolism slows down so you tend to chill easily. If you're someone who falls asleep easily I suggest you sit up for the meditations, with your back supported and straight. Some who are prone to fall asleep nevertheless prefer to lie down while meditating, so they hold an arm up (when it drops it awakens them). If you have trouble relaxing I suggest that you do the meditations lying down. Feel free to change positions in the midst of the meditations—with time you'll come to know your optimum position for relaxation and alertness. It is common to fall asleep while meditating for you're learning to maintain that edge between sleeping and waking consciousness. Don't worry, I've been doing this for twelve years and I still fall asleep more frequently than I'd like to. In fact when I originally went through the techniques of Silva Mind Control, I slept through two-thirds of it.

If you can't remember all that happened in a meditation it may help to read it over again. In so doing you'll find yourself remembering more easily what you experienced. If there are still large blanks in your memory you may want to do the meditation again.

If you find yourself thinking about all kinds of irrelevant things—feeling "spacey"—don't worry, that's the nature of the energy you are working with; it's very fluid—both active and receptive at the same time. With practice you'll be better able to choose where to focus your awareness.

CREATING YOUR OWN PRACTICE

In addition to going through the meditations in the book I think it's highly important that you also meditate on your own, i.e., without the outside stimulus of a tape or a group setting. This is so you will discover your capabilities for yourself and avoid becoming dependent on anyone or anything else for tapping your own inner resources. Because this book is to enable you to repossess your inner self, it is important that you practice daily on your own, entering and exploring the meditative state, hereinafter referred to as *your level*. When you do this by yourself it usually feels different—you may not feel as "deep"—this is because it's easier to follow someone else's instructions than to tell yourself what to do, and then do it. This is particularly true if you have been doing these meditations in a group setting, for exploring these energies is always more potent when shared with others. So in your independent practice, if you don't feel as if you're in a meditative state, *pretend* that you are and go through the motions anyway. If you do you'll discover that it becomes more and more effective each time you practice. It's important to remember that you never lose your ability to meditate for Applied Meditation is simply a matter of paying attention to and working with a part of yourself that is always present. However, it only works when you use it. You don't lose all your strength if you don't exercise, but when you do your body stays in shape—limber and strong. You can exert yourself with ease, rather than with effort. In the same way, the more you meditate the more adept you will be at using your deeper levels of awareness whenever you need to.

Some people meditate daily, some every few days, and some people meditate for less than five minutes at a sitting while others spend a half hour. I don't believe there is any magic formula for how often or how long you should meditate, but I do feel *regular* practice is important because then Applied Meditation will become a part of your daily routine. If you don't practice regularly it is not likely to occur to you to meditate when it would be particularly helpful. With time you'll come to know when and how long is best for you. Everyone has their own particular relationship with their inner dimensions.

It is my suggestion that after meditating you always take time to write down briefly what you've experienced in any combination of words and pictures that feels comfortable. Keeping a journal of your meditations will greatly enhance your ability to remember what occurred in them. This begins the process of moving your inner sense of well-being into the material world around you, enabling

you to bring these energies into your daily activities more easily—
that's what Applied Meditation is all about. Recording your experience will initiate and facilitate this process. It will also track your
progress which will help you develop the best possible working
relationship with your inner self.

As your practice evolves you will discover that there are more
and more things you want to work on, so you might find it handy
to make a list so you needn't remember all the different things you
wanted to do while meditating. Instead you need only open your
eyes for a moment and glance at your list (this is particularly helpful
for affirmations). Remember alpha consciousness isn't linear. As
you learn more techniques you can integrate them into your daily
practice, using as many in each meditation as you find helpful.

RELAXATION: WORKING WITH IT

When you are physically relaxed you are at the alpha level so the
first meditation is a basic relaxation exercise in which you will
learn a technique that will enable you, with just a little practice, to
relax in a matter of moments whenever you wish. The induction
that opens the meditation section of each chapter uses this same
technique. Soon you'll learn to recognize the particular quality of
alpha awareness so that you'll be able to tune into that part of
yourself at will, whether or not you're physically relaxed. You'll be
able to meditate on a rush-hour bus.

At *every* given moment your body is responding to whatever
you're imagining. If at one time you were terribly frightened by a
dog, every time you imagine one your body starts pumping adrenaline even when no real dog is actually present. This dog phobia
is an example of the intimate body-mind connection which is
continuously functioning. If you imagine yourself on a sunny beach
your metabolism will slow down. In the first meditation, you're
going to take advantage of this phenomenon. It will guide you
through each part of your body, giving you time to relax. Once
you're physically relaxed you'll create something that symbolizes
that relaxation for you: you can make up whatever you want, a
sensation, a picture—anything—be sure it's specific and easy to
recall (butter melting on a stack of pancakes). So the next time you

want to relax all you'll need to do is bring your physical relaxation symbol into your awareness, and your body will respond accordingly—this is what I mean by creating a language to speak to your inner experience. Next time you won't need to relax each part of your body separately. Instead all you'll need to do is focus on your symbol.

You're also going to relax your mind, this doesn't mean that it shuts up; only that it calms down a bit—expands—your thoughts no longer feel cramped or rushed. Instead they begin to meander. Then you will create a symbol for mental relaxation. Adding to this you will use a process for emotional relaxation, so that the entire meditation is not experienced through any strong feelings that may be present. If this is not done, strong feelings act like sunglasses, coloring everything. You want to be clear. Emotional centering *does not mean resolving the feeling*, it simply means taking care of it so that it doesn't dominate the rest of the meditation. For example, if you had an argument with a family member earlier, then you imagine putting the concern up on an imaginary mental shelf, or in a closet, or whatever may occur in your imagination to relax yourself emotionally. Remember, solving the problem is not necessary for this emotional clearing.

Now once your body, mind and feelings are relaxed you will create a symbol that represents the state you are in—your alpha level—in which you'll do your interior exploration and work. Many people feel that they have to wait till their symbol comes to them—only if it "comes" will it be correct. This is another one of the subtle ways we discount ourselves—believing what is right must come from an exterior source. In creating symbols give yourself full permission to *make up* whatever you like. There is no correct symbol; you're working with your *own* associative process. Therefore whatever you make up is the right one for you. If a number of symbols come to mind, arbitrarily choose one, or let them coalesce. If you keep changing, your innerconsciousness becomes confused. If we were to use a different word to represent the color green each time we referred to that color, the words would become useless. This does not mean you can never change your symbols. If you discover one you like better, use it, but just be consistent.

If you have the same symbol for each stage, i.e., relaxing your body, your mind and feelings, and entering your level, that's fine, just give each part of yourself time to calm down. By the time you focus on the symbol for your level you will already be there, and your inner self will come to know that after focusing on it you will begin to do your interior work. After your meditation if you don't remember your symbols, simply make them up in the next meditation (the ones you make up will, in all likelihood, be the same ones you created in the first place).

In this first meditation there'll be a number of suggestions which you can use to deepen your consciousness and explore your inner dimension, for the inner world is as expansive as the outer. The next meditation is designed for increased breath awareness. When you are tense, anxious, or off balance you are usually not breathing fully, cutting off oxygen—energy flow in the body—which only perpetuates further tension, anxiety, etc. It's amazing what simply stopping and breathing will do to alleviate stress and create a clear mental and emotional atmosphere in which to proceed. The fact that we take a deep breath before we embark on a difficult task is no coincidence.

Also, in the count-out of the meditation it is suggested that you "feel revitalized." The meditations *do* revitalize you, but it also takes time to adjust to outer consciousness levels, so if you don't feel chirpy right away, you needn't worry.

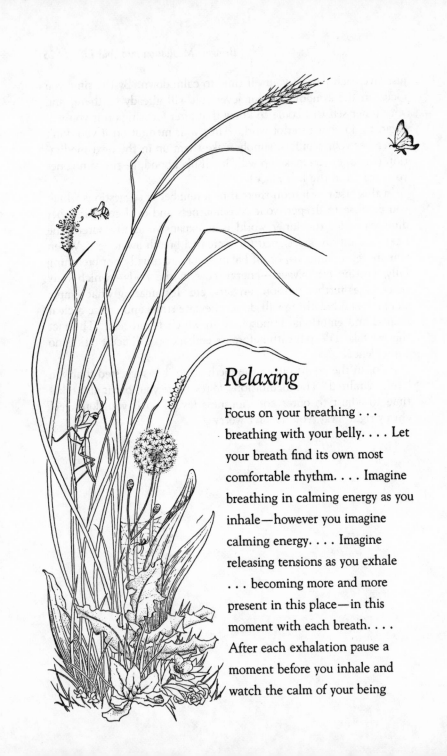

Relaxing

Focus on your breathing . . .
breathing with your belly. . . . Let
your breath find its own most
comfortable rhythm. . . . Imagine
breathing in calming energy as you
inhale—however you imagine
calming energy. . . . Imagine
releasing tensions as you exhale
. . . becoming more and more
present in this place—in this
moment with each breath. . . .
After each exhalation pause a
moment before you inhale and
watch the calm of your being

expand . . . peacefulness expand, as you watch the next inhalation approach slowly, bringing in more calming energy . . . your breath comes in and moves out taking more tensions away with it . . . washing them away like ocean waves. . . .

I'm going to direct your attention to different areas in your body. . . . If you wish you can relax these areas, becoming more and more relaxed as we move through this process, moving into a state of inner calm, of inner creativity. . . . Moving into a more and more harmonious state of being . . . a very good feeling of relaxation. . . . Very calm and very aware at the same time. . . .

First become aware of your feet, the weight of your feet pressing down on the floor, the space your feet occupy, clothing touching your skin, skin covering each of your feet, bones, muscles, tendons, blood, nerves, everything inside of your feet . . . aware of each of your toes. . . . Imagine asking your feet to relax. . . . Rather than breathing out through your nose, imagine as though your breath were moving out through the tips of your toes carrying with it any tensions you had in your feet . . . feel your feet relaxing more and more with each exhalation of breath. . . . It feels good to give your feet space to relax. . . .

As your feet continue to relax, now become aware of your ankles . . . your shins . . . your calves . . . and your knees . . . aware of the whole of each of your lower legs, the space they each occupy. . . . Feel the clothing touching your skin, skin covering your legs . . . and all the bones and muscles inside. . . . Imagine asking your lower legs to relax, give them permission to relax . . . feel them relaxing . . . let your exhalations of breath wash away any tensions in these areas, leaving each of your legs feeling very, very relaxed. . . . It's good to give your body the time, the space, it needs to relax. . . .

As your lower legs continue relaxing move your awareness up to include both your thighs . . . be aware of the space they each occupy . . . aware of the shape of the space between your thighs. . . . Be aware of the space inside of your thighs . . . be aware of the shape of each of your thighs . . . aware of the bones, of the muscles within . . . ask your thighs to relax, tell them they needn't carry you at the moment and they can have this time to relax. . . . Send your breath down through your thighs to help them relax. . . . Feel them relaxing more and more with each exhalation of breath. . . . It feels good to let them relax. . . .

As your thighs continue relaxing, move your awareness up to your pelvis. . . . Be aware of the space your pelvis occupies, the clothing touching your skin, skin covering your pelvis . . . aware of the bones, the muscles, the organs inside. . . . Notice the weight of your pelvis pressing down on the floor or chair. . . . Let your pelvis relax. Imagine your weight sinking a little more into the chair or floor. . . . You may wish to imagine breathing out through your genitals, your exhalations carrying away any tensions that you have in this area. . . . Feel your pelvis relaxing. . . . Feel yourself fully supported by the chair or the floor. . . . It feels good to give yourself the gift of this space for relaxation. . . .

As your pelvis continues to relax more and more, become aware of your belly and lower back . . . aware of the space that this part of your body occupies, the space between one side of you and the other . . . space between your belly and your back. . . . All the bones, muscles, organs within this space . . . all of them functioning in harmony with one another. . . . Relax your abdomen and lower back. . . . As your breath moves in and out of your body let the rise and fall of your belly massage this whole area into a deep state of relaxation, feel it relaxing, entering a calmer and calmer state of being, very relaxed. . . .

As your belly and low back continue to relax, become aware of the rest of your back and your chest. Be aware of the space that this part of your body occupies. . . . Feel the size and shape of your rib cage. . . . Move your awareness in deeper, become aware of your heartbeat, the pulse of your heart . . . sustained by continuous inexhaustible life-force energy . . . feel the rhythm of your pulsing heart . . . know that whenever you pay attention to your heartbeat you'll find yourself feeling calmer. . . . Now include in your awareness the rhythm of your breath . . . allow these rhythms to return you to yourself, wash through the whole of your being . . . let them dissolve any tensions you have in your chest and upper back. . . . Feel the whole of your chest and back entering deeper and deeper states of relaxation. Feel them relaxing. . . .

Now become aware of your shoulders, your arms, and your hands . . . aware of each of your fingers. . . . Notice the space that each of these parts of your body occupies. Notice what the different parts are touching. . . . Imagine your breath washing down through your shoulders, arms, hands, dissolving all tensions in its path and moving out through your finger tips . . as they become more relaxed it's as though they become ever so slightly heavier. . . . Feel these parts of your body becoming more and more relaxed with each exhalation of breath. . . . Tell them they can relax, feel them relaxing. . . .

As they continue to relax move your awareness up to your neck. Be aware of the space your neck occupies. . . . You may wish to roll your neck around letting it find its own most comfortable position. . . . Give your neck space to relax . . . acknowledge it for the hard work of holding your head up all the time . . . tell it it can relax now . . . feel it relaxing, relaxing more and more with each exhalation of breath. . . . It feels good to relax your neck. . . .

Now move your awareness into your throat, you may wish to swallow, becoming very aware of all the muscles in and around your throat. . . . Relax your throat, let it relax more and more with each exhalation of breath. . . . As your throat continues to relax move your awareness up into your mouth . . . let your tongue relax a little . . . move your mouth around so you can become very aware of the hinges of your jaws. . . . Breathe through the hinges in your jaws and feel them relax more and more with each exhalation of breath. . . . Let your mouth hang open if it is more relaxed in that position. . . .

Now imagine the many layers of muscles in your face, giving your face full range of expression. . . . Relax all your facial mus-cles. . . . Imagine a soft breeze caressing your face, soothing it into relaxation . . . relaxing your cheeks . . . your eyes, your eyelids . . . your forehead, your temples . . . relaxing your whole face . . . and letting that relaxation spread out over your scalp . . . let the relaxation soak in to all the muscles in and behind your eyes . . . the whole of your face and head relaxing. . . .

Notice how good it feels to be so relaxed and know that every time you relax you'll be able to enter deeper and deeper states of body relaxation with greater and greater ease. . . . Know that this is so. . . . It feels good to give your body the gift of time, of space, to relax. . . .

Now make up a symbol that represents this body relaxation. . . . Any symbol that you choose. . . . This symbol can be a picture, a place in your body, a sensation, a sound, whatever you like. If you have a couple of symbols, arbitrarily pick one or let them coalesce into one. . . . This is your body relaxation symbol which you can use whenever you wish to physically relax. . . . Now tell yourself that whenever you bring this symbol into awareness the whole of your body will relax as you are now relaxed in a matter of moments. . . . Tell your body this now, and know that it is so. . . . Know that your body will come to know this symbol and will always relax whenever you bring it into your awareness. Know that every time you use this symbol your whole body will respond to it more and more quickly, tell yourself you'll remember this symbol for the next time you meditate. . . . Whenever you bring your physical relaxation symbol to awareness, in a matter of moments the whole of your body will respond, relaxing just as you are now relaxed. . . . Know that this is so. . . .

Now you can also give your mind time and space to calm down, to feel peaceful. . . . Now imagine being in a place that feels very good to you, a place where you can feel quiet and peaceful. It may be in the country, in the city, at home—wherever you like—if you have a number of places that feel calming to you, pick one of them. . . . If no place is completely calm, make up an imaginary place that would feel serene to you if it were to exist. . . . Now choose one place to be. . . . Imagine being in this special place now. . . . Imagine what's below your feet . . . what's to your left . . . to your right . . . imagine what's in front of you . . . and behind you. . . . Imagine what's above you . . . how the air feels on your skin . . . the sounds present . . . the scents present. . . . Let your imagination make this place real, allow yourself to be fully there in your mind. . . . Create this place for yourself to enjoy. . . . Enjoy this place you've created. . . . Let yourself be fully there. . . .

Imagine that your body, your mind, the whole of yourself is like a sponge and you can draw into yourself all the peaceful feelings around you . . . breathe in the peaceful atmosphere . . . drawing in the good feelings of this place, into the whole of yourself . . . breathing it in . . . bringing in the serenity . . . the separation between you and this place is becoming hazier and hazier . . . as many of these feelings around you are now in you. . . . You are as much a part of this place as everything that is here . . . this place feels very good. . . . It feels very good to be part of it all. Feel how in this place the usual chatter of your mind has quieted down some. It's a good feeling to feel yourself mentally relaxing. . . .

Notice how your mind is very relaxed and at the same time very alert. . . . Here, sounds do not distract you, instead they enhance your inner calm and awareness. . . .

Here thoughts move in and out of your awareness as easily as you breathe in and out . . . in and out . . . no resistance, no attachment. . . . Here, thoughts, feelings, sensations move through your awareness as easily as puffy white clouds drift through the spacious afternoon sky . . . feel the peace in the sky of your mind. . . . Your mind is expansive, clear and calm. . . . Imagine your mind being the spacious afternoon sky . . . feel how relaxed and at the same time how alert your mind is. . . . It's a good feeling to be mentally relaxed . . . as your mind relaxes, your mind expands . . . imagine the sky of your mind expanding out as far as the horizon . . . and each of your thoughts like round and soft clouds. . . . Every time you mentally relax you'll enter deeper and deeper states of this relaxation with greater and greater ease. . . . Know that this is so. . . . It feels good to give your mind this time, this space to relax. . . .

Now make up a symbol that represents this mental relaxation. Anything you choose—a feeling, sensation, a picture, whatever—choose, create a particular symbol . . . this is your mental relaxation symbol. Now tell your mind that the next time you bring your mental relaxation symbol into your awareness it will relax in a matter of moments just as your mind is relaxed now . . . tell your mind this now. . . . Know that this is so. Know that every time you bring this symbol into your awareness your mind will enter calmer and calmer states of mental relaxation more and more quickly. . . . Tell yourself that you'll remember this symbol to use the next time you meditate. . . . Whenever you bring your mental relaxation symbol to awareness, in a matter of moments, your mind will relax, just as it is now. . . . Acknowledge that this is so. . . .

When you're ready, with your awareness go over the full range of feelings that are present for you now. . . . If any feelings, positive or negative, are clamoring for your attention, take care of them in whatever manner occurs to you. . . . You may want to imagine putting them away in a safe place like a padded box or you may want to imagine the rain coming through and clearing them away. . . . You can imagine all the "shoulds" soaking down into the ground . . . and then take a moment to nurture yourself, appreciate who you are . . . give yourself permission to feel safe and secure . . . emotionally relaxed. . . . Now create a symbol for emotional relaxation. . . . Know that whenever you bring your emotional relaxation symbol to mind your feelings will quickly relax. . . . Tell your emotional self this now. . . .

With your body, mind and emotions relaxed you are at the alpha level of consciousness. . . . This is your creative, self-restoring center—your level. Notice the quality of this space that you now occupy. . . . Notice how you're feeling, any particular sensations in your body, pictures, sounds, vibrations. . . . Know that whenever you feel these sensations, they'll reinforce this level of energy. And I want you to know that whenever you generate these sensations they'll quckly guide you to this place you now occupy—to your level. . . . Here you'll find you have access to a greater range of imagination and creativity. . . . Your powers of concentration are also enhanced and permit you to focus wherever you choose. . . .

Now create a symbol that represents your creative, self-restoring center—your level, any symbol you like, and know that whenever you bring your symbol for your level into your awareness, in a matter of moments the whole of your self will enter this stable level of innerconsciousness with ease. . . . Tell yourself this now, tell yourself that the next time you bring this symbol into your awareness you'll easily and quickly enter this state of being. . . . Know that this is so. Tell yourself that you will remember your symbol for your level and know that every time you bring this symbol into your awareness you'll enter your level with greater and greater ease. . . . This is your creative self-restoring center which you are learning to use for a purpose, any purpose you desire. You'll be able to recognize and work from this level with greater ease every time you practice. Acknowledge that all of this is so. . . .

To return to your creative, self-restoring center, to your level, all you need to do is first bring your symbol for body relaxation into your awareness and give your body the space it needs to relax, in a few moments bring into your awareness your symbol for mental relaxation and give your mind time to calm down some, then relax emotionally, then bring into your awareness your symbol for your level and notice that that particular quality of inner awareness is again present. . . .

Know that you have complete control at this level and every other level of awareness. . . . You may accept or reject anything I say or you may wish to put something aside for later consideration. . . . This is your alpha level—the threshold between your inner and outer realities.˙. . . Here you'll discover the rich and beautiful landscape of your inner dimensions. . . . Here you'll experience vivid and meaningful sensations and imagery . . . your own creativity, your own receptivity . . . new realities unfolding before you, guiding you to new dimensions of being. This is your creative self-restoring center—a stable level of inner consciousness. . . .

Your consciousness has total control of itself. Know that you can choose to move with it in any direction you like. You can return to your usual waking awareness whenever you wish and you can explore the many dimensions within. Know that you can enhance your inner awareness whenever and however you like. I'm going to suggest several methods you can use to deepen your inner experience. Then I'll give you time to use one of these methods I'm about to describe or you may wish to make up one of your own. . . . Throughout your exploration of inner dimensions you will remain alert and aware. . . .

You can imagine yourself to be a leaf upon a tree on a warm sunny afternoon. Imagine that a gentle breeze comes along and lifts you up. . . . Imagine floating through the air as long as you like and when you're ready, slowly fluttering down upon the ground, feeling that you're becoming increasingly aware of yourself with each descending layer of your movement toward the ground. Upon landing on the ground you'll discover yourself at a much more enhanced level of inner awareness—your inner experience will have become much more vivid. . . . And if you like you can land in a brook and softly, easily float through your inner dimensions, feeling yourself gently bobbing up and down as you safely rest upon the surface of the water, and being carried ashore whenever you wish.

Or you can imagine yourself to be in an elevator watching the elevator lights above the door, feeling the sensations as the elevator goes down, down into the depths of your being. . . . And you can choose to leave the elevator at whatever floor you wish, exploring what that particular level has to offer. . . . Or if you choose you can have the elevator go up, exploring the heights of your being.

Or you may wish simply to count on a descending scale from ten to one, telling yourself that at each descending count your aware-ness will go deeper and deeper within yourself until at the count of one you'll find yourself at just that level you wish to explore, a deeper level than before. And at the count of one you'll notice that, in fact, this has occurred. . . .

Or you may wish to watch your breath, to watch the rise and fall of your belly, to feel yourself entering an increasingly enhanced dimension of inner awareness with each breath, with each exhala-tion of breath, letting your breath soothe you into returning you to yourself . . . letting your breath wash away any distractions and settling into who it is that you are. . . .

Take time now to choose one of these methods or to explore one of your own creation, and use it now to enhance your inner awareness. As you do this you'll discover the expansive, fluid spaces within you. Take time to do this now. . . . Tell yourself you will remain alert and aware throughout your exploration.

◆ ◆ ◆

Begin to finish what you're doing and ready yourself to follow

what I have to say to you now . . . very alert and very calmly
listening to what I have to say to you now. . . . Know that every
time you enter these dimensions of awareness, that everytime you
enter your creative, self-restoring center, you're increasingly able to
control and maintain whatever level of awareness you choose. . . .
You'll be able to enter, recognize, and work from these levels with
greater ease every time you practice. . . .

Know that you never lose your ability to meditate, instead, every
time you practice your abilities are greatly enhanced. . . . You'll
discover that every time you meditate, the good feelings that you
experienced will carry over into your daily activities, enabling you
to more fully enjoy the life that is yours, enabling you to work
through any problems that arise with greater ease. . . . Know that
all of this is so. See yourself carrying this sense of well-being you're
now experiencing into your daily activities.

◆ ◆ ◆

Decide now when you will again go into your level. Decide when
in your daily routine would be good times for you to practice
meditating for a few minutes . . . once, twice, maybe three practice
sessions a day. . . . Tell yourself you will remember what you have
decided. . . . Imagine doing what it is that you decided. . . .

To return to your waking consciousness all you need to do is to
tell yourself, "I am now going to count from one to five and snap
my fingers . . . at the count of five I'll open my eyes feeling
revitalized and remembering all that I've experienced in this
meditation". . . . Then count slowly, giving your consciousness
time to adjust levels, just as I am about to do. . . .

Now make yourself ready to come out to outer levels of consciousness, knowing you can return to these inner dimensions
whenever you wish. . . . In a moment I'm going to count from one

to five and snap my fingers; at that moment you'll open your eyes, feeling revitalized, remembering all you've experienced and feeling a sense of well being that will carry over into your activities . . . know you can return to these dimensions whenever you choose. . . .
ONE—becoming more aware of the room around you. . . .
TWO—coming up slowly now. . . .
THREE—at the count of five you'll open your eyes feeling relaxed, revitalized, and refreshed, remembering all you've experienced. . . .
FOUR—coming up now . . . bringing with you your sense of well being. . . .
FIVE!—eyes open, feeling refreshed, revitalized, and relaxed, remembering all you have experienced . . . having brought with you your sense of well being.
[You may now choose to describe or draw your experience.]

Ocean Breath

Close your eyes and focus your awareness on your breathing, breathing with your belly. Feel the rise and fall of your breath. . . . Let your breathing find its own most comfortable rhythm. Breathing that is as relaxed as the breathing of a sleeping baby. . . . Let your breath come all the way down into your belly. Let the rhythm of your breath soothe the whole of your body . . . bring in what you imagine to be calming energy as you inhale . . . release tensions as you exhale . . . bring into your awareness your symbol for physical relaxation . . . feel all the associations of this symbol, this symbol for physical relaxation. . . . Let those associations spread

out through the whole of your body. . . . Give your body permission
to relax, for it can relax now, let the awareness of this symbol
soothe your body into relaxation. . . . It's good to give your body
space and time to relax . . . . Imagine the tensions sinking into the
floor. . . . Feel the weight of your body being fully supported by the
floor. . . . Know that every time you bring this symbol into awareness you will enter deeper and deeper states of physical relaxation
with greater and greater ease. Tell yourself this now. . . .

When you're ready, bring into your awareness your symbol for
mental relaxation. . . . Let all the associations of this symbol
permeate the whole of yourself. . . . Watch the chatter of your
mind becoming calm and quiet . . . where thoughts move in an out
of your awareness as easily as you breathe. . . . Let the rhythm of
your breath calm your mind, give your mind the permission and
space it needs to settle down into the source of itself. . . . Let your
symbol calm your mind. . . . Here sounds do not distract you,
instead they enhance your inner focus. Here, it's as though all your
thoughts were the puffy clouds drifting through a sunny afternoon
sky, the sky of your mind, spacious clear mind. . . . It's good to give
your mind space and time to relax . . . to respond to the calming
message of your symbol. . . . This mental relaxation is a very
harmonious state of being. . . . Tell yourself that whenever you
bring your mental relaxation symbol into your awareness, the
whole of your mind will enter deeper and deeper states of mental
relaxation with greater ease every time you practice. . . .

When you're ready, bring to awareness your emotional relaxation
symbol if you have one. With your awareness go over the full range
of feelings that are present for you now. . . . If any feelings,
positive or negative, are clamoring for your attention, take care of

them in whatever manner occurs to you. . . . Let yourself emotionally relax. . . . Let all the "shoulds" soak into the ground and
nurture yourself, appreciate who you are, give yourself permission
to emotionally relax.

◆

When you're ready, bring into your awareness your symbol for your
level . . . your creative, self-restoring center. . . . Now feel yourself
at a stable level of innerconsciousness. . . . Feel that special quality
of awareness that you have at this level. . . . Your symbol evokes a
special quality of awareness that you are learning to recognize, and
you can work from your level with greater ease every time you
practice. This is your level, which you are learning to use for a
purpose, any purpose you desire. . . . Here you'll find you have
command over a greater range of imagination and creativity. . . .
Your powers of concentration are equally enhanced and permit you
to focus wherever you choose. . . . This is your creative, self-
restoring center. . . . Here you have complete control and you may
accept or reject or put aside for later consideration anything that I
say. . . . Here you'll discover a rich and beautiful landscape of your
receptivity and creativity unfold before you, you'll experience
vivid and meaningful sensations and imagery . . . new realities. . . .
As these realities appear they'll guide you to new dimensions of
being. . . . Here you can make use of the wisdom of your inner self,
discovering the expansive power of your inner being. . . . Your
inner being is a part of the universal energy which permeates all
life. . . . The energy which can dissolve limitations, enabling you
to create change easily. Know that all of this is so. . . .

I will now give you time to explore and enhance your inner
awareness by any method of your choosing. . . . You can use the

falling leaf or elevator, deep breathing or a countdown—whatever you choose. . . . When you next hear my voice you'll be fully alert and ready to follow carefully all that I have to say throughout the whole of this meditation.

◆　◆　◆

Now imagine that you're at the beach—an ocean beach on a sunny summer day. You're sitting or lying on the sand—remember times when this has occurred . . . imagine as though you were transported to the beach instantaneously. . . . There right now . . . imagine the warmth of the sun shining down on you warming your forehead, your whole body; imagine the sound of the ocean. . . . Feel the warmth of the sand below you as the sun has warmed the sand, letting that warmth nurture you, your body soaking it up. You can sense the shape of the indentation that's made in the sand from the contours of your body, your body is fully supported. . . . You can see the glitter of some of the particles of sand. . . . Smell the salty air, feel the breeze that cools you . . . refreshes you, hearing the breakers and the occasional sound of the gulls. . . . Let yourself be fully present in this place. Let your imagination fully create this place. . . .

Now notice the ocean . . . how the waves build and break, the ocean waves build, break, roll on the beach, and roll back in again, building, breaking, moving out, moving in. . . . Roll out, roll back in . . . build, break, roll out, roll back in. . . . The rhythm of the ocean, the inexhaustible movement of the ocean. . . . As you experience the rhythm of the ocean simultaneously become aware of the rhythm of your breath, air rolling in, air rolling out, rolling in, building, breaking, rolling out. . . . The inexhaustible rhythm of your breath sustaining the whole of your being. . . .

Feel your breath as a part of the universal rhythm of the whole of everything. . . . Just as the ocean partakes in this universal rhythm, so too does your breath. . . . Rolling in, building, breaking, rolling out. Rolling in, building, breaking, rolling out. . . . Simply sit with your breath and let it soothe you, cleanse you. . . . Simply be present with your breath, letting your breath draw you into yourself, into beingness itself, moving in, building, breaking, moving out—just as the ocean does. . . . Imagine in fact that your breath is the ocean moving through you. . . . And imagine that your breath can move to any area in your body, rolling in, rolling out, washing away all tensions, all toxins, smoothing the surfaces, rolling in, rolling out just as the ocean waves smooth all rough edges, so too, your breath can wash them away. . . . And now take time to let your breath move to any areas in your body beginning the process of washing away all your tensions, smoothing the edges, pulling in calming energy as it rolls in, washing away tensions as it rolls out. . . . Imagine the air rolling out through the area of tension rather than out through your nose, taking the tensions, toxins, with it; they're slipping out . . . let them slip away. . . . Calm rolling in, they're rolling out. . . . Rolling in . . . softening, rolling out . . . relaxing. . . . And know that with each breath the tensions will continue to diminish and over time they will be gone all together. . . . Feel how each time you breathe the tensions become looser and looser, less and less. . . . And you sink deeper and deeper into the support of the earth. . . . Sometimes tensions, toxins, disappear very quickly, sometimes slowly, either way they have begun to disappear. . . . You are more relaxed, returned to yourself. . . . Just as the ocean washes down everything around it your breath moves through your body, relaxes it, revitalizes it, clears your body as the waves clear the beach. . . .

Feel your breath a part of the universal rhythms that are constantly present always. Let your breath soothe you, clear you, return you to yourself, to beingness itself. . . . Simply be present letting your breath draw you into yourself, into beingness itself. . . . Fully present with your breath, your breath that is constantly present, constantly renewing you, your breath that is the breath of life itself. . . . As the waves are constant, so too is your breath. . . . As your breath is continuously present, as you are present with your breath, you fully relax. . . . Know that whenever you ride your breath you draw all of yourself into your breath and so let your breath draw all of yourself into clarity. . . . Riding your breath continually, just as you can ride and balance on the ocean waves, you ride and balance with your breath. . . . Let yourself be soothed by the presence of your breath. . . .

And as you're present with your breath look out into the future and notice if there is anything that keeps you from being relaxed . . what you do to yourself to forget your breath, to forget yourself, forget beingness itself. . . . Notice what you need to do to remember your breath, to be present wholly, connected with your being and beingness itself. . . . Imagine doing this . . . remember to breathe, feeling yourself constantly in the present with your breath, remembering to breathe.

◆　◆　◆

I want you to know that everytime you meditate, you receive beneficial effects both physically and psychologically. . . . That every time you meditate, you're increasingly able to control your levels of conscious awareness and able to remain at whatever level you choose for as long as you desire. . . . Know that you never lose your ability to meditate . . . instead every time you practice your abilities are enhanced geometrically . . . and you'll discover that every time you meditate, the good feelings you've experienced will carry over into your daily activities enabling you to enjoy more fully the life that is yours, enabling you to work through any problems that arise with greater ease. . . . Know that all of this is so. . . . Imagine yourself carrying this sense of well-being into your daily activities. . . . Expect it to be so.

◆　◆　◆

Know that you are fully capable of acting on these energies. . . . Finish what you're doing and make yourself ready to come out to outer conscious levels . . . know that you'll bring with you all the energies you've contacted. . . .

Know that you can return to these dimensions whenever you choose. You may want to project when you want to meditate again. . . .

In a moment I'm going to count from one to five and snap my fingers . . . at that moment, you'll open your eyes remembering all that you've experienced. . . .

ONE—becoming more aware of the room around you. . . .

TWO—coming up slowly now. . . .

THREE—at the count of five you'll open your eyes feeling relaxed, revitalized, and refreshed remembering all that you've experienced. . . .

FOUR—coming up now, bring with you your sense of well-being. . . .

FIVE! (snap)—Eyes open, feeling refreshed, revitalized and relaxed, remembering all that you've experienced, feeling a sense of well-being, ready and able to act on the energies to which you've attuned yourself.

[You may want to jot down your reflections.]

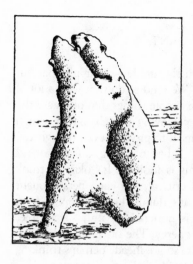

Chapter Three

Creating a Language to Speak to Your Deeper Self

Whenever you meditate you are predominantly at the alpha level, which is suggestible, so you may as well take advantage of this receptivity and develop your own programming—thereby, with an act of will, choosing to program your own development. If a TV ad can con you into buying some kitchen gadget why not choose to do something you really want? Using affirmations is one of the most powerful ways of doing this.

An affirmation is simply a positively stated sentence of how you'd like to be, such as: "The whole of my body is healthy." That may sound simplistic because you know the whole of your body is not fully healthy; all of us have something or other that ails us. However, since your innerconsciousness is noncritical it believes anything, and it's your innerconsciousness that directs your body. So if you cultivate a belief within that your body is healthy, it will enable your body to be more effective in fighting off potential sickness, and it will give you a little added strength to heal the ailments it already has. Our bodies are continually responding to our inner messages; remember that simply imagining what you're afraid of activates your adrenal glands. If you put in the message that you are healthy your body will respond accordingly, and this is simply done by *pretending* that it is so.

AFFIRMATIONS:
TAKE A STAND FOR WHAT YOU WANT

Working with affirmations is extremely simple—so simple that our tendency is to slough it off as silly. We tend to do that with a lot of things in our lives but it's just these simple things that often are the most enriching. We need to stop denying ourselves that which could so easily be ours. Permit yourself to proceed even though you may think it ridiculous. When I began doing affirmations I invariably thought to myself, "This is foolish." It's okay to think that—remember the beta mind is critical, but each beta thought has very little energy. Thinking it's dumb doesn't stop it from working—the innerconsciousness is noncritical, i.e., suggestible, and each alpha thought has more energy. The only thing that will stop it from working is not using it, so go ahead, perhaps thinking all the while that it is an absurd activity.

Awhile back I had an experience that reignited my knowledge of the power of affirmations. About a year ago I had a major disagreement with one of my closest friends, and for many months we talked about it often, never being able to come to any resolution. It made it close to impossible for us to be able to enjoy our friendship. We finally decided to go to a mediator who tried to help us work through our problems. That too was unsuccessful. All along our intentions had been good—we each sincerely wanted to work it out—but to no avail. Several weeks after that attempt it came to me in a meditation to use an affirmation. The specific words that came to my mind were, "I reside in the care we have for each other." I used the affirmation regularly, and wrote a postcard to my friend inviting him to join me in its use. About a month later we saw each other again and somehow, inexplicably, the year-old tension had completely dissolved. The affirmation must have drawn on the intuitive knowledge available at deeper levels, for we found ourselves moving along a new course. The use of that affirmation was the only new element in our relationship—nothing else had changed. If I hadn't known how to use these energies I might have lost a friendship close to my heart. It is experiences like this that humble me for the energy that is available to work with is powerful. In working with innerconsciousness I have come to realize that the solution comes about without my knowing *why* or *how*. It is never linear or reasonable—it simply is. Sometimes it's very subtle; I can't even point to the solution, but I can't point to the problem anymore either which—is solution enough for me.

It's good to make your own affirmations. To do this, think of aspects of your life that you'd like to change and how you'd like them to be instead. For each one create a sentence, stated *simply*, *positively*, and in the *present* tense, or think of a particular picture or sensation that represents each change as if it has *already* come about. This process will enable you to create a specific affirmation for any particular transformation of your choosing—take a stand for what you want.

Your innerconsciousness is not linear but instead very childlike so you don't have to have an analysis of why something is needed or how it will happen—justification is unnecessary. You simply need a statement of the desired end result. Always state it in the present tense because your innerconsciousness, being suggestible, takes things quite literally. You don't want to become healthy because that's perpetually in the future; you want to *be* healthy. As far as your innerconsciousness is concerned you only exist in the moment; time is meaningless to it. So don't say, "I will be healthy, because I eat well," but "I am fully healthy."

Because of the noncritical nature of your innerconsciousness affirmations should always be stated positively; it doesn't understand negatives. Notice what happens when I say, "Don't imagine a lemon." You immediately and unavoidably think of a lemon. If you use the affirmation, "I'm not sick," it will just hear "sick." It's easy to understand this if you think of young children who are much more responsive when you state things in a positive way. Rather than saying "Stop making all that noise," it is much more effective to say, "Be a little quieter." As a matter of fact we should begin to watch the negative suggestions we are constantly giving ourselves (a friend calls them neffirmations). For example, "Whenever I talk in groups, I sound stupid." Notice how this statement is positively expressing something you don't want. Similarly, if you want to feel secure speaking in public, saying, "I'm not stupid," is ineffectual, whereas saying, "I'm intelligent and articulate," helps enormously.

In addition, you don't want your beta mind to give your inner self a bunch of alternatives stating it one day this way and one day that. Your innerconsciousness, just like a child, will only become confused. You want to impress it with a *clear* message, using the same picture or statement time and time again (like a symbol).

When using affirmations, the important thing is that when you are repeating them you feel as much as possible that they are true. You concentrate on the power implied by the statement itself; pretend that it is so. It is not the words themselves (or the pictures) that have power, *it's the feelings they elicit.* You want to plant those feelings in your innerconsciousness as often as you can so new resources will grow for you to act out of. Be sure not to focus on the inaccuracy of the affirmation for that will only perpetuate the reality you want to change. If it were fully true you wouldn't need the affirmation. It's a given that there's a contradiction, but don't look at it and conclude that the affirmation is not working. Instead, move through your daily activities with the assumption that the power of the affirmation is working under the surface. When you say to yourself, "I am healthy," don't focus on your ailing knee, but concentrate on the vitality your body does have. When you are going through your daily activities and your knee starts to hurt, don't decide that the affirmation has been ineffective, but remember it and assume its power is gradually working and that its reality will slowly manifest itself.

It is crucial to be ever aware that we always respond in terms of our beliefs. This is operative with affirmations and with all other techniques in this book. We always go through our activities in terms of our attitudes. Thus, if you use an affirmation with the attitude (belief) that it probably won't work—it won't. So try to suspend judgment and just experiment with the process watching for its results instead of trying to prove to yourself that it's not working. If you do this, the contradiction between your daily reality and the affirmation will slowly dissolve. Since each of us is constantly looking to have our point of view validated, I'd rather work on the side of proof of benefits than detriments. If you can keep your attitudes positive, you won't give up your power.

Some people prefer to speak the affirmations aloud, for hearing the words gives them an added power. Or you may want to make up a jingle. You know that method works; how often have you caught yourself singing a TV commercial in your head, unable to get it out of your mind? ("Double your pleasure, double your fun.") You might also want to use just one word that connotes the kind of quality you want to bring into your life, such as trust, cooperation, love, joy, generosity, etc.[1] I suggest that you write down (or draw) your affirmations and post them in places that you regularly see, like the door of your refrigerator or your bathroom mirror; simply catching sight of them out of the corner of your eye will enhance the process of bringing their energy into your life.

You can also repeat affirmations while doing rhythmic activities such as exercising or cleaning, as you are in the alpha state and it will be just as effective as it is when you are meditating. You can use a number of affirmations, one right after the other, or you may want to use just one, repeating it over and over again. Either way, stick to the same wording, which doesn't mean that you can't refine them. As you experiment with the use of affirmations you will discover the format that's most comfortable for you.

The important thing is that you use them *repeatedly* because one characteristic of our innerconsciousness is that it is extremely responsive to repetition. That's one reason why rituals are universally practiced—a major part of every religious tradition is the use of ritual. And a major element of ritual is the repetition of certain words—as in chanting—or the regular use of certain gestures. These chants and gestures always have a specific meaning behind them. Their purpose is to evoke a particular energy. Similarly, repetition of affirmations is a powerful way to create a channel through which deeper knowledge surfaces. In time you will come to a fuller realization of the power that you are speaking of in each affirmation, moving beyond intellectual understanding and creating conditions in the whole of your being in which the affirmation will manifest itself. None of this occurs logically. Although we do not yet understand the process of the all-knowingness of the collective unconscious, we can dip into it to improve our lives, and affirmations do just that, like tapping an underground spring. You will find yourself unconsciously behaving differently, intuitively acting in alignment with the affirmation. In the induction for each meditation section there are new affirmations that address the particular issues dealt with in that chapter. It's good to use affirmations every time you meditate.

Here is one affirmation which I think is of particular importance, "I only respond to *positive* suggestions." This protects you from your own negative thoughts and those of others. We all find ourselves acting in ways we don't really approve of; if we tap our own wisdom we'll find ourselves always behaving to the best of our abilities, for on a deep level we *do* know what's best. Even if you forget everything else in this book and use only this affirmation, it will change your life.

Another powerful affirmation is, "I maintain balance amidst change." This enables you to be relaxed rather than stressed out so you can respond creatively with the whole of yourself in the midst of turmoil.

One which will move us out of loneliness into trusting both ourselves and others is, "I believe in myself; I believe in my family and friends; we believe in our community; there is a free flow of support among us." This will create an atmosphere of sharing our powers and collectively better enable us to resolve whatever needs changing in our lives.

To combat any mystification or suspicion of the innerconsciousness an affirmation such as, "I have complete control of all levels of awareness," will be helpful.

In today's apocalyptic times we can create a safe future by believing in it and thereby working for it. Using the affirmation, "I trust the future," cultivates this belief.

In the first meditation at the end of the chapter, which you may want to do now before you proceed further, you will focus on numerous affirmations.

SYMBOLING:
USING THE POWER OF SYMBOLS

A symbol is something that represents more than itself. For instance, anything you feel sentimental about is a symbol. There may be a kind of flower that has particular significance to you because it represents the person who gave it to you and the relationship you had with that person, more than simply the look and smell of that variety of flower. Our lives are full of symbols, some are very personal while others have come to be almost universal like the wedding ring, or the American flag.

A symbol, being more than itself, is a converging point, the focal point of meaning. A symbol does not need logical or sequential thought processes in order for it to evoke its full meaning. Because our innerconsciousness is holistic, nonsequential and more focused its predominant language is symbols. By definition a symbol elicits a particular set of associations and responses when you bring it to awareness. Therefore if you want to behave in a particular way you can create a symbol to represent that behavior, bring it into your awareness at the opportune time, and you will then discover yourself acting the way you want to. Your behavior and your inner messages have moved into alignment by use of the symbol. You won't need to go off and meditate about the kind of energy you want or the changes you'd like to make; all you need do is bring into your awareness the previously created personal symbol you have for the energy. This is very important to be able to do because when you're in the midst of a situation you don't have the time, space, or inclination to go off and meditate about it. For example, I am a very goal-oriented person—this trait is often useful because it enables me to accomplish a lot, but there are situations where it becomes a detriment. I feel like I want to be there already and I am very impatient. Often it's when I'm working in groups that this problem surfaces. To resolve this tendency I created a symbol at a deep level of consciousness—a sailboat. The meaning of sailboats to me is that they get to their destination by utilizing the natural forces around them. So whenever I bring this sailboat into my awareness it causes me to trust the organic process and to adjust myself to the energies around me rather than "pushing the river." As a result I find myself calming down, feeling more a part of the process, and understanding how the process (symbolized by the wind and the current) is in fact necessary to bring me to the goal. If I hadn't already created the symbol of the sailboat in a meditation, to use whenever I might need it, I would continue to be impatient in meetings.

A woman in one of my classes had an image of herself as a klutz. She played left field on a softball team and her body kept responding to this self-image, sabotaging her ability to play well. In class she went through a fantasy of feeling extremely coordinated and created a symbol for it. She moved from being the klutz on her team to being a star. Every time a fly ball was hit she brought this symbol to mind and to everyone's amazement she started catching those flies. It worked because when the ball was in the air she didn't have enough time to give herself a pep talk, but she could remember her symbol instantaneously.

For you to be able to understand the power of symbols, it's important that you remember the *intimate* connection between what is going on in your awareness at any given moment and its effect on the rest of you—your body, your behavior, etc. Again, the example of dog phobia makes it clear that simply imagining a dog will set the adrenaline pumping. You've probably come to experience this connection yourself by using your induction symbols.

You have numerous associations with any particular behavior you want to elicit. In the symbol they converge creating a focal point out of which the concrete action you want emerges. Whenever the symbol is in your mind it creates a channel for you to become intuitively aware of what is needed to behave in accord with the energy. The symbol acts as a flashlight illuminating that information from the depths of knowingness. The trick is first to get in touch with the energy and then create the symbol in a deep level and tell yourself that next time you bring it to mind you'll respond accordingly. And you can create an affirmation telling yourself you'll remember and bring it into your awareness at the opportune moment. Never forget that it's your inner messages that you act out of. The symbol is more than just a beta thought. Instead it becomes a source of behavior.

You can have specific symbols for many kinds of energy: for creativity, for personal power, for trust, for cooperation, for clear communication, for anything you may need. For example, if you're about to go through a round of interviews, it's a good idea to have an appropriate symbol to use while being interviewed. It will increase manyfold the likelihood of being chosen for the job you want.

In the Symbol-making meditation you can create a symbol representing any particular kind of energy you choose. To help you connect with that energy the meditation will guide you through experiences of your past when you felt it most strongly. If there are no such times, *pretend* there were, or do whatever occurs to you to help you to *feel* the energy. After focusing on the energy, make up a symbol to represent it. Whatever symbol you create is the *right* one, for it's what you associate with the energy, and it's *you* that you're working with. Symbols don't necessarily have to be pictures but it is important that they be specific and easy to recall. You may wish to use a place in your body or a physical gesture or a particular tone—whatever your inclination. I also suggest that you create an affirmation that says that you'll remember to bring your symbol into your awareness whenever a situation arises in which it will be of help; for obviously it only works when you remember to use it. (A separate affirmation for each symbol.)

The first symbol-making meditation is for general use; be sure to choose in advance what you want to create a symbol for. I also recommend that you increase your vocabulary of symbols gradually so your deeper self comes to know each one, rather than confusing it with too many to begin with. Like affirmations it is good to post your symbols in places where you'll see them.

If you do this you'll find their effectiveness growing more rapidly, for each reminder strengthens the energy, and you'll be better able to act on its power. It's also good to take time to focus for a few moments on the power and quality of the symbol every time you meditate.

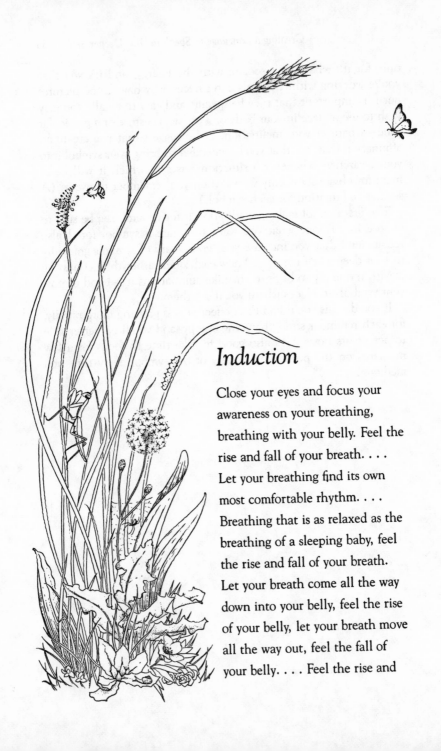

Induction

Close your eyes and focus your
awareness on your breathing,
breathing with your belly. Feel the
rise and fall of your breath. . . .
Let your breathing find its own
most comfortable rhythm. . . .
Breathing that is as relaxed as the
breathing of a sleeping baby, feel
the rise and fall of your breath.
Let your breath come all the way
down into your belly, feel the rise
of your belly, let your breath move
all the way out, feel the fall of
your belly. . . . Feel the rise and

fall of your breath. . . . Let the rhythm of your breath soothe the whole of your body. . . . Bring in what you imagine to be calming energy as you inhale, release tensions as you exhale. . . . Bring into your awareness your symbol for physical relaxation, feel all the associations you have with this symbol, your symbol for physical relaxation. Let those associations spread out through the whole of your body. . . . Give your body permission to relax, for it can relax now. . . . Let the awareness of this symbol soothe your body into relaxation. . . . It's good to give your body space and time to relax. Imagine the tensions sinking into the floor. . . . Know that every time you bring this symbol into awareness you will enter deeper and deeper states of physical relaxation with greater and greater ease. . . . Tell yourself this now. . . .

When you're ready, bring into your awareness your symbol for mental relaxation. Let all the associations of this symbol permeate the whole of yourself. . . . Watch the chatter of your mind becoming calm and quiet . . . where thoughts move in and out of your awareness as easily as you breathe. . . . Let the rhythm of your breath calm your mind and give your mind the permission and the space it needs to settle down into the source of itself. . . . Let your mental relaxation symbol calm your mind. . . . Here sounds do not distract you, instead they enhance your inner focus. Here, it's as though all your thoughts were the puffy clouds drifting through a sunny afternoon sky, the sky of your mind. . . . It's good to give your mind space and time to relax. . . . This mental relaxation is a very harmonious state of being. Tell yourself that whenever you bring your mental relaxation symbol into your awareness, the whole of your mind will enter deeper and deeper states of mental relaxation with greater ease every time you practice. . . .

When you're ready, bring in your symbol for emotional relax-ation, with your awareness go over the full range of feelings that are present for you now. . . . If you discover any feelings, positive or negative, that are clamoring for your attention, take care of them in whatever manner occurs to you. . . . Let yourself emotion-ally relax. Imagine letting all the "shoulds" soak into the ground, and nurture yourself, give yourself permission to relax emotion-ally. . . .

When you're ready, bring into your awareness your symbol for your level, your creative, self-restoring center. . . . Now feel yourself at a stable level of innerconsciousness. . . . Feel that special quality of awareness that you have at this level. . . . That special quality of awareness that your symbol evokes; you are learning to recognize and work from your level with greater ease every time you practice. This is your level, which you are learning to use for a purpose, any purpose you desire. . . . Here you'll find you have command over a greater range of imagination and creativity, your powers of concentration are equally enhanced and permit you to focus wherever you choose. . . . This is your creative, self-restoring center. . . . Here you have complete control and you may accept, or reject, or put aside for later consideration anything that I say. . . . Here you'll discover a rich and beautiful landscape of your receptivity and creativity unfold before you, you'll experi-ence vivid and meaningful sensations and imagery. . . new real-ities. . . . As these realities appear they'll guide you to new dimen-sions of being. . . . Here you can make use of the wisdom of your inner self, discovering the expansive power of your inner being. Your inner being is a part of the universal energy which permeates all life. . . . This is the energy which dissolves limitations, enabling you to create change, know that all of this is so. . . .

I will now give you time to explore and enhance your inner awareness by any method of your choosing. . . . You can use the falling leaf or elevator or countdown—whatever you choose. . . . When you next hear my voice you'll be fully alert and ready to follow carefully all that I have to say throughout the whole of this meditation.

◆   ◆   ◆

Finishing what you're doing . . . your consciousness is very receptive, very creative, very relaxed and very alert. . . . You will easily follow all that I have to say to you now, you will remember the whole of your meditative experience and be able to work with the energies you are going to experience in this meditation whenever you choose in the future.

Affirmations

One powerful way of working with this energy is in using affirmations. I'm going to suggest several affirmations. If you wish to affirm them repeat them to yourself after me. And at the same time, as much as you're able, feel as though each affirmation is fully true . . . bring into your awareness pictures and sensations that represent each affirmation as you speak the words to yourself. If you don't like the affirmation simply don't repeat it and wait for the next. Remember not to focus on the difference between any affirmation and your life, but look instead for a grain of truth in your personal experience and let your inner consciousness expand it, making room for new energies to flow through. Feel the power of the words. In so doing you'll discover that as time goes by you'll find yourself living in ways that conform to the affirmations, and you will find affirmations materializing in your daily reality. You'll intuitively be acting out of the power of each affirmation. . . .

I believe in myself; I believe in my family and friends; we believe in our community; there is a free flow of support in creating change. . . .

I trust the whole of myself. . . .

I am enriched by my deepest dimensions. . . .

I have complete control of my awareness, abilities and activities on all levels. . . .

I am aware and alert when I meditate. . . .

I only respond to positive suggestions. . . .

The whole of my body/mind is healthy. I have all the energy I need to do as I choose. . . .

My negative feelings guide me to changing their sources. . . .

I face my fears; they are challenges; they guide me to new dimensions of learning. . . .

My life is full of joy. . . .

A spring of creativity continually flows through me and out into the world. . . .

All that I know is available to me whenever I need it. . . .

All my needs are always met—there is enough for everyone. . . .

I am in tune and responsive to my intuition—my deeper knowingness. . . .

Every day the powers of the depths of my consciousness become more and more available to me. . . .

I act on my knowingness in my life. . . .

My increasing personal power is for making the world a better place to live for everyone. . . .

I maintain balance amidst change. . . .

I trust the future. . . .

Know that in focusing on affirmations you've evoked patterns of energy that'll begin moving through your life, materializing in your daily experience. . . . Know that these energies have already begun to move and their movement will be empowered every time you focus on the affirmations. . . . You'll find yourself intuitively acting in alignment with the affirmations.

Now create one affirmation of your own choosing. Pick one particular area in your life you'd like to improve . . . imagine how you'd like it to be . . . feel it as a present reality. . . . Create a statement . . . simple, positive and present tense, of how you would like it to be. If you're more inclined, choose a picture or sensation instead, best of all do both. Take time to do this now.

◆ ◆ ◆

Bring your awareness back to my words knowing that you'll remember this affirmation for future use, knowing that the energies have begun their movement. Knowing you'll find yourself intuitively acting in alignment with the affirmation the more you use it. Tell yourself this now.

Internalizing a Quality

Imagine soothing energy, whatever that means to you—it may be sounds, feelings, vibrations, a knowingness. Imagine soothing energy, whatever that means to you . . . calming energy . . . the softness of velvet, imagine yourself surrounded by this energy, soothing energy and letting it soak into your body, absorb its

softness . . . feel it gently returning you to yourself, nurturing you
. . . soothingness soaking deeper and deeper into you . . . comforting you, healing you . . . soothingness gently moving through you,
through the whole of your being, deep into yourself. Enabling you
to simply be receptive to yourself . . . receptive to this soothing
energy. As though, if you listen, the soothing energy opens up
within you very soft and soothing music . . . you can sense the
tones of your being, you can almost hear the quiet hum of beingness
itself—the music, the tones of life itself. . . . Let the music soothe
you, let the cells of your body sway with it . . . surrounded by
soothing energy, gentle energy, almost as though you're floating in
it, soft soothingness. . . .

From this place give yourself permission to be fully receptive,
take care of yourself however you need to, so that you can allow
yourself to be fully soothed, all your edges smoothed, fully receptive, soft . . . quiet in yourself, receptive and soothed. . . .

And as you are receptive, quietly residing in yourself, bring to
awareness a quality you would like to work with, a quality that
you'd like to bring more of into your life. Choose a particular
quality you would like to cultivate. Love or joy or grace or humor
or another quality . . . whatever quality you like. . . . Choose just
one now, and know you can work on others another time. . . .

Now simply meditate on this quality in this receptive state.
Repeat the word to yourself several times. . . . Experience its
meaning . . . experience its meaning from many sides of it . . .
repeat the word over and over and over again. . . . Know the
meaning of the word. . . . Reach out to it intuitively. . . . Feel the
energy inherent in the quality. . . . You can almost feel the quality,
sense it . . . see it. What color is it?. . . . Feel it . . . listen to it,

how does it sound?. . . Taste of its energy . . . let it touch you . . .
how does it make your body feel? What parts of the whole of
yourself resonate with it?

◆ ◆ ◆

Let the quality share the space you occupy, call it by repeating its
name—the word—over and over and over again. . . . Share your
presence with one another, let it be present with you, let its full
meaning be next to you, let yourself be fully present with it . . . let
it be all around you . . . beside you . . . above you . . . below you
. . . let it be all around you, let it surround you.

◆ ◆ ◆

Create a vessel into which to put the meaning of the quality. . . .
Imagine putting the energy, the vibrations, the knowingness, the
full meaning into this vessel. Fill up the vessel with the quality. . . .
Now imagine drinking out of the vessel, feel yourself absorbing the
quality, let it move through you just as soothingness moved through
you earlier. . . . Imagine the quality circulating through the whole
of your body, breath it in. How would that feel? . . . Let your
breath, let your blood carry it to all the nooks and crannies of your
body. . . . Let your breath, let your blood carry the contents of the
vessel through the whole of your being, feel it flowing, sifting,
settling throughout the whole of your being, feel it vibrating
through you . . . sense it emanating from your center.

◆ ◆ ◆

Know that you are endowed with its power; you are empowered
with this quality. Imagine for a moment that you have *become* the
energy, *become* the quality—being the energy, the knowingness.

◆ ◆ ◆

Know that as you become more and more familiar with the energy
it will sink deeper and deeper into yourself, into the core of your
being. Now extend your awareness to include how it is you can act

on this energy in your activities, notice how you can incorporate
into your life what you sense and feel, what you know. . . . Decide
if you're willing to do that. . . . If you are, feel yourself doing
it. . . . Become aware of how it is to have the energy present in
your actions . . . to have your actions be receptive to the presence
of the energy.

◆   ◆   ◆

Know that you are fully empowered with this quality, this knowingness and you will become even more so, the more you include it in
your awareness. Know that this is so.

Symbol-making

Now you are going to create a symbol for a quality or ability you
would like to cultivate. You are going to use the vast receptive and
creative powers available to you. I want you to know that from this
place time is very fluid. You can remember and relive experiences
vividly as though they were again occurring, bringing their powers
to bear . . . using their powers and projecting them into the future;
retaining their powers by containing their powers in a symbol, a
symbol that you can use time and time again to call upon the
power inherent in the quality. . . . And in fact as you use the
symbol you create you'll discover yourself feeling and acting in
ways that are fully in accord with the energy of the symbol. Know
that this is so. For symbols are the language that speaks to your
deepest knowingness—they are the language of your inner self and
you can tap the power of knowingness itself and bring forth
whatever power you would like, and empower yourself and empower

the situation. Know that you can create a symbol to evoke whatever you choose for symbols are the language of your inner self.

Now get in touch with the quality you would like to work on, the quality you would like to create a symbol for. . . . What does it mean to you?. . . In a moment you'll remember a time in your life when this quality was present, or you can create an imaginary time. Feel this time now . . . create this time now . . . feel the atmosphere of the scene, notice how your body feels, exaggerate the quality. . . . If there seems to have been no time when this quality was present, pretend that there was.

◆ ◆ ◆

Now, either remember another scene where the quality was present or become even more deeply aware, even more in tune with the scene you've been experiencing. . . . Sense the quality, sense its vibrations, its tone. . . . Does it have color, or sound?. . . As you hear the sounds of these words you'll get further in touch with this quality. Discover the personality of the quality. . . . Now, experience a time in the future when the quality is present. . . . How does this time feel? What are you doing? Exaggerate the quality, feel the scene unfold and the quality getting even stronger. . . . Feel the quality's energy in your body. Feel its power.

◆ ◆ ◆

Now create a symbol that represents this quality. . . . If a couple come to mind, either choose one or let them coalesce into one; if nothing comes to mind, make one up; What you create is *right* for you. . . .

This is your symbol, feel its power. I want you to know that whenever you bring this symbol to mind, you'll find yourself feeling and acting in total unity with this symbol. . . . Tell yourself that this is so, that whenever you bring this symbol into your awareness you'll find yourself acting in accord with it, intuitively knowing whatever you need to, to act in this empowered way. Tell yourself you will remember to use your symbol whenever you need it. . . . Know that everytime you use it, it becomes increasingly power-ful. . . . Feel your power; you are fully able to act on this quality.

Enjoyment

Know that as you hear these words you will get in touch with times in your life where you have fully enjoyed yourself. . . . The sounds of these words will evoke from the depths of your being the quality of enjoyment . . . deep enjoyment. Remember a time where you fully enjoyed yourself. . . . Remember this time . . . feel as though it were occurring all over again . . . feel the pleasure this time has for you, delight in the pleasure . . . once again you can appreciate this time, feel your body as though you were reliving this time again. . . . Notice what's around you. . . . Feel the expansiveness of the atmosphere you're in. . . . Feel your connection to others, your connection to yourself. . . . Just experience the lighthearted energy. . . . Moving into deeper and deeper levels of enjoy-ment. . . . Letting the energy of enjoyment move through every layer of yourself, feel pleasure. . . . Feel the satisfaction of enjoy-ment. . . . Remember other times or remember even more vividly this time you've been experiencing. . . . Relive joyfulness, feel the rich satisfaction, having fun, playing. . . . Letting the spontaneity carry you, uplift you, trusting these good times of joyousness, times of enjoyment. . . . Celebrate life.

◆ ◆ ◆

Now bring these feelings of enjoyment into the present, fully opening your life to the pleasure you can have now. Bringing enjoyment into your life now, in the present. . . . Notice the times, the places in your daily life that can burst with enjoyment or that can softly fill you with deep, rich satisfaction. . . . Notice the different situations in your life that you like, that are enjoyable, expand these times, exaggerate their goodness. . . . Feel how others can also appreciate these times, can share your joy.

◆   ◆   ◆

Now, let the enjoyment flow out into the future, enriching it; enriching the future, a future you can look forward to. . . . Let this enjoyment permeate the future, flow into the future, opening yourself to enjoyment, letting it heal the whole of your being. . . . And as it heals the whole of yourself, the energy moves out and heals what's around you. Lighthearted energy . . . playfulness . . . laughter . . . sensuality . . . sexuality . . . sharing, sharing enjoyment. . . . Rejoice in life. . . . Letting this enjoyment permeate the whole of yourself and all those around you. . . . Imagine it permeate the whole of life itself.

Now create a symbol that represents all that you've been experiencing, that represents all this enjoyment, this pleasure, this goodness. . . . If a couple come to mind either choose one or let them coalesce into one. . . . If nothing comes to mind, make one up, and know that what you make up is right for you.

◆

This is your symbol of enjoyment. . . . Know that it contains all the feelings, the energies that you've been experiencing. Imagine its power. . . . And know, that whenever you bring this symbol into your awareness you'll unleash the enjoyment contained in whatever situation you're in . . . whenever you bring this symbol to mind, you'll find yourself feeling and acting in unity with this symbol. . . . Tell yourself that this is so, that whenever you bring your enjoyment symbol to mind, you'll find yourself feeling and acting in unity with this symbol. . . . Tell yourself that this is so, that whenever you bring your enjoyment symbol into awareness, you'll find yourself acting in accord with it, intuitively being receptive to whatever you need to know to enjoy yourself. . . . Tell yourself this now. Know that this is so.

♦

And tell yourself that you'll remember your symbol whenever you need it.

Creativity

Now imagine yourself in a very comfortable, quiet, warm place in the countryside; there is a stream there. There is a refreshing feeling about the whole place. . . . You can smell the subtle scent of flowers in the air; you can hear the sound of the water, notice the colors and textures of everything around you. . . . Let yourself fully create this place, let yourself really appreciate this place.

♦

Now focus on the stream. I want you to know that this is a very special stream, this is a stream of your imagination . . . the stream of your consciousness, the source of this stream is nearby—a spring that continually feeds this stream, go to the source of the stream. . . . Find this spring, this spring can be whatever you imagine it to be, a spring of creativity . . . water, color, sound, vibrations, energy, this is a spring of creativity. So pure you can't

quite grasp it, but you can sense its power. . . . Imagine experiencing the very source of creativity itself . . . beyond yourself, the
source of creativity coming from a universal place, the source of
this spring is the very depths of collective consciousness of all
people, all living things . . . the source of collective knowledge,
collective creativity, primordial, infinite energy, energy that
extends vastly through the universe of the past, of the present, of
the future . . . however you imagine it to be. . . . Imagine going
into the very source of creativity itself, however you imagine that,
however you create that. . . . Feel the vibrant source of creativity
. . . sense it, imagine it, create it.

◆

Let yourself emerge from this source of creativity and make yourself
a comfortable way of floating on the stream of your imagination,
the stream whose source is primordial. . . . As this stream has an
infinite primordial source, it too can carry you to the vast reaches
of the world, discovering the unknown, revealing new energies. . . .
You may want to float down it on an innertube or by any method
you choose. . . . Imagine yourself floating down this stream, this
stream of creativity carrying you, floating down, down, down, pure
forms of creativity floating through your being . . . this stream
comes from the depths of the earth, the depths of the collective
consciousness of all life. . . . Letting the water you're floating upon
cleanse your entire being, moving through you, connecting you to
your *own* creativity. . . . Pure forms of creativity moving through
your being . . . so pure you can't quite grasp what they are, just
sense them, feel them, know that creativity moves through you,
experience this creative energy below you, around you, in you,
surrounding your entire being, however you imagine it, as you

move down, down, down the stream. A very magic, special stream coming from the depths of beingness itself, this stream constantly flowing, constantly changing, expression of life, the spontaneity of life itself . . . never twice the same . . . creativity. . . .

As you move further and further down this stream, you can begin to experience ways that this creativity can reveal itself in your life. You may see these ways played out as scenarios on the banks of the stream. . . . You may see imagery in the water as you float over it. You may sense things in the air. . . . New ways, richer ways for creativity to express itself in your life, for you to bring this energy that you're floating upon into the world. New ways to express it . . . richer ways to express it, expressing creativity on many dimensions, clearly asserting this energy. . . . Manifesting this energy in all aspects of your life. . . . Notice all the different areas of your life in the light of this creativity, let it enlighten your life . . . relationships with different people . . . responsibilities that you have . . . new things you may want to do, or old things you may want to do in a new way. . . . Projects you're involved in . . . simply bring different areas of your life to mind and in so doing you let this creativity shed light on them, giving rise to new experience.

◆ ◆ ◆

Notice if there are any activities you can do that will help the creativity flow out into your life. . . . Is there anything you need to be disciplined about?

◆ ◆ ◆

And as you float down the stream, and you experience your creativity evolving in new forms, in richer ways, you are now going to discover those ways which get in the way of this energy flowing. What blocks the energy from flowing, from moving, from expressing itself in your experience, from your acting on it, from your experiencing it?

❖

And as you experience what blocks the flow of this creativity, you will also experience what you need to do to remove this block, to let the energy flow. You'll discover exactly what needs to be done with these blocks, releasing the flow of energy in your life. . . . Knowing just what needs to be done to let this energy that you're experiencing move into your life, move into the world.

❖

As you continue to move down the stream and the creativity is manifesting all around you, you can begin to see the effects of this creativity. You can begin to experience how this creativity moves into the world, how people receive the energy and in receiving the energy are also inspired to create. All making the stream grow and expand, and become richer and richer. Feel the rewards of creativity, of yours, of everyone's, everyone's creativity building on the creativity of others, creativity spreading everywhere. . . . This stream moves through all consciousness, through all lives. Feel the excitement of expressing this energy. Letting creativity flow through each of us. . . .

Now create a symbol that represents all that you're experiencing . . . that represents creativity, your creativity. . . . If a couple come to mind, choose one of them, or let them coalesce into one, if nothing comes to mind, make one up. It can be a sound, a gesture, a picture. . . . This is your symbol for creativity, your creativity. With this symbol you can tap primordial creativity. Feel the creative power inherent in this symbol. Take time to imagine talking to your symbol, personify it . . . ask it questions whenever you are stuck and you'll find yourself knowing the answers. . . .

Talk to your creativity symbol now, talk to it about any quandaries
you may have and sense change begin.

◆   ◆   ◆

Whenever you bring this symbol into your awareness you'll discover
creative energies beginning to flow, for you will have tapped
universal energy and you'll find yourself able to act on these
energies, riding the movement of creativity . . . expressing creativity in your life. Tell yourself that this is so. . . . Tell yourself that
whenever you need creativity you'll remember to bring this symbol
to awareness and know that when you do you'll find creativity
flowing through you from the source of beingness itself.

Countout

Take time now to imagine using what you have worked with in this
meditation and imagine the difference it will make in your ability
to be as you choose. . . . Know that every time you work with these
energies you become increasingly empowered.

◆

Go over all you experienced in this meditation . . . insights,
feelings, sensations. . . . Make yourself ready to come out to outer
conscious levels. . . . Know that you can return to these dimensions
of awareness whenever you choose. . . . Know that whenever you
enter these levels of consciousness, you receive beneficial effects
both physically and psychically. You become a more centered
being. Each time you meditate you are increasingly able to control
degrees of conscious awareness and remain at whatever level of
awareness you choose, for as long as you choose. Every time you

work with your level your abilities are enhanced. . . . Know that all
of this is so. . . .

In a moment I'm going to count from one to five, at the count of
five you'll open your eyes feeling refreshed, relaxed and revitalized,
remembering all that you've experienced . . . bringing with you
the energies you've attuned yourself to . . . being fully ready and
able to act on these energies in your life, and knowing you can
return to these dimensions whenever you choose.

ONE—coming up slowly now. . . .

TWO—becoming aware of the room around you. . . .

THREE—at the count of five you'll open your eyes feeling
revitalized, refreshed and relaxed . . . bringing with you all the
energies you've connected with, having full memory of all that
you've experienced. . . .

FOUR—coming up now. . . .

FIVE!—eyes open, feeling refreshed, relaxed and revitalized, ready
and able to act on the energies you've become attuned to.

[It is a good idea to write down or draw any affirmation or symbol
you created.]

Chapter Four

The Nature of the Inner Dimension

There is a contradiction in working with your innerconsciousness that is best described by trying to drink water without a glass—it goes right through your fingers. Innerconsciousness is fluid and it feels extremely nebulous. Sensations are gone as fast as they come. However, you know that if you concentrate and focus your attention you *can* get a drink of water without a glass. Because the nature of our inner dimension is qualitatively different from the material world around us, we have no framework for understanding what we experience when working with it. There's a vulnerability, an insecurity, that you feel when working with the innerconsciousness, for there is no objective world to knock up against so you can know your position and what you're dealing with. Instead you find yourself in a shifting, amorphous reality with no immediate feedback. If you apply the usual definitions for how things work you find yourself believing that you are not doing it correctly, but this is not the case. When you understand the dynamics of innerconsciousness you will find yourself more able to trust and work with your own inner powers.

CONFLICT BETWEEN INNER
AND OUTER CONSCIOUSNESS

What this work is all about is maintaining a state of relaxed attention, the stage between sleeping and waking awareness—the alpha level equally active and receptive. However, your beta consciousness does not go away, instead, as you've probably discovered by now, it continually judges everything you experience. In our society beta consciousness is what we've been taught to use and value most—it's been given full control. Your beta consciousness feels extremely threatened by your beginning to pay attention to, and use other parts of yourself since it doesn't like to lose power. So it immediately begins discounting: "I'm not relaxed," "I just made that up," "That's dumb," "I'm gonna be late." Usually people respond to these messages by trying to shut them up and arguing with them—"I am too relaxed"—feeling that they are a reflection of not meditating properly. But argument isn't a very relaxing activity. It's a full-time job to try to shut up the beta mind because it has an infinite store of such distractions, and as long as you're trying to deal with them you're not focusing your attention on your inner work. The beta mind succeeds in diverting you, thus maintaining its power. You can let yourself off the hook by not responding to everything the beta mind says—just let it run on with its critique; let your beta voices take a back-row seat while you focus your attention on your inner work. *You choose what takes center stage in your awareness.*

You've probably spent your whole life ignoring the innerconsciousness so you need to be patient with it as it needs time to get used to the idea of working for you. All the while the beta mind is discounting, your innerconsciousness is rebelling. It's not fair to come along and expect it to shape up instantly. It is carefree and would much rather play around than be disciplined. Since it is free to do what it pleases when you're not focusing your attention on it, it now tries to evade you. One of the diversionary tactics of innerconsciousness is to bring in off-the-wall images. Sometimes it gets even more rambunctious and tries to scare you with grotesque pictures. The result of this is that, on the one hand, you get your beta voices in a back-row seat; on the other hand, you then have to contend with the spotlight bouncing at random all over the theatre (off-the-wall); your innerconsciousness doesn't want to be still and focus. When you find this happening, don't worry about it. Just move your attention back to center stage.

At all times notice what you're *choosing* to focus your attention on. You're at the controls behind the spotlight and you can choose to focus wherever you wish. We tend to take our consciousness for granted, not even aware that there are controls, to say nothing of using them. Leaving the stage in darkness or finding the beam bouncing around aimlessly on occasion doesn't mean you have to go back to the beginning of the scene—innerconsciousness is not linear. It just means you left center stage in darkness, but you can choose to re-illuminate it, going back to where you left off.

Understand that *awareness and attention are different*. You can be aware of a noise while attending to your inner work. Notice if your center of attention is within you or outside you—remember, just because you have noisy neighbors doesn't mean you have to listen to them. (As I suggested earlier you'll soon find yourself able to meditate on a rush-hour bus.) Again, it is a matter of what you keep at center stage. As with beta discounts, you needn't answer them all; you can simply let them stand in the wings. If you become too distracted by sounds or discomfort, turn them around and make them work for you. Remember you're in a suggestible state, so just tell yourself, "All distractions will cause me to be *even more* focused on my inner processes."

There are two other common ways innerconsciousness succeeds in avoiding disciplined work. It might make your body feel restless or itchy, or your throat congested—again distracting your attention. Being suggestible, you can imagine drinking warm syrup and pretend that it is soothing your scratchy throat. To your amazement you will find your cough receding. The other way innerconsciousness evades you is that sometimes you'll find yourself feeling as if you had been asleep and you'll come out of the meditation with large blank spots (the play goes on, but the stage is dark). There are several things you can do to avoid this. You can give yourself a regular suggestion such as, "When meditating I remain aware and alert to all that occurs." Sitting up while meditating may also be of help. However, if you continue to have blank spots there are some procedures you can use to fill them in. Logic won't work because innerconsciousness doesn't have a story line with a beginning, middle and end; it's more like a patchwork quilt. But being present and hanging out with an image, word, or vibration that you know was a part of the meditation will often bring the rest to mind. Simply letting an image linger in your mind will sometimes draw up the rest of what occurred, since memory works associatively, not sequentially. Conversely, when you're meditating and you're fully aware of your experience, feeling as if you'll easily remember it, all too often you return to waking awareness to find that it has slipped away. Pick one specific detail of the experience *while* you are meditating and tell yourself you'll remember it. This is a lot easier than bringing out a whole scenario. Then when you come out to outer consciousness you'll remember that detail and when you focus on it the rest of your inner experience will surface. It's similar to recalling a dream—when you encounter an object that was in the dream itself the whole dream floods into your awareness. The remembered detail or the familiar object acts as bait on a fishing line, drawing up the rest of your deeper experience, for each detail is, in fact, part of a whole.

It is very important to understand the conflict between your inner and outer consciousness, so you won't interpret it as a reflection of not doing your work properly. In fact, I've discovered that the more effective my work is, the stronger the conflict becomes. Innerconsciousness is frightened by the responsibilities and outer consciousness fears it is losing control. This conflict tends to make meditating feel like a chore. It doesn't matter how it feels—the question is whether or not you do it. There are two things related to this that are important to watch for. Sometimes when a story that seems off-the-wall pops into your mind, before bringing your attention back to center stage, you should look at it carefully for it often metaphorically contains an insight into the issue you are working on. Another thing that sometimes happens is that even when you have blank spots in your memory the changes you were intending to work on manifest themselves in your life anyway. (The play does go on.) This happens when your innerconsciousness finds it easier to work below the surface because your conscious awareness encumbers its effectiveness. In time you will come to recognize when you're experiencing rebellion or when it is constructive work—trust your intuition.

THE CHARACTER OF INNERCONSCIOUSNESS

In learning to do inner work there is often much emphasis on visualization (the word often used to refer to these techniques), not because picturing things is the only effective way to work with innerconsciousness, but because when one is leading a meditation or just talking about the experience it's much easier to describe what something looks like than what it feels like. But consciousness works in different modes—some of us predominantly feel things in our bodies, some hear things, some simply know things, and for others, seeing is predominant. I happen to be a visualizer, so the meditations I write are likely to be slanted towards that mode, rather than sensations, knowingness, etc. The important thing is that your imagination works in some way, and whatever mode is most natural for you is what you need to pay attention to. This is not to say you can't develop the ability to work with other modes, the point is not to discount the ways that your imagination does experience reality.

The symbolic language of innerconsciousness often expresses itself in metaphors or puns. One person's symbol for mental relaxation was a train entering a very peaceful countryside (train of thought). In fact one of the more pleasurable characteristics of striking up a relationship with your inner self is that it has a good sense of humor.

When some people meditate they often experience various physical sensations and responses. They may feel as if their body has grown bigger or heavier, some get tingling or heat sensations, and some find that they start to nod and rock, or feel as if they are whirling, or their eyelids may flutter or their bodies twitch. Whatever the sensations, they are no cause for worry, they are simply natural responses to energies beginning to move in new and unfamiliar ways. If you find yourself uncomfortable imagine the antidote, e.g., if you have a whirling sensation grow roots through the floor and into the ground.

In the material world things take time to happen. Time and space create limits and maintain within themselves linear and logical progressions. The inner world is altogether different; as it's holistic, and sequence is not something within its experience—it operates in *simultaneous* patterns—time is meaningless. If I say, "yellow balloon" you don't have to go looking for it to imagine it; it's there the instant you hear the words.

Since you're accustomed to everything taking time, when you do work in a meditation the chances are you'll feel as if you didn't do it very well because it didn't seem to take any time or follow any logical progression. All too frequently, when you focus on a healing image, for example, the image is very fleeting. It has no duration so you feel you must recapture it to ensure its effectiveness—but then it is redundant and feels stupid. Don't worry, that's just part of the process.

In these meditations you're often directed to imagine talking to your inner imagery and sensations and to ask questions of your symbols. Like improvisation, this creates the context which evokes creativity. But since processes occur simultaneously on the inner levels you will find that *as you're formulating the question you already know the answer.* This makes you feel as if you made it up or knew the answer all along; since it's the symbol you're asking, you expect the symbol to answer and therefore discount your know-ingness. Alas, inner conversations are non-linear. The point is that you find yourself knowing the answer, not how you got it. If you discount it, you are not allowing yourself the use of your inherent personal power. When you feel as if you knew it all along the chances are you were discounting it and ignoring your own know-ledge. Having known it all along doesn't make it wrong either. The issue is whether you heed it; the point is that you *know* the answer is right. Remember the process is non-linear and simultaneous. It's not as if you ask the question and then get the answer; both usually occur at the same time. It is like when you move the spotlight (attention), it doesn't take time to illuminate the new area. So when asking a question within, simply be receptive and sensitive to what you're experiencing inside simultaneously. That experience will contain the answer.

If you don't seem to be experiencing anything, *make something up.* Don't wait for it to come to you, for if it were going to come to you it would *be there already.* I've done psychic case work for many years, and I've guided hundreds of people through the same exer-cise. Some people feel as if the information just comes—seemingly out of the blue. Other people feel as if they had made up the whole thing. It doesn't matter how it feels, the *content is always the same.*

In both situations the psychic reading is just as accurate—it just takes longer and feels more laborious to make it up. So when you don't sense the answer to your inner question, give yourself full permission to *invent* it. Listen to your fantasies, for they have the answers. It is impossible to exaggerate the importance of this. If making something up is wrong by definition that's the height of not taking yourself seriously.

Often the answers you come to are simplistic. They may be obvious or they may be cliché, or corny, or trite. We've all been systematically conditioned to discount these qualities (only complicated things can be worthwhile). What we need to remember is that ideas become trite or corny *because* they have been universally experienced and expressed. Innerconsciousness gives us cliché answers because it resides in the realm of universality and, when questioned, dips into the collective knowledge of the human race. When we say something corny it is somehow suspect—not to be taken seriously—or downright wrong. This is one way we keep ourselves isolated from one another. When we discount an answer only because it is cliché we divorce ourselves from the lessons others have learned. When meditating about the difficulty with my friend the affirmation that came to me certainly was corny: "I reside in the care we have for one another." Had I not taken it seriously it's likely I'd no longer have the friendship. The assumption that answers to problems must be unique or complicated and that simple answers won't do, keeps us powerless. If we listen to our corny, simplistic answers and take action, we'll pull ourselves out of our isolation and be able to resolve our difficulties. If we'd allow ourselves to act on the obvious we wouldn't have so many problems. But remember just as power unused may as well not exist, answers and insights not acted upon will be of no value. The purpose of Applied Meditation is to bring the knowingness from the universal realm to the particular realm of our daily lives, and this requires acting on our own insights.

INTUITIONS, THOUGHTS, AND FEELINGS

One of the most important aspects of this work is developing a sense for your intuitions and learning to keep beta consciousness or your emotions from suffocating them before you're even aware of their existence. Otherwise you won't realize you had an intuition until it's too late. How many times have you come home from a party saying to yourself, "Why did I go? I knew it would be awful." When you've learned to recognize your intuitions, you'll be able to avoid many undesirable situations, but you need to sense them fully before you can respond to them in time. For me it feels like keeping an eye focused toward the back of my mind.

Part of the process of recognizing intuitions is being able to distinguish them from your beta thoughts and your emotions. Intuitions, thoughts, and feelings are all different aspects of ourselves. Beta is intellectual, categorical, complicted, either-or, sequential, and logical. Its messages are easy to recognize for they are never subtle, but always straightforward. Emotions are pushy; they always have a charge to them—attachments, desires, shoulds. When you find yourself with a message and you want to be clear where it is coming from—whether intellectual, emotional, or intuitive, ask yourself questions like these: Is it critical? Does it set up an either-or category? Is it complicating? Does the voice seem to be coming from my head (intellectual)? Does the answer have a lot of force behind it? Is it pushy? From my parents? From my boss? Is it difficult to ignore (emotional)?

Inner messages are never pushy. They're always holistic—not logical or sequential. They are without conflict, subtle but clear, with no shoulds—they simply *are*. You can ignore them but you *can't* argue with them. You can easily take them or as easily leave them. They are background awarenesses that create a sense of the whole. They are often the first impressions that come into our minds, but in this society the first to be discounted, for their knowingness doesn't have reason attached to it. When you don't know why you know something you assume you don't really know it. With intuitions you will have an unquestionable sense of knowing that it is so. Ask yourself how or why you know what you know; if you *can't* answer then it's an intuition.

With time you'll learn to distinguish between your intuitions and other aspects of yourself, for each one is different. You'll discover the particular individual quality of your intuitions. To get at them, always ask yourself what you *sense* (intuit)—not what you think or feel. Unlike your intellect or your feelings, your intuition will rarely get you into trouble; instead it will almost always keep you out of it.

This is not to say your intellect and feelings are unimportant and better ignored, but that when you recognize which you're dealing with you will learn to respond appropriately.

We have been programmed to look for drama in our lives so we expect it in our meditations. But as I have pointed out, our inner-consciousness is subtle, never forceful, and rarely dramatic, so people often conclude that they must not be meditating properly. You usually will not discover the effectiveness of meditation *while* meditating. Look for its power not in how it feels when you're doing it, but instead in the changes that begin to occur in your life. So if you don't think you're meditating correctly, *pretend* you are, go through the motions anyway. If you do, you'll find the changes begin to manifest themselves.

Unlike other activities (the more you do them, the clearer they get) it seems that the more you meditate the less distinct the different levels of awareness become. Going deep doesn't feel so deep any longer, and you also find yourself with more profound insights in your regular waking awareness. This is because the channels are clear and the movement of awareness from one level to another has become so smooth it all feels like the same level. Another contradiction to working with your innerconsciousness: the more you meditate the less you need to.

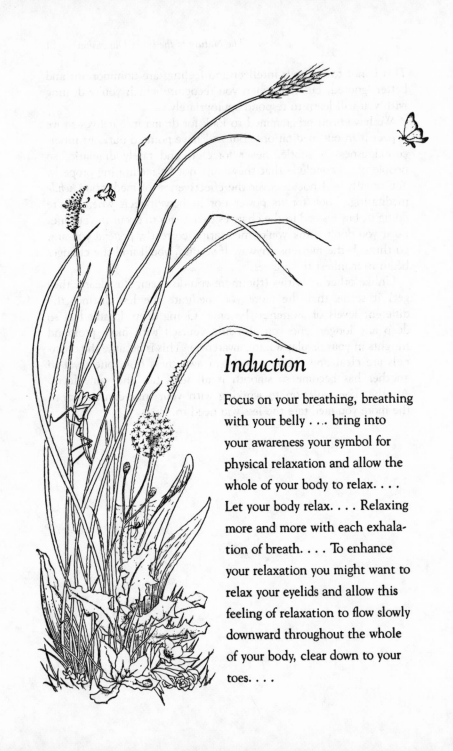

Induction

Focus on your breathing, breathing
with your belly . . . . bring into
your awareness your symbol for
physical relaxation and allow the
whole of your body to relax. . . .
Let your body relax. . . . Relaxing
more and more with each exhalation of breath. . . . To enhance
your relaxation you might want to
relax your eyelids and allow this
feeling of relaxation to flow slowly
downward throughout the whole
of your body, clear down to your
toes. . . .

And when you're ready, bring into your awareness your symbol for mental relaxation . . . feel your mind begin to relax. . . . Feel the chatter of your mind become calm and quiet. . . . Feel your mind become clear and spacious, as spacious as the sky and your thoughts are like puffy clouds, drifting in and out, in and out the sky of your mind. . . .

And then when you're ready, bring in your symbol for emotional relaxation. Go over the full range of your emotions. . . . Pay attention to your feelings and if there are any feelings that are calling for your attention, take care of those feelings in whatever way occurs to you. . . .

Then focus on your symbol for your level. . . . You are now centered at a stable level of innerconsciousness where you find faculties and senses opening out far beyond those that you usually use in your waking awareness.

You are now consciously developing psychic skills you have always had. . . . You are at your level—the threshhold between your inner and outer realities. . . . Here you discover a rich, beautiful landscape of your receptivity and creativity. . . . Here you experience very vivid, very meaningful sensations and imagery, new realities. . . . As these realities unfold they guide you to new dimensions of being, as your being opens, more and more of these energies shall flow through you. . . . Just as using your muscles keeps your body strong and resilient, so too, using your level keeps your intuitive and psychic powers fully accessible and fluid. . . . From here you can make use of the wisdom of your inner self. . . . From here you realize the calm expansive power of your inner being. . . . Your inner being is a part of universal beingness. . . . From here you experience yourself as part of the pure universal energy which permeates all life. . . . From here you gain the wisdom to make this world a more harmonious place to live. . . .

Now listen very carefully, paying attention only to these words and your responses to these words. . . . If other thoughts drift through your mind just let them drift and gently, easily bring your attention back to these words. . . . Even when you're not paying attention to these words your innerconscious mind is taking in this information and these instructions, and you'll be able to use these techniques in the future. You are going to fully remember all that you are about to experience. You will absorb new energies, assimilate and understand these energies. . . . You are going to do all of these things with the whole of your being as you explore these new dimensions. . . .

In a moment I am going to count on a descending scale from ten to one; at each descending count you'll feel your awareness move deeper and deeper into your inner dimensions. . . . Ten, moving down now . . . nine, deeper and deeper . . . eight, relaxing into yourself . . . seven, returning to yourself . . . six, deeper and deeper . . . five, moving deeper . . . four, very aware and very alert . . . three, moving down . . . two, into your deeper dimensions . . . one, deep in yourself. . . . Here your imagination is extremely fluid and you can direct it where you choose. . . .

I'm going to suggest several affirmations. . . . If you wish to affirm them to yourself repeat them to yourself after me, and at the same time, feel as though each affirmation is fully true. Bring into your awareness pictures and sensations that represent each affirmation and as you speak the words to yourself, feel the power of the words. . . . In so doing you'll discover that as time goes by you'll find yourself living in ways that conform to the affirmations, and

the affirmations materialize in your daily reality. You'll intuitively
be acting out of the power of each of the affirmations.

I believe in myself; I believe in my family and friends; we believe in
our community; there is a free flow of support among us in creating
change. . . .

I trust myself, I am enriched by my deepest dimensions. . . .

I am aware and alert when I meditate. . . .

I can focus my consciousness wherever I choose, for as long as I
choose. . . .

My imagination is fluid and free. . . .

I am in tune and responsive to my intuition—my deeper knowingness. . . .

Every day the powers of the depths of my consciousness become
more and more available to me. . . .

I remember my symbols when I need them and call them to
awareness. . . .

I act on my knowingness in my life. . . .

A spring of creativity continually flows through me and out into
the world. . . .

My increasing personal power is for making this world a more
harmonious place to live for everyone. . . .

I maintain balance amidst change. . . .

I trust the future. . . .

Now take time to focus on any of your own affirmations. . . .
Knowing that in focusing on affirmations you cause yourself to
conform to the affirmations at all levels and you'll discover yourself
acting in alignment with the affirmations. Or, you may want to
spend time reviewing and working with your symbols.

Stretching the Imagination

Imagine holding a piece of fruit in your hand. . . . Imagine the texture of the skin, imagine the feel of it in your hand . . . the size, the weight of it. . . . You may literally want to move your hand around as you imagine these things. It is as though you were literally holding that piece of fruit. . . . Feel its size . . . its texture . . . its temperature. . . . Imagine it . . . its weight, its consistency. . . . Imagine taking your fingernail and breaking the peel, bring it up to your nose and imagine what it would smell like. . . . Imagine the juice, the temperature, the feel of it. . . . Notice the quality of this fruit, almost as though it had a tone to it, a vibration to it. . . . Compare it to the quality of other fruits, the vibrations that they have, the tone. . . . If each kind of fruit were to have a sound to it, a note to it, a tone to it, what would you hear? . . . Imagine the sound if you were to squeeze the juice out of the fruit. . . . How would it sound when the juice dripped? . . . What kind of sound would the fruit make as you crushed it? . . . Imagine drinking the juice, what would it taste like? . . . How would it make your mouth feel? . . . How does it compare to imagining the taste of other juices?

Now I want you to imagine creating a mental shelf. . . . You can place anything on this shelf that you would like to refer to at a later time. . . . Now, put the fruit up on the shelf, if you wish to, you can come back to your exploration of it later. . . . Anything you put on this mental shelf at any time you'll be able to remember. You can then come back to it and it will still be there, ready for you to continue your exploration. Tell yourself this now, that whatever you place on your mental shelf will remain there— retained; ready for you when you return to attend to it. . . .

Know that your imagination is fully fluid; you can choose whatever direction you want it to go. To further explore the fluidity of innerconsciousness we're going to experiment with body sensations. . . . Feel your body, aware of the position your body is in, aware of the space you occupy. . . . Now imagine your body to be the consistency of a stone . . . a smooth stone that's at the bottom of a stream bed . . . water rushing over it, rushing over it, always making it smooth and round. . . . Feel your body as though it were a stone on the bottom of a stream bed. . . . How does it feel?

◆

Now let your body become the water that rushes over the stone . . . fluid, moving, clear, clear running water, taking the shape of whatever is around it . . . water, crystal clear water that washes all that it passes by . . . bringing out all the subtle colors of the stones below you. . . . Let your body be the water of the stream . . . feel it, hear it, sense it.

◆

And above the stream imagine a breeze . . . let yourself become the breeze, let yourself be the breeze, blowing over the stream, over the land, the open breeze, it goes everywhere . . . let your body be the breeze . . . the wind, it goes everywhere, blows everywhere.

◆

Now notice the rays of the sun . . . penetrating the breeze with the vitality of fire, the penetrating warmth of the sun. . . . Let your body become the rays of the sun. Feel it in your body, be it in your body . . . fire, warmth, radiant light, brilliant fire, warmth. . . . Let your body be it.

◆

Now bring your usual body sensations back into your body . . .
feeling your usual physical self. . . . Now, listen, listen to the
crackling of the fire . . . listen to the blowing of the wind . . .
listen to the gurgling of the stream . . . listen to the crackling rocks
as they roll over one another where the stream moves very rapidly.

♦

Know that your imagination is extremely fluid, that your psychic
senses are extremely keen—the more you work with them, the
sharper they become. . . . Your inner awareness perceives the very
deepest subtleties of reality itself. . . . Know that all of this is so,
and that as you work with your inner senses they become more and
more agile. . . . As you work in directing your imagination you can
change the imagery, feelings, sensations, and sounds moving in
whatever directions you choose, and you are increasingly able to
direct your inner awareness as you choose each time you meditate. . . . Know that all of this is so. . . . Now with your deep
knowingness sense the different aspects of your consciousness.
Discover their character. Your intellect . . . notice its abilities to
figure things out, notice its ability to make distinctions. . . . Your
emotions . . . they are always moving, full of color, full of
desire. . . . Your intuition . . . it simply knows, it experiences
wholeness, the whole of what is so. . . . Bring different issues in
your life to awareness and discover what you think, what you feel,
and what you *know* about these issues. . . . Notice when different
aspects of yourself are active, when you respond to which.

♦   ♦   ♦

Now go back to your mental shelf and if there is anything there,
your can attend to it or do any other inner work of your choosing.

♦   ♦   ♦

Know that everytime you meditate, you receive beneficial effects both physically and psychically. . . . That every time you meditate, your imagination becomes increasingly agile and your psychic/ intuitive powers grow in sensitivity. Know that you're increasingly able to control levels of awareness and remain at whatever level you choose for as long as you choose. . . . Know that you never lose your ability to meditate, instead every time you practice your abilities are enhanced geometrically. . . . And you'll discover that every time you meditate, the good feelings you've experienced will carry over into your daily activities, enabling you to enjoy life more fully, enabling you to work gracefully through any problems that arise. . . . Know that all of this is so. Imagine all of this, tell yourself these things now.

Countout

Finish what you're doing and make yourself ready to come out to outer conscious levels knowing that you'll bring with you all the energies you've contacted, going over the insights and feelings you've had in this meditation.

◆　◆　◆

Knowing you can return to these dimensions whenever you wish. You may want to project when you will again meditate. . . . In a moment I'm going to count from one to five, at the count of five, you'll open your eyes remembering all that you've experienced . . . feeling refreshed, revitalized and relaxed. . . .

ONE—becoming more aware of the room around you. . . .

TWO—coming up slowly now. . . .

THREE—at the count of five you'll open your eyes feeling relaxed, revitalized, and refreshed remembering all that you've experienced. . . .

FOUR—coming up now, bringing with you your sense of well-being. . . .

FIVE!—eyes open, feeling refreshed, revitalized and relaxed, remembering all that you've experienced, feeling a sense of well-being.

Chapter Five

It's All Energy

When I first had the experience of successfully reading a case it was awesome because it meant I was *part* of the universe. If I could perceive in detail someone of whom I had had no previous experience, no longer was I a separate entity simply moving through the world. Instead, I was somehow intimately connected to everything. My experience taught me that we are all a part of a cosmic whole. Consciousness all of a sudden lit up with magic; my consciousness was infinitely more than I had ever imagined. Until then I'd always taken my own awareness for granted and paid attention only to the external world. It all turned around. All of a sudden my imagination was as real as the ground I stood on. If I could get to know someone so well by simply directing my imagination, there was much more to the intricacies of the universe than I'd ever been taught by rational explanations.

The scientific era has taught us to make clear separations between the subjective and objective, the body and mind, the personal and political, the organic and inorganic, fact and value, spirit and matter, heaven and earth, God and everything else. Western rationalism has taken the life, the soul out of everything. Before the onslaught of dualism, most inhabitants of the world experienced it as charged with spirit—everything possessed consciousness and was part of a living whole. The scientific revolution ushered in a new viewpoint: the world is simply made up of separate parts that have been put together into a vast machine of matter and motion obeying mathematical laws. Science has succeeded in separating us from the whole and getting us to view the objective as inert, value-free—in other words dead. Not only have we lost our place in the world, the world itself has died and has therefore become exploitable—this is the beginning of alienation. As Fritjof Capra describes:

> To Descartes the material universe was a machine and nothing but a machine. There was no purpose, life, or spirituality in matter. Nature worked according to mechanical laws, and everything in the material world could be explained in terms of the arrangement and movement of its parts. This mechanical picture of nature became the dominant paradigm of science in the period following Descartes. It guided all scientific observation and the formulation of all theories of natural phenomena.
>
> The drastic change in the image of nature from organism to machine had a strong effect on people's attitudes toward the natural environment. The organic world view of the Middle Ages had implied a value system conducive to ecological behavior. In the words of Carolyn Merchant:
>
> "The image of the earth as a living organism and nurturing mother served as a cultural constraint restricting the actions of human beings. One does not readily slay a mother, dig into her entrails for gold, or mutilate her body. . . . As long as the earth was considered to be alive and sensitive, it could be considered a breach of human ethical behavior to carry out destructive acts against it."[1]

ALL THAT EXISTS IS ALIVE

Western culture views women as closer to nature, and both are suspect. Women are "naturally" emotional and intuitive; men are more rational. The scientific method teaches us to exploit nature, but not to trust our own natures. To know is, by definition, not to feel—not to be involved—for feelings cloud the issue and make it immeasurable, and scientific methodology only deals with that which is quantifiable. The degree to which the human element enters into the experiment is the same degree to which it is invalidated. And science holds a monoply on knowledge. Therefore, by definition, *knowledge resides outside of ourselves.* If knowledge is exclusively attained externally that effectively cuts us off from the vast knowingness that consciousness has *direct* access to. Not trusting our own nature we find ourselves dependent on the authorities (usually men).

Only experiments reveal the "facts," not experience. How often do we discount one another for not being "objective?" Our experience is suspect and useless until it is scientifically substantiated. Witness:

> During a six-month period in 1973, the New York Times reported the following scientific findings:
>
> A major research institute spent more than $50,000 to discover that the best bait for mice is cheese.
>
> Another study found that mother's milk was better balanced nutritionally for infants than commercial formulas. . . .
>
> A third study established that a walk is considerably healthier for the human respiratory and circulatory systems, in fact for overall health and vitality, than a ride in a car.
>
> A fourth project demonstrated that the juice of fresh oranges has more nutritional value than either canned or frozen orange juice.
>
> A fifth study proved conclusively that infants who are touched a lot frequently grow into adults with greater self-confidence and have a more integrated relationship with the world than those who are not touched.[2]

Western rationalism teaches us to believe only that which has been proven (never trust the obvious); in consequence we no longer believe in our own experience. The result of separating ourselves from our own experience has finished the job—alienation fully completed.

I don't mean to imply that we throw out what science has discovered over the centuries, but that we be very clear that science is neither the sole purveyor of truth, nor is it neutral. It is important to understand the philosophical premises upon which it rests for they have profound implications on how it is we view our own experience and our relations with the world around us. But now that science has rejoined the cosmic whole, the fact is that we can all return to our connections. Science has come around on itself, for contrary to Cartesian thought, everything at once contains within itself its opposite. Now the purest of sciences—physics—has observed (discovered) that the observer is part of the observed (discovery). It began with $E = MC^2$ and continues with quantum mechanics. The world has come back to life. In the words of Fritjof Capra:

> Physics has gone through several conceptual revolutions that clearly reveal the limitations of the mechanistic world view and lead to an organic, ecological view of the world which shows great similarities to the views of mystics of all ages and traditions. The universe is no longer seen as a machine . . . but appears as a harmonious indivisible whole; a network of dynamic relationships that include the human observer and his or her consciousness in an essential way.[3]

It is not only innerconsciousness that functions in simultaneous patterns, but the very building blocks of the material world also seem to do so. Gary Zukav describes:

> The distinction between organic and inorganic is a conceptual prejudice. It becomes even harder to maintain as we advance into quantum mechanics. Something is organic, according to our definition, if it can respond to processed information. The astounding discovery awaiting newcomers to physics is that the evidence gathered in the development of quantum mechanics indicates that subatomic "particles" constantly appear to be making decisions! More than that, the decisions they seem to make are based on decisions made elsewhere. Subatomic particles seem to know instantaneously what decisions are made elsewhere, and elsewhere can be as far away as another galaxy![4]

Not only does material, i.e. atomic particles, appear to be conscious, but in addition, our consciousness seems to be connected to theirs—objectivity itself is discovered to be impossible. As Capra explains further:

The crucial feature of quantum theory is that the observer is not only necessary to observe the properties of an atomic phenomenon, but is necessary even to bring about these properties. My conscious decision about how to observe, say, an electron will determine the electron's properties to some extent. If I ask it a particle question, it will give me a particle answer; if I ask it a wave question, it will give me a wave answer. The electron does not have objective properties independent of my mind. In atomic physics the sharp Cartesian division between mind and matter, between the observer and the observed, can no longer be maintained. We can never speak about nature without, at the same time, speaking about ourselves.[5]

Our dualistic objective worldview has trained us to ignore aspects of reality that have now slowly seeped into the scientific laboratory where there are experiments with results that fully defy the classic materialist explanation. We are now told that the very building blocks of matter—the atoms—have no separate objective reality. It can no longer be an issue of cause and effect when separate sub-atomic particles respond to one another instantaneously. This is also made clear by the scientific experiment in which a mother rabbit responded the *same* instant that each of her babies were killed miles away from her in a submerged submarine that even radio waves could not penetrate.[6] Psychokinesis (PK) is the term used for the direct influence of mind on matter. PK research with Gellor, Mikhailova, and Kulagina,[7] have proved that objects can be moved simply with the power of mental concentration. All of these objective occurences necessitate rearranging our ideas of the nature of the universe as well as of what is possible. It is only because of our narrow frame of reference that we define such occurrences as paranormal. We are all part of a whole and consciousness itself is a participant in what occurs—not simply reflective and responsive—a participant in the creation of the phenomenon.

Silva Mind Control techniques teach the power of positive thinking—if you want something all you need do is imagine it and you'll get it, whatever it is—be it a parking place, an apartment, a job, or whatever. So after I had discovered the powers of my imagination—its ability to receive information—I was inspired to experiment and see what other powers it might have. All of a sudden "coincidences" became commonplace. All kinds of things started manifesting themselves in my life after I had projected them with my imagination. I didn't understand how or why it was working, but my experience showed me that it did, indeed, work. It was as if the world, up until that point, was out of sync—everything was random—and when I began taking responsibility for what my imagination was projecting everything moved into synchrony. Random events ceased to occur and coincidence was suddenly pregnant with significance. This is why I like Carl Jung's term "synchronicity," a causal, meaningful coincidence. His illustration:

> A young woman I was treating had, at a critical moment, a dream in which she was given a golden scarab. While she was telling me this dream I sat with my back to the closed window. Suddenly I heard a noise behind me, like a gentle tapping. I turned round and saw a flying insect knocking against the window-pane from outside. I opened the window and caught the creature in the air as it flew in. It was the nearest analogy to a golden scarab that one finds in our latitudes, which contrary to its usual habits had evidently felt an urge to get into a dark room at this particular moment.[8]

Osmosis is occurring, is always occurring. Consciousness permeates the material world, affecting which of the myriad possibilities transpire. And our past experiences of the material world limit the possibilities we can imagine—what's conceivable. Your imagination not only affects how you behave in the world, but conversely it affects how the world behaves towards you. And what has happened in your past affects what you imagine. Matter affects mind; mind affects matter. But contrary to Jung, I think we can consciously participate in the process—in this sense it is no longer acausal but does remain simultaneous, i.e. not occurring within the sequence of cause and then effect.

Native American tradition places the people inside the whole—working with the connections. Rationalism patronizingly views their rituals as "primitive." As a child I went to many Pueblo rain dances in New Mexico where, by the end of the day, rain usually came down upon us all—often the first rain for many weeks.

Our imagination affects what happens to us whether we choose to participate in the process or not. Consciousness is always interacting with the environment—I think of it as electromagnetic energy continually radiating out from each of us, *magnetic* energy drawing to us particular probabilities while repelling others. The law of this phenomenon is the attraction of opposites within the unity of opposites—energies that resonate with each other attract one another. In the words of Kammerer, "We thus arrive at the image of a world mosaic or cosmic kaleidoscope, which, in spite of constant shufflings and rearrangements also takes care of bringing like and like together."[9] So from now on when I refer to thoughts and attitudes, know that I mean a *material* force affecting the environment.

This can easily be seen if you look into your past; you'll notice how events happen in rhythmic sequences. Seemingly unrelated positive events congregating together, and so too the opposite, bad incidents happening together. You could call them streaks of good or bad luck. Well, it's true except that luck is by definition something operating by chance—randomly, disconnected from ourselves. The energy you're putting out is a major ingredient in causing these "random" circumstances to occur. Notice that some people you know are optimists and have lives full of good fortune, while others are melancholic and their lives are full of misfortune. Coincidence does not exist—things don't happen by mere chance. Things occur out of the coalescence of energies. We always hear, "What goes out, comes back," "As within, so without," "As you sow, so shall you reap." What this looks like concretely is that the day you're in a bad mood is the day your car gets sideswiped while parked, and the plumbing gets clogged, and likewise the day you're feeling good you get offered a promotion and a dear friend whom you haven't seen in years unexpectedly arrives in town. I'm not saying your moods created these events, but that it is part of the whole—it is likely that part of your mood was psychically, on a deeper level, being aware of these probabilities.

Synchronous events frequently occur as puns. If you're in a bad mood there's likely to be a connection between what you're feeling and the particular event that occurs. A friend of mine recently expressed how tired and deflated he felt; he got two flat tires that week. Any residual scepticism I had evaporated when I was reading a book called *The Seth Material* which was the first of a series of books to come out by Jane Roberts. This book was the first material I had come across that enabled me to understand rationally why I could imagine something and then it would occur. While reading it I described to several friends, "This book has been turning my idea of reality upside down!" After reading the first one I was anxious to get the second, *Seth Speaks*. Many people apparently were going through the same process as I was, for I went to numerous bookstores only to discover they'd all just sold out. Returning home, I called a number of others and finally found a store that had one copy left. I asked that they hold it for me. When I picked it up I discovered that this copy's binding had been put on upside down.

A woman in one of my classes said that when she was younger her life was full of what she'd always thought were coincidences but they all stopped when she took the advice, "Don't expect anything, you won't be disappointed." For the first time she understood why they had disappeared. Now she was delighted at being given permission to have positive expectations again. Yet we let ourselves worry, having no idea that our fretting is adding to the likelihood that the very things we fear most will in fact occur. It's time we turn it around.

Most religious traditions have a pervasive belief that prayers work. *If* you believe, your prayers will be answered. What that means is that you don't always get what you want, but you *do* get what you expect. Wherever your attention is focusing, wherever your imagination goes, how it is that you're subjectively feeling, all of this is a feeding power of probabilities—wherever you focus your awareness, that's the probability you attract. It's not as if there's a judge in the sky deciding what will and what will not occur; it's a matter of the coalescence of energies, for our consciousness en masse creates a sea of probabilities. Where the greatest amount of energy exists is where the probabilities materialize into events. If we know that this is so we can participate and take responsibility for energies we put out into the atmosphere so that we can decrease the likelihood of negative events occurring and increase the likelihood of positive events occurring. It's of paramount importance that we take *responsibility for our consciousness and direct it in positive ways.*

CULTIVATING FAITH

Getting what we expect is always called a self-fulfilling prophecy. True, but it's time we stop being victims and realize that in fact *we are the prophets.* Greater amounts of energy lie in deeper levels of awareness—remember the deeper you are the more focused and concentrated your consciousness is. (People do not pray intellectually.) So when we direct our imagination while meditating, it has that much more force than in our usual waking consciousness. Our innerconsciousness is totally malleable; we can choose where to focus it, thereby increasing manyfold our influence on what happens in the world around us. The power we give up within will be reflected without and vice versa, the power we don't have without will be reflected within. We cannot afford to leave untapped any power that we have to affect change, given the crisis the world is in today.

Some people voice the protest that by visualizing something that isn't in existence you are deceiving yourself by not facing reality. It's not an issue of denying what is—it's an issue of projecting what could be—taking a stand for what could be better. What you're doing is being self-directed—choosing where you want to go. You can't move forward if you have nothing to strive for. Becoming a visionary you have moved from being a victim to being an active participant.

I don't expect you to believe right now that if you imagine something you greatly increase the odds for its occurring, *for belief comes from experience.* But I suggest that you temporarily suspend your skepticism and try it. This does *not* mean trying it with the attitude that it *won't* work, for you will only prove your own expectations. Instead it means making room in your point of view that just *maybe* it *will* work.

I promise you that within a month of regular practice you will observe patterns of events that correspond to your projections, and you'll be convinced that in fact your imagination does have an effect.

This is all a two-way street. The imagination (expectation) is not only the stuff probabilities are made of, but is also the *medium* through which you perceive information psychically. It is the seeding ground of probabilities. When you use the power of positive thinking you not only *create* probabilities, you also familiarize your-self with those that already exist—positive thinking always operates in a context. You are familiarizing yourself with the situation ahead of time—psychically attuning yourself to it. Not only is the envi-ronment responding to you, you are responding to it. You and your environment are moving into sync. For example, if you're project-ing a parking place, you'll intuitively make the correct turns in discovering it. Remember your imagination is also a *receiver* of information: you didn't create the parking place, you became at-tuned to it.

We get what we expect, the trick is to expect what we want. Wishful thinking and expectations have opposite results. The differ-ence is that a wish has an attitude behind it that says it's beyond possibility—the cow looking over the fence at the green pastures, whereas expectation holds the attitude of assuming it will occur—no fences. It is the vibrations that are at play here. Where you are simple and specific in your projection you'll find it easier to get into the sensations and feelings associated with what you want. Simply imagining a feeling of well-being by focusing on a smiling sun which has little personal meaning doesn't work. Well-being doesn't happen in a void, it happens in a context. It's a result of specific conditions. So to feel good you need to imagine *what* will bring this about. Perhaps living in a new space will make you rejoice, so imagine what it feels like to be *already* living there.

All of this works vibrationally; it's not logical. So you don't need to worry about how, why, where, or when something's going to occur—leave that up to your beta mind. All you need to do is to *feel* as if it has already occurred and endeavor to take it for granted, just as you do with your memories. If you do that you'll project the appropriate energy to draw to you what you want, and for you to move intuitively in the right directions to bring it about. Always be specific, simple, and positive in your projections. The clearer you are about your goal—how it feels to have attained it—the more powerful your projection is. If you have confusions and conflicts associated with the goal the power of the projection is diminished proportionately. Likewise, the more you expect your goal to man-ifest itself, the more likely it will—i.e., all of this works proportion-ately to your faith in it. It is therefore good to begin with small issues because they are easier to be clear about. The clearer you are the more it will work, the more it works the more you believe it's going to work the next time. *Belief comes from experience.* You need to cultivate your belief by successful projections, and as you do, you can take on bigger and bigger problems—otherwise you're likely to throw the baby out with the bath water. So start with parking places and bus connections, then slowly work up to the issues that really do make a difference in your life. For it is the faith in its working that makes it work.

Your primary focus should be on what you're wanting/expecting rather than on what you're currently dissatisfied with, which is not to say you should deny what is happening, but that you should expect change to occur. Always have your last image be one of movement towards the positive reality. Be careful you don't look to see whether or not your projections are working by watching to see if the problem has begun to dissolve. This is a focus on the problem and as such does nothing but perpetuate it. Instead simply assume it is working under the surface whether you experience it yet or not.

I had an experience a number of years ago in which I learned this well. As it all too often does, my problem boiled down to economics. At the time, I was making a living doing odd jobs. I spent many of my waking hours worried about how I was going to get the rent together; I spent many of my meditative minutes imagining money coming in. The fact that I didn't know how I was going to pay the rent was entirely more real and had a lot more energy connected to it than all my imaginings of money did. After I finished meditating I still had to face the reality of my bills, and I decided this was one projection that I was somehow doing wrong; it just wasn't working. Then one day it dawned on me: I was focusing more on the problem—the bills, than on the solution—money coming; understandably so, for that was the situation. Having more money simply wasn't believable in the face of all those bills. I had to make it believable, so I changed my tactics. I decided exactly what I needed to feel economically secure and projected it to occur in six months, so my experience didn't deny the possibility of change. I needed three things: to be out of debt, to have a functional car and to feel like I didn't have to take every job that came in, enabling me to put my primary attention on developing Applied Meditation. I had three pictures representing this: I imagined taking my friend out to dinner in celebration of my repaying the debt; I imagined driving around in my dependable car; and I imagined saying no to a job that came in because it interfered with my focus on Applied Meditation. Given my particular lifestyle it was fully plausible that in six months I would have it together. I didn't know how I would have it together, I just assumed I would. No longer did I feel that my projections weren't working for I didn't need to compare them with my current conditions. For the ensuing months I momentarily pictured each of these three situations in my meditations. It wasn't hard; it was momentary, and after a while I did it less often for other things superseded in my meditations. After about four months I stopped focusing on it altogether—I had just spaced it out.

Exactly six months later—not a week early, not a week late—it all manifested itself. I was in the process of rebuilding an engine for my car. I had been energizing finding a volkswagen bus with a blown-up engine, so I could put my new engine in it as I didn't want to install a new motor in my beat-up old car. I had exactly two-hundred dollars to spend and the last possible day when I was deciding to give up and put the engine back in the old car I found just what I was looking for—a volkswagen bus with a blown-up engine for sale for two-hundred dollars. I bought it and it turned out that there was nothing wrong with it—the oil light wire had grounded out simultaneously to the bus running out of gasoline—so the previous owner assumed that the engine had blown up. I called him and told him what had happened and asked him if he wanted his bus back; he said he didn't, so I put its engine into my old car. The friend to whom I owed money happened to be in the market for a car, so I gave it to her (I neglected taking her to dinner). Because the car was worth more than the debt, she gave an additional two-hundred dollars to the previous owner of the bus, as it was worth more than I had paid for it. In the end I had a functional car, I was out of debt, and that was the first week that I began teaching Applied Meditation on my own—and it's been the central focus of my life ever since.

Don't ask me how it worked, it just did, and as is usually the case in projection, events occur in surprising ways. I didn't spend hours in meditation; as I said before it was momentary, not only in my meditations but also as I went through my activities. Whenever my frustrations came to mind, I would think of my three pictures and know that behind the scenes that energy was at work. Each of those pictures had very real emotional feelings connected to them. One thing that is important to understand is that the projections are part, but not all, of the process. The next step is to act on the energy. It doesn't just come to you; you've got to meet it halfway. If I hadn't been actively looking for a bus, I would never have been told about the one I found. It seems to me that energizing realities does two things: It creates a probability and it also sensitizes you to knowing intuitively in what directions to go to bring the reality into being.

The irony: though the imagination is seen as unreal we're supposed to be able to imagine anything. This is not so. We can't imagine anything, either because there are external limitations or because there are internal limitations. You may *think* you can imagine anything. You can think it, but to feel what it would be like is quite another matter. If you can't imagine it, don't blame yourself. On the one hand your imagination is psychically attuned to what is possible. The environment may not contain the possibility of your desire yet. On the other hand, your past experiences, your memories are the raw materials used by your imagination to cook up new meals. If there's no flour in the pantry it will place severe limitations on the bread you bake. Someone who has lived in poverty all her life *cannot* imagine what it would *feel* like to be economically secure. She knows only what it's like to wish for it, which is quite a different matter.

Don't blame yourself for not being able to imagine what you want. Instead, if you inspect your projections carefully you'll find that they are a valuable barometer for what you need to work on in order to bring about the change. If the problem is your limited experience rather than objective limitations then what you want to do is expand your consciousness using other areas of your experience. Let's say you know how it feels to have your life full of an abundance of love and family support; imagine transferring this same sense of emotional security into the economic side of your life. Imagine that same sense you have of knowing they will be there when you need them to knowing money will be there when you need it. It will take you a while to do this but it can be done.*

---

*In this chapter I am dealing with the dynamics of individual energy projection and do not mean to imply that the solution to our economic malaise resides in the way we each project our imaginings—this is a political issue and will be dealt with in the last chapters.

Your imagination is a material force affecting the environment, but we mustn't forget that we're social beings living with others who, needless to say, also have imaginations. Your individual imagination does not create reality, it simply interacts with it. By focusing it you increase the likelihood of things occurring; *you do not create the events.* If there are more people imagining otherwise, the event will not come to pass. I'm not saying that our imagination isn't effective, I'm just reminding you that it's only a part of a sea of probabilities. When you participate with it you increase those probabilities which will materialize as a result of the concentration of energies.

As you come to understand the potent energy of consciousness it becomes important not only to take responsibility for your own thoughts, but also to watch how you describe yourself to others. You don't want them carrying around negative images of you. Notice if you ever portray yourself as a helpless victim just for the dramatic effect. Do you want that thought form—the idea that you're a victim—floating around potentially compounding your problems? I am not saying that you shouldn't share your problems but that when you do, you should also share what you are doing to solve them, so that that is the image people will carry around with them, thus giving you added support for the change.

As the innerconsciousness is quite literal, it is of extreme importance that you inspect your projections and be sure that you are ready for them to occur. Make your projections detailed enough that you can experience the whole of their implications. Be sure you really *do* want them, otherwise, if they should be manifested you may discover there are aspects that aren't quite what you bargained for.

CONSCIENTIOUS CONSCIOUSNESS

It's extremely important to understand the fact that we get *what we expect, not necessarily what we want.* For example, as women we've been taught to experience ourselves as vulnerable and weak, expecting to be overpowered and needing protection. Now I know that this is the *last* feeling I should have when I walk in the streets. I don't blame myself for feeling vulnerable—there are very *real* reasons for my feelings, but I know that vulnerability is just the energy that will draw an assailant (remember the unity of opposites: energies that resonate with each other attract one another). Therefore whenever I feel vulnerable I notice the feeling and do whatever I need to do to feel powerful whether that be exploring and transforming my worries, carrying a weapon, learning self-defense, or being with friends—whatever, but I never allow myself to go into the street alone if I'm feeling insecure.

When I was describing this dynamic in one of my classes a student told of a friend of hers who'd been raped and afterwards was so afraid she refused to leave her home. A few days later my student, with all good intentions, convinced her friend to go out—just next door—and when she did she was raped again, this time by a different assailant. Her fearful energy psychically drew him in, which is *not to blame* her—she clearly had *real* reasons to be fearful. But the way to get over it was not to allow herself to be prematurely persuaded to venture out. First she needed support to learn to feel she was strong and able to defend herself, thereby changing her energy. When she was raped her survival was threatened, she went into theta and subsequently her projections about her physical vulnerability had a lot of potency. She needed time to change those projections.

When you care it's only natural to have some worries. Worries are a double jeopardy—you're already troubled and now you realize that the concerns themselves are adding to the likelihood of the actual occurrence of what you fear most. You want to know whether your worries come from your own emotional limitations or from your intuitive/psychic awareness. That's not the issue. The very fact that you are thinking them means they are a probability. So what do you do in order not to collude with the problems? First let your imagination give shape to your anxieties, then look closely at the scene you're afraid might transpire—know it in detail: the atmosphere, the place, the weather, the people involved, and what everyone's doing. Then you do what you can externally so that the particular ingredients of your worries never have a chance to assemble themselves. *Do not dwell on your worries*, but take them as messages and attend to them. Then in your imagination *change* the scene itself as best you can to a positive outcome, thus changing the energy—working both inside and outside. If you cannot change the quality of energy in your imaginary projections I suggest you be very cautious about the situation. If you have changed it but still have a little residual negativity hanging around, you'll want to transform it.

The most powerful method I have discovered for transforming negativity is what I call *mental housecleaning*. Years back I was teaching a class with a friend of mine and we were not getting along at all—which was bad enough in itself—but impossible to tolerate if we were to do a good job in our shared work. I couldn't figure out rationally what to do. Every time we were together after a class I'd find myself angry at him, or myself, or both for one thing or another. So I tried a problem-solving technique I'd learned from the Silva Training called the Glass of Water. After using it the next time I meditated, a champagne-glass-shaped fountain just appeared in my awareness. It was not one of those off-the-wall images that so frequently move through one's mind while in alpha; I knew exactly what it was for. I proceeded to put my image of my friend in the fountain to be washed and cleansed by the water that sprung up through the stem. As I imagined all this I wasn't struck by anything specific, it was not one of those "Aha!" experiences—there was no great emotional feeling when I did it. As usual, it just felt like a little story I made up—as, indeed, it was. One more time I relearned that the results of meditation are discovered later in the world around me, and not during the meditation itself. Subsequently every time I interacted with my friend I felt okay about it; no longer did I plague myself with our difficulties. To this day I have no rational explanation for what happened to change the situation. The only thing I can point to is my use of what I now refer to as my mental housecleaning device. Needless to say we were better able to collaborate with one another.

Using the mental housecleaning device cleared a space in my consciousness and made new experiences possible. It was a symbolic gesture to give my deeper levels the message to transform my stuck position and provide space for new perspectives to come in. The innerconsciousness takes things quite literally so in order to create a mental housecleaning device, imagine something that *transforms* energy and doesn't simply store it—for example, a fire, a compost pit, a fly-eating plant, whatever, so that what goes in, comes out transformed. Always use the same device so your innerconsciousness will come to know it better and better. This technique is one that drives the beta mind bananas, discounting it in every way. Use it anyway—the discounts of beta are ineffectual for the alpha level is non-critical, but it does respond to symbolic messages. Some people have problems with the idea of putting a friend in an imaginary fire, but you are simply putting *your* idea of your friend in, not the friend himself. When working with innerconsciousness it is your *intentions* that always create the effect. They form the vibrations. The specifics of your visualization are simply the framework for channeling the energies; the issue is your intention. Are you genuinely trying to resolve the relationship, or are you trying to hurt your friend? Actually it is benefitting your friend to change your attitudes towards him, whereas it does not benefit either of you to be stuck in negative attitudes toward one another. Doing mental housecleaning will enable you to communicate clearly to resolve whatever issues are problematic. Otherwise, what frequently happens is that even when you've discussed your problems with your friend and made agreements to change, you still find yourself being irritated at the drop of a hat. This is because your innerconsciousness is still in the habit of being irritated so mental housecleaning is called for.

You can also use this method to clear yourself of any attitudes by simply creating a symbol and putting it in. Or you can use it to clear your vocabulary of any words you'd prefer not to use. For example, if you are trying to stop referring to women as "girls," imagine putting the word "girls" into your device.

After using the mental housecleaning device, refocus your attention to a positive outcome. Some people use devices that produce positive results. A friend uses a waterfall that he puts things in, and then he gets something different out once it has bounced around on the rocks in the stream below. My process is such that I simply put stuff in, and then with an act of will move my awareness to other concerns, letting time create new positive directions. I warn you to refocus your attention either on a positive outcome or something different altogether—if you don't, you'll find yourself habitually acting out of the familiar, thus recreating your problem. Mental housecleaning clears your mind of bad habits but it does not necessarily solve the problem itself; instead it provides space for a resolution to appear, a resolution that otherwise you probably would not notice. You always want your last thought to be positive and moving and therefore the last directive to which your consciousness will continue to respond.

If ever you find you are still plagued with a problem you have mental housecleaned and you are sure you have properly followed the instructions for using the technique (that your last thought was positive or something else altogether) the chances are your inner-consciousness knows that whatever you're working on is not exclusively a negative habit on your part but has something positive to offer you—some lesson is still to be learned. Some closer attention is called for. In this case I suggest that you inspect the problem further, for within it are the seeds of insights you need in order to move on. Once you've acted on the insights your mental house-cleaning will succeed.

MASS MEDIA = MASS HYPNOSIS = MINDLESS MASSES

There is great concern these days about environmental pollution. It is of at least equal consequence that we address ourselves to the pollution of our minds. If we are to take control of our consciousness we cannot do so without concerning ourselves with the images constantly emanating from the mass media and penetrating our awareness. Television has become a most trusty companion for all too many of us. It may feel good to have a friend who is always there for you, doesn't argue, and is full of entertainment—the problem is you are not in the habit of arguing with it either.

I've already said that we move through the world in terms of our inner messages. When we watch TV we are in the alpha level and much to the gratification of Madison Avenue it is a highly program-mable state of awareness. We don't distinguish between the real and the unreal—we simply act in accordance with our images, whether we're actually confronted by a mad dog or simply imagine that we are, as far as our adrenal glands are concerned it's the same thing. Notice the bodily sensations you get when watching a horror show. Once I understood the power of the imagination, I stopped expos-ing myself to such atrocities for they are genuine pollution of the mind. Witness the number of children afraid to swim in pools after seeing *Jaws*. I even met a boy who was afraid to sleep on a waterbed.

There are already so many dreadful things going on that I have to be careful how I carry them in my awareness. I don't need to compound the problem. I don't want to draw toward me events that resonate with the horror shows.

Inventions make life easier to live. Now we have television, which has gone a step further and replaced it. We may as well not live life at all, as we can't ever live up to the image of the "good life" brought into our homes in full living color. So why not sit back and let the box do the living for us—it's easier that way. As Jerry Mander says, "The people who control television become the choreographers of our internal awareness," and "by (television's) expropriation of inner experience, advertising makes the human into a spectator of his or her own life. It is alienation to the tenth power."[10]

When listening to the radio, or reading, we have to provide our own images; TV does the whole job for us. We've become passive receptacles for the images it bestows on us. How often have you heard someone say, "Just like on TV!" as an expression of how *real* something was? Now we hardly live life, we just watch it, but when we do live a little the most exciting moments get compared to what we saw on TV. "Life itself has become a spectacle."[11]

How bad is the problem, really? "More American homes have television than have heat or indoor plumbing," and, "The average TV set is turned on for six and one half hours per day."[12] Recently the TV informed me it was up to eight hours per day.

> The spread of television unified a whole people within a system of conceptions and living patterns. Because of it, our whole culture and the physical shape of the environment, no more or less than our minds and feelings, have been computerized, linearized, suburbanized, freewayized, and packaged for sale.[13]

We're bombarded everyday with messages we don't want to internalize—from billboards, magazines, newpapers, but the prime offender is TV. An expert in biofeedback tells us that:

> The horror of television is that the information goes in, but we don't react to it. It goes right into our memory pool and perhaps we react to it later but we don't know what we're reacting to.

When you watch television you are training yourself not to react and so later on, you're doing things without knowing why you're doing them or where they came from. [14]

So what is it that we are reacting to later without knowing it? We've become mindless consumers, but there's an even scarier aspect:

If commercials are the appetizer and dessert of each TV time slot, violence is its main course, the meat and potatoes that make the sponsor's message stick to your ribs. "To the advertiser, violence equals excitement equals ratings." [15]

And why are we horrified when we read in the papers stories like that of the boy who killed a schoolmate and then brought his friends to see the corpse?

An appalling number of juvenile crimes—torture, kidnapping, rapes, and murders—have been traced to events portrayed on televisions. . . . A boy's television habits at age eight are more likely to be a predictor of his aggressiveness at age eighteen or nineteen than his family's socio-economic status, his relationship with his parents, his IQ or any other single factor in his environment. [16]

TV teaches that women are helpless victims, that men are the saviors and that the solution boils down to a shootout. This kind of scene is literally programmed into us in a million ways. We become numbed to violence and eventually look at mangled bodies with total indifference.

Schools have lost their primary role in teaching problem-solving skills. Their impact has been replaced by 1984's Big Brother in disguise. Now we're taught not to solve problems at all—take an aspirin or shoot him instead. "By the time a child graduates from high school, he or she will have spent less than 12,000 hours in front of a teacher and more than 22,000 hours in front of a television set." [17]

We don't need to be mesmerized by Madison Avenue and homogenized by prime time. Just because the drug, heroin, feels good doesn't mean you have to indulge yourself. If we don't want to be homogenized the best thing to do is turn off the set or talk back to it for your own self-protection so your deeper levels of consciousness don't absorb it all noncritically in the name of reality. The people responsible for the programs won't hear your arguments, but your deeper awareness will. So talk back! And take back your consciousness! Every time you compare yourself to John Wayne or Marilyn Monroe bring in the affirmation, "I believe in myself." There is nothing more frustrating than trying to live up to something that isn't real. You can protect yourself from the destructive messages by imagining yourself surrounded by an invisable mirror that bounces back the ones you don't want to absorb.

Keep in mind that whatever images we carry around inside are what we act out of. In your suggestible alpha state it is imperative that you don't sit back and allow yourself to be filled with the garbage of the media, then later find yourself mindlessly regurgitating it out into your life. There is more to life than how much you weigh, or how strong you are, or getting the latest gadget on the market. Your creativity won't get plugged up if you consciously choose what to let through your alpha awareness. But if you don't take control you leave it up to television. If our creativity isn't buried under the sludge we'll have better ways of spending our time than in front of the tube. Remember our creativity comes from deeper levels. We have to give it space to surface. And on the other hand we don't want to energize all the junk we watch by carrying it around in our real imaginations.

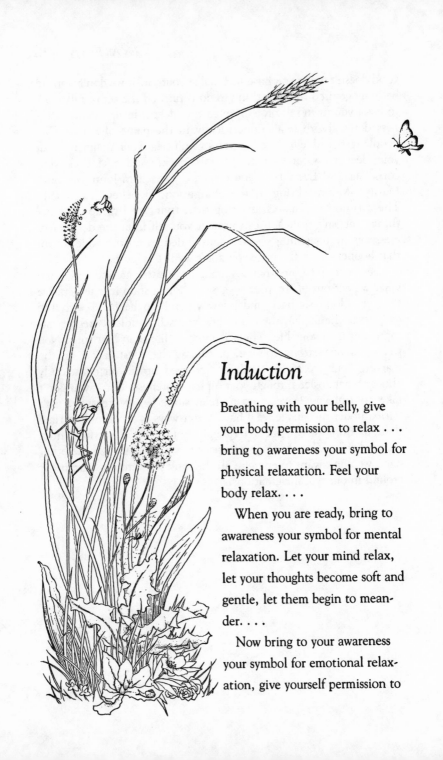

Induction

Breathing with your belly, give
your body permission to relax . . .
bring to awareness your symbol for
physical relaxation. Feel your
body relax. . . .

When you are ready, bring to
awareness your symbol for mental
relaxation. Let your mind relax,
let your thoughts become soft and
gentle, let them begin to meander. . . .

Now bring to your awareness
your symbol for emotional relaxation, give yourself permission to

feel safe and secure . . . emotionally relaxed. . . .

Now bring to awareness your symbol for your creative self-restoring center. Here your consciousness is fluid and free. You will remain alert throughout this meditation, tell yourself this now. . . .

I am going to suggest several affirmations. If you wish to affirm them, repeat them to yourself after me knowing that in so doing you create patterns of energy both within and around you causing your life to align itself with the power of the words you are speaking. And the affirmations will manifest themselves in your life.

I believe in myself, I believe in my experience. . . .

I trust my nature, I trust nature. . . .

I am a fully intelligent, creative being. . . .

I live up to my fullest potential. . . .

I expect the best. . . .

I listen to my intuition. It knows what is so and guides me in the right direction. . . .

I only respond to positive suggestions. . . .

My fears are transformed into my teachers, empowering me to move forward with courage and knowingness. . . .

I always successfully protect myself. . . .

My life is in harmony with the life around me. . . .

My life is whole, my life is embraced by the whole of life. . . .

All my needs are always met, there is enough for everyone. . . .

I maintain balance amidst change. . . .

I trust the future. . . .

Now take time to focus on any of your own affirmations, knowing that as you focus on affirmations you create patterns of energy to which your life will conform. Or you may want to focus on any quality symbols you have been working with.

❖ ❖ ❖

Finishing what you're doing . . . alert and ready to follow what I have to say to you. . . .

In a moment I'm going to count on a descending scale from ten to one. At each descending count you can descend deeper and deeper into yourself—into your center of knowingness—into the center out of which your personality emanates. Ten, moving down deeper now, feeling the qualities of who you are . . . nine, relaxing into yourself, returning to yourself. . . eight, acknowledging the particular essence of your being, the special way you are an expression of life . . . seven, feel the deepest tones of your being, like musical chords . . . six, moving down deeper and deeper into your center . . . five, your center of knowingness . . . four, your center of receptivity, creativity, all knowingness . . . three, deeper and deeper into yourself, who it is that you are . . . two, moving into your center out of which your energy emanates, drawing to you particular events, resonant events . . . one, this is your center of knowingness, potent energy resides here. Here you can adjust energy, align energy, create probabilities. This is your center of receptive knowingness. Here you can feel yourself as a part of all that is. . . .

This is a very powerful place to do your interior work. From this place you have access to all knowingness, to your own knowingness. To the wisdom that's yours. Here you can experience all that you know. Here you can look at any aspect of your life and know it's true nature . . . know your own true nature. Here your wisdom resides. You can look at any fears, any anxieties, any particular feelings, anything, and you can discover what to do. Here, all your knowingness resides.

Bathe yourself in all the universal knowingness you have access to. Discover what you know, what you already know, feel your knowingness. Here your inquiring mind can acquire whatever knowledge you need in your life now. And as you imagine your knowingness, imagine your knowingness filtering down into the whole of yourself. . . . Honor your knowingness, give yourself the space you need to come in tune with what you know, and be able to act out of your knowingness, bringing this knowingness into the world. . . . You can shape your life so the knowingness can flow through easily. Just like a spring comes up from the depths of the earth, water flowing, let your knowingness flow up from the depths of your being, from the depths of beingness itself. Keep within yourself a clear open channel for this energy to surface and flow through you, out into your life. . . . Keeping clear, drawing to you events that resonate with the goodness of life itself. Trust your experience.

Rehearsing the Future

Feel the quiet space you now occupy, fully relaxed—yet there is much potency—like the atmosphere right before the morning sun rises, the dawn of a new day . . . very peaceful, yet pregnant with potential. Very quiet, yet charged with possibilities . . . feel this very quiet, receptive space you now occupy and know that this very space is full of creative energy, here you can create possibilities, here you can create probabilities, for this quiet space you now occupy is very powerful. . . .

Know that you have different vortexes of energy inside of

yourself and in particular a vortex of energy in the middle of your forehead, sometimes called the third eye. Imagine going into that vortex of energy with your awareness. Imagine letting your awareness reside in your third eye, whatever that means to you, feel the quality of energy that's present in this area. From here you can best create probabilities. It is from here the future dawns. Imagine that you are sitting in a theatre, where you have control of the spotlight. Imagine as though this were a magic theatre, where the future rehearses, and this spotlight is very powerful, for you can direct it to illuminate the future—all the possible futures. . . . The future is the stage this spotlight illuminates and you can set the stage however you choose. Know that you can also make the light brighter or duller.

Begin to imagine what your third eye illuminates, look down the beam of light as though it were a flashlight. Wherever you turn this light it can illuminate possibilities that already exist. Then you can create probabilities of how you'd like things to unfold for yourself, your family, your community, the world. You can focus this beam of light personally, collectively, and planetarily. You can focus it here, you can focus it there, seeing possibilities that exist, and you can create positive probabilities. . . .

First observe possibilities as they already exist and let your third eye illuminate the immediate future . . . notice the probabilities. Let the next week unfold before you, and watch it occur . . . watch what you do . . . watch what happens. . . . Let the scenes arise in your awareness . . . sense the atmosphere around each . . . as though you're watching previews. . . . Notice how each day unfolds . . . be aware of the atmosphere surrounding the unfolding of scenes.

◆   ◆   ◆

Now go back to the beginning of the week and this time let the spotlight illuminate day by day exactly how you would like it to be. Let you and the world around you move into synchrony, familiarize yourself with the best of possibilities. Feeling good about yourself, energize what you would like to have occur, how you'd like to feel. Endeavor to expect it to truly occur. Illuminate it with the spotlight . . . imagine this happening.

❖   ❖   ❖

Feel yourself being very deserving of all this that you would like to have occur. And know that in experiencing it occuring in this way, you have energized it, you move into synchrony with the best of probabilities—for consciousness is magnetic energy. You are drawn toward circumstances that resonate with the good qualities you imagine and so, too, circumstances are drawn into your goodness.

❖   ❖   ❖

Now let the light illuminate how, if it unfolds in this manner, it will affect others. If you discover any detrimental effects on others, make whatever adjustments are necessary, so that all that occurs is good for everyone.

❖

Now once again go back to the beginning and this time enter the scene. Travel down the beam of light and enter into the image of yourself that you've been watching, feel all the events unfolding around you. Notice what you're wearing, how your body feels . . . any sounds, smells, vibrations that are present as the week unfolds around you. . . . Feel yourself going through the events, feel the excitement of these events developing in this desirable manner, feel your connection with all those that you share these events with. . . . Feel it all happening, experience it happening, happening around you. Feel as though it were happening right now . . . from the beginning of the week to the end.

❖   ❖   ❖

Now project yourself into the future beyond the coming week. Feel your life, how it has been effected by the occurrences of these events that you've projected. . . . These events have already entered the past, they are now memories. . . . Imagine how you'll feel about yourself, about your life after all this has transpired.

♦   ♦   ♦

Know that you have set energy into motion, that you intuitively know how to bring these events into reality . . . know that these energies are already moving into the environment creating probabilities that can manifest themselves . . . drawing in all that resonates with your imaginings. . . . Allow yourself to believe in yourself, believe in your experience, believe in the world, believe in the future. Suspend any residues of skepticism and believe that the very fact that you can imagine these experiences makes them real, your imagination is real, imagination is the stuff probabilities are made of. . . .

Now notice what you need to do to bring these energies into your life, in a way that feels good to yourself and to all those around you. Ask yourself what you personally need to do to bring these events into reality . . . or maybe there's something you need to give up. . . . Make agreements with yourself about what you're willing to do to bring all this into the world. And notice how and when you'll do it . . . and know that in so doing you bring this energy out into the world . . . knowing what you have to offer the future . . . knowing what the future has to offer you.

Tell yourself that if ever you find yourself frustrated with the way it has been that you'll move you're attention to a sense of change that has already begun to take place . . . believing in a better future. . . .

Now give yourself permission to have faith in these probabilities, to have faith in yourself. . . . Know that the world is full of goodness, know that soon you'll find yourself living inside of these events. . . . Know that this is so. Expect it.

Mental Housecleaning

Know that your consciousness is *your* consciousness, your dominion. . . . Your consciousness is loyal to your choices . . . you can choose the qualities of energy that reside here. The whole of your innerconsciousness is your realm, your sphere, and fully responsive to your influence. Your innerconsciousness is responsive to your suggestion.

Now create a ritual of transformation in your consciousness. Create a mental housecleaning ritual—use the transmuting powers of nature. . . . Create something like fire, a compost pit, whatever you like—be sure it transforms energy . . . recycling the old making space for the new.

◆　◆　◆

This is your mental housecleaning device. Know that you can use your mental housecleaning device to convert, to transform any negativity, making space for new creative perspectives to reveal themselves. Tell your deeper consciousness this now, tell your deeper consciousness that whenever you symbolically put anything through your mental housecleaning device your consciousness will then transform the constricting energy, making space for new energy to emerge. . . . Know that this is so, trust it. . . .

You can use your device whenever you are stuck in negative patterns; simply symbolize the habituated pattern and put the symbol into your mental housecleaning device. . . . When you do this keep your intentions clear and positive. After using your device always move your consciousness in a positive direction or focus on an entirely different concern trusting that deeper within you a conversion is taking place. . . . Your imagination is real and when you imagine a transformation you speak to the deepest levels of knowingness within you which respond; the energy shifts and a metamorphosis occurs. You've transformed the old and created space for the birth of new liberating experiences to manifest themselves. Know that this is so.

Whenever you do mental housecleaning always be specific. . . . Recreate the concern in your awareness, be aware of the atmos-phere in which it lives, symbolize it and put the symbol through your device, then move your consciousness into a new direction expecting the transformation to take place deeper within you. You can take time to work with your mental housecleaning device now. . . . Choose one specific area of habitual negativity that you wish to free yourself of.

◆   ◆   ◆

Know that you have released yourself from patterns of the past . . . transformation is taking place within you. New experience is available to you now. Expect it. . . .

Tell yourself that you will remember to use your mental house-cleaning device whenever you need to clear the debris in your mind and it will enable you to be fully present, clear and creative in the situation. . . . Your consciousness is *your* dominion and you can choose the qualities that reside within you.

Self-Protection

Think of times when you've felt very safe, what safety means to
you, protection, security, safety . . . feel yourself safe, secure,
protected. . . . Let these qualities move through your awareness.
Like snapshot pictures, remember times of safety, protection,
security. The times in the past where you've felt these qualities
present. Let them be present now. . . . Breathe in the sense of
safety. . . . Feel yourself increasingly aware of what it feels like to
be safe, how it feels in your body. . . . Bring the energies of safety
and protection into the present, into the room right now . . .
feeling your body filled with this sensation of security and
safety. . . . Fill yourself up with that sensation as though you are in
a bubble of protection or a warm cozy firelit room, or white light, a
loved one's arms, soft music—whatever security is to you. . . . In
fact you may want to literally imagine yourself in a bubble of
protection. You may want to imagine yourself in a bubble of light,
energy, music, however you wish to imagine yourself surrounded by,
and immersed in protection.

◆

Create a symbol for this experience. It may be the bubble itself or
it may be something different. . . . Know that whenever you bring
this symbol into your awareness, you'll bring this energy of protection into your sphere, into your space, and in so doing you'll
protect yourself from any influences that may restrict your movement. You will find yourself intuitively knowing what you need to

do to protect yourself. . . . Whenever you use your symbol of protection you fully possess your space, you engage your dominion over who it is that you are, you cause others to respect your integrity. . . . Whenever you use this symbol you create boundaries allowing only positive influences to penetrate. . . . Know that this is so, that this symbol energetically creates a quality of dignity around you, to which everything responds, bouncing off the negative and absorbing only the positive. . . . With your symbol of protection you become immune to all detrimental influences. Suggest to your inner self that whenever you bring this symbol to mind you will receive the information you need, knowing just what is necessary to remain safe and secure. . . .

Wherever you are, you can protect yourself from other people's energy, from germs, from attack, from advertising . . . whatever it may be, by simply bringing this symbol into mind and in so doing you surround yourself with this energy of protection and safety. . . . Know that this is so, tell yourself this. Whenever you need the energy of protection you can make it so by simply bringing the symbol to mind and your space will be honored. . . . You'll command your own space, release your courage whenever needed and successfully stand your ground, for your symbol not only protects you from the outside but releases your power—power within to be equal to power without—equal to whatever might challenge your integrity. Give yourself permission to believe this.

You can also use this symbol to protect anyone who may be threatened, anything that may be threatened. You can use this symbol to surround anything with protective energy. . . . Imagine using this symbol now, moving through your activities to see how it feels. . . . When you use it, you intuitively know what to do to protect yourself or others. . . . Tell yourself the next time you bring this symbol to mind the whole of your being will respond, doing what's needed to protect yourself and everything around you. . . . Know that everyone will respond to this energy.

Stretching your Confidence into a New Area

Experience the warmth you feel for the beauty of life, the wonder of the world, spectacular landscapes . . . delicate flowers . . . a child fumbling as she learns to make her own way through the. world. . . . Feel your compassion, feel the compassion you have for all of life, your love of life itself.

◆ ◆ ◆

Draw this quality you are now experiencing into yourself. . . . Breathe in compassion for who it is that you are, breathe it into the whole of your being . . . breathe in tenderness for your own nature . . . immerse yourself in compassion, let yourself be affectionate towards who you are. . . .

Remember yourself in the past, all the years that have gone into making you who you are. Unique experiences, a combination of experiences that only you have had, believe in the lessons of your experience. . . . Recognize your intelligence. Appreciate who it is that you are, love yourself. Acknowledge the true nature of who you are, *your* nature, what you have become because of the choices that *you* have made. Tell yourself what you appreciate about who you are. Simply enjoy liking yourself, respecting yourself.

◆ ◆ ◆

Notice how you receive this acknowledgement, sense if there are any places that this love bounces off, where it doesn't go in . . . or any place that needs the love to go in even deeper. . . . Now imagine having X-ray vision and penetrating right into those areas that haven't accepted this acknowledgement; infuse the areas with caring energy, feel them softening, becoming receptive, let them be nurtured with loving compassionate energy . . . massage yourself with loving energy.

◆   ◆   ◆

Now bring into your awareness your sense of competency, your sense of intelligence. Become aware of your sense of security with your abilities. To do this you may want to remember an area in your life in which you are fully competent, an area you have fully mastered. Choose an area in your life where you believe in your experience; don't worry if the area seems trivial or unimportant— what is important is that you are fully proficient. . . . Believe in yourself, believe in your capability, trust your experience. . . . Now create a symbol for self-confidence.

◆   ◆   ◆

Now choose an area in your life that you would like to enhance, be it creativity, a skill, whatever you choose . . . choose one particular skill that you would like either to acquire or to expand what you already have—a way of being with people, a way of being in the world that you would like to be, enabling you to move in new directions of your choice.

◆

Know that within you, you have the ability to tap universal collective consciousness and that within it resides the knowledge, information and energy that will enable you to acquire just what you need to develop yourself, to express yourself through the newly acquired ability. . . . You have the ability to tap knowledge, know that you can tap the source of all knowingness. Pretend that you can. . . .

Your symbol for self-confidence enables you to be fully receptive to insights and qualities that will help you bring about this new way of being. Your symbol acts as a magnet drawing to you exactly what you need from deep within and from without. . . . Sprinkle this confidence into the arena you have chosen to embrace, as though your symbol were to rain upon it, however you imagine this.

Now imagine your symbol flooding the area with the powerful energy of competence. . . . Imagine it glowing, charged with knowingness. . . . Now imagine your future self and let her/him be empowered by all this energy. Let your future self be fully able in this new area, let your future self be dynamic . . . imagine yourself newly able in this area. . . . How does it feel? Now be your future self, let your confidence symbol make your steps steady in this new area of your life. . . . Let your confidence give you courage to manifest your desires, to believe in yourself. . . . Feel how you allow all this to occur . . . slowly your steps are no longer tenuous but instead steady and strong.

◆   ◆   ◆

Talk to your future self and your symbol for self confidence to discover what it is you can do in your life to bring all of this about. . . . Sense if there is anything you need to give up in your life or in your self-image to make room for this new way of being. . . . What can you do to cultivate this attribute?. . . Are you willing to do these things?

◆   ◆   ◆

Know that if you can imagine it you can create it. . . . You'll find yourself knowing intuitively just what to do, just where to go, just what to ask, just what to say. . . . Your body, your mind, your feelings and your spirit are now all aligned with this energy. Know that this is so. . . . Give yourself permission to believe in yourself, to believe that in fact all this can come about, will come about. You deserve it. . . . Let any residual skepticism soak down into the ground to be transformed by the soil or put through your mental housecleaning device making room for this new energy to come through.

◆ ◆ ◆

Know that as you are confident in some areas you can become confident in all areas that you choose to focus on; confidence can spread throughout the whole of your experience, throughout the whole of your life, believing in your experience in all areas of your life. . . . Know that your potential grows every day. . . . Believe in yourself. You have transformed a wish into a belief.

Fear as Challenge

Now imagine a spot that's a very powerful spot for you, a place of power. . . . It could be one that you create in your imagination, one that you've been to before, a place of power. . . . A place that's charged with energy for you. Create your place of power. . . . Let yourself be in this spot, feel the power of this place. . . . You may remember times in your life when you felt very powerful, strong, creative. . . . Fill this place with the qualities of those times. . . . Sense what power, what strength, what vital forces mean to you, feel them here in this place. . . . Feel the power around you, move your awareness within yourself and sense what places within you vibrate with the power around you.

◆

If you like, imagine yourself standing in this place and drawing up all the power it has to offer you, through the arches of your feet, the palms of your hands or anywhere it's inclined to come in, breathe it in. . . . Infusing the whole of yourself with the power, letting the energy move through you in such a way that it is dispersed very evenly, rhythmically, equally, throughout your whole self. . . . Feeling extremely powerful and balanced, fully balanced yet charged with a vital force. . . . Empowering the whole of your being, every cell, every thought, every feeling—the whole of your experience charged with strength. . . . Feel how centered you are with this energy moving through you. . . . Feel that quality of being fully powerful and balanced all at once.

◆

Now bring to awareness your symbols for protection and confidence. Or if you have none bring into the scene the quality of safety and feel your confidence. . . . You are courageous; it is from these wellsprings of energy that your courage emerges. Experience courage, experience your courage.

◆

Now choose one particular fear or anxiety you would like to work on. . . . Bring into your awareness something that you find very intimidating, scary, fearful; recreate the times you've felt this particular fear. . . don't bring the fear too close so that you find yourself losing touch with the powerful energy moving through you. . . . Just bring it close enough so that you can keep your energy moving smoothly. . . . Continuing to feel courageous and protected. . . . Feel this fear . . . take the fear and look at it. . . . Separate yourself from it and look at it. . . . Let whatever anxieties you carry drain out of you and in turn give the fear form, color and aliveness, give it a personality, the anxiety moving out of you, now you can talk to the fear and see what it has to offer you . . . where it comes from. . . . The fear is no longer within you at all but personified before you.

◆   ◆   ◆

Be receptive, listen to what you need to know from your place of power, from your symbols to let this fear become a challenge so it gives you more power. . . . Ask the fear for a gift, notice what it has to offer you. . . . Know that in fact your fear is your greatest teacher, and from your center you gain courage, from your friends and family you gain courage. And from your fear you learn lessons . . . keeping your power so that the fear becomes a challenge and moves you forward in your life. . . . Become friends with this fear you are confronting now. . . . Let it give you power, let it teach you. . . . As if it were a door through which you can discover new ways of being.

◆

Imagine the fear having a beam of light. . . . Now if you wish you can aim this light into any situation, into the imagined future and see what it illuminates. . . . See just what the fear can illuminate— what you can learn. . . . It may illuminate caution, it may illuminate old things you can now let go of. . . . Notice what inside of you resonates with the fear, vibrates with the fear. . . . Notice what the fear is protecting you from.

◆   ◆   ◆

Transform constricting energy into positive light. This light can be used to tune yourself very finely to potential situations. It can give you the knowledge that you need to move through those situations in a very courageous and protected way. . . . It can give you the information you need to rearrange probabilities, making the potential scenes positive.

◆   ◆   ◆

If you wish you can decide to walk down the path created by the beam of light emanating from the fear and embrace the challenges, make them your own, let that beam of light empower you to move forward. . . . With the light the unknown is illuminated and all becomes known and you become wiser. . . . See where you can go with it.

❖

Appreciate the fear that has become a challenge, giving you the gift of the lessons that you have learned. . . . Create positive probabilities. . . . Believe in yourself, appreciate your power, your symbol of protection, your courage, appreciate the support others have for you to move forward and learn.

❖ ❖ ❖

If you choose, you can imagine moving forward in your life until you come across another fear and when you do, give it personality too, talk to it, let it give you the gift of the challenge that it has hidden within it; learn from it and let your place of power, your symbols and your friends give you the courage to move forward through that fear, becoming a wiser fuller human being.

❖ ❖ ❖

Know that you can always do this, protected, powerful, courageous and yet learning. . . . Remember the support around you. . . . Remember to transform the negative into a positive light. . . . And all you ever fear is transformed into challenge which in turn is transformed into the wisdom of lessons learned. . . . Acknowledge that this is so.

Countout

Just as the sun gives birth to a new day, your imagination gives birth to a new future . . . your imagination is real, in it probabilities are born. Appreciate your imagination for all that it gives you . . . in it your knowingness resides and you can sense what is so and work with it, creating positive transformation. Go over all that you have come to in this meditation, insights, choices . . . know that the very fact that you imagine it makes it real, the energy now exists . . . trust it, expect the best.

◆   ◆   ◆

Finish what you're doing and make yourself ready to come out to outer conscious levels by knowing that you'll bring with you all the energies you've contacted.

In a moment I'm going to count from one to five, at the count of five, you'll open your eyes remembering all that you've experienced . . . feeling refreshed, revitalized and relaxed. . . .

ONE—becoming more aware of the room around you. . . .

TWO—coming up slowly now. . . .

THREE—at the count of five you'll open your eyes feeling relaxed, revitalized, and refreshed remembering all that you've experienced. . . .

FOUR—coming up now, bringing with you your sense of well-being. . . .

FIVE!—eyes open, feeling refreshed, revitalized and relaxed, remembering all that you've experienced, feeling a sense of well-being.

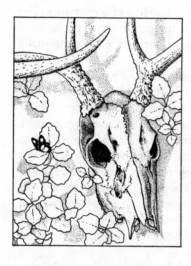

Chapter Six

Tapping
Universal
Energies

It is in meditation that you become aware of your intuition, which is an aspect of yourself that won't get you in trouble. How do you put it in charge so you can act in the best way possible *amidst* your activities? Intuition resides in the realm of universality—the imagination is real. So all you need do is imagine universal energies continually moving through you. The technique of *running energy* does just that.

For most of us our natural inclination is to spend our energies primarily focused on our personal lives, our trials and tribulations. We tend to forget our connection to the earth, to the sky, to each other, to the life that's constantly percolating in and around us. When we forget our connections, we wind up feeling drained and isolated. When we remember our connections, we become energized, inspired, and feel a part of all that's around us.

RUNNING ENERGY:
SHIFTING OUT OF EGO ATTACHMENT

Running energy resolves this problem, that is, it moves us out of
our personal isolated niches and into a position of universality. The
process itself is simply imagining the energies of the earth and sky
to be constantly moving through you, just as the air continually
moves through you.

A couple of years after I had begun working with the power of
consciousness I took a class where I learned this technique. Until
then, whenever I taught a full-day workshop I would be so burnt
out at the end of the day that I would not have the energy to cook
dinner for myself. I'd just collapse into bed. The next time I had to
teach an all-day workshop it occurred to me that there was all this
energy around so I needn't depend only on *my own*. So right before
I started my class I ran energy and continued to run it throughout
the day. When the workshop was over I made myself dinner and
went out dancing for the next four hours. The difference it made
boggled my mind; never again have I become exhausted from teaching because now I always run energy.

For me, when I'm running energy I don't feel anything; it's just a
picture I make up in my head—I'm a visualizer. But, as with mental
housecleaning, the results are profound and are felt in the midst of
activities, not in the meditation itself. When I first applied the
technique I didn't understand why it worked because I still ex-
pended as much physical energy as I ever did. In retrospect I can
see why in the past my teaching so exhausted me—my ego had
been too involved, and I had let it take a front row seat. Most of
my energy was engaged with how people were hearing me, and
what people thought. The fact is I have no control over how people
hear me, or of what they're going to think of what I say—nor
should I. All I can do is present the material in as clear a way as
possible, respecting people's choices as to how they will respond.
It's only natural for me to want both approval and agreement, but
it confuses my clarity and drains my energy and it certainly doesn't
help people hear me any better; instead, it hinders them.

Before I started running energy in my classes, if I had information
which I knew would help someone with a problem I'd restate it
many different ways in order to convince them to follow my sugges-

tions. Now when I run energy it doesn't *occur* to me to try to convince anybody of anything. Instead, I find myself communicating with much greater clarity than ever before and with a sense of security, knowing that's enough. My expression is precise for the very reason that I'm not caught up in the opinions of others. Running energy causes me to respect people's processes automatically because my ego is no longer separating us. If someone doesn't take good advice, that's okay, it's their choice, not mine. Clear communication occurs because my personal feelings are not clogging up my process; it isn't as though they go away, they're just no longer in the driver's seat. Running energy automatically moves you from a position of emotionality to spirituality, from the emotional to the intuitive, moving from a position of individual isolation and ego-attachment to a position of universality—enabling you to view the world in a clearer way.

Running energy is the single most effective technique for overcoming stress, for most stress comes from a sense of isolation—you're out there alone, fending for yourself. It is particularly helpful in difficult situations, for instance being around relatives who are hard to get along with. If you run energy in the midst of such a situation you'll surprise yourself, you might actually enjoy being with them. Or you may find yourself in a conflict with your boss or your landlord and you know that if you express all that you're feeling you'll end up paying for it—a position you cannot afford to be in. On the other hand you know you need to assert yourself. If you run energy you'll find yourself intuitively knowing exactly what to do and say that will most likely influence the other person in a positive way.

Just as running energy reduces your need for approval, it also enables you to steer clear of negative energy so you won't find yourself internalizing other people's problems. These two things are extremely important in working with people, particularly if you're doing healing, teaching, or are in a position of leadership.

The essential thing about this practice is that energy is constantly moving *through* you; you've created channels so that nothing gets stuck. It is particularly helpful in overcoming bodily problems such as headaches, or even more severe problems like epilepsy that are the result of stuck energies. I know of epileptics who learned to run energy and no longer have seizures. It is also effective to use when you feel that you are picking up too much information and you are unable to deal with your psychic abilities.

In learning how to run energy it's good to begin by sitting with your back straight, either in a chair or on the floor, if the latter you may find it more comfortable to sit on a pillow with your legs on the floor; this way they won't fall asleep so easily. It's important to have your spine as straight as is comfortable.

You can run energy as a substitute for going into your meditative state or in conjunction with your three symbols for mind/body/emotional relaxation. If you use it in conjunction with your symbols connect with the earth while relaxing your body, and connect with the sky while relaxing your mind. When you use it in your daily life, before you start any activities take a few moments to close your eyes and begin the energy moving with the intention that it continue. Then occasionally pause for a moment in the midst of what you're doing and focus your awareness on the energies moving through you. With time you will find that you'll automatically run energy when you need to. It is also helpful to use if you tend to fall asleep when meditating. It will enable you to enter a deep state of consciousness while at the same time maintaining your alertness.

This technique can also be used if you don't have all the energy you need to take care of your responsibilities and don't have the time to get the rest you need. However, I would like to caution you that running energy is not a substitute for rest, though it does result in a more efficient use of physical energy because you won't find yourself being burnt up by stress.

Running energy can be used as a barometer to reflect your state of being. If you find it easier to imagine the earth energy, the chances are that all the practical affairs in your life are covered: your kitchen is clean, but you may find yourself frequently bored. On the other hand, if you find it is easier to imagine the sky energy, you probably have a sink full of dirty dishes but lots of good ideas, few of which are put into action—you are spaced out. Everyone needs a balance of both. If you find it hard to imagine the earth energy then that's what you need to work on; as you do you'll be less absent-minded and no longer walk into glass doors. If you have a lot of ideas and don't know where to start, ground yourself and you'll find you are able to focus. On the other hand, if you're in the midst of a project and you get stuck, bring through the energy of the sky. It will help you move on. In my experience with people who are very depressed, they can't imagine a future that is desirable and it is understandable that they remain low, for they have nothing to strive for. They will find it difficult to focus on the sky energy, but forcing themselves to do so will in time bring about a change of heart. Some people have an easy time imagining both earth and sky energy, but have trouble mixing them together; invariably these people's lives feel compartmentalized. To move to a sense of integration mixing the energies is called for.

Running energy is helpful in meetings; if ever you are stuck on one issue and you can't seem to bring it to resolution, stop the discussion for a few moments and have everybody bring in sky energy. Afterwards, you'll find yourselves knowing how to move forward. And, similarly, if you seem to be working all over the agenda, unable to take one thing at a time, stop and bring in earth energy.

All this may sound a bit weird and esoteric. It still feels that way to me. But now I look at it just as I look at my beta mind discounting—my judgment doesn't matter because my experience has proven to me the power of running energy. Running energy may not feel particularly significant, but I promise you that if you do it you'll notice its effects.

ENERGY CIRCLES:
CONCENTRATING CONSCIOUSNNESS

Meditating in a group feels a lot more potent than it does when you're alone so if you have a whole group meditating on the same thing at the same time it becomes extremely powerful. Everyone's deeper experience merges, dissolving isolation. The best way to get the energies vibrating on the same wavelength, so to speak, is to use energy circles, where people sit in a circle, holding hands, and run earth and sky energy through themselves and then imagine the collective energy they create together moving around the circle. Once all of this is operating, you bring into the circle whatever concerns people would like to focus on. As I have mentioned, our individual consciousness creates probabilities. Needless to say, when you have collective consciousness focused on creating probabilities, they are much stronger.

I've been leading energy circles in weekly meditation support groups for seven years and if I didn't lead them I'd certainly join one. I'm a junkie for them now; their potency amazes me. Working consistently with one another for a length of time, we've come to develop an entirely new kind of relationship; we know each other psychically; we're intuitively attuned to each other, an attunement that grows with time—an experience of knowing other people in a wholly different way. We intuitively witness each other's growth from the *inside out*, instead of from the *outside in*—an amazing perspective to experience!

Circles are a powerful antidote to the isolation endemic in our society. They have become the major source of support in my life. In fact, if it weren't for them this book you are now reading would never have materialized. They not only provide me with easy access to my own knowingness, but also I get the benefit of everyone else's insights. The effects of energizing and the insights gained are extremely helpful, but just as important to me is the uncanny sensation I get in the circle itself; it feels as if I'm being fully supported by the energy—suspended in it—for the duration of the circle. I'm relieved of the responsibility of carrying my own weight. Sometimes it feels like the whole room is filled up with energy. Once right in the midst of a circle an unopened bottle of wine popped its cork. To me it feels as if this energy that I'm suspended in extends out beyond the space and time of the circle itself and becomes an underlying support as I go through my activities of the week.

In general, an energy circle allows us to do two things: energize events and investigate situations. This investigation leads to helpful insights in finding a strategy for how to deal with a given situation. It is particularly powerful because, in my experience, it is virtually impossible for individuals to hide their intentions from psychic perception. So if ever you're in a quandary about what or whom to trust in a situation, an energy circle will provide very helpful insights. Sometimes the information gained in these circles is something you may not want to hear, but despite that it is important information to pay attention to.

You can use circles for whatever you wish; they can be as large or as small as you want—two people to hundreds. They are very effective for unifying people—however diverse—before everyone goes about their common task. They enable groups to be more effective in their work, as well as providing support for individuals. If your sole purpose is to unify people, you won't want to take the time to focus on more than the common commitment and the tasks at hand. Beginning with a circle will greatly enhance everyone's ability to work well with one another. They are the best method I know of to combat the isolation and separateness that permeates our society as they induce people to shift into a more collective frame of mind thus pooling their individual powers.

Energy circles are good for starting a meeting or any kind of collective planning. It should take only five to ten minutes, yet shorten your meeting overall by enabling everyone to work together so effectively. I was in a group which was to do an all-day workshop and rather than having the usual long drawn-out discussion in planning an event like this, we did a circle. We all went into trance and then every few moments one of us would throw out a question like, "How many people are there?" "What's the mood in the room?" "What are the different roles each of us is playing?" We came out of trance about fifteen minutes later, went around the circle and each of us shared what we had imagined. Clear patterns emerged and we planned the day in about a half hour. The whole process was fun and took us forty-five minutes rather than the usual two or three hours. Needless to say, the workshop couldn't have come off better. You can use this same process to explore the best ways to work together both in the present and in the future. All too often in conferences the energy generated is great, and so too is the frustration of leaving and returning to our individual lives. This contradiction can be resolved by using a meditation which gives people space to deal with their feelings on a deeper level, make internal commitments to carry on with particular actions of their choice, and discover where support lies for them. This final exercise will channel the power generated by the conference, and close the gap between it and people's individual lives. It makes it possible for all that was shared and the power created by the conference to be more easily carried over into the communities. People won't leave in isolation, but instead with renewed and specific commitments to their communities.

If you have already been doing the meditations in a group context, begin your meetings with a circle, otherwise get some friends together and try it for support. I recommend doing it regularly because it takes time to get the hang of it and time to discover how powerful circles can be. When you are using a circle for energizing probabilities and gaining insights, there should be a leader who gives the cues as each individual takes a turn to ask the group for energy for specific purposes, e.g., healing energy for herself or others, energy to be more centered, energy to find a better job, to improve a relationship, whatever she feels she needs. Talking while in the meditative state will not disturb either your process or anyone else's, although it may feel a bit clumsy at first.

When you are working with influencing probabilities that involve other people, questions arise as to whether it is ethical to use psychic energies to influence others. On the one hand it is important to understand that we are not playing God; everyone chooses on some level whether or not to respond to psychic suggestion. On the other hand when we focus our energies on a desired probability, this concentration of energy strengthens that probability and makes it more likely to be chosen simply because it becomes louder and therefore harder to ignore.

I feel you have to be careful when asking for energy when someone else is involved. For instance, if you are asking for energy to deepen a friendship, you must respect the autonomy of the other person, so you would add, "in a way that is mutually agreeable." It is important to put forward any request concerning others in the spirit of respecting everyone's will, and only ask for those things to be manifested that are *agreeable to everyone involved.*

Although it is ethical when you value the free will of your equals, asking only for mutually beneficial results, I do feel that it is appropriate to energize things with the spirit of a "should" when you're working with a situation in which the other person is in a more powerful position specific to your problem. It is okay to energize that your landlord remember your leaky faucet, or that the surgeon be clear and coordinated, or a potential employer be impressed with you. For example, one evening a couple of years ago I did an energy circle with friends to channel energy to a judge so that he would give lenient sentences for civil disobedience by some anti-nuclear protestors. Five hundred people had been arrested, and when the judge began levying sentences everyone was startled at how stiff they were. The day after our circle his sentencing had greatly improved. All of the above relationships are *not* equal. On the other hand, energizing your friend to call you or lend you money with a *should* behind it is inappropriate.

Before the circle it's wise to discuss what you are going to ask for. There are two reasons for this: First, because you want to describe the general scenario so you can be brief after the circle begins—expressing the whys and hows in the circle is just distracting; second, frequently you'll need help in figuring out how to state your request in brief and *positive* terms. Most of the time we are more aware of what we don't want than what we do want. This is another place where the group is really helpful. Everyone else has a fresh perspective and can help you figure out how to state the issue positively, giving you a vision to move toward rather than reacting against where you are. Remember innerconsciousness doesn't understand negatives. Don't ask for energy to stop being lazy, for all people will hear is "lazy." Replace words like "effortlessly" with "easily," or instead of saying "heal my headache," say "my head be clear and comfortable." Each request needs to be to the point and positive. If you want an apartment, don't say "energy to acquire an apartment because I don't have enough room to do my sewing and artwork." Tell people ahead of time the reasons why and in the circle simply say "energy to acquire a spacious apartment." It is also good to target the energy by giving times, full names and addresses in the circle itself. If you're applying for a job, name the employer, the company, the address and the job title. If someone is to have surgery, give the full name, the home address, then the part of the body (*not* the disease), the time of surgery, the hospital and the surgeon's name. For example, "I would like healing energy channeled to Jennifer Burton of Santa Monica Avenue in Berkeley, particularly to her abdominal area for her surgery with Dr. Tom Blake at Highland Hospital at three o'clock on Friday." Then repeat just her name. If you don't have all the information, simply give what you do have. It may seem superfluous to give all the details, but it's my experience that it's a lot easier to focus when the specifics are mentioned in the circle.

You can ask for energy for as many issues as you like. Because of the simultaneity of innerconsciousness, it doesn't take long to focus on the different requests (maybe seven seconds for an average). In my support groups there are usually about five of us and each of us asks for about half a dozen things apiece. All of this takes an average of about fifteen minutes for the whole circle to be completed. People often write down each of their requests and when it is their turn open their eyes and read them. You can ask for the same thing week after week. One would expect this to be boring, but to the contrary, it is a very interesting way of tracking the progress of an issue.

If you ask for energy for a number of issues, put them in a sequence from the general to the specific. For example, if you're asking to be calm and clear and you are also asking to state your case as well as possible in court, ask in that order. It is also important to clear your awareness between each request—it's easy to do, just takes a moment, but you need to remember to do it. For example, if you have more than one request to be energized, it's necessary to ask for one thing, be silent for a few moments to give people time to imagine it—trust your intuition as to how much time is necessary—or simply imagine the energy moving around the circle twice and then suggest that people re-center, and then ask for the next issue to be energized. Psychic energy knows no boundaries so we must create them. That's why it is important to focus on one thing, re-centering between issues, one person at a time; otherwise the energy from the last person or issue gets carried over to the next. If you're channeling healing energy to someone, she doesn't need the residues of the energy for the job you just focused on.

When moving from one person to the next in the circle, there should be a few moments of silence so that everyone can focus on the new person and their consciousness can adjust to her energy. When you are making your requests, consciously imagine yourself receptive to the energy, for our programmed inclination is to believe we must fend for ourselves alone, which effectively bars us from receiving support.

During the circle itself, as with individual meditation, your beta consciousness will discount what is occurring—it may seem silly or bizarre—that's okay, just go through the motions anyway. All that is happening in an energy circle is that everyone is focusing their attention simultaneously. After you've experienced the power of a circle, the messages of your beta mind will become less relevant. Channeling energy simply means focusing consciousness; there is no right way. But it is important to think of it as *channeling* energy—universal energy—not as sending your own; you need your energy, and others don't. Awhile back a counselor, who works primarily with people's emotions, joined one of my groups. The first few circles exhausted her. When it was pointed out that she was to channel energy—as opposed to "being there" for each request, she no longer was drained by the circles.

So once again, I emphasize that you let yourself make up pictures, sensations, sounds, however you imagine the different things people are asking for. You may not feel your imagination has any connection to reality, but I assure you it has a profound connection. *It is the medium of both psychic awareness and probabilities.* Make it up, keep an eye tuned to the back of your mind to see what transpires there, create little dramas as though what is being asked for is playing out right in your mind's eye. *Embellish* whatever feelings or images you become aware of—those first impressions that come to you. Remember consciousness is energy—that is all you are working with. It's not a lot of hocus-pocus, nor is it mysterious or hard to do. It is simply concentrating consciousness to empower probabilities and to sense what tendencies are already present. Everyone has his own individual way of channeling and focusing energy. Some people simply experience a knowingness, a well-beingness, others experience body sensations, others visualize colors, and still others visualize symbols or miniature dramas. In whatever way your imagination is inclined to focus on the positive outcome of any given request is what's right for you. Trust whatever occurs and play with it—if you get an image, embellish it. If you don't get an image or a sensation, create one and embellish that. Your first impression is like the outlines in a coloring book—when you color it in, it brings it to life. Trust your own process.

If you ever imagine a scene or have sensations that do not feel good to you, that is, when things don't seem to be moving in a positive direction, but are stuck, it is important to try to change it as best you can so that you improve the probabilities. Don't come down on yourself if you can't come up with a positive outcome—it's not your fault. The conditions in the given situation are simply not ready and able to change and you're psychically attuned to this current fact (which doesn't mean the situation is negative forevermore). So whenever you contact negativity in the circle simply do what you can to create movement. It's at times like this that you'll often find you did not have enough space to work with the sensations when an individual was asking for energy, so remember at the end of the circle before you open your eyes to go back and finish what you did not have time for earlier, remembering to re-center yourself afterwards so that you do not carry that energy with you after the circle is finished. If you change the negative imagery— moving to a positive outcome—after the circle share how you worked with the images/sensations. What you did with them will be significant—symbolically representing a course of action that the individual can use in problem-solving.

Circles are a very good method for discovering the psychic nature of the imagination. Afterwards you will feel as if all that happened was just in your own head, totally disconnected from the outside world, and therefore insignificant. That's how it feels, but that's not how it is; your consciousness *is* connected to the outside world. So after the circle you should share with each other what happened, for it is only by taking the risk and expressing what you imagined that you get validation for your psychic awareness. It helps people remember, right before they give feedback, if each person repeats exactly what he said in the circle. Often more information comes to people in the process of describing what happened in the circle, and that's okay too. If you're a sensitive rather than a visualizer, make yourself describe what you felt even though it is hard to put in words—when you do this it will be helpful to the recipient, for more insights will come in the process of articulating your experience.

In the sharing after the circle you'll discover in what ways your experience is significant to the receiver of the energy. For example, Janet was asking for energy to feel good while working. Clara had imagined her smelling roses in the midst of work; when asked what color the roses were she said they were orange. Janet then told the group that the boss had just brought orange roses and placed them on all the tables in the restaurant where she was working. This was very validating for Clara, enabling her to trust her intuition that much more, and it was helpful to Janet as an idea she could use to maintain her well-being while working. When Clara had seen the roses, she didn't feel there was anything particularly significant about them; one never discovers the significance of one's imagining in the midst of the circle—that only comes later through the feedback process. So take the risk and express whatever you get in touch with or make up, and you'll find the experience of doing energy circles enriched manyfold.

It takes a while before you can be aware of what is going on in the circle and articulate it. Give yourself time to become comfortable with the process. I think circles are the best way to experience the power of the imagination and, to repeat, the more you experience it working, the more you'll believe it will work again and the more your powers are enhanced. Circles cultivate our sensitivity to what's true at the moment while at the same time making us visionaries.

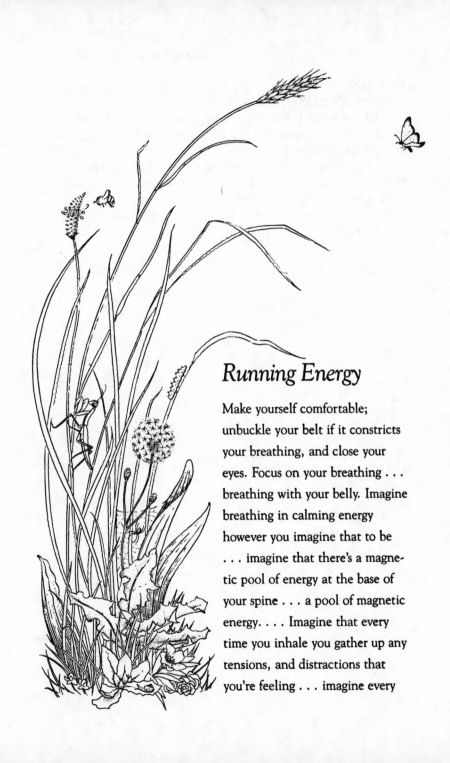

Running Energy

Make yourself comfortable;
unbuckle your belt if it constricts
your breathing, and close your
eyes. Focus on your breathing . . .
breathing with your belly. Imagine
breathing in calming energy
however you imagine that to be
. . . imagine that there's a magnetic pool of energy at the base of
your spine . . . a pool of magnetic
energy. . . . Imagine that every
time you inhale you gather up any
tensions, and distractions that
you're feeling . . . imagine every

time you exhale that all these tensions, all these distractions get drawn into this pool of energy. . . . Now imagine that this pool of energy begins to sink down through the floor, and gravity draws the band right down into the earth, sinking further and further down with each exhalation of breath however you imagine this to occur. . . . Like water that soaks down into the ground. Every time you exhale, tensions, distractions go down this band of energy into the earth. . . . Gravity draws down all the clamor of the day. . . . This band of energy goes further and further down as if gravity were drawing it down through all the layers of the earth, through all the elements in the earth, until it settles and connects with what you imagine to be the very center of the earth . . . however you imagine that. . . . Feel it, sense it, see it, pretend this is occurring, feel yourself become more and more relaxed with each exhalation of breath. And know that down this band of energy you can continue to release tensions, distractions into the ground to be dissolved and transformed.

◆   ◆   ◆

Now imagine that you have roots, roots like a tree, roots that branch out through all of the earth, through all the layers of earth and you can pull up the earth's sustenance into your body, nourishing earth energy, pulling it up into your body as you inhale, enabling you to feel as connected to the earth as a tree is connected to the ground. . . . Pull earth energy up into the whole of yourself, however you imagine earth energy to be . . . you can have the energy of the earth come up that band of energy creating a circuit, or up through your feet, whichever is more comfortable, however you imagine earth energy coming into your body, tuning you to your connection to the earth, to your connection to your body, to the substance of which you're made. . . . Feel the supportive, nurturing, sustaining energy of the earth flowing through the whole of your body, supporting you, relaxing you, enabling you to focus. . . . Experience how the earth always supports your weight, your whole being. Feeling the substance of which you're made, the calming supportive energy of the earth; the strength and power, the support of the earth below you, supporting every cell in your body.

Notice how it makes you feel to draw earth energy up into your body. . . . Adjust the cord so it's just the way you like it . . . the right color, texture, shape, sound, flexibility, rhythm. . . . This is your grounding cord. . . . You can use it whenever you wish, to help you focus and relax. . . . You can also use it like your mental housecleaning device, letting whatever you symbolize go down your cord to be transformed in the earth. . . . Know that your grounding cord will continue to be here as you move your awareness on . . . intend that this be so.

◆   ◆   ◆

Now become aware of the sky. Imagine that there's no ceiling above your head but instead just the vast sky is above you. . . . Be aware of the air, the breeze, the patterns of weather, the radiant sun, the luminous moon. . . . Each and all of the planets and the stars beyond, the millions of stars. . . . Be aware of the whole sky . . . the movement of the sky, the energy of the sky, and bring into the room a concentration of the sky energy and imagine the top of your head opening up like a funnel and the sky energy begins to pour into the whole of your body tingling down your spine . . . mixing with the energy of the earth. . . . Feel yourself becoming attuned with the energy of the sky, becoming aware that each molecule of your body moves with the same rhythm as the solar system, the sky. . . . Feel the energy of the sky move through you. . . . Feel the movement within you. . . . Let the energy of the sky mix with the energy of the earth throughout your body. Just as the earth and sky mix all around you, let them mix within you. . . . Feel yourself as open and vast inside as the sky above you.

◆

Now let the energy of the sky move out as more energy moves in through the top of your head, and it also moves out, moving out either through your feet, through your hands, down your grounding cord, or back out through the top of your head, however you are inclined to let it move back out. . . . Just like breathing air, continually moving in and out, let the sky energy continually move in and out. Notice how it feels to have the energy of the sky moving through you. Whenever you bring through the sky energy, it will clear you and enable you to be open and insightful. Know that this is so.

◆　◆　◆

Energy of the sky, energy of the earth constantly moving through you . . . universal energies constantly moving through you. . . . Know that now that you've created these channels for the energy to move in this manner, that the energy will continue to move through you as you focus your attention elsewhere. . . . Intend to have the energies continually move through you. When you're ready you can open your eyes knowing that this energy continues to move through you, and if ever you need to reinforce this energy, all you need do is momentarily focus back on these channels, and in so doing you'll clear the path for the movement of this energy through you. Know that this is so. . . . Open your eyes when you're ready and inclined.

Energy Circle

*[The person designated to begin the circle can suggest an approxima-
tion of the following.]*

Focusing on your breathing, breathing with your belly, breathing in
calming energy, gathering any tensions and distractions, breathing
them out and down your grounding cord . . . sinking your grounding cord down into the center of the earth, all the way down
through all the layers of the earth . . . letting your grounding cord
carry any tensions, any distractions into the ground to be transformed by the earth. . . .

Imagine that we are all a circle of trees—roots intermingling in
the ground, drawing up earth energies, up our grounding cords, up
our roots, into our bodies . . . feeling the earth energy in our
bodies . . . feeling our connection to the earth, feeling attuned to
the substance of which we're made . . . feeling attuned to our
bodies . . . feeling the support of the earth below us, the nurturing
energy of the earth, focused and relaxed. . . .

As we continue to release tensions into the ground, drawing up
earth energies into ourselves, let us move our attention to the sky
. . . to the air around us, as trees reach to the sky, feel the air
around us, be aware of the vast sky above us, the radiant sun, the
luminous moon . . . the planets . . . the millions of stars . . . the
rain . . . the clouds . . . the whole sky . . . ourselves in tune with
the sky. . . . Bring through the energy of the sky into our bodies,
mixing it with the energy of the earth, let it move in and out

continually, just as air moves in and out continually, however we imagine this to occur, creating channels through which to focus, receive and channel support . . . earth and sky moving through us . . . each of us becoming clear channels of energy. . . .

As the energy continues to move through us in this manner, feel the energy we create together. . . . Imagine the energy moving around the circle, as though it were moving in your left hand and out your right hand . . . around and around, potent energy . . . magnetic energy . . . building momentum as it moves round and round, getting stronger and stronger. . . . Feel the pulse of the energy . . . the life of the universal energies moving around the circle, the energies of the earth and sky moving through us . . . energy moving around and around . . . suspended in this energy . . . energy we can use to support each other . . . to gain insights . . . to energize realities . . . energy moving around and around . . . energy that will continue to move around as we focus it on the different issues of our choice. . . .

[Now the leader can suggest to the first person that she state what she would like energized. Then the first person asks one request at a time, saying "re-center" after a moment of silence, before going on to the next. After that person's requests have been energized, the next person can imagine the energy moving around the circle a couple of times and then say the following.]

Re-center yourselves . . . clear your awareness . . . feel the energy of the earth and sky moving through you . . . moving around the circle . . . in your left hand and out your right . . . around and around . . . powerful energy. . . .

[Then she can ask for whatever she wants energy focused on; then the next person does the same thing. Proceeding all the way around the

circle in the same manner, going through the clearing process each time, i.e., when the next person to ask for energy is finished sending energy to the person before her, she leads the group in clearing their minds and feeling the energy continuing to move around the circle. When the last person's (the leader's) requests have been energized the first person who requested energy can lead the following ending process.]

Re-centering yourselves . . . feeling the energy moving around the circle . . . go back over in your awareness what you sensed each time you channeled energy for each of us. . . . Finish anything you did not have time to finish earlier, having your last sensation be a positive one. . . . Take as much time as you need. . . .

Know that the energy we've generated will continue to move as we move on. . . . Open your eyes when you're feeling ready and inclined.

Starting a Meeting or Group Planning*

[Either have someone read or ad lib an approximation to this. To begin, use the first section of the Energy Circle meditation (up to the brackets) and then continue with the following, starting after the pause marks. If the group is uncomfortable holding hands or running energy, sit in silence with eyes closed and substitute the next paragraph for the Energy Circle part.]

Let our silence give us the space we need to adjust ourselves to the tasks at hand. . . . Feel the energy we create together in this room . . . letting ourselves settle into being together, affirming our common concerns. . . . Feeling our collective power, feeling what connects us, creating a greater whole of powerful energy we can use to create change.

◆   ◆   ◆

For group planning replace the second paragraph about the agenda with the suggestion that everyone imagine the future event(s) as though they were unfolding right now in their mind's eye. Set the context by naming some specific plans or times in the future. Then suggest that each person around the circle ask a pertinent question, one at a time, with silent time in between, e.g. What is the atmosphere? What are each of us doing? What roles do the different people play? How does everything unfold? How many people are there? What are they doing? What is happening to us a year from now? etc. When finished, read the rest of the meditation. After the circle, share how each of you imagined the event. You may want to do this by speaking one at a time without interruption and then discussing it later after everyone has had a chance to share. This will insure not losing any insights. (Obviously this meditation can also be easily adapted for opening a conference.)

Now focus on our intention of coming together today, our common purpose . . . what brings us together . . . what goals we share . . . be aware if there is anything coming up that needs addressing, that is keeping our energies from unifying. Decide when and how to work on this issue. . . . Imagine us moving through our work creatively and efficiently. . . .

Go over the agenda in your mind. *[Name items on the agenda slowly.]* See us working through issues with ease and creativity, making clear decisions, harnessing and organizing our energies for our shared tasks. Sense how all this is happening. . . .

Notice how you need to be to best support the group, what concerns you need to put aside, what concerns you need to share. . . . Decide if you are willing to do these things. . . . Imagine us all working together in an atmosphere of warmth and mutual respect.

◆   ◆   ◆

Sense the timing being smooth and easy. . . . Sense everyone energized, feeling good about our shared work, a renewed re-energized commitment to our shared purpose, feel the spirit of our group. . . . See ourselves succeeding in our overall goals. . . . Notice what needs to happen for this to occur. . . .

Review your feelings/thoughts, any choices you've made, and open your eyes when you feel inclined, knowing that this energy will continue to be present, enabling us to fully cooperate and work together creatively.

Closing a Conference

[Use portions of Energy Circle Meditation that are appropriate and proceed with the following.]
Remember your choice to come here . . . remember your arrival, everyone from different places coming together to share, to learn, to grow. . . . Go over in your mind's eye the events that have transpired, what has happened between us . . . the collective power we've created.

◆   ◆   ◆

You may want to name some of the specific activities now. Remember the connections you made . . . the leaps of understanding you experienced . . . what inspired you . . . what still needs work. . . . Remember the sparks in you, between you, among us.

◆   ◆   ◆

Now imagine these sparks becoming little seeds which we can each plant in our own communities, and all we've shared here, all that's grown out of our collective experience takes root in each of our communities and grows. Grows even bigger than it is now. Envision it.

◆   ◆   ◆

Notice what you personally want to do to carry on. . . . Choose what you will commit yourself to in cultivating all that we've begun together . . . notice how you can make space for this new growth to take place . . . notice what support you have for this, both here and at home.

◆   ◆   ◆

Imagine the ripple effect of all our work . . . feel how the energy
we share transcends space and time. Feel our collective power . . .
it creates a pool of support we can dip into whenever we need to
replenish our spirits. Feel our collective commitment—it transcends space and time; it always feeds our spirits . . . and we have
the power to create change.

◆   ◆   ◆

Know this energy continues to be present. You can open your eyes
when you are so inclined.

Chapter Seven
We're All Healers

Health is the result of living in harmony with yourself and your environment. Health is to be in sync with life: all the rhythms harmonizing . . . breath with body functions, body functions with life activities, and life activities in rhythm with the cycles of the earth. But it isn't exactly easy to be in sync with modern living— we're lucky if we can just keep up . . . the idea of being in harmony has become fully foreign.

I recently saw a graffiti: "Civilization is carcinogenic." Our society is producing a lethal environment. We get it on all sides—we risk our lives every time we get in a car—there are nearly fifty-thousand highway deaths a year.[1] Work debilitates and threatens to kill us— each year fourteen-thousand workers killed on the job and another 2.2 million disabled; and, separate from accidents, another half a million workers develop "official" occupational diseases.[2] And modern medicine makes us sicker.

Our society is becoming increasingly stressful. The most pervasive health problems are related to stress in one way or another.[3] The body's natural self-protective system, the immunological system, is suppressed by the presence of chronic stress, compounding suscepti-

155

bility to illness.[4] To patch it all up 120 million prescriptions for tranquilizers are dispensed each year.[5] The modern method of moving into sync is to numb out. But sitting back and drinking or taking downers so you can recoup to be able to make it through to the next day does nothing but add your name to the casualty list.

To be healthy one must live a harmonious life-style, but living a completely healthy life-style in a carcinogenic environment is obviously impossible. Health is a socio-political issue, not a private one; what is called for is *change*.* But we have to survive long enough for us to make it. That means maintaining our health in as many ways as are currently possible.

Taking a victim, powerless position only increases your susceptibility to the very real hazards which surround you.[6] How do you think your body feels when you say, "Oh it doesn't matter how much I smoke, the pollution is so bad anyway"? How can any of us expect to make progressive changes toward healing our environment if we don't honor our bodies even in the immediate ways in which we *do* have control, such as minimizing ingesting junk food, exercising, and meditating?

With the mystification of innerconsciousness came the mystification of the healing process. When we repossess our inner selves we will repossess our healing powers. Since I've come to learn how to use the power of consciousness, one of the most significant changes in my life has been my health. I used to feel that whenever I got sick it was something that happened *to* me; I had to follow the doctor's instructions, go to bed, take medication, and wait until my illness left. I used to be sick an average of ten days a year. Now I virtually never get sick for more than a day at a time. If I get the flu I particpate with it, passing it through my body very rapidly so I don't need to wait a week for it to go away. I've learned that I'm not a victim of whatever illnesses cross my path, instead I can participate with my body in its healing processes or avoid responding to potential illnesses altogether.

Scientific thinking makes all that is mysterious become invisible. The regenerative healing process is one of life's greatest mysteries.

---

*This chapter deals with improving individual health within existing limits. The last chapters deal with removing the limits with political work.

To understand it rationally is like trying to understand colors with your ears, but just as your eyes can know color your deeper self can know healing. Shamans throughout the ages have used trance states to understand and heal ailments. It is in our interest to stop regarding such behavior as primitive. To mystify the innerconsciousness is to kill the mysterious. When we dip into our psyches we are no longer victims but participants, for there true knowingness resides.

DEFROCKING THE DOCTORS

The advent of rationalism took the life out of the objective world, justifying exploitation, so too the body got divorced from the mind to become a machine that only the mechanic-doctor understands. You, the inhabitant of the body, have nothing to do with the inception of any malfunction and, further, nothing to do with the healing process, and the environment rarely enters the picture at all. Only the white enshrined doctor is able to save the day and if others try they are quacks, liable to arrest for the high sin of practicing medicine without a license. The patient is assumed to have no intelligence to judge for herself what's in her best interest— no, the heroic doctor must protect the patient against all others (herself included). Doctor knows best. I don't mean to paint the picture that doctors are evil individuals; my intention is to expose the philosophy of the medical profession which isn't in the best interest of the patients (though you couldn't ask for a better kind of job security for the doctors).

Science develops technology. Medical science has now developed such sophisticated equipment that due to its high cost, health care has had to become centralized—"health" is produced in huge hospitals and the family doctor is nowhere to be found. Our health care system takes good care of medical science but people's health has inadvertently been kicked out the back door. Witness:

> The pain, dysfunction, disability, and anguish resulting from technical medical intervention now rival the morbidity due to traffic and industrial accidents and even war-related activities, and make the impact of medicine one of the most rapidly spreading epidemics of our time. ... only modern malnutrition injures more

people than iatrogenic disease in its various manifestations. In the most narrow sense, iatrogenic disease includes only illnesses that would not have come about if sound and professionally recommended treatment had *not* been applied.[7]

It has also been established that one out of every five patients admitted to a typical research hospital acquires an iatrogenic disease, sometimes trivial, usually requiring special treatment, and in one case in thirty leading to death. Half of these episodes result from complications of drug therapy; amazingly, one in ten comes from diagnostic procedures.[8]

Medications in hospitals alone kill between 60,000 and 140,000 Americans a year and make 3.5 million others more or less seriously ill.[9]

In one instance, autopsies showed that more than half the patients who died in a British university clinic with a diagnosis of specific heart failure had in fact died of something else. In another instance, the same series of chest X-rays shown to the same team of specialists on different occasions led them to change their mind on 20 percent of all cases.[10]

The majority of appendixes that are removed for "acute appendicitis" turn out to be uninfected.[11]

The figure of the surgeon fighting death in the operating room has always made for high drama on TV and in the movies. The grim reality is that more than half the surgery performed in this country is unnecessary. This washes an estimated 12,000 lives and $4 billion down the operating room's drain each year.[12]

America's health is so poor and so closely policed by the medical profession that a sane national health insurance plan ought to include a periodic moratorium on the practice of medicine just to give itself a fighting chance. . . . In 1976 there was a doctor strike in Los Angeles over malpractice rates. . . . This caused a $17.5 million loss to the hospitals. . . . One analysis of the data concluded, "On balance (the strike) was responsible for more deaths prevented than lives lost."

A week-by-week analysis by another investigator concluded that there was "an almost steady decline in death rates during the doctor slowdown, followed by an abrupt leap upward (from 14 to 26 deaths per 100,000) in the very first week that surgery as usual was resumed."[13]

The technical effectiveness of medicine is very limited. Hospitals could release 85% of their patients without harming them from a strictly medical point of view.[14]

A doctor friend of mine was warned by the hospital he uses that he wasn't bringing in enough patients—certainly the ultimate absurdity that patients are needed to keep hospitals running, not the other way around. Unintentionally creating illness and then turning around and trying to heal it is a cycle that guarantees continuous profit. Promoting health has no such advantages. Self-healing is bad business for the "health" industry, one of the largest industries in our country, which is the only one in the world to include it in the gross national product.

Medicine, getting off to the wrong start, has made much progress along the wrong road. Medicine is not the study of health; it is the study of disease. It's as if anyone promoting cooperation did so by exclusive preoccupation with its opposite—competition—and set up a twenty-four-hour surveillance for whenever competition reared its ugly head, and then scrutinized its every aspect. Remember that whatever you focus on is what you create as real. Obviously it would be more useful to focus on the elements of cooperation. With the concentration on disease, health itself recedes over the horizon.

The medical model defines health as the absence of disease, which gives you about as much understanding of it as defining exercise as the absence of rest. It's as if the medical establishment, in the face of continual burning, studied all the most efficient means of performing skin grafts, rather than simply turning off the heat.

The biomedical model is firmly grounded in Cartesian thought. Descartes introduced the strict separation of mind and body, along with the idea that the body is a machine that can be understood completely in terms of the arrangement and functioning of its parts. . . .

Following the Cartesian approach, medical science has limited itself to the attempt of understanding the biological mechanisms involved in an injury to various parts of the body. These mechanisms are studied from the point of view of cellular and molecular biology, leaving out all influences of nonbiological circumstances on biological processes. [15]

The complexity of the body/mind is reduced to a series of mechanical parts. If it goes wrong, introduce a new ingredient or replace the part. When our bodies are ailing they are generally regarded by both ourselves and the doctors as malfunctioning machines to be taken into the shop to get fixed.

The public image of the human organism—enforced by the content of television programs, and especially by advertising—is that of a machine which is prone to constant failure unless supervised by doctors and treated with medication. The notion of the organism's inherent healing power and tendency to stay healthy is not communicated, and trust in one's own organism is not promoted. Nor is the relation between health and living habits emphasized; we are encouraged to assume that doctors can fix anything, irrespective of our life styles. [16]

If doctors know so much about health care, why is it that their life expectancy is ten to fifteen years less than that of the average population? [17] No, the doctors know much about the "alien" illness which "invades" the body but this is an entirely different issue from that of health care.

Avoidance of the philosophical and existential issues that arise in connection with every serious illness is a characteristic aspect of contemporary medicine. It is another consequence of the Cartesian division that has led medical scientists to concentrate exclusively on the physical aspects of health. In fact the question 'What is health?' is generally not even addressed in medical schools, nor is there any discussion of healthy attitudes and life styles. [18]

75% of physicians do not recognize or inquire about stress in their medical workups. The *more* experienced the physician the *less* likely he or she is to acknowledge the relevance of stressful life events to clinical practice. [19]

The doctors understand the disease process and in many cases how to intervene. But when one gets down to basics they neither understand nor acknowledge the healing process itself. This is reflected in the concept of "spontaneous remission." The medical model promotes beliefs that encourage suspicion of the body and of nature itself. The intrinsic healing powers of life itself are systematically ignored. Our birthing process has been ripped off while labor is now looked upon as if it were a disease. Our health is ignored, while there is an obsession with illness. And lastly our death—medicine's ultimate goal is to eliminate it. One cannot be healthy without being life-affirming; one cannot be life-affirming and at the same time death-denying. Life and death are united opposites, you cannot have one without the other.

> Disease is viewed as an enemy to be conquered, and medical scientists pursue the Utopian ideal of eliminating, eventually, all diseases through the application of biomedical research. [20]

We are mesmerized by the knight in white, here to take control and lead the battle to put any "invading" disease in its rightful place. We've been taught to regard illness as a problem that only doctors have the expertise to understand and solve. Our complaint is often diagnosed with a four-syllable word that we can't even pronounce, but we are given a play-by-play account of the progression of destruction the disease is likely to take through our bodies. We get all the appropriate messages we need to remain ill; *knowing precisely what to expect, we join the doctors on the wrong road.*

It is common knowledge that the placebo effect is due to the patient's belief in the doctor, but how many diseases are created for the same reason: a loyal response to the doctor's search and prediction of malfunction?

> Another study, looked at the following train of events. They examined 4,000 people who were feeling well and confirmed that 30% were clearly ill without being aware of it, and that 60% had latent diseases to which they were well adjusted. Only 10% were in clinically good health. The authors' conclusion: when these people who were feeling fine were informed of their clinical profile, that was all it took to transform 90% of them into patients and bring on in most of them the appearance or worsening of symptoms that they had ignored up to then. [21]

In 75% of all cases the usefulness of the prescribed medication is not the active principles but in the *faith* that the patients have in the technology. In other ages people *believed* in miracles; today they *believe* in science, and so the medical ritual takes on the appropriate guise.[22]

The only problem is that our belief in medicine is making us sicker, at least as often as it is making us well. It's in our best interest to understand that the agent of change is *belief*. If we pull ourselves out of our entrancement with the all-powerful doctor—stop being spellbound—we can begin to believe in ourselves.

Medicine has succeeded in wrenching the healing process out of nature—an impossibility, but modern man has a genius for achieving the impossible. Healing is a natural phenomenon. It's our bodies that do the healing. It's time we own our bodies; illness is not the property of doctors, but belongs to us and plays an important role in our lives.

MAKING MIRACLES COMMONPLACE

How do we retrieve our bodies? By learning to respond to the messages our maladies are giving us. We must learn to communicate with our bodies rather than relying exclusively on the doctors.

Unlike tranquilizers, meditation puts you in an acutely receptive state of awareness where you can hear the subtle messages of your body. Both meditation and tranquilizers calm you down and make you feel good. With tranquilizers you numb out and are that much further away from knowing the needs of your body, to say nothing of the abusive side effects. On the other hand, one of the side effects of meditation is to steer you clear of all those stress-caused diseases.

As with any other issue, when concerned with health, working with innerconsciousness always flows in one of two directions: active or receptive. When you can imagine what you want, that is, *feel* what it would be like, then you project it. When you can't, an insight is called for, so you ask questions, tune in, and then respond to the information you get. Your body can respond to the messages you give it; you can respond to the messages your body gives you.

When I was younger, every year I had a runny nose all winter long—that was what winters were for me. During the winter after I learned the techniques of Silva Mind Control, when my sinuses started to act up I meditated, imagining my mucous membranes drying up—I had a picture that was like cotton evaporating. I did this maybe four or five times. My nose cleared up, and ever since I haven't had a runny nose all winter. Until I learned the power of consciousness it never occurred to me to imagine the problem clearing up. Instead, I continually gave my body the message: "This runny nose will be here all winter," for that had been my experience.

Effecting change with the power of consciousness works in direct proportion to how strongly you believe that it will work. The more you believe something is going to work, the less confusing your inner messages will be; clear messages are directives for your body to respond to. The catch is your belief comes from your experience of it working. So I recommend you begin by doing little experiments, ones that do not have a lot of emotional charge like telling yourself exactly what time you wish to awaken in the morning (assuming your mother didn't continually tell you that you always slept late). It is easy to give clear messages when you start on something simple. One thing I did was work on mosquito bites, imagining an impenetrable wall around me so that the mosquitoes could not get through and bite me. That didn't work—the mosquitoes didn't seem to see the wall—so I tried another tactic. I imagined talking to my skin, telling it that these mosquitoes were going to come and that both myself and it would be happier if we let them come and go without responding. This method worked and from then on whenever a mosquito bit me, a welt would appear for perhaps twenty minutes, go away, and the bites never itched. This is a good example because it's no big deal whether or not you get mosquito bites.

The more you experience success the stronger your belief in the power of your body/mind becomes. The stronger the belief the more powerful you are—remember, the agent of change is belief. Eventually, with the accumulation of experience you'll find yourself spontaneously giving clear messages—without premeditation—always expecting what you want. Instead of being a victim to whatever dangers may cross your path, you will always be able to keep your power.

Three years after I began meditating I had a profound experience that revealed to me the degree to which I had come to know the power of the body/mind and how much I had *regained* mine. I was moving a refrigerator on a dolly, pulling it backwards down a driveway into the street. The driveway, rather than the gradual decline I had expected, moved from sidewalk level to street level very quickly. All of a sudden the refrigerator was pushing me—I wasn't pulling it—and then I tripped on a four-by-four beam. As I fell, I instantaneously called on healing powers. Under "normal" material conditions (whatever that is) the leverage created by the bars of the dolly and the corner of the four-by-four was such that the bones of my legs would have snapped under the impact of the refrigerator. If I had responded with fear, expecting to hurt myself, my body would have responded by receiving the full impact and my legs would have been crushed. Instead, when I landed on the pavement I felt an incredible mushroom of energy holding up the refrigerator. Afterwards my legs didn't hurt and that energy continued to buzz through me for the rest of the move we were making that day—almost as if I'd taken a psychedelic.

A friend of mine had a similar experience on his motorcycle a couple of years ago. He made a left turn in downtown traffic, not seeing the car coming toward him—nor did the driver see him. When my friend realized what was happening, he stopped the bike and put his foot down on the pavement while screaming at the driver. The driver hit his brakes and the front tire of the Chrysler stopped on top of my friend's left foot, where it remained. At the moment of seeing the car approach his foot he flashed a feeling-sense through his mind: "My foot is safe and sound and will stay healthy and strong." When the driver realized he needed to pull up slightly, the tire rolled off my friend's foot. He shook it gingerly, discovered that his foot was not even sore, and then proceeded to drive on. At home later, he took his shoe and sock off and found that his foot was not even bruised, nor did it ever cause him any pain or impairment.

The vital thing to understand about each of these examples is that the last and prevailing message was a positive one, expecting what was wanted, one of trusting the body and its power to maintain itself, one where there is *no* space for the idea of being victimized and out of control. In a study of 152 cancer patients "the most significant finding was that a positive attitude toward treatment was a better predictor of response to treatment than was the severity of the disease." The Simontons, who conducted this study, pioneered working with cancer by visualization. Their patients have a survival rate twice the national norm.[23] As long as we're taught to believe we are victims to whatever health hazards come our way we won't have the necessary strength to change the conditions that give us the trouble in the first place.

A few years ago I attended a lecture by Jack Schwartz who taught a class called Voluntary Control of Internal States. He has spent many years in refining directive consciousness. He often demonstrates the control he has by sticking a knitting needle through his biceps. He might as well be pulling the needle through a pincushion. Doctors had been trying fruitlessly to discover what was biochemically different about him that would account for his extraordinary abilities. One day he was in the lab, again doing this demonstration, and halfway through it a doctor walked into the room and asked, "Don't you ever bleed?" In the many times he had done this it had never occurred to Schwartz that he would bleed. This time the needle was halfway through his arm, and to respond to the doctor's question he had to think, "Do I ever bleed?" The moment he questioned whether or not he bled, he bled—because in order to decide if he did, the image of bleeding was present in his awareness, and his body responded accordingly. As soon as he decided he didn't bleed, moving his awareness to other concerns, he stopped bleeding.

At every given moment, our bodies are continually responding to the messages of our minds. So what messages is your mind giving your body? Prevailing wisdom says: You got a problem? Have a drink. Got a stuffy nose? Take Contac. Got indigestion? Take Alka Selzer. Can't sleep? Take Sominex. There is a chemical solution for everything. These messages promote total distrust in the body's own ability to heal itself. We're led to believe that the innate wisdom of the body/mind simply doesn't exist. "A drug ad denies your ability to cope. . . . The result is that you become further separated from yourself. . . . Your ability dies for lack of practice and faith in its efficacy." [24] Instead of believing in your body you probably come close to hating it because it's not the right size or shape. Schwartz bled in reponse to his thoughts; what do you imagine your body does in response to your distrust and dissatisfaction?

These powers are not exotic; it isn't as if only a few exceptional individuals are endowed with them. They are sleeping inside each of us and we can awaken them. Just as muscles atrophy with lack of use and exercise brings them back to life, we just need to *use* this power that each of us has. So-called miracles can become commonplace if we choose to take responsibility.

HEARING THE VOICES OF YOUR BODY

When you're meditating on a health problem you need to give your body a clear message of what you want. Imagine what it would be like to be healthy in that particular area—problem free. If you can't experience yourself healthy (what you want), then going in and talking to the ailment will move you forward. Your body is not ready to heal yet—there is a message that needs attending to. Whenever you get sick it's because you've come in conflict with the environment. It's a message that something around you and in your behavior needs to change to enable you to return to living in health. Our bodies are barometers keeping us on course to lead harmonious lives. There's *always* a message there. If you tune in, get the message, and respond to it, you'll find that your life changes profoundly. With any illness or pain your body is talking to you, you just need to listen. Your life will be enormously simplified if you take a moment to pay attention and respond to the messages. If you keep taking aspirin for headaches, not stopping to discover why it is you have headaches, your body doesn't give up signaling you. Its reactions (symptoms) will get louder and louder until you can no longer ignore them. Down the road you may find yourself with a screaming úlcer which, needless to say, is much more difficult to heal.

Doctors spend their time looking for the symptoms of illness, rarely acknowledging that *illness itself is a symptom*. We all know how ineffective it is just to treat the symptom. Our automatic reaction whenever we get sick is that something is wrong with our bodies rather than with our lives. This is an incredible discount of our bodies, for they are our early warning system and know just what is healthful. If being sick is thought of as wrong we give away a part of ourselves relegating illness to be forever out of our control. To repossess our healing powers we must repossess our illnesses.

Might not the illness be the inevitable response of a healthy individual to a situation that is not? Aren't the digestive troubles, headaches, rheumatism, insomnia, and depressions that switchboard operators, key punch operators, assembly line workers, and electronics solderers suffer from, more than anything the "healthy" protests of an organism that cannot adjust to the violence done to it daily, at an eight hour stretch?[25]

Ill health should be taken as an invitation for introspection. If you reflect deeply you will find what in your life is out of sync. This can be done easily while meditating, by simply imagining a talk with the ailing part of your body. Be inquisitive and imagine what it would say—let yourself make it up—your fantasies will tell you what is happening. You'll discover simple things, some easier to respond to than others, like needing more rest or better eating patterns or changes in a relationship. Make an agreement with your inner self as to what you'll do about it. Some of the messages are harder to respond to—they may be about your working environment which usually is out of your control. If this is the case, at least you've discovered the specific cause of the problem and can take protective measures against it. Maybe you're plagued with headaches and discover they're from the fumes at work. Use your imagination to find out what can be done to compensate. *Notice your inclinations* (other than telling off your boss). Maybe your head will tell you that a regular run in the countryside will be of help, or that you should get your lungs to be on guard so they can push the toxins back out, before they make it into your bloodstream. Ultimately what's called for is clean air, so don't neglect to organize simultaneously to get proper ventilation at work. But political change takes time; if you listen to your inner messages you'll know how to compensate for the problem in the meanwhile.

You've got to be careful neither to fully blame yourself for getting sick and ignore the conditions of your life that need change, nor to blame the conditions entirely, leaving you in a powerless, victim position. The way out is to get rid of the detrimental influences and at the same time discover how it is that you *collude* with them. Just like the victim of rape who neither created the rapist nor asked to be raped, her feelings of powerlessness were her collusion. What is called for here is *both* her empowerment and the elimination of rapists. Your internal response to an event is as important as the event itself. The clothing of two people catches on fire, one person panics, runs, and fans the flames, severely burning herself. The other remains calm and consciously chooses to roll on the ground, thus smothering the fire and ending up with only minor burns.

The environment increasingly is full of substances that are hazardous to our health. Everyone exposed to carcinogenic sub-stances does not develop cancer. (This doesn't mean it is okay to continue to pollute the atmosphere.) No matter what is going on, despite how we may feel, we are not victims but participants.

Sometimes you're getting more out of having the problem than you would from being healthy. Usually the problem itself provides a solution for something else. So ask yourself what it is that made you come down with the malady. What is the ailment protecting you from? What are you getting out of it? Your immediate reaction to this question is likely to be defensive, but blame is not the issue here. Even the worst of things have their positive side. If you allow yourself to look under the surface you can answer the question. Maybe it is a much needed rest, or alleviation from overwhelming responsibility, mourning a loss, or a way out of a seemingly irresolv-able situation. When you find out what the advantages are for you, you can take steps to get your needs met in healthful ways. Then you'll be able to focus your energy effectively on healing yourself and your environment.

It is important to understand that your body is intimately tied to your deeper levels of consciousness and not to your beta level. If this were not the case you could easily twiddle your thumbs, each revolving in a different direction at the same time. The beta mind operates with separate entities while deeper consciousness operates only with whole patterns. You know the experience of not being able to "think straight" when sick. This is because when you are sick you are operating out of deeper levels of consciousness so you can heal better.

With this in mind I recommend that you regularly tune in to the current condition of your body. This needn't take long; it can be momentary in the midst of the rest of your meditative work. Notice how your body feels, where the energy seems to be—if there's too much or too little anywhere, or if it's getting stuck someplace. Then try to imagine balancing out. Focus on any areas that you're working toward healing, tune in, and sense how the process is going—give it a little added support.

To understand the messages of your body it is helpful to know that there is a direct correlation between the particular ailment and the message. If your sexual organs are out of balance you need to change your sex life, not your work life. It's often helpful to think of clichés and plays on words: if your neck hurts, is there somebody in your life who is a pain in the neck? If your stomach is giving you problems, is there something in your life that you can't stomach? If you have a sore that seems to refuse to heal, is there someone getting under your skin? Are you sore about something?

In meditating on healing yourself it's good to have a framework to work with: find a doctor with whom you can collaborate, not one who regards you as irrelevant and is only focusing on the part of the body that is ailing. Instead, be sure the doctor knows you are an integral part of the healing process. Form a partnership with the doctor, assert yourself and make the doctor work *with* you, not *on* you. Rather than asking her what's going to happen with the illness find out what needs to happen for your body to return to a healthy condition—what it will feel like, what it will look like.

If you don't want to go to a doctor, then give yourself a framework by reading up on the subject or talking to people who have success-fully healed themselves of a similar condition. Or find an anatomy chart—you need to give your imagination food for thought.

A couple of years ago I got a toothache. I went to the dentist and was told that I had an abscess and would need to have a root canal done, which was going to cost five-hundred dollars—money I didn't have. I asked him to explain the physiology of what was occurring in my mouth—exactly what a root canal was. He was very coopera-tive and took the time to explain in detail what was going on. Then I told him that I wanted to try healing myself with medita-tion. He wasn't very optimistic, but I appreciated his giving me a chance. He drained the abscess and put in a temporary filling, saying he would give me two weeks and if I had no further problems he would make the filling permanent, which would avoid doing any of the root canal work. I went home with a clear picture of what to imagine when I meditated. I was motivated—I didn't want to borrow five-hundred dollars. So I meditated three or four times a day for the next two weeks—each time I visualized the details of my tooth healing. When I returned to the dentist the problem had disappeared and he put in a permanent filling. Each of us gained more respect for the body/mind's regenerative healing powers.

On another occasion I was exposed to infectious hepatitis. I've never liked having shots and once again I wanted to prove to myself the power of my body/mind. I asked the nurse what gamma globulin shots actually do. She told me that gamma globulin is simply something that the body already produces to ward off disease. Had I had little trust in my ability to protect myself I would have gotten the shot; instead, I wanted to exercise the powers I knew I had. I imagined my body producing gamma globulin overtime—armies were being created. I imagined little armies of gamma globulin marching through my blood and standing in formation around my liver creating an impenetrable fortress. It worked—I didn't come down with the hepatitis I had definitely been exposed to. I again confirmed my power to maintain my health, and thus my power was further increased.

YOUR BODY IS THE HOME OF YOURSELF: HOME MAINTENANCE

In beginning to use your consciousness for healing, you must cultivate patience, particularly if you have quite a number of conditions bothering you. As it took time for your problems to develop, it will also take time for your body to develop and maintain healthy habits. Your body has become accustomed to the problem, and it will need time to become accustomed to the solution instead.

I relate to my *whole* self as conscious—not just my brain, but every cell in my body—as possessing an intelligence, as indeed it does. (You don't need to explain to your cells how to replenish themselves—in fact it is the opposite.) Consciousness moves along habitual grooves. Sometimes healing is simply a matter of re-educating your cells, letting them know the situation has changed. When your body goes through some trauma it responds in the same way as your consciousness does. You find yourself acting as though the threat is still present because the scene remains in your theta level even though the situation has changed. Think of your cells in the same way, storing trauma and behaving as if their lives are under constant assault when that is no longer the case.

It's very important to keep the agreements that you've made with your body to help it return to a state of health. If you don't, your body will feel duped, and stop cooperating with you. It's the same as when a friend makes promises that she doesn't keep; eventually you get fed up and write her off. Often people discover that it's hard to keep the agreements they have made. This is because when you go inside you become aware of *all* the solutions; inside lives all-knowingness. You find out all that needs to happen to return to health, making lots of agreements. A week later you find you haven't been keeping them. It's as if you tried to eat a banquet in one mouthful—inside there are no limitations of space and time, but in the outside world you have to contend with lots of limitations. If you find yourself not having kept all the agreements, go to your level and talk it over with the ailing part of your body and come up with a more realistic and manageable course of action so you can take it one bite at a time. Remember, patience is called for.

Since your body is always responding to whatever is in your awareness at every given moment, it's important to watch how it is that you think as you move through your activities. Notice if you're spending more time and energy thinking of the problem, being irritated and victimized by it, than you are focusing on its moving into a state of health. In other words, do you spend more time thinking about the problem or the solution? Your body simply is going to respond to the strongest messages you give it, and whatever you spend the most time on will have the most energy. It's hard to focus more on the solution when you're experiencing the problem, but the important thing is the prevailing last message whenever the area of concern comes to mind. If you think of the problem always have your last image be your recovery—your sense of power and change, and that will be the direction your body goes in, cutting new grooves for consciousness to move in.

Remember Jack Schwartz deciding whether or not he bled, and bleeding. Don't focus on the problem to see if it has begun to heal yet. I learned this lesson well when trying to rid myself of headaches. In Silva Mind Control you learn that to get rid of a headache you just go to your level and tell yourself that at the count of five your headache will be gone. So, whenever I got a headache I would do just that: go to my level and tell myself that at the count of five my headache would be gone. Then when I came out of my level it was only natural to check to see if I were successful. I had just had a headache; I knew full well what it felt like, and there it was as soon as I looked for it. It took me a while to discover what I was doing wrong. Now, whenever I get a headache I go to my level and tell myself that over the next half-hour my headache would slowly dissolve. When I come out of my level it is okay that my headache is still there because I know it is going to take a while to go away. In a half-hour I am occupied with other events and there is no line to be drawn between success and failure, yet my headache disappears in the same amount of time it takes to digest an aspirin.

If you have any constant problem, chronic pain for example, tell yourself that the pain is dissolving ever so slowly, that it's imperceptibly getting better, and over time it'll be gone altogether. This way you haven't let your experience of the problem become a reflection of your inability to heal it; instead, you've allowed yourself to experience the problem while *knowing* that it's continually getting better.

Another way of working on a recurring health issue is to work on it at a time when it is not present. Do the necessary inner work ahead of time so when the need arises you're ready for it—the same principle as working with symbols. The first day of my menstrual period I used to feel really awful. Once I was scheduled to do a new kind of workshop with a group of people I'd never before worked with. My period was due to start the same day; I could not afford to be under the weather when working. So I began talking to my uterus three weeks in advance. I was feeling fine at the time so it was *believable* that I would feel fine later. And, in fact, I did. This approach is particularly good because when you're feeling bad you're not inclined to meditate at all, much less convince yourself that you could feel otherwise. It's difficult to believe in how good things could be, in the midst of feeling bad. It only works when what you project is *believable*. Remember the agent of change is belief.

Since your body is tied to your mind it's important to bring your attitudes and beliefs into conscious awareness. They pave the road that your thoughts move over, leading them in very specific directions. They're subtle, but you can become fully aware of them if you take the time to bring them to light. It's important to know that what you discover is *not* reality, but your attitude *about* reality—which you can change. Once you become aware of a negative attitude, you can change it by inserting the opposite attitude with an affirmation. To help you uncover the defeating beliefs about your body that you need to change, ask yourself some of the following questions: Is my ability to be healthy different from that of others? Am I victimized by anything? Do I think of bodies as degrading and impure? Do I think of food as fattening or nourishing? Do I think of exercise as a strain or a game? What does the word "illness" mean to me? What does the word "health" mean to me? Am I stuck with any burdens? Do I like my body? Am I fully vulnerable to all germs I am exposed to? Think of three negative feelings about your body, then think of their opposites and notice how you can cultivate those. What do they feel like? Whatever insights you come up with will be food for your meditations and you'll find that as you take action to change these attitudes you'll increase your health manyfold.

In describing the ways to heal ourselves I am well aware that if you are struggling with a terminal disease you are unlikely to experience yourself as healthy in your imagination. You may wish for it passionately, but expecting it is another matter. It is only possible to heal when you can sense what it would be like. Whatever the problem you're working with, if you can't imagine being well in the area of your body that is afflicted, then you can use the resources of your innerconsciousness to come to terms more easily with what is happening to you, discover what you need in order to live in more comfort, and/or come to a sense of completion with your life and let go.

In our youth-worshipping, death-denying, secular culture there is a way that we deny ourselves the ability to come to terms with the natural processes of our bodies—we all die sometime. When death is imminent we go into a frenzy and rob ourselves of death with dignity.

I don't mean to imply that being given a medical prognosis of imminent death means you have no choice. Many people whom M.D.'s "put in their graves" years ago are still alive and well, but every one of them, you may be sure, made the choice to live on a deep level. When you make a choice on a *deep* level to defy prognosis, whatever your process, your imagination will reveal to you in what direction you are going, and then it will help you come to terms with what is going on. The Meeting the Wise Self meditation is designed to ease the process of death.

All ailments are messages we *need* to hear to keep a harmonious balance in our lives. Ailments are *not* something wrong, but signposts pointing to what is right. When we follow their directions we live in health; when we ignore them we get lost and wander around aimlessly in a hazardous environment on a collision course, getting even sicker. It is our ailments that know how to live in health. Health problems are always a reflection of the innate wisdom of life itself.

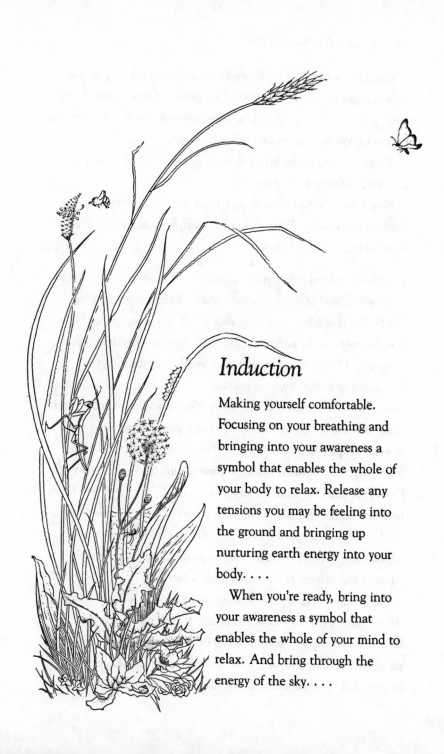

Induction

Making yourself comfortable.
Focusing on your breathing and
bringing into your awareness a
symbol that enables the whole of
your body to relax. Release any
tensions you may be feeling into
the ground and bringing up
nurturing earth energy into your
body. . . .

When you're ready, bring into
your awareness a symbol that
enables the whole of your mind to
relax. And bring through the
energy of the sky. . . .

Bring to awareness your symbol for emotional relaxation. Go over the full range of feelings that are present for you now, if any feeling is calling your attention, take care of it in whatever manner occurs to you so you can emotionally relax. . . .

When you are ready, bring to awareness your symbol for your creative, self-restoring center. . . .

Now take time to enhance your level on your own by whatever method you choose. When you next hear my voice you will be fully relaxed and fully alert.

◆   ◆   ◆

Beginning to finish what you're doing. . . . You are now consciously developing psychic skills you have always had. You are at your level—the threshhold between your inner and outer being. Here you discover a rich, beautiful landscape of your receptivity and creativity. Here you experience very vivid, very meaningful sensations and imagery, new realities. . . . As these realities unfold they guide you to new dimensions of life. As you open, more and more of these energies shall flow through you. Just as using your muscles keeps your body strong and resilient, so too, using your level keeps your intuitive/psychic powers fully accessible and fluid. From here you can make use of the wisdom of your inner self. From here you realize the calm expansive power of your inner being. And you can feel yourself as a part of the pure universal energy which permeates all life. From here you discover the powers to heal yourself and others. Here you become a healer. . . .

I'm going to suggest several affirmations; if you wish to affirm them repeat them to yourself after me, feeling as though they are fully true; knowing that in focusing on affirmations you'll create patterns of energy that will move out into your life, materializing in your daily experience both within and around you.

I believe in life. . . .

I believe in myself. . . .

I believe in my body. . . .

The whole of my body/mind is healthy. . . .

My life is whole, my life is a part of the whole of life. . . .

Energy flows easily and clearly throughout the whole of my being. . . .

I am in harmony with the natural rhythms of life within and around me. . . .

I honor my sexuality and celebrate the joy of life. . . .

I give myself the time I need to remain centered. . . .

I honor my body with care. . . .

I eat only those foods that nourish my body. . . .

I rest all I need to replenish my body. . . .

I exercise all I need to maintain my vitality. . . .

My body is a self-healing, self-clearing organism. . . .

I hear what my body tells me; my body hears what I tell it. . . .

All the needs of my body are always met. . . .

I maintain balance amidst change. . . .

I trust the future. . . .

Now take time to focus on any of your own affirmations or symbols.

◆   ◆   ◆

Know that in focusing on affirmations you have created patterns of energy that will move out into your life and materialize within and around you. . . .

In a moment I am going to count on a descending scale from ten to one. At each descending count you'll be able to relax into yourself, into your body even more than you now are. As you relax you become increasingly sensitive to the state of your being, to the state of your body. At the count of one you will be fully attuned to the healing powers of life itself, aware of the healer that resides deep within you.

Ten, moving deeper now . . . nine, returning to yourself . . . eight, relaxing into who it is that you are . . . seven, relaxing into your body . . . six, your body relaxing into the universal life energies that carry it . . . five, deeper and deeper . . . four, moving down into the center of your life . . . three, relaxing . . . two, very aware . . . one, feel the expansive energies of life itself.

Tell yourself you will remain alert throughout the whole of this meditation and you will remember all that you experience.

Vitality of Life

Now become aware of whatever you imagine to be the very source of your vitality, the spring from which your life forces come. However you imagine that, create that, the source of your vitality, the source of the life force energy within you. . . . You may wish to imagine the radiance of the sun, imagining that you have a golden sun within you, emanating this life force energy . . . brilliant energy that your life rides upon . . . radiant energy that is your life, feel the spring of energy, the source of vitality . . . it's the continuous flow of your being . . . animating who it is that you are. . . . Watch it, feel it, sense it, as though your energy were coming up from an underground spring . . . continually coming up . . . continually moving, like a river that is never twice the same . . . the continuous spontaneous flow of your being. . . . The spirit of life itself . . . every moment of your life being different than the moment before, every moment a part of this river of energy . . . let yourself be carried by the excitement of life itself . . . radiance moving up and out through your body, out into the life that is yours. Feel the continuous and inexhaustible resilient life force energy that is yours . . . however you imagine that to be, vibrant energy.

◆

Feel the life force energy moving through the whole of your being . . . every cell of your body infused with the pulse of life. The spontaneous, inexhaustible energy . . . vibrant, radiant energy moving through you like a river that's never twice the same. Feel the rhythm of this energy . . . energy which your life rides on from moment to moment to moment. . . . Feel it teeming in every cell of your body, through every pore, every organ . . . energy, radiant vibrant energy. . . . Feel this energy's connection with all of life energy that permeates everything. . . . The glow of life.

Identify with the constantly new life being born within you. The cells, of which you are composed animated by life, vibrant with life . . . cells continually being created, continually growing, as old ones die . . . the continuous transformation of energy . . . constantly transforming energies, bringing energies in . . . and releasing, discarding what's no longer needed. Life is fully resilient, it rejuvenates itself, acknowledge this. . . . Feel the constant movement, the self-perpetuating, self-healing regenerative powers that your body has . . . how it continually renews itself . . . the innate wisdom that your body possesses, its ability to heal itself . . . the intrinsic intelligence of every cell of which you are composed . . . the continuous movement of energy, the resilience of life itself.

Feel the energy expanding, bursting forth, feel the celebration of life . . . feel it surging through you, the movement of this energy . . . the dance, the sound, the rhythm, the music of life.

Pulsating energy moving through you . . . celebrate life . . . feel the wisdom of this energy, how it is that it always knows how to regenerate itself. . . . This energy's ability to heal, to return anything into a harmonious balanced condition, fully vital, yet balanced, maintaining an equilibrium. . . . Acknowledge the wisdom of life itself. Let yourself trust life. Let yourself reside in the sanctity of life itself.

◆

Now create a symbol, make up a symbol for all that you're experiencing, a symbol for your vitality, for your health, for the vitality of life itself.

◆

Know that whenever you bring this symbol into your awareness it will enable you to move into harmony with the life forces within you . . . and whenever you bring this symbol into your awareness it will revitalize you, energize you . . . that whenever you bring this symbol to mind it creates a channel to receive the information you need to regain your health and vitality. Tell yourself this now . . . that the more you use this symbol, the more you'll live in health. . . . Feel the energy of this symbol. . . . Let the energy of this symbol pour into the whole of your body . . . feel the life forces vibrating within you, throbbing in every cell of which you are composed. . . . Acknowledge life. Trust life.

Developing Rapport with Your Body

You are going to direct your awareness to different areas in your body. . . . As you do this sense them, feel them, see them, experience them in good health. In the next meditation you will have time to go over any areas you may be having difficulty with so that you can understand the difficulties and energize the healing process. As you move through the different areas within you, you may wish to imagine yourself very tiny, as though your whole self were moving through your body . . . you may wish to imagine riding a pinpoint of light . . . light that illuminates the internal workings of your body. . . . Know that it is fine—in fact it is good—simply to make up what you imagine it to be like inside yourself . . . you needn't imagine it literally, you may instead wish to symbolize the internal parts of your body.

Bring to mind your symbol for health and vitality and keep it in the background of your awareness as you explore the inner workings of your body, in so doing your symbol will enable you to fully experience the innate intelligence of each area within you.

Feel your bones . . . explore what they look like . . . imagine what they'd feel like if you were to touch them with your fingertips. . . . Become aware of the strength, the durability of your bones, of the whole of your skeleton giving your body a frame to stand on. . . . Sense the strength of your bones . . . experience your bones . . . know that within them they create your blood, your life blood.

Imagine the layers of muscles connecting to your bones . . . be aware of their strength, their flexibility, their texture, their color, their tone. . . . Feel how it is that your muscles give you movement . . . explore the whole of your musculature . . . its strength and durability. Notice how it shapes your body. . . .

Become aware of your heart, the rhythm of your pulse . . . the sound of your heart beat. . . . Imagine all the blood branching out throughout the whole of your body. . . . Imagine moving through a vein and exploring the whole of your circulation, feeling the blood moving easily and rhythmically throughout the whole of your body . . . keeping the whole of your body fully nourished . . . bringing to each of the areas in your body what they need as it carries away the wastes . . . carrying on the regenerative processes of life itself, keeping your body in a harmonious balance. . . .

Feel the rhythm of your breath, like waves rising and falling . . . feel your breath cleansing and sustaining your body . . . feel your breath moving through the whole of your body, carried by your blood . . . as though each cell of which you are composed is breathing in clean, fresh air. . . .

Now become aware of your digestive system. . . . You may wish to imagine riding on a piece of food. . . . Go through the whole of your digestive system . . . notice its feel, its color, its sound . . . experience your digestive system transforming food into energy . . . keeping every cell of your body well nourished. . . .

Become aware of your reproductive system, its harmonious balance . . . how it looks, how it feels, where it is in the cycle of life . . . appreciate your sexuality as a celebration of life itself. . . .

Become aware of your brain, sense it, feel it. . . . Become aware of your spine . . . aware of the whole of your nervous system branching out to the full reaches of your body. . . . Feel how alert and responsive your body is. . . . Imagine the networking of impulses throughout the whole of your nervous system keeping your body in clear communication, all your body parts in communication. Feel how acutely aware your body is. . . . Acknowledge the intelligence residing within you. . . .

All of your senses are sharply attuned, intimately connected to your nervous system. . . . Explore your five senses, see them, feel them, fully sense them. . . . Explore each of your senses, your sight, your eyes, your hearing, your ears, your touch, your skin, your taste, your mouth, your smell, your nose. Now take time to explore them.

◆

Now become aware of each of your glands exploring them one at a time . . . however you imagine each, producing the appropriate fluids for all of your body to function in cooperation. . . . And keeping you immune to detrimental forces, notice how your glands each play a role in keeping your body in a state of balance.

◆

I will now give you time to go in further and explore on your own, areas you've been through or areas you have not yet gone into. Remember your symbol for health and vitality and explore with it. Take time to do this now.

◆ ◆ ◆

Bring your attention back . . . take time to finish what you're doing. Take time now to fully appreciate the nature of your body, the home of yourself . . . feel its integrity. . . . Believe in your body, make friends with it . . . feel how all the areas in your body cooperate with one another, always able to replenish itself, providing you with a good home for yourself. . . . Love your body for the home it gives you.

Self-Healing

From this place be aware of the innate health that is intrinsic to life itself, for life is healing, self-clearing, regenerative. . . . To heal yourself, know: each symptom is the clue to the conflict behind it, containing needed knowledge to create a constructive solution to the conflict. . . . Each problem contains within itself the seeds of its own healing. Any ailment you might have is a signpost pointing you towards just what is healthful. Trust your body's ability to heal itself. . . . When you cut your skin, it rebuilds itself of it's own accord, your body knows how to regenerate itself. . . . Experience, acknowledge the self-healing capabilities intrinsic to your body. Remember times when your body has healed itself. . . . The cells with which you are made are fully influenced by your attitudes. . . . Trust the nature of your body . . . in so doing, you treat it kindly. Your trust gives your cells added support for their healing work. Give yourself permission to believe in your body.

◆

Now become aware, fully aware, of the whole of your body, the position it's in . . . the condition it's in . . . the pulse of life percolating in your body . . . the pulse of life percolating in every cell of which you are composed . . . Know that you are becoming as aware of your internal physical environment as you are of your external physical environment. . . . It is now an established fact that you have an inner awareness of the internal workings of your body. Feel the sense of unity that this awareness brings you . . .

with this sense become aware of any areas in your body that you would like to heal. . . . To promote and maintain good health you can communicate with any area of your body. . . . You can hear its messages, gaining insights to problems, discovering what you need to do to heal yourself. And you can also put in new messages and your body will respond to these messages.

Choose one particular area you would like to work on. . . . If you have a number of different areas, choose one, and know that you can work on the others another time. . . .

Visualize that part of your body, imagine what it looks like, what it feels like. You needn't imagine it literally—imagine it however you like. . . . Feel the area of difficulty . . . sense its condition. . . . Be aware of the atmosphere in which it lives. . . . Be aware of the quality of energy present in this part of your body. . . . What mood would it be in if it had a mood? What color would this mood be? What sounds or vibrations are present in this part of your body? Let your imagination create a sense of how this area is doing. . . .

Imagine it having a consciousness of its own, an intelligence of its own, as indeed it does. Imagine that this part of your body sends out a messenger who represents its consciousness. Talk to the messenger; listen to what it has to say about the mood of this part of your body. . . . Ask it how it feels . . . imagine what it would tell you. Use your imagination, make up a story . . . give yourself full permission to pretend that indeed you can talk to this area. Let the child within you make up this conversation. Imagine what the two of you would say if you were to talk. Trust what happens, even if it feels simplistic. . . . Ask the messenger what is going on . . . be receptive to the area's experience.

◆

Ask if there is anything it is defending you against . . . anything in your life this ailment is protecting you from . . . or what it wants protection from. . . . Be receptive to whatever you sense, for it may not answer you verbally . . . you'll find yourself with a better understanding of the problem and knowing how to create a more constructive solution to the conflict.

◆   ◆   ◆

Ask it if there are particular exercises, foods, rest or whatever it may wish to help it return to a state of vital health. . . . Ask what it wants, sense what it has to say. Trust your sense.

◆

Decide if you're willing to give it what it wants . . . decide if there is anything you want from it and ask for it. . . . You can tell it how you feel, what you want. . . . You may need to re-educate the cells—tell them what is happening now or reassure them about the future.

◆

Sense if the area is willing to give you what you want. . . . What kinds of agreements might you make so that you can cooperatively take care of one another? Compromise when need be . . . ask it what you can now expect of it . . . tell it what you're willing to do. . . . Be patient with one another . . . endeavor to make life easier for one another. . . . Put any feelings of self-blame, frustration or powerlessness through your mental housecleaning device.

◆   ◆   ◆

You may wish to bring your symbol of health and vitality into the scene. Imagine asking the symbol if it has any light to shed on the healing of this area. . . . Come to agreements with the area, and when you come to agreement, imagine acting on it. Notice what that feels like. . . . Imagine how the mood in this part of your body changes, feel the area healing.

◆

Now, notice if there is any resistance. . . . Imagine what it is you
need to do to take care of the part of yourself that does *not* want to
heal. . . . Decide how you are going to act on this . . . and imagine
doing so.

◆   ◆   ◆

Now imagine your vitality symbol hovering above your body . . .
let it pour its healing energy into the area. . . . Feel vital, healing
energy coming into the area, healing the area . . . this healing
process will always be what's last in your mind whenever you're
aware of this area in your body. Tell yourself this . . . and know
that whenever you bring this symbol to mind it will help your body
in its healing process. . . . Know that this is so.

◆

Now take the time to finish anything that you hadn't time to finish
earlier or begin this healing process in another area.

◆   ◆   ◆

Now create a line of communication, open up a channel so that
you can continue to be in tune with the needs of your body and
your body can continue to be in tune with the needs of your life
. . . able to meet each other's needs. Know that you can keep this
channel open, and in consequence you will always be fully aware,
mind of body, body of mind. Create this channel of communication
now and tell yourself you will continue to use it. . . .

Now if you have any remaining ideas, sensations, or feelings of
frustration, discomfort or ill health, put them into your mental
housecleaning device . . . leaving you with only trust and faith in
your body's health.

◆

Know that every day you're getting better, expect the best. . . .
Your body/mind is united. . . . Trust your ability to heal yourself
. . . to be in harmony with the whole of yourself and all that's

around you. . . . Now, if you have one, bring to awareness your symbol for self-protection, experience what it feels like to be fully protected . . . feeling very safe and strong—taken care of, fully protected . . . whatever that is to you . . . a loved one's arms, warmth, a cozy room, a sound, white light, whatever you imagine to be protective energy.

◆

Now surround yourself with this energy, let it form a protective bubble around you . . . create/focus on your symbol for self-protection and know that it creates a bubble of safety, security and strength. Immerse yourself in the energy. . . . Know that whenever you wrap yourself with this energy you protect yourself from danger . . . know that this is so . . . that this symbol keeps you safe by shielding you from any threats to your health. This energy keeps your body's immune system strong and sound. . . . You have protected yourself by creating a protective bubble enclosing this safe energy . . . imagine yourself fully protected. This is your symbol of protection, in fact, it can protect you from any influences that may threaten your health, protecting you from germs, bites, whatever may come your way. . . . Acknowledge that you can protect yourself with this energy. . . . You may imagine asking the energy if there's anything you need to do to protect yourself from any influences that may hinder your health. . . . Sense what you can do to keep yourself safe and healthy.

◆

Decide if you are willing to do this, and if you are, experience yourself doing so. . . . If you're not, see what alternatives there are and experience yourself acting on those. . . . Know that you do have the ability to maintain your health and to protect yourself from any threats. Imagine that this is so.

Healing Attitudes

In this state you are very clear, much clearer than usual. Here you can discover the patterns of your own consciousness. Here your beliefs, your attitudes become sharp and clear. Not only are the patterns of your consciousness revealed to you here but you can repattern your awareness so it moves only in positive directions. You can discard negative ideas and pave new roads for your consciousness to move down—moving in a healthful direction. . . .

I am going to ask several questions. Notice your responses . . . notice when you respond in such a way that you give up your power and feel bad about yourself or your body or your life. Notice when you feel vicitimized. First simply reflect and then at the end of the meditation you will have time to create positive and powerful beliefs—new directions to move in.

What do you think about your body—how do you feel about it? Its size, shape?. . . What don't you like?. . . What do you like?. . .

How strong, flexible, durable are you?. . . What limitations do you have to contend with?. . . What are you always vulnerable to?. . .

When do you get sick?. . . How come?. . . What does illness mean to you?. . . Can you be fully well?. . .

Further explore your attitudes towards healing and dis-ease.

◆ ◆ ◆

Now transform any attitudes that limit your health with your mental housecleaning device, or ground them with your grounding cord, know the earth transforms them.

◆ ◆ ◆

Bring to awareness your symbol for vitality. Remember the resilient qualities of life itself. Life regenerates itself—heals itself. Life is vitality. . . . Now construct specific beliefs and affirmations that speak to how you would like it to be, how you will it to be. . . . Repossess your power, the power of life itself. . . . You may also want to talk over this new way of being with particular parts of your body.

◆ ◆ ◆

Believe in your ability to change . . . believe in your body, believe in your wellness . . . imagine exaggerating your belief. Stretch your faith, make it even greater. . . . Feel how your life will be after these changes have come about.

◆ ◆ ◆

Notice what you can do in your life now, to acknowledge this new power you're cultivating. Think of a symbolic act that is in alignment with your new beliefs. Imagine doing it.

◆ ◆ ◆

Expect change to occur over time. . . . Expect the best. . . . Trust yourself, trust your body, trust life itself.

Food, Rest, Exercise

You are now going to explore the routine of your life—the life of your body. You now occupy an extremely receptive, and knowing state of awareness. Acknowledge the fact that within you lies the knowledge of what you need, to care for your body, to care for yourself, to honor your life. . . .

Focus in on food now. Some food your body will resonate with, some food your feelings may resonate with. Some foods may hum, some may scream. Be aware of what part of you is desiring different foods. Simply bring a food into awareness and you'll be aware of whether it's your body that desires what this particular food has to offer or another aspect of yourself that desires this food. Explore what parts of you desire the different foods in your life. Bring to awareness one at a time.

◆   ◆   ◆

When you are finished exploring the different foods, if there are foods that you are wanting with other parts of yourself than your body, talk to those parts of yourself and see how you can meet their needs in new ways, so you only eat those foods that your body wants. . . . Choose what you want to eat for healthful life, meeting the needs of all of yourself, your body and your feelings.

◆   ◆   ◆

Choose how you want to relate to food as you move through your daily routine. . . . Focus on meals, on that part of eating that is connected with others. . . . Imagine that everything is a part of a healthy process of living, of sharing, of nourishing yourself, nourishing others. . . . Choose how you want to relate to food in a fully healthful way, healthful for all the parts of yourself, your body, your feelings, your mind, your spirit, your family and community. . . . Feel, see yourself acting on your knowingness, caring for the whole of your being as you nourish the life within you with food. . . . Acknowledge the earth for sustaining your life, providing your body with food.

◆   ◆   ◆

Now take time to be aware of what your body needs in rest and relaxation on the one hand, and activity and exercise on the other. Talk to your body about it, notice how it feels . . . sense what resonates well with your body. Create a routine in your life that is balanced with vital activity and replenishing rest. Create rhythm in your life.

◆   ◆   ◆

Decide what you are willing to do. Make agreements with yourself. Imagine acting on your choices . . . caring for your body, the home of yourself. . . . Acknowledging what you need, honoring the life that is yours, honoring life itself.

Sexuality: The Dance of Life

Imagine going to a place that's extremely sacred; create this place for yourself now; imagine a temple . . . a temple that is so quiet all you hear is the silence of its enchantment. This place you create is your temple to become fully whole within.

◆

Not only is this place sacred, but it's extremely sensual. Life is vibrant here, energy is revealed in its pure, naked forms . . . here you can affirm all life-giving sensuous energies. This place is a powerful place, a sensuous place. Create this place now, let it be enchanted. . . . And know that this place may reveal new insights, new energies for you to experience, that are particularly important in healing, integrating, and growing with your sexuality. From here you can make peace with your sexuality and celebrate it at the same time . . . a very safe, splendorous and sacred place. Bring your mental housecleaning device to mind so whenever constricting feelings or thoughts come up you can transform them by putting them in your device or simply letting them soak into the ground. . . .

In this place you can be extremely aware of the connection your body has to the life cycles of the earth and heavens, the cyclic nature of life itself . . . the coming into being and the passing

away—birth and death. Sexuality is the richest experience of life
itself. Feel your attunement to the rythmic nature of life. The spirit
of the movement of life, the cyclic nature of life itself, your sexual,
sensual self. Affirm your love of life . . . sexuality is a celebration of
life itself. . . . Feel the spark of joy within you. . . . Make yourself
fully comfortable in your temple and now move your awareness
inside of yourself to what you imagine to be the center of your
sexuality. . . . Let yourself experience the motion of the vitality of
life itself. Your sexuality that springs from the source of life, the
regeneration of life. Affirm your physicality, affirm your sexuality.
Affirm the life force which surges up through you. . . . Let your
sexuality spring from the core of your being. . . . To bring forth
your sexual experience remember good times you have had, times
sexuality—sensuality—has brought you pleasure.

◆

If there's anything blocking you from affirming your sexual energy,
if you wish, you can release those blocks, you can transform them.
You can visualize them dissolving; you can remove them; you can
put them through your mental housecleaning device; you can
imagine talking to them and discover what you need to do in your
life to release each of these blocks. It may be releasing pain, it may
be giving yourself permission to experience sexuality in new ways.
You can give the negative messages back to whoever told them to
you in the first place. . . .

Whatever it may be, balance the center of your sexuality so that
you can fully experience it as a gift for yourself, or a gift for you to
share with another—a gift from life force energies themselves.

◆ ◆ ◆

Feel the splendor of life itself. As though your sexuality were the
music of your body. Know that as you heal your sexuality, as you

clear your sexual center, you become fully connected to the earth
and the spirit, to the dance of life your body naturally moves to,
that the earth and spirit are one and the same. And that you merge
with the cosmic whole with loving orgasmic energy. . . . In merging
with the whole of sensual, sexual orgasmic energy you empower
yourself, power from within rises up and yet you are open and
receptive and life energies are received—sexual, sensual, intimate
energy is received and all meets within you and you are one with
the pulsating dance of life.

◆

Now imagine that as you heal, you'll be more and more able to be
fully present and attuned to your sexuality and the sexuality of
those around you. Honoring it as a sacred part of our lives. Honoring your choices and those of others; feel how you can do this.
Enabling yourself to become a fully spontaneous, sexual being,
connecting where it feels good, where you're attuned to another,
where loving energies flow . . . letting that connection express
itself. . . . And you may choose to experience your sexuality within
yourself, letting it reveal all the levels of yourself and your self-love.
Loving ourselves, loving each other, our bodies dance with soul
. . . intimacy vibrates within and around us. We are sexual beings,
we celebrate the joy, life within ourselves and with others—sexual
alone, with another of the same sex or the opposite, sexually
connecting where it feels good and we dance our love of life
together. . . .

Respecting your choices, and knowing that in healing your
sexuality your choices are very clear; you know what you need.
Affirm where you are, and affirm your ability to express your
sexuality, while fully sensitive to others and respecting another.
Knowing that there's enough for everyone, that we are all sexual

. . . that life is sexual. Affirm your choices to commitment to one
in particular . . . attachment, independence, taking care of
yourself, taking care of the sacredness of your sexuality, while
honoring the sacredness of the sexuality of everyone . . . honoring
the bonds that sexuality creates. Knowing that in affirming sexuality you affirm life itself. Take time to imagine expressing your
sexual energy in ways that are a celebration, an integration into
the wholeness of life itself—the orgasm of life. . . . Sexuality is so
powerful, so potent, that it is only in sexuality that life itself can
be created. . . . Honor sexuality—both yours and others'.

◆ ◆ ◆

Create whatever you need to protect the integrity of your sexuality;
if you wish, do an imaginary ritual to protect its sacredness. . . take
time to protect yourself from all those ideas in the world around
you that degrade and hurt your sexuality.

◆

In protecting your sexuality, you let it flow, flowing from the depth
of your being out into a joyous celebration of life. You choose when
and when not to act on your sexual energy, in tune with the
choices of others. . . . And with all these energies moving through
you and connecting you with another you can explore your feelings
of love, your feelings of celebration, your feelings of intimacy, the
bonds your sexual sharing creates, your spirit, your soul alive in
your body. . . . Take time to explore and choose the ways you can
be in the world that affirm your sexuality, your life, that affirm the
richness of life itself.

◆

In this exploration, this affirmation of your sexuality, you may
choose to create a symbol for all that you're experiencing, and you
can bring this symbol into your awareness whenever you wish to
heal and affirm your sexuality. You may wish to ask your symbol

what you need to do in your life to affirm and protect your sexuality. Decide if you're willing to do it, and if your are, see yourself doing so; if you're not, decide what compromises you're willing to make.

◆ ◆ ◆

Take time to acknowledge yourself as a sexual being; to thank anyone you've been sharing this energy with. Knowing that in affirming sexuality you affirm life itself—for life is sexual.

Meeting Your Wise Self

Create a very sacred place for you to be in; it may be a temple, a place in the country, or a place you've been, or a place you'd like to be able to be. Create a place, a special sacred place, a very peaceful place, so peaceful you can almost hear the quiet of it. So quiet, the quality heals your spirit. Create it, imagine what is all around you. Create a very comfortable place with your imagination—the colors, the textures, the sounds of life that are here, be aware of the qualities of energy here. . . . A very special place, a wonderful environment for you to be, a temple, your sanctuary, where you can come to feel your spirit, to be very peaceful . . . to gain the knowingness you need for your life. Let your spirit be replenished by this place.

◆

In a moment I am going to snap my fingers, and at that moment you're going to meet an aspect of your knowingness, an aspect of yourself, which may be manifested in many ways. This aspect of yourself is very, very wise, all-knowing. This aspect of yourself may come to you in the form of light, an imaginary being, an animal, a

spirit or maybe another you. *[snap]* Imagine this aspect, very, very
wise, very gentle, and yet very powerful and strong, very, very
compassionate. Meet this part of yourself now, very wise and
all-knowing, sense the wise, compassionate self. . . .

Ask this aspect of yourself how it is that the rest of you can gain
the courage you need to either keep up the fight, or to let go, to
move on, to trust the future. . . . Imagine what this aspect would
tell you, sense your knowingness. You may receive answers in
energy form, they may not be verbal; you may simply find yourself
knowing, feeling, having the courage that you need to keep up the
fight or to let go, to move on, to trust the future.

◆   ◆   ◆

As you breathe, imagine breathing in this new knowingness . . .
imagine breathing in this courage. . . . Breathing in this strength
so that it spreads through every aspect of your being . . . every cell
of your body . . . every thought in your mind . . . every feeling in
your emotions . . . your whole being, vibrating with courage, with
patience, with knowingness. . . . And your whole self becomes as
wise as your wisest, deepest self. . . .

Notice things that you need to do in your life to be able to come
to completion in any areas of your life . . . to let go, to move on, to
move forward.

◆   ◆   ◆

You may want to imagine doing some kind of ritual or ceremony or
dance with your wise self. . . . As you imagine this you empower
yourself, trust the future, let go. You evoke the deepest knowingness
of your being, of beingness itself. . . . You are courageous and at
the same time compassionate with yourself. . . . Imagine performing
a ritual with yourself, a ritual that acknowledges your life, expresses
any rage you may feel . . . transforms any blame you may feel, and

acknowledges your power, all that you've done, letting go and moving on. . . . You can create this ritual in your mind's eye in whatever way occurs to you—however you are inclined.

◆   ◆   ◆

You may want to take time to ask your wise self how it is you can be more comfortable in your body. . . . How it is you can take charge of the life you have left . . . how you can create peace in your life now. . . . If you're in pain, imagine your lungs bringing in lots of oxygen, your breath spreading through your whole body . . . your breath carrying relief throughout your whole body . . . each breath massaging the whole of your body with relief, with calming comfort. . . . Send your breath wherever your body needs it. . . . With your wise self you may want to imagine creating a channel—a channel down into the ground to let the pain begin to drain out. . . . Breathe out the pain; expect the pain to lessen over time, expect it to be a little easier, a little more comfortable, as time passes. . . .

Notice whatever may be holding you back from coming to peace with yourself, with your life . . . anything that's bothering you. . . . Imagine speaking to that quality, that quality of yourself, that part of your life, that person, whatever it may be. . . . Discover what you need to do to come to peace with yourself, with your life.

◆

You may want to imagine transforming it, you may want to imagine it soaking into the earth . . . you may want to imagine doing something . . . taking care of something . . . allowing yourself to move forward. You may need to imagine doing something or saying something you never had a chance to. . . . You may want to take time to simply remember your life. . . . Taking time to focus on any concerns you may have . . . communing with your wisest self.

◆   ◆   ◆

Go over all you've come to know in this meditation, any choices you may have made. . . . Imagine setting the stage for this day and the next, where you can carry this energy you've experienced in your meditation out into your life. . . . Knowing that this energy is there for you always, that it transcends time and space. . . . Acknowledge the support of your wise self, knowing your wise self is always with you, knowing your wise self is you . . . all you need do is tap into your deeper self.

Countout

Go over in your awareness this new-found sense of well-being. . . . The whole of your body/mind functions as harmoniously as you desire and expect it to . . . it can function as harmoniously as the rest of the whole of nature. Believe in the intrinsic healing powers of life itself. . . .

Go over in your awareness the meaning and the associations of the different symbols you've created. . . . Review the lessons and insights you gained. Go over any agreements that you've made.

◆ ◆ ◆

Notice how this new way of living is going to affect your life . . . how it will affect your activities. Now notice how it will affect those around you. Notice if any adjustments need to be made . . . if anyone, needs to be spoken to . . . what support you have for these changes . . . what support you'll now be able to give others.

◆ ◆ ◆

Know that it is an established fact that you have full power to live in harmony. . . . Feel how this is so, and it will increasingly be so as time moves on . . . choose when you will again focus in on the well-being of your body when you meditate. . . . Trust yourself, trust your body, trust your mind, trust nature.

In a moment I'm going to count from one to five, at the count of five, you'll open your eyes remembering all that you've experienced . . . feeling refreshed, revitalized and relaxed. . . .

ONE—becoming more aware of the room around you. . . .

TWO—coming up slowly now. . . .

THREE—at the count of five you'll open your eyes feeling relaxed, revitalized, and refreshed remembering all that you've experienced. . . .

FOUR—coming up now, bringing with you your sense of well-being. . . .

FIVE!—eyes open, feeling refreshed, revitalized and relaxed, remembering all that you've experienced, feeling a sense of well-being.

Chapter Eight

Making
Your Life
Work for You

Just because everything is a unified whole does not mean that contradiction is eliminated: contradictions between feeling peaceful and the problems we have to contend with in our everyday lives; contradictions between subjective problems caused by unresolved feelings, ignored lessons, or inappropriate outdated beliefs on the one hand, and on the other, limitations in the objective world around us, like having to go to a demeaning job forty hours a week in order to survive; contradictions within ourselves between the complacent side and the courageous side. It is out of contradiction between the real and the ideal, that all creativity emerges and the visionary within each of us is awakened.

EMBRACING CONFLICT

With our awareness of the possibility that things could be better *struggle is born*. Out of the constant struggle to resolve conflict between the real and the ideal *change is born*. And from the resolution of conflict and the overcoming of limitations, *development is born*. It is through conflict that all learning, change, and development occurs.

Having successfully grappled with one conflict by creating a new condition within and around us, no longer limited by the old, new ways of improvement emerge—new limitations, new contradictions, and new resolutions. Change is developmental, not cyclical—never do we find ourselves back at the beginning (we'd still be living in the Stone Age), which isn't to say that we don't make mistakes. There is no state of final fulfillment; each change opens new doors and ushers in new possibilities, and the eternal contradiction between the actual and the potential continues to fuel development. *Nothing is permanent but change itself.*

We all have problems; they are real—we don't make them up. They come from the world we live in, the material conditions of our lives, both past and present. Life is in a constant state of change and because of our awareness of this we get the idea that things could be different. Otherwise we would unquestioningly take things as they are. The product of a malfunctioning machine does not experience a problem, but we are not at the mercy of circumstances because with consciousness we do have choices: we can decide which aspect of ourselves to act out of; we can get clear where to address our energy to bring about change, i.e., discover whether the primary cause of a problem is due to subjective or objective limitations.

Some people, when they are trying to resolve personal problems, spend all their time remembering and reliving the past, believing that all they need to do to change is to understand what went wrong in their childhood. Understanding why you are as you are only makes you more comfortable with your limitations. Solely focusing on the past only reinforces the problems that now face you. Understanding why it was the way it was doesn't tell you how you can be different now or in the future. It gives you no vision to strive for. It is the equivalent of focusing on disease rather than health. Remember wherever you focus your consciousness is the reality you perpetuate—your attention is the feeding power of probabilities. Are you preoccupied with what is wrong or with what could be better?

I approach things from the opposite direction: going into the future and only working with the past if it blocks my ability to imagine and believe in the future. When that happens the past is truly getting in the way and must be attended to.

The resolution between the real and the ideal can only happen over a period of time. Before any movement occurs you have to come to the realization that a particular unsatisfactory aspect of life doesn't *have* to be the way it is, that it *could* be different, thus allowing for the possibility of change. At this point you *can't* imagine your life otherwise but at the same time you don't feel fully victimized because you know that conditions can be amended. You've begun to be open to new realities—you know they exist but you have the feeling they are elusive, just beyond your grasp. As you continue to focus on the possibility of a new reality you gradually see/sense more clearly what it could be like. When you get to the point where you can imagine it vividly—really *feel* what it *would* be like—the change is imminent.

During this process, as you focus on a better vision of yourself, the future, old beliefs come in echoing such sentiments as, "Oh, I can't do that, no one will like me anymore." (This is where the past enters the scene.) Whatever messages you give yourself that discount the possibility of a better life, they are keeping your awareness from experiencing the new reality, and they are the very same beliefs that are sabotaging your actions as you work toward bringing about change. Remember you act out of your inner messages.

So just as you personify an ailment and take care of it, you use your imagination to personify each of the beliefs and negotiate with it. Ask the blocking belief what it is *protecting* you from so you can then create new ways of taking care of yourself. Notice what you need to let go of in order to make room for change. Make clear agreements with yourself and stick to them, and you will then find that the old beliefs become amenable to change. This process usually brings up the same things that one looks for in classic therapeutic settings, but rather than scrutinizing and analyzing them you *transform* them, for your imagination is pliable. You create new attitudes that will meet both your old and new concerns not only allowing forward motion, but, in fact, fueling it, rather than merely explaining and justifying why you are stuck. You have now created new beliefs giving you foundations for new ways of being in the world. Sometimes the easiest way of doing this is simply to imagine the past as having transpired differently—the way you would have wanted it. This gives you new resources out of which you can act. We can be thankful that innerconsciousness is not critical. It dictates our behavior but we can dictate its contents.

What this means in practice is that whenever you are grappling with some unsatisfactory condition, you don't approach it by looking into the past to try and figure out what brought it about, but you ask yourself how you would *like* it to be instead. Then cultivate a vision of yourself in the new situation. I assure you if there are any beliefs attached to stuff from your past that need to be attended to, they will make themselves known loud and clear, and then you can deal with them as I have described. As you transform each discount the vision of the desired future becomes increasingly real and plausible. If no discounts come up you needn't go looking for them, but be happy that you are already capable of bringing about the change and the more you focus on the vision the more you will align your energies so that you act intuitively in new ways. Soon you'll find yourself living in a new reality.

Many times in imagining the ideal what comes into your awareness saying it's impossible is not old beliefs from the past, but instead real *objective* conditions in the present that need to be overcome to make space for the ideal to be cultivated. Again it is the imagination that is the medium of psychic awareness. Your life exists in an objective context which you are subjectively, i.e., intuitively aware of—there are limitations beyond your own personal ones. When this occurs you need to look at why those external limitations exist, and what else can be done to address the original concern they are a result of. They are usually someone else's idea of the resolution between the real and the ideal. Alternatives must now be sought and *objectively* worked for.

To illustrate, let's say that the ideal is to be calm and relaxed at work but you find yourself scattered, rushed, and stressed out all the time. You lie back and meditate, visualizing yourself fully relaxed at work, then you extend your fantasy to include the context of your workplace—suddenly an image of your boss appears bustling through the office and asking you for a cup of coffee. Don't blame yourself for not being able to imagine yourself relaxed because your inner self is telling you that in actuality no matter how relaxed you're going to get yourself, your boss is going to disrupt your space.

You now know that needs to change objectively and in order for that to happen you need to know *why* he is asking you for coffee, i.e., does he need to assert his authority, or doesn't he know how to make coffee? Or what? Then come up with an alternative course of action so his needs get met. If you can't find a way to do this, use your imagination to come to terms with the situation—as I did with the mosquito bites. If this doesn't work I suggest you start looking for a new job, or meditate (on your own time) twice as often to compensate for your stress.

Problems arise when you are confronted with a reality you don't like. However, you have the capacity to learn from it and resolve the conflicts by changing the conditions. The trouble is that we have been taught to believe that we, ourselves, are at fault, and that the sole source of our problems lies in our own limitations. When you feel bad you probably assume that there is something inherently wrong with you, blaming yourself because it doesn't occur to you that the source of the problem is in the environment. The reason for this is that generally we are taught to accept the status quo— that everything is supposed to be as it is. However, when you think about it your experience certainly teaches you otherwise. Things simply are not how they are "supposed" to be, and they never were. Everything is in constant flux.

Still, whenever I have a problem my immediate reaction is to think that there is something wrong with my nature. While we have been taught that our problems are our own fault, we have also been taught to be suspicious of our inner selves. We get it coming and going—we see ourselves as at fault and powerless at the same time. We need to turn all this inside out and realize that inside each of us is the creative power to overcome problems originally caused by conditions on the outside.

If, too often, we find ourselves looking inside for the source of our problems, further isolating ourselves by withdrawing, not only does that feel terrible because we feel incompetent, victimized, and lonely, but it doesn't solve the problems either. They will continue until they are directly addressed and the conditions themselves are changed. That means choosing to take the power we have on the inside and using it to reorder what's happening on the outside.

If you address the circumstances causing disharmony and "listen" carefully, you will learn how to create harmony. You don't want to get stuck *in* conflict, feeling inadequate and that circumstances are beyond your influence, making you brood and commiserate with yourself (hoping something or somebody will come along and fix it for you) anymore than you want to get stuck *avoiding* conflict. Only when you choose to *embrace* it openly will the solution become apparent. Ignoring and repressing negative feelings will not do, for underneath they will do damage. All of a sudden you will find yourself with a sty in your eye. You can ignore intuitions but feelings are another matter. Avoiding conflict doesn't make it disappear, but participating with it carries you to resolution. You learn, life becomes more meaningful, and you have become more adept at overcoming the issues. It feels very good to stop being a victim and take charge. Listening directly to the message in the irritation will enable you to work at creating the necessary changes so you'll no longer be plagued with it. Like taking aspirin for headaches may give temporary relief, but leave the problem festering beneath where it's only a matter of time before it reasserts itself—perhaps this time as an ulcer. The same holds true for stress: avoiding it doesn't resolve it; embracing it gives you the needed information as to which changes are necessary to solve the problem.

It is the perpetual denial of conflict that leads to the compulsive behavior of any addiction. Not allowing ourselves to face and come to terms with what is really bothering us, we drive ourselves to focus *elsewhere*. One can't relax and deny at the same time because the festering problems that need attention will naturally come into awareness. Not willing to be centered inside ourselves we compulsively eat, keep things clean, or constantly socialize (as if there is no choice), or maybe numb out with alcohol or drugs. The longer the original problem goes unaddressed the more neurotic we become and the more the problem gets buried under all the sludge that results from the side effects of the compulsive behavior—compounding our problems. Needless to say, it makes it that much more difficult to address the original problem and get our lives back on a healthy course. Instead we find ourselves caught in a vicious circle.

Only by confronting conflict head-on will you be able to empower yourself to take charge of your life and change it for the better. We must all use our awareness creatively to discover how to change the material conditions that give rise to our problems—that is, to use the inner power common to us all to guide us in changing external limitations. Not only is there conflict between the ideal and the real around us but it resides within us as well. There is a part of you that would just as soon things stay the way they always have been, not wanting to contend with the new and different, no matter how much better it would be. Then there is your courageous and visionary side that is ready to work for change. Only you can choose which aspect of yourself to act out of. If you want to act out of your courage find the spark of joy within you, for life's natural state is one of replenishment, creativity, development and change— the celebration of life which gives you the strength to move forward.

BELIEFS ARE OUR ROADMAPS

Understanding what conditions gave rise to a certain problematic behavior on your part is important in the sense that it alleviates the depressing effects of blaming yourself for your problems. But just because you drew some conclusions to limit your behavior and/or expectations in the past because of what was then happening around you doesn't mean it is appropriate to continue operating out of those same conclusions. Now they are likely to be inappropriate assumptions. Hopefully, your interpretation of circumstances will enable you to deal creatively with problematic conditions. But too often you add to your problems because (along with the rest of us) you have so much debris in your consciousness that you are unable to view the situation clearly. This is usually because you haven't fully dealt with some conflict out of your past and you are projecting rather than clearly perceiving. You find yourself carrying the old problem around—viewing everything through it—and it's as if you are replaying the old dramas. How often do you say to yourself, "I think I've been here before." In all difficulties there is always a real conflict going on outside of you which triggers feelings inside of you whose source is something out of your past. But using your past as a source of wisdom instead of letting it perpetuate emotional charge and confusion will enable you to clear your consciousness so you can stop adding to your problems, and be able to employ your creativity to deal directly with the external source of stress. This can only be done when conflict, past and present, is embraced, that is, the message heard, the lesson learned. This is the source of wisdom.

Each of us has a network of beliefs, beliefs we've come to through our past experiences. It is our beliefs through which we interpret all that comes to our awareness, and out of which we always act—the assumptions we operate out of. They are the framework through which everything moves—the maps we use to navigate through our lives. We're not even aware that our consciousness is a vehicle taking us in a particular direction; it's in our interest to understand that this is the case. We *can* put our hands on the steering wheel and stop being rattled about. There are only certain landscapes that can be viewed from a particular road and you want to be sure the vistas are to your liking, and the maps are not outdated. Some beliefs are functional and constructive, while others perpetuate problems we'd prefer to leave behind, in which case it's time to reroute yourself.

Beliefs are like machines stuck in the "ON" position, so you want to be sure that they are churning out the kinds of experiences you want to embrace. Consciousness is always moving, moving like a river through the channels of *habituated* beliefs. During most of our waking hours our consciousness simply moves through familiar channels; i.e., we act out of habit. That's fine if it is taking you in the direction you want to go, but if it's not, then you must dig new channels for your consciousness to move through, making new vistas of experience available to you.

No matter what it is, the *natural state* is one of movement. So watch for any attitudes, thoughts, or feelings that are static—when you get stuck life passes you by. One of the best ways to discover this is to notice whether your thinking is moving in a circular direction, i.e., is it repetitious? Circular thinking is closed in on itself and has no opening for new ingredients to break the unsatisfactory cycle and move on. Typical of this kind of thinking is having clarity about all the reasons why something is wrong and only focusing on why it is the way it is (classic therapy), with no room for positive ideas that recognize the possibility for change. It's easy to discover these thoughts if you notice yourself continually becoming irritated or cynical or if your thoughts have all-inclusive words in them such as "can't," "never," "always," "nobody," "all," "every," etc. When these words are present you won't even *recognize* any new ideas or information that will break the circle, for they are *excluded* by your belief and will go right by unnoticed.

To clear your mind of such debris identify defeatist thinking by continually being aware of your internal dialogue. What messages are you giving yourself? As life is in constant change, movement and growth, you can discover negativity by simply noticing if whatever you are thinking or feeling is life-affirming. Is it moving or static? Does it expand or contract? Is it opening or constricting? Is it warm or cold? (Read the vibes.)

Become aware and keep in check the constant chatter of your internal dialogue for it is a continual stream of suggestions. Being aware of it will reveal all of your beliefs and attitudes, both positive and negative. What messages are you giving yourself? If you want to keep your consciousness working for you rather than at cross purposes then when you notice yourself saying "can't" change it to "haven't been able to." If you say "always" change it to "usually." If you say "never" change it to "haven't yet." If you find yourself fearful, imagine yourself feeling excited and challenged instead. These simple changes will have profound results for they will enable you to recognize new input, and you will find your situation becoming flexible and amenable to change.

Since we are creatures of habit it's good to get and give support in changing any habitually uncreative thinking. Usually each of us is the last one to notice how our personal thinking limits us—we just take it for granted. I suggest that you make agreements with your friends to point out to one another circular, static thinking. When you hear your friend say "can't" bring it to her attention. I always appreciate people pointing it out to me, for it makes me aware of how I am unconsciously letting myself get stuck, and as soon as I realize what I am doing I know I can choose to stop.

We must bring to light and change all our negative attitudes because they attract circumstances that resonate with them. There is nothing mysterious or hidden about such beliefs, they're constantly present. We just need to take the time to notice and be aware that they are *interpretations of reality*, not reality itself. When we make an effort to look it is appalling how apparent they become. For example, a few years ago I made a commitment to myself to discover my own racist attitudes. Aware that I had grown up in a racist society, I knew that there was no way that I did not have some racist assumptions. The world around us is mirrored in the world within us, i.e., our inner landscape is a reflection of the outer world. I found underlying attitudes that had been invisible to me because I had always taken them for granted rather than choosing to notice them. For example, I discovered that it had never been *fully* plausible to me that there were people of color who ran governments. It was an understandable attitude since my experience had shown me only white people in decision-making positions. If I hadn't taken the time to explore my racism I would still be unable to take for granted that people of other races hold leadership positions. It was subtle, but it was there and all I had to do was look. If I hadn't, and didn't continue to examine and clear out my racist beliefs I would still not be taking people of color seriously and would be relating to them in a limiting way, offending them as well as depriving myself of a whole range of experience. And worse, I would be unconsciously legitimizing a racist system.

Unacknowledged negative beliefs are insidious. You need not get down on yourself for having them—there is always a reason for their existence as their sources are real past experiences. Beliefs dictate your activities but you need to be careful they don't become dictators, that's when you will become a dogmatist. Just because it was so in the past doesn't necessarily mean it has to be so in the future. Bring your negative beliefs out into the light and then use your mental housecleaning device to transform them, thus enabling you to act in new ways. When you are not *acting* out of the old beliefs they simply become background echoes, eventually fading altogether for you have withdrawn their lifeblood. They only receive sustenance when you act out of them. *Without action they die.*

One of the most direct and obvious ways to become aware of your beliefs is simply to keep asking *why* you think, feel, and act as you do in any given sphere of your life. Your feelings are the results of your beliefs, but they are not carved in stone revealing eternal truths. If you pay attention to them you'll uncover the beliefs you hold. When you feel bad ask yourself, "How come?" If you keep asking why, you'll peel the onion and find yourself looking straight at core attitudes you carry. Then you'll want to ask yourself if these are attitudes you want to keep. This may seem simplistic, but remember it is our beliefs that we take for granted—they are not mysterious, just unacknowledged.

Another powerful technique for uncovering negative beliefs is for you to go over all the affirmations listed in this book and notice your responses to them. Notice if you feel as if they're within the realm of possibility. If you don't, that feeling will clearly point to a negative belief which you will need to change before you can fully avail yourself of the positive situations that the affirmations can create.

If you find yourself caught in trying to distinguish between a belief and reality don't worry about it. Take anything about yourself or the world you don't like—they are all beliefs, not reality itself, for reality is constantly changing and you can influence the course change will take. Your beliefs come from what happened in the past; it doesn't follow that things have to stay the same. Following are some examples of beliefs you may have that you could work on: The world is a hostile place. I am ugly. Everybody is smarter than I. I don't deserve love. The world is out of control, so why bother. Politics are dirty. Money is corrupting. I am always tired. People can't be trusted. All of these are ideas about reality, not reality itself. But each will cause a chain of emotional, mental and behavioral reactions as well as attract circumstances that conform to the belief. Life would certainly be better if the opposite were so. Working with consciousness is the first step in changing the course of things.

Seth suggests:

In those areas in which you are dissatisfied, you feel that you are *powerless*, or that your will is paralyzed, or that conditions continue despite what *you think of* as your intent. Yet if you pay attention to your own quite conscious thoughts, you will find that you are concentrating upon precisely those negative aspects that so appall you. You are hypnotizing yourself quite effectively and so reinforcing the situation. You may say, horrified, "What can I do? I am hypnotizing myself into my overweight condition (or my loneliness, or my poor health)." Yet in other facets of your life you may be hypnotizing yourself into wealth, accomplishment, satisfaction—and here you do not complain. The same issues are involved. The same principles are operating. In those positive life situations you are certain of your initiative. There is no doubt. Your beliefs become reality.

Now: In the *unsatisfactory* aspects, you must understand this:

there is also no doubt. You are utterly convinced that you are sick, or poor, or lonely, or spiritually opaque, or unhappy.

The results, then, as easily and effortlessly follow. Natural hypnosis, in the terms given here, operates as well in one case as in the other.

What should you do, then? First of all, you must realize that *you* are the hypnotist. You must seize the initiative here as you have in other positive aspects of your life. Whatever the superficial reasons for your beliefs, you must say:

"For a certain amount of time I will momentarily suspend what I believe in this area, and willfully accept the belief I want. I will pretend that I am under hypnosis, with myself as hypnotist and subject. For that time desire and belief will be one. There will be no conflict because I do this willingly. For this period I will completely alter my old beliefs. Even though I sit quietly, in my mind I will act as if the belief I want were mine completely."

At this point do not think of the future, but only of the present. If you are overweight, insert the weight that you think is ideal for you while you are following this exercise. Imagine that you are healthy if you have the belief that you are not. If you are lonely, *believe* that you are filled with the feeling of companionship instead. Realize that you are exerting your initiative to imagine such situations. Here there can be no comparison with your normal situation. Use visual data, or words—whatever is most natural to you. And again, no more than ten minutes is required.

If you do this faithfully, within a month you will find the new conditions materializing in your experience. Your neurological structure will respond automatically. The unconscious will be aroused, bringing its great powers to bear, bringing you the new results. *Do not* try to overdo this, to go through the entire day worrying about beliefs, for example. This can only cause you to contrast what you *have* with what you want. Forget the exercise when it is completed. You will find yourself with impulses that arrive in line with these newly inserted beliefs, and then it *is* up to you to act on these and not ignore them.[1]

Now that you know the power of your consciousness you can take a stand and insert the beliefs you want to act out of. If you don't transform your interior environment the changes you create around you will only be replicas of the same old problems dressed in new clothing. How often do you find yourself with the same script but with different actors (different friends, or lovers)? If you change your interior environment using new scripts you will free yourself to create *lasting* change around you. *Change must happen both inside and outside.*

Unlike the world of inner consciousness where everything is simultaneous (you imagine something the instant the idea occurs to you), the material world, alas, is altogether different: change takes time. The important thing to remember is that the energy generated by your imaginings does not in and of itself create the change — it simply creates the probabilities and sets the stage. It is still up to you to do the *acting*. I don't mean to discount the importance of the imagining, for without this stage there would be no context in which to create change. The work of the imagination creates new channels through which energy can move, breaking new ground, giving you new resources (beliefs) from which to act out of. The energy is the first step, then it is up to you to do the acting to bring about substantive changes.

In today's therapeutic times there are a number of techniques that focus purely on the discharging of old negative feelings. Letting go of those feelings *is* important, but once you let go of them, if you don't refocus your energy by filling up the spaces you created with new beliefs you will find yourself automatically refilling them with those same old feelings, for they are the ones that are familiar. You are functioning with the habit that something is wrong even after the original material cause is no longer present and the feelings have been expressed. It is of paramount importance that you move to a vision of the ideal.

Materializing your imaginings takes a conscientious act of will — if you are not conscientious you'll find yourself behaving in the same old way. We are creatures of habit; if we don't *choose* to act differently we simply behave in known familiar ways. But with an act of *will* choose to put yourself on the new stage. Since beliefs are born out of experience it is good to do something that is symbolically in line with the new belief — new actions create new experience which further roots your new belief. If you are trying to get over being shy *make* yourself strike up a conversation with someone on the bus.

At first it is likely to feel foreign — you may feel clumsy, but with time the new stage will become as familiar as the old and you can move your creative will on to other areas because the new habits you have cultivated have become strong and automatic. You now have enough experience to solidify the new beliefs and they will stand on their own. Your activity has made your belief move from the ideal to the real. For action is the lifeblood of belief.

If you find yourself sliding back into old patterns, don't interpret it as a sign of failure, quite to the contrary, if you weren't changing you wouldn't *notice* the backslide. In other words your center of consciousness is now in a new place. In the past you took that behavior for granted and didn't see it. Give yourself a break, be patient with yourself—it all takes time. Whenever you discover yourself in old patterns just focus on the new patterns and choose to act out of their power.

In dialoguing with problems and beliefs to gain the insights you need to solve them it is important to notice your attitude when asking questions. Are you coming from a clear, open, receptive place or is there an emotional charge present? What goes out messy will come back messy. Now if you find yourself just as confused or conflicted at deep levels inside, as you are in your usual waking consciousness, what is probably happening is that either you need to discharge emotionally or you have no previous experiences stored in that level which enable you to *recognize* insights derived from the collective unconscious. If you have a clear question it acts as a spotlight illuminating a path for your consciousness to discover an answer, but there must be some thought forms, experiences of the past, already there to render the information recognizable and comprehensible.

At times like this don't be discouraged but make a point of getting support for it is clear that the answer is not yet available within you. Talk to friends about the problem. They have led different lives and their experiences will open up channels within you to receive new insights.

As we repossess the power that resides in us all, within all life—we are no longer incompetent victims determined by circumstances. As we learn that contradiction can be the source of creativity in each of us, as we become open to the present, updating our assumptions, as we have the courage and wisdom to envision a better world, and then work for it, we can re-create our world just as we can re-create our beliefs. We find ourselves moving out of our isolation and becoming a part of a world of dynamic relationships.

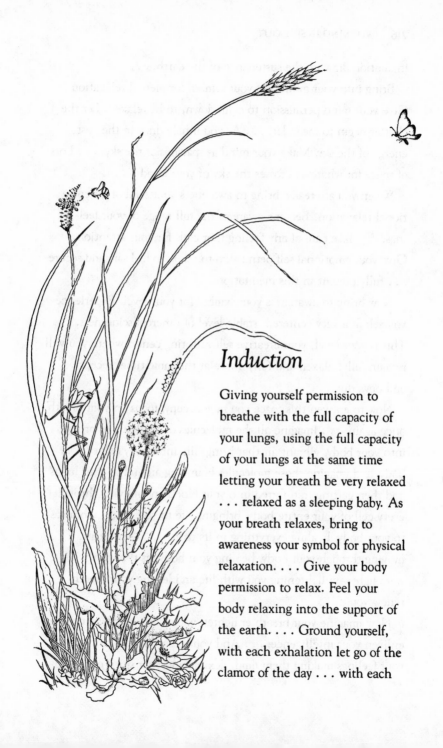

Induction

Giving yourself permission to
breathe with the full capacity of
your lungs, using the full capacity
of your lungs at the same time
letting your breath be very relaxed
. . . relaxed as a sleeping baby. As
your breath relaxes, bring to
awareness your symbol for physical
relaxation. . . . Give your body
permission to relax. Feel your
body relaxing into the support of
the earth. . . . Ground yourself,
with each exhalation let go of the
clamor of the day . . . with each

inhalation draw up the sustenance of the earth. . . .

Bring into your awareness your symbol for mental relaxation.
Give your mind permission to calm down, to be relaxed. Let the
chatter begin to meander. . . . As you inhale draw in the vast
energy of the sky. Make your mind as spacious as the sky. . . . Lots
of space for whatever crosses the sky of your mind. . . .

When you are ready, bring to awareness your symbol for emotional relaxation. Become aware of the full range of your feelings. . . . Take care of any feeling that calls for your attention.
Give your emotional self permission to relax, to feel safe and secure
. . . fully present in this meditation.

Now bring to awareness your symbol for your level. Experience
yourself at a very centered, stable level of innerconsciousness. . . .
This is your level, your creative self-restoring center where you will
remain fully relaxed and fully aware at the same time, receptive
and powerful. . . .

Now to enliven this space you now occupy, focus on your breath
once again. . . . Imagine all the molecules of air that you bring
into your body, vibrant air that brings life into every cell of your
body, and imagine those molecules bouncing around in your lungs
and then getting transferred into your blood and moving through
every cell of your entire body, bringing life to your body, vibrance
to your body, healing everything in its path. . . . Your breath
moving through your body, healing your body, as though the air
were light—enlightening you with life and letting your breath
renew you. . . .

Now imagine your breath enlighten your mind, clear your mind,
enliven your intelligence. . . . And your breath moves through
your feelings making them fluid, flexible and your spirit opens up

and flows through you. Riding your breath, the breath of life, the spirit of life flows through you, through the whole of your being, renewing you, clearing you, for your interior work. It feels good to simply be present with your breath, your breath that constantly renews your being, every moment of your life.

You settle into your breath, as your breath settles into you. Let yourself be carried by the rhythm of your breath. . . . Extend your awareness to include the whole universe, as though the universe was carried by breath. . . . Everything breathes. . . .

Breath is universal to life . . . feel universal energy, knowingness, all knowingness, all pervasive knowingness, all around us, within us, beneath us, between us, above us, throughout the whole of our being, throughout beingness itself . . . the order of everything, the rhythm of the universe, the natural movement of the universe . . . all the planets moving around their sun, each atom of which you're physically composed, each atom with electrons that move around the nucleus, the order of the universe, the continuous, inexhaustible, changing order. . . .

An order that contains within it spontaneity. The universe is dynamic, within everything is contradiction. Within life is death which, in turn, gives life to another. . . . There is no life without death—no death without life.

Focus in on what you imagine to be your vital, dynamic center. . . . Focus in on that place within you that is very quiet . . . and potent at the same time. Your center, extremely peaceful and vital at the same time, excited yet quiet. . . . Feel your center as though it is full of magnetic energy, a great concentration of energy that radiates out from your center, moves through the whole of your being, centering you, clearing you, returning you to your power, receptive in your power, open and focused. . . . And imagine this magnet in the center of your being pulling in universal energy—as indeed it does—drawing in universal knowingness . . . as without so within, you are in rhythm with all that is . . . your dynamic center roots you in the ground of life. . . . Feel yourself fully present with yourself, self-contained and yet sharing, fully grounded and yet open. Notice how that is; powerful and receptive, grounded and open. Self-contained, yet sharing. Separate yet a part of all that's around you. . . .

Sense the dynamism within you. Contradiction exists every-where, through the calm quiet, power from within emerges. . . . Your mind is full of content yet it is receptive, ready to move wherever you choose. . . . Discipline and order create channels through which artistic creativity spontaneously erupts. . . . Feel the dynamism within you . . . the balance . . . the equilibrium. This magnetic center of receptive power within you enables you to maintain a fluid balance amidst constant change. Experience how this is so. . . . Imagine a concentration within you of vital life force, the focal point of your life, whatever that means to you, the magnetic center of your being that roots you to life itself, imagine the tone, the quality, the colors of this center . . . your center. This center keeps you balanced through all the ups and downs of your life. The fulcrum of your life . . . your center that enables you to maintain balance amidst change. . . .

Affirmations evoke qualities and draw on powers attuning you to express their energies in the world around you. Feel the potential of the affirmations, pretend they are already manifest . . . exagger-ate the qualities . . . receptive to the powers . . . activating them in yourself. . . .

My life is on purpose. . . .

I am acutely attuned to my intuitive knowingness and impulses. . . .

A spring of creativity continually flows through me and out into the world. . . .

I believe in the ideal. . . .

I am courageous. . . .

My beliefs are grounded in the present. . . . I am aware of all that I say to myself and always move my consciousness in positive directions. . . .

My attitudes are constructive, they enable me to be clear and open in the present situation. . . .

I am in touch with my inner source of nourishment and knowingness. . . .

I learn from conflict; everyday my wisdom grows. . . .

My feelings flow easily and clearly throughout my being. . . .

My negative feelings guide me in creating harmony. . . .

I perceive the true source of discord both within and around me and know where to direct my energy to create harmony. . . .

I always make clear choices. . . .

I can create the changes I choose in my life. . . .

I maintain balance amidst change. . . .

I trust the future. . . .

Know that in focusing on these affirmations you have evoked deep powers. These energies will materialize in your experience . . . making the ideal more real. Take time now to focus on any of your own affirmations, or if you prefer focus on any symbols you have been working with. . . .

Meeting Your Potential Self*

Now move your awareness deeper into your self, into the vast landscape within you. And as you explore this landscape within you, all the different terrains of your inner dimensions, sense a place where there seems to be an extreme focus of energy, some place within you where you sense the energy to be extremely magnetic—it just draws you to that place. In this place you'll find a descending staircase. This stairway is going to take you into a power spot within you somewhere—a very comforting place for you to go. It is in this place that your fullest potential resides . . . deep within.

Now I will count down from ten to one and as I do, you will lower yourself down into a power spot, a place where you will be fully in tune with your power, with universal power. At the count of one you will be very aware of your fullest potential lying hidden inside you, and the source out of which your talents spring. At the count of one you will be very aware of your potential, in fact you'll meet your fullest potential as though she's another being. Ten, deeper . . . nine, descending deeper into yourself . . . eight, down the stairs, beginning to feel the strength surging up as you go down . . . seven, deeper and deeper into the person that you are . . . six, very soothing very strong energy here . . . five, down deeper, very vital, very strong energy . . . four, you can almost hear the power resonate . . . three, down into this very special, very powerful spot

When appropriate replace feminine pronoun with the masculine.

within . . . two, a very powerful, very special place inside of you
. . . one, feel the energy of this place, the power, the vibrations
around you. This place is full of potential . . . feel its resonance.

Imagine meeting your fullest potential as though she is before
you; notice her, create her; she is fully dynamic, sense her charisma
. . . create her and let her inspire you; her strength, her creativity,
her intelligence, her emotional richness. Let her inspire you.

❖

What is she doing exactly? Where does she usually hang out? Talk
to her, maybe different aspects of her spend time in different ways.
Imagine what she's doing.

❖

What has she given you in the past? Does she like you? Does she
believe in you? Do you like her? Do you believe in her?

❖

What would she like to do? Sense how the two of you can begin to
work, to play, to live together.

❖　❖　❖

Ask her about those aspects of yourself you don't like. . . . What
advice does she have for you? How can you make room for her in
your life, so that her expression can dynamically come through you
and clearly manifest itself?. . . What can you do so that you and
your potential are the same? Decide if you are willing to do these
things. If you are, imagine yourself doing so.

❖　❖　❖

Let yourself receive her power, your power, receiving it into the
whole of your being, as though your potential power were to pour
into the whole of your body . . . the whole of your mind . . . all of
your feelings . . . your spirit. . . .

And if any areas have trouble receiving the energy, the power
that is yours, ask them what they need to receive the energy . . . to
allow yourself to fully manifest your potential power. Decide if you

are willing to give them what they need. Imagine yourself doing what you're willing to do.

◆   ◆   ◆

When you're ready, let yourself merge with her. . . . Constantly living on the edge of a new frontier, the frontier of creativity, the frontier of new experience always pushing yourself and trusting yourself at the same time . . . always learning, always growing. . . .

Notice how it feels to have her move through you. Let her be you, feel yourself, see yourself, experience yourself living out your fullest potential, continually expanding the experiences life has to offer you . . . continually extending that experience as though you keep pushing the horizons farther out, creating a larger world to play in, to explore in, to work in, to learn in, to grow in. Decide where you first want to exercise your fullest potential.

◆   ◆   ◆

As you do all this notice what kind of support you can now give others so that they may be able to lead lives expressing their fullest potential.

◆

Notice how it is others can support you in expressing your potential. Notice how it will affect others if you live up to your fullest potential, what you need to do to make space for that in your life.

◆

Know that as you can imagine it, you can make it so. Take time to acknowledge your potential self. Tell her you'll be getting to know her, getting to be her more and more as time goes by. Know that this is so.

Exploring the Terrain of Your Life

Imagine as though you were to begin to float up above your body, above the roof and look down on a clear day, look down at all the buildings . . . and float a little higher up and look down on the whole area . . . the water, the shape of the land, and a little higher . . . seeing the layout of the land, the hills, the waterways, the roads, the vast ocean, the weather patterns. As you get higher, the land seems to be so small. Imagine that you even move out of the atmosphere of the earth and as you move out you can see the earth getting very small and you're immersed in the whole of the cosmos. Feel the expansiveness of the cosmos. Open your consciousness to include the whole of the cosmos, surrounded by it, just as the earth is surrounded by it let yourself be surrounded by it. . . . As you experience the vast and spacious cosmos draw into your awareness a sense of how vast time is, centuries and centuries of time, before us, ahead of us, time is as vast as space. Experience your cosmic consciousness, that includes the infinity of space and time. . . .

Now in your imagination come back a little closer to earth. . . . Know that with the consciousness you now possess you can view the terrain of your life—terrain of the past, of the present and of the possibilities in the future. Imagine your life symbolically translated into landscapes. . . . You can see quite distinctly where the different aspects of your life are going. Just as if you were a bird, you flutter around and above different areas of your life and see how you are doing down there. . . what replenishes you. . . what drains you. . . .

Explore the emotional climate of your life. . . . How is it in different areas? Notice the color, the quality, the vibes . . . in your work life . . . your family life . . . your friendships . . . your responsibilities . . . your routine . . . your creativity . . . your leisure . . . your play . . . your health. . . .

Notice if one area bleeds out into another. . . . How is the emotional climate of your life? As you discover your feelings in the different aspects of your life notice the beliefs behind them.

♦ ♦ ♦

Where is it stuck?. . . Where does it flow?. . . Notice if anything of the past is littering the landscape. . . . Is there anything objective and outside of your control that's blocking the sun or causing a drought?. . . How's the weather of your life?. . . Are there any weather patterns you hardly get to experience any more?

♦

If you find yourself getting caught up in any aspects of your life go back into the sky, into the cosmos of timelessness and spaciousness and you'll find you can see with clarity once again.

♦ ♦ ♦

Look down on the terrain of your life, notice the quality around your different experiences. . . . How are you feeling about yourself?. . . Are you learning or are you stagnant?. . . Are you complacent anywhere?. . . Are you living up to your potential?. . . Which aspects of yourself are active?. . . Are you feeling confused and lost anywhere?. . . Isolated on your own?. . . Are there any areas in which you seem to wander aimlessly?. . . Are there any areas that are disconnected, off on some side road?. . . Are there experiences and people nearby you would like to share with?. . . Are there any constricting beliefs taking you where you don't want to go?

♦ ♦ ♦

Are there any greener pastures?. . . Now be aware of how you would like things otherwise. . . . Notice if you need to adjust your attitude, or reroute yourself, or if something in the world around you needs to change. . . . What is getting in the way of what you want?

◆

Find the soft spot, where the situation is amenable to change both within you *and* around you. . . . Make change be within the realm of possibilty. . . . Create the probability.

◆ ◆ ◆

Trust your nature, trust nature. . . . Celebrate the life that is yours, the life we share.

From Impasse to Insight

Now bring to awareness the problem you chose to work on for this meditation, an area in your life you would like to be different. Remember times where this concern has been present. Recreate these times. Notice the atmosphere in which this problem thrives, the qualities, vibrations present, your sense of self, which aspect of yourself is prominent. . . .

Now let the qualities of this problem coalesce into a symbol. . . . Now put the symbol through your mental housecleaning device. Sense all the troublesome, tangled-up, heavy, stiff straining energy draining out—soon to be gone altogether. . . .

Now project yourself into a time of the future—don't worry about where or when it is, simply experience a time in the future in which you're living in a liberated way . . . liberated from that familiar concern from the past. Don't worry about how or when this comes about, just experience yourself living in a new independent way—this area of your life has become easy. What used to be the wished-for ideal is now real. Feel what this is like. . . . Notice the atmosphere of this time, the quality of this new time, your sense of self. Which aspect of yourself is prominent now? Resolution has already occured . . . pretend this is so, imagine it, exaggerate it. What does your life feel like? Your routine, your relations, what does it all feel like? Give it more detail, more life, embellish on the feel of it. . . .

If you have *not* been able to imagine a time in the future that is problem-free recreate the symbol of the problem itself. . . . Talk to it now, imagine it has personality and can communicate with you. This symbol may communicate with words or with direct knowingness—trust your imagination. Ask the problem symbol what it's doing . . . what it gives your life . . . what it is protecting you from . . . how it's feeling . . . what it believes . . . what it teaches . . . what it wants. . . . Tell it how you're feeling, what you want. . . . Negotiate so that the two of you can cooperatively co-exist.

◆ ◆ ◆

Now create a symbol of the problem-free future, or the cooperative harmony you are now experiencing. Create a symbol of this new way of being, an easier way of being. . . . Imagine as though this symbol is charged with knowingness, knowingness of resolution. Imagine it hovering above your body and beginning to pour its energy into your body . . . however you imagine that . . . resolution energy pouring through the whole of your body, re-educating the cells of which you are physically composed. . . . If any areas have trouble receiving the energy imagine asking that part of your body what it wants from you in order to receive the energy.

◆

Make agreements with the reticent areas of your body and let them receive as much of the energy as they are currently willing to.

◆

Feel your body empowered by the energy charged with this liberating energy. . . . Now let the resolution energy of the symbol spill over into your mind. However you imagine this to occur. Merge all of your beliefs with the energy. Begin to take on the attitude of this energy. . . . If any voices or ideas pop up unwilling to take it in, sense what it is they want . . . negotiate . . . make agreements. . . . Let the energy spread through the whole of your mind.

◆

Feel your mind full of resolution, believing in this new way. . . . Now let the energy of the symbol spread through your emotional self. Immerse all of your feelings with the energy. If any feelings have trouble receiving the energy ask them what they need so they too can celebrate this new energy. . . make agreements.

◆

Feel your whole emotional self charged with this energy of resolution. . . . Now let it spread out and flow through your spirit, let the energy emanate from your spirit. . . . The whole of your being filled with the energy of resolution. Your whole self vibrating in a new way. . . .

Now if you wish to gain further insights you can bring back one of the original problematic scenes, bring it back into your awareness. . . . Now ask your solution symbol what to do about the situation. Let yourself know what to do to empower yourself, to change the quality of the situation . . . to move forward in new ways.

◆

Acknowledge what you have learned, what you've chosen to do about it, any agreements you've made. . . . Is there is anything you

need to give up to make room for the new ways of being?. . .
Notice how your life will feel as you act on this new energy. . . . Is
there anything you want to do to symbolically root the energy in
your experience?. . . Notice how all of this will effect others . . . if
there is anything that needs to be said so that others can also be in
alignment with this energy. . . . Be aware of people in your life
who will support you in this change. . . . Mental houseclean any
residues of the old way and make whatever additional choices you
wish to.

❖ ❖ ❖

Give yourself permission to have faith . . . to believe in change, to
believe in yourself and your ability to change. . . . The very fact
that you have imagined these things makes them possible. The
energy exists, and you can use all that you have experienced in this
meditation to encourage, to advance, to make the ideal real in
your life. It is possible; it is probable; it is your choice.

Diminishing Past Trauma
Increasing Wisdom

You are now in a very magical level of innerconsciousness where
the limitations of time dissolve; you can become fully aware of the
past, using its power to move into the future. Imagine yourself now
to be a leaf on a tree in late fall—on the edge of winter. The leaf
flutters down onto the ground; feeling as though you are the leaf
gently fluttering down, and as you flutter down your inner awareness
becomes more and more aware of time, of your own personal time

in your life, chapters in your life . . . and as you move down deeper into yourself, when you land upon the ground you are going to land in a very special place where the limitations of time have disappeared. Feel yourself descending . . . a very magical space with lots of leaves that have fluttered down onto the ground, feeling each layer of your descent down into this special place. This is the autumn of time itself. Here you can re-experience and remake the seasons of your life.

◆

This place has very different qualities. And now imagine, discover, or create a shelf or a mantlepiece with a mirror towards the back of it. This mantlepiece is very special. Your imagination can use this mirror to reflect your life. If you look into it you can see what's behind you . . . all that leads up to where you stand at this juncture in your life—the path of your life, the twists and turns of your past.

If you choose, you can enter the looking glass, go back into the past and view it with what you know now, thereby learning more. You can rearrange it so the quality that resides there is different and you'll find that you'll carry your past around with you differently. Know that by reviewing your past your wisdom becomes wider and wider, it encompasses more and more and you'll find that you move into the future with great foresight . . . know that this is so.

Now play back any particular time, event, or chapter of your life in the past that you carry strong feelings about—that still upsets you. Choose one particular time, and just watch it unfold in front of you in the mirror . . . scenarios of the past, just take a moment and watch them unfold, watch yourself in the scene. Watch it like you were watching a movie of someone else's life. Watch everyone, watch it unfold as it did unfold. . . . Replay it in the mirror on the mantle, the mantle of the past. And now choose any particular episode that you saw, that you're seeing, that you need to work with. If there are several, choose one and tell yourself you will work on the others another time . . . choose an episode that you need to fully digest within you, so you can let it go into the past where it belongs, so you can carry the strength of its lesson into the future, so you can transform your energy, be grounded in the present and live in new and different ways. . . . So the past is never repeated. . . .

Replay the scenes once again . . . notice how you felt, what you believed about yourself . . . about others . . . what you believed was possible at the time. . . . Notice which aspect of who you are was prominent . . . remember what you decided at the time . . . notice if you felt victimized . . . if you had given up your power . . . or if you weren't taking into account where any of the other participants in the scene were coming from.

◆   ◆   ◆

Let the pain, the hurt, the anger, the disappointment drain out through the ground . . . or imagine expressing it. . . . Let yourself mourn the scene . . . let it go. . . . Put any stuck feelings into your mental housecleaning device. . . . Imagine the emotional storm beginning to dissipate leaving behind cleared, fresh, cleansed air. However you imagine this . . . send compassion back into that scene, compassion for yourself, for others. . . . Know that you can heal your past, you can heal your memories. In fact as you give compassion to this episode of your life you are healing your past and you are enriching who you are in the present. Know that this is so.

◆

Acknowledge what you have learned from this chapter of your life. Experience the positive side of this episode of your life. Imagine as

though it were a gift, a gift to your pool of wisdom. . . . Allow
yourself for a moment to appreciate this time in your life . . . what
lesson has it given you? Will you give yourself permission to accept
it? Will you let it settle into who you are?

◆

Now pretend that you are the choreographer. . . . Let yourself
remake this time . . . let the dance be different . . . how you wish it
had been . . . change the quality of energy that transpired. Imagine
how it would have been had you known what you know now. . . .
What would you have believed? What would they have
believed?. . . Imagine saying, doing, what you didn't give yourself
permission for at the time. . . . Imagine how people would have
interacted in this new scene.

◆ ◆ ◆

Now focus on what you learned from this time, how you can now
grow from it, let this time add to your pool of wisdom. . . . Bring
the lesson into yourself, into your whole self, almost as though it
were to become cellular knowledge . . . let it nourish who you are,
gaining strength to move into the future. Take on the gift of the
lesson of this time past. Bring lessons learned into the present so
you can move into the future with greater wisdom . . . and in so
doing know that you can now let go, for you've gained the gift of
the past.

◆

You may want to imagine your past as a golden thread of your life.
Let your past weave a golden robe of wisdom. . . . Immerse yourself
in wisdom . . . transform the weight, the baggage of the past into
this golden robe of wisdom. . . . As you let go of the past, embraced
by the lessons it offers, you move into the future with grace, with
ease, with foresight. . . . Know that this is so.

◆

And as you finish these rituals of letting go of the past, celebrate the lessons you've learned; feel the energy of the past filling up the whole of your mind, feelings, body, your spirit, filling the whole of yourself with strength and openness to create the space to move into the future with grace, feel yourself filled with the gift of the past . . . project this wisdom into the future. . . .

As you do this become aware of what needs to be done in your daily activities to carry this energy, this movement into your life . . . embracing the lessons, letting go of the times, creating new spaces in your life. Let go of the past, creating space in the present to move into the future in new and liberating ways. . . . You may in fact decide to communicate with some of the participants in that episode of your past. . . . What do you need to do to make room for this new way of being in your life?

◆

And imagine yourself doing whatever you need to do to have this occur in your daily activities. Feel yourself living with this new-found wisdom. . . . Notice how it may affect those around you.

◆

Lessons change who you are. . . . You change the future, moving forward in new ways, in grace, ease, with forsight. Acknowledge your past for letting you know what you now know . . . acknowledge change.

Transforming Defeating Messages

Focus your energy now on this moment, right here, right now, your present reality. . . . Realize that your present which you are now focusing on at this moment, this place, right here, right now is your place of power . . . this present reality. . . . Realize that always, always you live in your present reality; your energies are always focused through your present reality, this moment, this place, this present reality, your continuous, inexhaustible present, is your place of power, each present moment giving birth to the next. It is always your present moment where you effect change both inside and outside of yourself. Right now, right here, is the accumulation of all of your past experience focused right now . . . all of your past experience focused right here. . . . Your power is always in the present. . . . Feel the reality of these statements . . . your power is in the present. Take full possession of your power right here, right now, where you can effect change both inside and outside of yourself. . . . You are always responding in your present, responding to the imagery of your consciousness, to the messages from your inner being. . . . You always act out of your inner messages. . . . Now with your consciousness, realize that you can create messages that enable you to act the way you choose . . . creating attitudes within you exactly as you would like them to be . . . creating inner messages that say exactly what you want them to. . . . Know that consciousness is fluid, flexible, amenable to change . . . creating new channels through which to move.

You are now going to work on an attitude . . . an attitude that you have about yourself or the world or both, that's defeating, that's limiting, an attitude that perpetuates a way of being that you know you need no longer carry. . . . Knowing that things can be better than that outdated attitude allows, knowing that you can act in more liberating, free ways, knowing that you can be more open. . . . As you hear the sounds of these words your consciousness is now adjusting itself to exactly that level where you can transform these outdated attitudes; you can change them and create new inner messages enabling you to act in new and emancipated ways in the world . . . enabling you to act the way you choose. . . . Your consciousness is now at a very creative dimension where you can create new realities, where you will create new realities. . . . Pick one particular attitude you need to work on. . . .

Bring into your awareness now the belief that you have chosen to change. . . . Notice how that belief makes you feel . . . makes the world feel. . . . What kind of atmosphere does it thrive on?

◆

As I speak to you now, the sounds of these words are evoking a specific episode from your past that was significant in creating this limiting attitude. You are now becoming aware of a scene of the past that was significant in the formation of this old attitude that you are going to release from your being. . . . Create, remember these times now, notice how you're feeling . . . notice all the details of the scene . . . notice the atmosphere. . . . Now imagine as though this scene and the attitudes it engendered created stiff, armouring clothing. . . . Take off the constricting garb, imagine taking off the belief . . . and put it all through your mental housecleaning device.

◆ ◆ ◆

Let your body, your mind, your feelings and spirit be released from constriction; give yourself permission to be comfortable. . . . Now assure yourself that just because it happened that way before does *not* necessarily mean it will again. You can choose to reroute your consciousness and you can also change the magnetic atmosphere so different kinds of circumstances coalesce. Now, assure yourself that this belief is not reality. That instead it is a way of interpreting reality. Tell yourself that this is a belief about the *past*. . . . Tell yourself that *now* is your point of power. . . . That *now* things are different. . . . This was an idea about reality, not reality itself. . . . The future is to be different. . . . Know that this is so.

◆

Now in whatever manner occurs to you, change the scene you've experienced so that it feels good, so it includes what you *now* know. . . . Put on new clothing, create a comfortable situation that allows you to realize your fullest potential . . . so that it allows everyone in it to realize their fullest potential. Now, in whatever manner occurs to you create an atmosphere that is the opposite of the one you felt earlier which caused the belief. Create the opposite atmosphere, the opposite emotional feelings . . . the opposite thoughts. . . . And let yourself be expanded and opened by these feelings . . . receptive to these feelings. . . . Fill yourself up with the opposite quality. . . . What would have happened had this belief been prevalent?. . . Change it so that you are harmonious with all that's around you, and all that's around you is harmonious with you, free of old limitations.

◆

If any other scenes arise from this old attitude, change them as you changed the first scene. . . . Know that by changing the pictures of the past in your imagination . . . by changing those pictures you change the messages you give yourself, changing the way you relate

to the world. You repossess your power, the power that you know
can be, that you know is yours . . . you take your power in the
present. In replacing constricting imagery in your consciousness
you leave old patterns behind, making space to act in new, open,
and liberating ways. In so doing, you've changed your future.
Consciousness is powerful, flexible and fluid. . . . Now is your point
of power. . . .

   Keep transforming memories, thoughts, feelings of the past . . .
use your mental housecleaning device to make space for the power
of this energy. . . . Project the power of your new belief into the
whole of your past . . . fill up all the holes, the wounds, the gaps
until you find yourself standing fully present on the steady ground
of your new experience, *now*.

◆   ◆   ◆

Your new belief is fully rooted. . . . Now experience this new found
self that you are now. . . . Know that you have changed. . . . How
do you feel about yourself now?. . . Let your imagination move in
the direction that this new belief causes you to go. . . . What new
kinds of things can occur?. . . How will they feel?. . . What will
you do?. . . What will unfold around you?. . . How will it effect
others?. . . The relationship you'll have?. . . What will the world
be like?. . . Let yourself energize probabilities that can occur with
this new belief in place. . . .

   Now, create an image, a symbol representing how you're now
feeling, or use the picture of yourself feeling harmonious as a
symbol of your new way of being. . . . This new image will enable
you to act in new ways that you choose. You have left the old
attitude behind; it is relegated to the past. . . . Feel the liberation,
the wholeness, the harmony, of this new self who you now are. . . .
Know that if ever you find yourself acting in old ways, that you can

bring this symbol into your consciousness and it will give you the messages you need in order to act in the new ways, put you back on the new ground. . . .

Now take time to talk with this symbol, personify it, create it as an independent being. Ask what specific things you can do to bring this new way of being into your life. . . . What symbolic acts could you perform as a gesture in good faith?. . . What experience can you give yourself to strengthen your belief taking root? . . . Sense the answer. . . .

Decide if you're willing to do it; if you're not, notice an alternative. See yourself doing these things . . . how, when, where, you will do them?. . . What support do you have for these changes?

◆ ◆ ◆

Tell yourself that you will recognize impulses that arrive in tune with your new belief. . . . Tell yourself you'll respond to these impulses further rooting this belief.

◆

Ask your symbol to come into awareness spontaneously if ever you slip back into old patterns. . . . Know that this new way of being is soon to become as familiar as the old—in fact more familiar . . . thank your symbol, go over any agreements you've made and acknowledge yourself for making this change, for you've created this energy. Now all you have to do is act on it.

◆ ◆ ◆

Know that your consciousness is energy, energy creating realities, know that you have now changed your consciousness, changing your reality, energy moving in new directions, know that in changing your consciousness your environment will conform to this new way of being, new realities materializing. Know that the symbol will come into your awareness whenever you need it, bringing with it the energy that enables you to act the way you

choose. . . . Know that you have left your past behind and created
the future of your choice, for *now* is your point of power. . . . Know
that this is so.

Purpose, Choice, Habits

Take time now to bring into view whatever you sense, imagine, and
know to be the purpose of your life right now. . . . The important
tasks and goals that you have right now, your commitments. . . .
Feel these greater purposes and goals . . . sense their meaning,
their energy . . . know what they are, the creativity within these
goals . . . experience the quality of this overall purpose. You may
simply feel energy, you may see yourself in different activities—
however you experience this greater purpose. Becoming more
intensely aware of your purpose, the direction of your life, the
changes of your life that are right for you to be in harmony with
the universe, with those around you, with the inner growth of your
being . . . and the practice of your life, with your daily activities.
Experience this energy, this purpose, the refinement of yourself,
the refinement of your will, of your connections to the earth and
everything on it, to the people around you, to your creativity.

◆

Now imagine this greater purpose forming a symbol, something
that represents your greater purpose. Imagine all the energy that
you're experiencing, sensing, knowing, coalescing into a form—this
form having an energy of its own . . . maybe in a picture, maybe
light, maybe a being. Create it now. Know that you can let this
symbol of your purpose illuminate a path for you, enabling you to

act easily on your priorities. Keep this symbol in your awareness. . . . Now focus on the concept of *choice* . . . *choice* . . .
choice. . . . What does choice mean to you?

With this in your awareness, notice what part of you chooses
. . . what's doing the choosing when you are moving in a particular
direction down the path of your life? What's at the steering wheel?
Which parts of you are making the choices in the different aspects
of your life?. . . Take time now to look into your life, your daily
life, your daily routine, all the things that you do . . . all the
aspects of your life . . . your work . . . your relationships . . . taking
care of your body, your habits, your projects, all the different
aspects of your daily routine.

◆

Notice which part of you is doing the choosing. . . . Are your
head, body and heart all involved?. . . Or is one involved and the
others left out?. . .

Notice if any areas of your life are not on the enlightened path
of your purpose.

◆   ◆   ◆

Choose a particular aspect in your life that is off track to work
with. . . . What's doing the choosing in this particular area of your
life?. . . What qualities are prominent?. . . Is there another part
of you that is more suited to be at the steering wheel in this area of
your life? Bring to awareness your symbol of purpose and let it
enlighten you. If there's another part of you that needs to do the
choosing have that part of you talk to the part of yourself that was
doing the choosing before. . . . Be aware of how the new part can
take care of the old, so that the two can cooperate and you can get
back onto the right path. . . . What does the other part of you
need, if it's not going to choose—what will it do instead? What

can you give it to keep it satisfied—occupied?

◆　◆　◆

Now what choices do you want to make in regard to this area of
your life?. . . What do you have to give up?. . . What are you
willing to do?. . . Focus on your purpose symbol experiencing
what it resonates with so you can make a clear choice.

◆　◆　◆

Feel, sense how this commitment that you have made reroutes you,
breaking new ground that is in alignment with your purpose. . . .
What feelings are present as you move forward in this new way?. . .
Notice what new vistas of experience are now available to you. . . .
How will your relations with others change?. . . Make adjustments
if need be.

◆

How are you going to make time and space to honor your choice,
to keep on this path and not get drawn off by other parts of yourself
choosing at the wrong times, disregarding what's your greater
good?. . . You must take care of all parts of yourself. If you neglect
some they will take over at the controls. . . . Take time to see to it
that the right part of you is at the steering wheel in this area of
your life, moving on down the path in the direction that you
want. . . . Notice what gets in the way of this change as you move
on down the road, if anything beckons you off course . . . notice
what needs to be done about it. . . . What danger spots do you
foresee?. . . You may discover old ways of behaving that are simply
habitual, familiar and so more comfortable than the new ways. . . .
If you find this happening you may wish to do mental housecleaning,
to recycle the old ways, making space to act on the new
choices, allowing yourself to stay on the path, to stay on purpose,
to stay in alignment with your choice.

◆　◆　◆

As you experience this new direction notice what supports you to stay on the path. It may be friends, it may be a symbolic act, it may be rewards you can give yourself for staying on the path, to honor yourself, to make the choices that are right for you.

◆

Extend your awareness to include all your life activities now. Keep the symbol of your life purpose with you. Imagine moving into the future of your life; as you move on down the path of your life purpose take time to note what is a comfortable pace for you to move in, so you can be patient and energetic. . . . Having the activity that you need, having the rest that you need. As you choose to move on down the path it may become very clear to you that there are some things that you need to let go of, that there are some things that are simply baggage weighing you down, making your movement cumbersome, awkward. . . . Notice what you might be carrying with you that you need to let go of, or carry differently, so that you can move through your activities more gracefully. . . . Maybe habits, maybe a relationship, a particular activity—what do you need to do so that you can be light footed on your path of life?. . . Are you willing to do it? And if so, imagine doing so now, be aware of what you need to do in your life to carry out this choice.

◆   ◆   ◆

Keep on going down the road until it's very familiar to you, noticing the kinds of experiences that transpire. Noticing how it feels good to be on this road—what bumps come on the road, what turns come on the road, what vistas come into view in this life that you're leading. . . . You may notice particular occurrences that are likely to have happened as you've moved on down the road, that have made it easier to travel this road. Ride on down the road till it's very familiar and easy to be on this particular road, till it's such a part of your life that it becomes nearly instinctive, and you don't need to make choices so conscientiously.

◆

And now, go over any agreements that you have made or need to make to follow through on the choice that you've made, this direction that you're going in. Projecting this path into your life, bringing it out of the meditation and into your life, moving along down this path in your activities. . . . Know that you do have the choice to be able to bring this energy into your life. Choose if you're willing to do that. Go over the agreements with yourself. Know that in imagining it, the energy for change has already been set in motion. . . . Know that it will be very easy for you to bring into your awareness your symbol of your greater purpose, and it will illuminate this path that you've been moving along in this meditation, in bringing this into your awareness, you'll very easily be able to give yourself the internal support that you need to act on your priorities, and make choices that are for the greater good.

Countout

Finish what you're doing and make yourself ready to come out to outer conscious levels by knowing that you'll bring with you all the energies you've contacted, going over the insights, choices and feelings you've had in this meditation. . . . Know that the very fact that you have imagined these things makes them possible . . . makes them probable. . . . You are fully capable of bringing these visions into your life, making the ideal *real*.

◆   ◆   ◆

Knowing you can return to these dimensions whenever you wish. . . . You may want to project when you will again meditate. . . .

In a moment I'm going to count from one to five, at the count of five, you'll open your eyes remembering all that you've experienced . . . feeling refreshed, revitalized and relaxed. . . .

ONE—becoming more aware of the room around you. . . .

TWO—coming up slowly now. . . .

THREE—at the count of five you'll open your eyes feeling relaxed, revitalized, and refreshed remembering all that you've experienced. . . .

FOUR—coming up now, bringing with you your sense of well-being. . . .

FIVE!—eyes open, feeling refreshed, revitalized and relaxed, remembering all that you've experienced, feeling a sense of well-being.

Chapter Nine

How We Are With One Another

"The great majority of murders (88 percent according to one survey quoted in the President's Crime Commission Report) are committed within the family or among acquaintances. The same is true of other crimes of violence: a District of Columbia study showed that two-thirds of rape victims were attacked by boyfriends, members of the family, or other acquaintances ... which prompts the fanciful speculation that one might be safer out alone in the dark city streets than waiting cozily at home for a convivial troop of relatives and neighbors to drop in.[1]"

THE CORROSION OF OUR RELATIONSHIPS

It is clear our connections are fully corroded. Trust is an alien feeling, and alienation itself is now an experience that has become as American as apple pie. Alienation means separation; if we can't count on our personal relationships, what do we have left? How is it that this depressing state of affairs has come about?

We live in a competitive society, relegated to being "out there"

245

all alone, fending for ourselves, trying to survive—to make it. As a result our culture has twisted us to the point that deep down, inside each of us, there inevitably resides a gnawing sensation that tells us, "I am not good enough." So we must constantly prove ourselves in order to justify the life that is already ours. We find ourselves compelled to participate in the exhausting, never-ending treadmill of upward mobility, a rat race that also exhausts the limited resources of the earth at a rate vastly faster than nature's ability to replenish itself, or if we can't seem to get our lives moving anywhere we hate ourselves because we're convinced we're just not smart enough.

We can't trust ourselves; we can't trust each other. No longer is our personal integrity a given. Instead we find ourselves having to buy it on the installment plan, putting much more in than we're getting out. We don't honor our own basic humanity. We trivialize those of another race or sex and we don't respect the integrity of all life, no matter what the form. These attitudes constitute an installment plan for a long slow suicide of the whole human race and a downright murder of the earth.

We've traded in our relationship to each other and to the earth for "plastic substitutes at marked-up prices."[2] The name of the game is to buy and sell, not to enjoy and cherish. The agreement has a built-in obsolescence—it won't work because we still live on the earth and are forced to breathe the smog we ourselves have created. Modern man's attempt to conquer nature is a contradiction in terms, for to conquer nature is to conquer life, and the way to do this is commonly known as suicide. The whole human race, along with all other species, lives in an interdependent environment. We have not succeeded in extricating ourselves from the immutable laws of nature, but we have wreaked havoc on the intricate webwork of mutually supportive relationships that each life-form is a part of—the miracle of life itself.

In the depth of our hearts and souls we each know the truth of what I say, and it is very painful to be in touch with this knowledge. So we avoid our deeper experience and instead find ourselves killing time—perhaps by getting together with friends not because we genuinely want to see them but because we want to avoid being alone. The depth of our loneliness is proportional to the depth of our separation from our own nature, from nature itself and from one

another. We let TV fill the space created by the separation, numb-
ing our pain while it insidiously implants an insatiable appetite for
the ultimately depleting game of consumption. We find ourselves
buying things—*anything* to soothe our alienation. We buy something, feel better for awhile, but alas, the effect wears off and we're
out there again buying something new. The TV keeps the gears of
our society well lubricated. Life used to be the source of replenishment; now money makes the world go round.

Sometimes we consume one another, turning in an old friend for
a new one for the sake of novelty. Or how much of the time do you
find yourself pretending interest—engaging in small talk, the contents of which you don't really care an iota about? How often do
you smile, saying something else under your breath?

We deserve more. Life offers more. We know that avoiding conflict doesn't make it disappear, much less resolve it. We can relax,
getting off the treadmill and then our alienation will catch up with
us, forcing us to face it head-on. If we are to become whole we have
no choice but to heal our alienation. People wouldn't be so bored if
they felt a part of the human condition rather than apart from it. If
people took on social responsibility their lives would quickly fill
with meaning. To restore ourselves and our community, to avail
ourselves of dependable, loving relationships we will have to take a
good long look and re-evaluate the codes we live by—the values
and behavior we have always taken for granted.

We all make up the social fabric of our times; we are as determined by it as it is by us. Nothing exists in isolation; we are not a
bunch of unrelated automatons free to pursue our own destiny in
space, occasionally colliding and bouncing off one another, but we
are continually interacting. On what basis does this occur, that is,
what moral codes are we acting out of? What codes form the
criteria of our choices?

We are prisoners and we will remain so if we take these codes as
immutable facts of life, instead of consciously choosing the values
we want to live by. The first step is to look deeper and become
aware that these old codes are not immutable, but actually
programmed beliefs. Programmed because we had little or no
participation in their creation. All programmed behavior comes
automatically—remember you're acting out of your inner messages.
But just because it comes naturally it does not necessarily follow

that it's right or that we can't change it. It could simply be a bad habit. If we take social codes as facts of life and they are no longer serving us then they become invisible bars that keep us all in prison, so we need to ask if these beliefs are serving society, i.e., meeting fundamental human needs. Defeating social beliefs are to be treated no differently than defeating personal beliefs—they can be discovered and worked with in the same way that is explained in the previous chapter. All ideas go somewhere, the eternal question is are they taking you where you want to go? We are always working out of some policy, whether conscious of it or not. Ask yourself *why* you are responding as you are in any given situation and you will become aware of your values. The question is *who* do they serve in the long run? I think it's quite clear that many of the codes we live by are no longer functional; they don't just need a tune-up; they are long overdue for a complete overhaul.

None of us is lucky enough to have grown up in this culture unscathed. The world around us is mirrored within us so we need to examine those values and attitudes we tend to have which have particularly adverse effects on our relationships.

To me the bottom line is endeavoring to respect the integrity and dignity of *all* life. That means changing the "me-first" attitude most of us have been taught, to the reality of "me-as-a-part-of-it-all." When we belong, we have social responsibilities.

Watch yourself for feelings that tell you you are better than someone else—feelings that all of us constantly have and must change if we are to experience truly cooperative living. Think of it this way: it's absurd to think of tigers as somehow better than, or more deserving than bears, and even sillier to think of one tiger as better than another tiger. They both live on the earth, and we don't question their relative value. If you prefer tulips to daisies does that mean that a tulip is better? Each one of us is a creature that lives on the earth, and it is presumptuous to decide that one is better than another. This competitive thinking is so pervasive we tend not to recognize it when we see it. How often have you been at meetings or in groups where someone gets up (after a particularly impressive statement) saying, "That's a hard act to follow." Anything that is alive *belongs*, by definition. Whenever you feel that you are a better person than someone else, it is simply arrogance.

The same goes for groups—or countries. From the beginning,

America was a place where the settlers had the gall to assume they deserved the land more than the indigenous people whose home it had been for more than a thousand years. It is arrogance that provides the footing for the rationalization for any unjust act. It trivializes and stereotypes every culture and individual that happens to be residing in the path of "progress." The arrogant further bolster their position by believing they are rescuing the "lowly" from their own limitations. Arrogance digs the footholds for all the backclimbing that goes on in our competitive society. Personally, I'd rather walk on solid ground than try to balance precariously on the backs of others. Conversely, it hurts to be walked over—to be treated arrogantly, as though your life were devoid of value.

Arrogant ideas are fully ingrained in each of us: "I'll make it despite the group," or the praise, "he pulled himself up by his own bootstraps!" When someone appears to do this, he doesn't do it as a hermit in a cave. Others gave him a break, or worked for him; he didn't do it alone, but alone he gets the credit. A star wouldn't be a star without the recognition of the group. *Though we feel isolated, we are social beings with a relationship to one another.* If someone is rich it is not because he is inherently better and more deserving, it is because he's usually taking a disproportionate amount of the money for the work he has done. He is in a position to pay himself more while underpaying others. It is because he has stepped on more backs as he clambers up the ladder of success.

The flip side of the coin (me-last) is to have feelings of inferiority. If your back has been used for years to support the splendiferous standard of living of others, you become downtrodden, believing you don't deserve more than you get. Instead you find yourself convinced that it is an honor to be allowed to serve the important ones.

It is no wonder that we are alienated from each other; ideas like these are woven into the very fabric of our belief systems. They render us lonely, isolated individuals suspicious of each other and unable to connect in a meaningful way. It is stressful to be relegated to being alone and always on guard.

No one knows more about your life than you do. (You're the expert on yourself.) If ever you feel someone else is more qualified to know what's best, you've given up your power and insulted your own integrity. You are not using your own ability to decide what *you* feel and think about what the "authority" has to say. In the same way, if you ever put yourself in a position of judging what is best for someone else, feeling your judgment is more qualified than theirs, you have done violence to that person's integrity. You have not honored her ability to choose for herself. This doesn't mean that we can't help each other out. As our lives consist of different expriences some of us know more about one thing while others know more about something else. But we're in it together as social beings, and everyone involved should participate in decisions.

Power dynamics where people are in one-up or one-down positions frequently are very subtle, but to whatever degree one of these is going on we've objectified and dehumanized each other. Never should a person define another. When that happens we've turned in the natural harmony we could be living in for a pecking order.

"Respect authority!"—We've been brought up by coercion—"Don't ask why, just do it!"—institutionalizing objectification and ostracizing all genuine respect.

Saying, "If you don't do this I won't give you any dinner," totally obscures the purpose for the desired action and keeps people in line so that authority can manipulate however it sees fit. How much better to say, "I'd like it if you'd do this because I'm tired." The former creates an atmosphere that fully negates the fact that people are intelligent and able to make their own decisions. This "have to" mentality obstructs choices and each person's social responsibilities, effectively preventing the development of judgment and discrimination. Following the dictates of authority made it possible for Hitler to get as far as he did. In fact, it is *because* we are intelligent that this kind of authority is necessary for the maintenance of a hierarchical society.

If we were to use our heads we would discover that it is not to our own interest to follow instructions blindly. If it were, they wouldn't need to resort to coercive tactics ("Don't ask why, just do it"). How often did we hear that at home or in school—preparing us to accept what we now get at work. People willingly cooperate and "get the job done" when they know it to be in their interest. But because the authorities don't care what people think—nor is it usually in their interest—they use coercive tactics. If everything were *really* in our interest, wouldn't it be easier for them to explain why, so we would become their allies? In which case, they wouldn't have to expend energy in backing up their threats.

Our training is to respect authority, not leadership. Authorities dictate to a bunch of mindless individuals the immutable laws of society (there aren't any). Rather, everything is always changing, so we constantly need to question what is appropriate for any given situation. On the other hand, leadership respects the choice of those being led, and they in turn respect the fact that the leader is more knowledgeable in the area of concern and will be helpful to them. This is a cooperative, not a hierarchical relationship. True leadership thinks *with* people not for people.[3]

FROM COERCION TO COHESION

To keep yourself in check, subjectively observe your feelings when dealing with others: Do you feel smaller or bigger? Do you feel worthy? Or like a klutz? Is the other person perfect and you're sure she's right before she opens her mouth? Are you just trying to prove a point or are you sharing? Are you interested in the other person? Are your intentions warm or cold? Do you feel as if you have anything to offer or that the other has something to give? Are you overwhelmed? Maybe you've made him more important than yourself. Are you impatient? Maybe you're making yourself more important than him. Then ask yourself what is needed so that the integrity of each of you is equally respected, i.e., an awareness that one of you is no more deserving than the other. This does not mean that one of you doesn't know more about something—living in such a commodity-oriented society we tend to confuse knowledge with value—a very basic and common mistake. How often do you feel you aren't as important because you don't know as much about the issue? Notice if your thoughts move toward connection—from "I" to "We"—or toward isolation—"I" at the expense of others, or others at the expense of "me." "I-only" and "you-only" thoughts are inevitably prescriptions for trouble. Asking these questions will point to the times when you need to use mental housecleaning, making space for establishing good connections with others that allow you to respect the differences and to affirm life.

We tend to fall into ways of thinking that make equal relationships very difficult. One of them is categorical thinking which is the same as tunnel vision and does not take into account all the ingredients of the situation. If "progress" took into account what it was wiping out in its development we'd be in a different place today. It is fully understandable that this one-sided thinking comes naturally to us, given our specialized society. It is the extreme of beta thinking to take only one aspect of a relationship into account and use it exclusively to follow a sequential line of logic. We are taught to think in terms of "either/or," not "both/and." We find ourselves thinking, "It's either your fault, or mine," forgetting that both of us play into the situation.

If someone is one-up then necessarily someone else is one-down. It is this very thinking which provides the ground for objectifying one another: "You're a fool!" If you look into your past all kinds of situations will come to mind in which you dealt with conflicts with this kind of thinking. In all likelihood they did not end amiably, nor did either of you learn from the confrontation. But if you think in terms of both then you necessarily have to deal with the dynamics of the relationship. That's where all change comes from.

This one-sided thinking is the cause of the static circular thinking which I discussed in the preceding chapter. It doesn't take into account the other side of the contradiction. Change is constant, coming out of contradiction, therefore you must deal with relationships. It is understandable that you get stuck when you don't attend to the other aspects of the situation. If you're focusing on only one side you become blind to movement and convinced that things can't change. This kind of thinking erroneously assumes that things are the way they are: "That's life."

If you're not always blaming the other person when you have negative feelings, you turn against yourself, thinking the world is fine and it's all your own fault when something goes wrong, saying, "If I weren't so stupid . . ." Feeling this way promotes a kind of dwelling in the past and more circular thinking. It just isolates you further, making it all even worse than it already was, causing you to get more removed from the true source of your problem. No one is ever the sole source of any problem (it takes two to tango). Remember, we are social beings and there are two sides to everything. What we need to do is focus on the dynamics. We don't live in isolation, we only *feel* isolated. Whatever the problem is, there is a reason for it in both you and the people you're relating to;

problems never reside in one or the other place but in both. Blaming yourself as the sole source of a problem feels bad, but equally destructive, although it may superficially feel better, is the idea that it is all "their fault." This victim mentality effectively keeps you powerless—change is beyond your grasp.

It is in the interest of the corporate establishment that we continue to think in either/or terms. It keeps us oblivious to change, so it doesn't occur to us to question the status quo—not upsetting their apple cart. Believing change to be impossible creates a real contradiction between our negative feelings and our belief, because any negative feeling always calls for change as anything that feels bad makes you prefer it to be otherwise. The result of this contradiction is that negative feelings have become taboo; we find ourselves not wanting to express them. The easiest way to deal with that is to become oblivious to them altogether, further perpetuating the myth that things are the way they're supposed to be.

DENIAL OF FEELINGS

Denial of feelings is another essential ingredient for a hierarchical society. It goes part and parcel with dominant/submissive relationships: "It's okay to step on the next guy, he won't feel it anyway," or "If I were smarter I wouldn't have been there to be stepped on; he was just doing his thing." These attitudes take over when feelings have disappeared from the scene, leaving plenty of space for objectification. When one is on the receiving end it makes change seem impossible: "I'm just dumb, they know what's best." When one is on the sending end it makes oppressing others seem okay: "If they were smarter they wouldn't be there." Either way responsibility is avoided.

Anger is the emotion we have the least permission to express. *Anger is life-affirming*, for it's a healthy reaction when your sense of justice has been violated, when you *believe* in your own integrity and it has been stepped on by someone else's presumptuous and patronizing behavior. It's a moving energy, and when we let it move it certainly does upset the status quo, for it moves us toward justice. It is for this reason that it is the emotion most forbidden, as it always calls for change. But most of the time what happens is that because we don't have permission to release it, instead of some positive movement it gets convoluted and we store it, and then it builds up and overflows, suddenly getting dumped in the wrong place. It is stored-up anger that creates inappropriate outbursts and mindless violence. If you feel angry and just say to yourself, "That's life," it doesn't allow for change, so you become resigned, your anger never gets expressed, but it stays inside and gets twisted, turning into depression, cynicism, bitterness, hatred, and hostility. All these emotions carry the implicit message, "Don't care so much." These feelings are insidious because they certainly don't create positive changes (those directed at the original problem), as does anger. In fact, life shrinks from them as they always lead toward isolation, tearing the insides out of both the holder and the beholder.

We must choose positive channels for our anger, transforming it into fuel to energize and direct us to change the source of injustice. Just as illness is a positive signal to keep you on the road to a healthful life (if you are receptive and responsive to its message), so, too, is anger a sign pointing the way and moving you in the direction of harmony and justice. Just as having a tendency to have headaches won't disappear by ignoring them (the message gets louder), anger won't go away by controlling it. You must choose a positive outlet for it. Ask yourself, "What's the injustice?" and then, "What's the opposite?" Give yourself a vision of how things could be, and then move in that direction. The same can be said for all negative feelings. Instead of allowing them to be signposts pointing toward what would make us genuinely feel better, we find ourselves ignoring them, expressing only the positive even if it means fabricating it to fill in the blanks. It's fully ingrained in all of us to respond to the question "How are you?" by saying without a moment's hesitation, "I'm fine," even when feeling absolutely wretched. So we find ourselves continually acting in superficial ways which create hollow relationships. It all adds up to our viewing our own feelings as vague, alien, uncontrollable forces that need careful supervision. We think we have to be objective and leave our feelings out of it (that is if we have any left). This makes it impossible for us to maintain any meaningful relationships, isolating each of us rather than allowing us to connect and help each other change the real sources of our distress. The tragedy is that we've come to the point where we don't even know how to behave when we need each other the most. We find ourselves *wanting* to talk about the weather when we're with a friend who's going through hard times. We find ourselves trying to cheer up our friend not because that's what she needs or wants but because it will make us feel more comfortable around her.

If you have the courage to express your real feelings you will discover what a relief it is to break through the barriers of communication because you will receive some real human understanding when you feel bad.

We all want better relationships. We need no longer tolerate shallow or unpleasant ones. As everything changes, so can your relationships; this means that you, your family, and your friends can change. We can move out of our isolation and into close connection if we learn viable ways to relate. Now our differences separate us instead of enriching our lives.

BRINGING CLARITY INTO COMMUNICATION

We need to learn how to communicate with one another with respect, honesty, and clarity. Here too we are taught the opposite, but behaving one way toward someone and thinking another way is neither clear nor respectful. Any good relationship is dependent on clear communication which always moves us forward toward connection. You need to know what you are thinking and feeling about other people and what you want from them, but just as important, you need to know how to express yourself simply. Respect also means knowing how to provide ample room for people to choose how to respond to you.

It's gotten to the point that we don't know what direct communication is, much less how to do it, but we're great at bribing, threatening, punishing, and guilt-tripping. We don't simply manipulate one another, we *think* in manipulative terms. As it pervades our subjective environment, the first thing we need to do is untangle our minds so we can begin to communicate directly. This means cleaning up the way we think so we don't find ourselves saying things like, "Wouldn't you like to go for a walk?" A question like that doesn't provide room for the other person to think for herself. Instead it manipulates her by indirectly telling her what to decide. Leading questions are commonplace and contain two elements that are the principle sources of communication problems: negatively expressed questions, and "You" statements rather than "I" statements. This is how we objectify one another, avoiding responsibility for where each of us is at. This perpetuates the isolating, one-up/one-down relations and makes respectful, equal connections almost impossible. So, "Wouldn't you like to go for a walk?" should be translated into "I would like for us to go for a walk, what would you like to do?" Notice how this way you are taking a clear position and at the same time allowing the other person plenty of room for her own process.

So first we need to try to stop objectifying one another ("You" statements) and take responsibility for where we individually stand ("I" statements). Try to catch yourself whenever you're drawing a conclusion about who or what someone is. When you find yourself doing that, backtrack a few steps and move your attention from the other person back into yourself to discover how you got there. Ask yourself what actually happened and what you felt and thought about it that made you draw that conclusion. Then ask yourself what you want.

I have chosen a very simple one dimensional situation as an example because it makes it easier to see the dynamics of communication at work. If you find yourself thinking, "Joe is a selfish person," that is objectifying him. If you stop and reflect you'll remember that he often doesn't wash his dishes, which makes you feel angry, since you use the same dishes and have to wash them before you can cook. So you figure he isn't thinking of you because if he were he'd have washed them. Now that you've discovered why you decided Joe is selfish, ask yourself what you'd like from him. Obviously you'd like him to wash his dishes as soon as he's finished eating. If you never communicate your process, you will keep having to deal with dirty dishes and feel increasingly angry with Joe, something I'm sure he wouldn't want. Now if you simply tell Joe to stop being selfish you'll add to your troubles. Joe will get defensive. So, knowing your own process, you can say, "Joe, when you leave dirty dishes in the sink it makes me feel angry because I don't think you've taken into account that I use the same dishes and when I want to cook I first have to clean up after you. So would you please wash them as soon as you're finished eating?" This he can respond to relatively easily, and the chances are you'll end up with a clean kitchen instead of a lost friend. All this may seem cumbersome, but I assure you that by keeping to "I" statements as well as communicating your full process, you'll avoid unnecessary interpersonal conflict. Though it appears troublesome you'll no longer find yourself in *real* trouble.

Basically, clear communication means keeping your *center inside yourself.* When you objectify Joe ("he's selfish") the focus of attention is on him. I'm not saying you can't make judgments; I am saying you need to present them for what they are and refrain from presenting them as facts—Joe is not selfish, that's *your* evaluation of him. The only fact here is that Joe leaves dirty dishes which you also use. *Facts are always observable actions.* Evaluations are always conclusions drawn from actual occurrences. Whenever you say something about somebody, if it's not describing an action, you can count on it being an evaluation. Watch out, be sure you keep your center in yourself.

It's also common to express our judgments as if they were feelings—"I feel you're selfish." This is not better than presenting judgments as facts. Judgments are judgments. If you keep yourself in your center you'll discover the basic emotion going on inside of you—in this case, anger. Thoughts in the guise of feelings obscure where you're really coming from. Just as we have to separate our judgments from actions, we must separate our feelings from thoughts. You don't "feel" Joe is selfish, you *think* he is. You *feel* angry. Clear communiction must include expressing what our basic feelings are. When we put out our *real* feelings we'll be expressing our vulnerability, no longer able to objectify each other. Our relationships will quickly move from being hollow to being full of substance. We'll come to know one another in a *real* way. We will regain our humanity.

Asking for what you want is another taboo; instead the person is supposed to guess what it is. We all have wants, and there is no reason to hide them. If you express your desires directly you infinitely increase the likelihood of having them met, and you won't expend all your energy trying to figure out where the other person's coming from. So when you find yourself asking leading questions, dropping hints, or making negative assessments, backtrack and reflect; ask yourself what you want and why. Express that, take a stand, own where you are, keep your center in yourself. If we all do this we'll know where each other are, and we won't have to beat around the bush all the time or search for others in the bushes to discover where they stand. Instead we can use our energy in genuine communication.

Communicating with your friends is like communicating with your innerconsciousness. They'll be more responsive when you state what you want in positive terms—"I'd like you to wash your dishes," rather than "Stop leaving dirty dishes." They'll have a positive vision to move toward rather than banging their heads against an injunction.

Positive relationships are dependent on clear communication. Clear communication is dependent on your knowing and expressing the observable acts, your own feelings, your evaluation, and then exactly what you want. And similarly you'll help others communicate with you by asking questions to elicit this information from *their* experience. In doing this be careful not to ask leading questions; your intention is not to push your perspective, but instead to help them discover their own, so that you can interact on an equal basis.[4]

Clear communication will quickly lift the fog and reveal where everyone stands. You'll come to know when your differences stem from simple misunderstanding and when they are *real* differences that need to be addressed. This is where politics enters the scene.

If we only pay attention to our consciousness and immediate relationships then the battle will be never-ending, for the root source of our problems lies in the institutions that dictate our lives in dehumanizing ways. The very institutions that have wreaked havoc on our relationships are now leading the whole of the planet into disaster.

"It is often more comfortable to avoid the truth. However, it is well known that the condition of the world is in dire need of change. It is my deepest belief that it is absolutely necessary for us to heal our alienation . . . to become whole people—no longer fragmented—living in supportive communities enabling us to work creatively together to put the world into some kind of liveable order."

Now that we know how to repossess our inner selves, now that we know how to heal our relationships, the challenge is before us to heal our planet—we have the power to do so " . . . by moving our reawakened insides out."

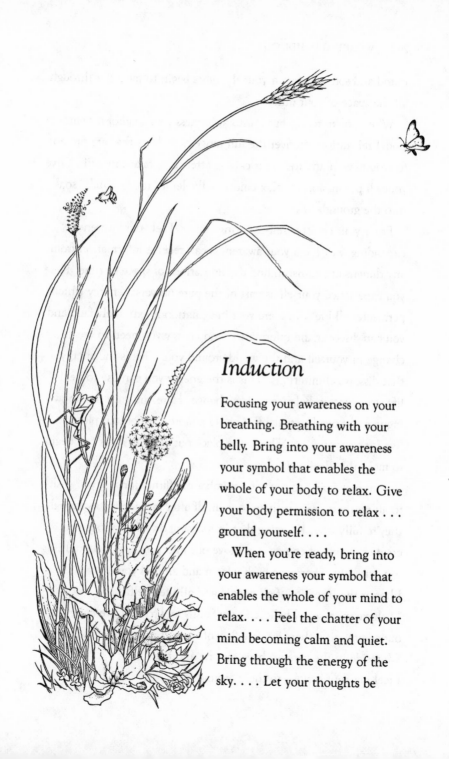

Induction

Focusing your awareness on your
breathing. Breathing with your
belly. Bring into your awareness
your symbol that enables the
whole of your body to relax. Give
your body permission to relax . . .
ground yourself. . . .

When you're ready, bring into
your awareness your symbol that
enables the whole of your mind to
relax. . . . Feel the chatter of your
mind becoming calm and quiet.
Bring through the energy of the
sky. . . . Let your thoughts be

round and soft . . . watch your thoughts begin to meander through all the space of your mind. . . .

When you're ready, bring into awareness your symbol for emotional relaxation, go over the full range of feelings that are present for you now. If any feeling is calling attention, take care of it. Give yourself permission to relax emotionally, let all the "shoulds" soak into the ground. . . .

Enter your creative self-restoring center. Feel your awareness expanding. . . . Here your awareness can receive information from any dimension, transcending the limitations of space or time. Here you experience yourself as part of the pure universal energy which permeates all life. . . . Here your imagination is extremely fluid and you can discover the information and energy you need to create change in yourself and the world around you. This is the energy that dissolves limitations. This is the energy you can use to heal life, to maintain balance amidst change. Here you gain the knowingness you need to make this world a more harmonious place to live for everyone. . . . This is the place out of which you can begin to make the ideal *real*. . . .

I am now going to suggest a number of affirmations. If you wish to affirm them, repeat them to yourself after me, feeling as though they're fully true. Knowing that in focusing on affirmations you create patterns of energy that move out into your life, materializing in your daily experience both within and around you. . . .
I honor the integrity of all people and all life itself. . . .
I believe in myself, I believe in my family and friends, we believe in our community; there is a free flow of support among everyone. . . .
We reside in the care we have for one another. . . .
I feel my connections to those around me. . . .

I am a cooperative person. . . .

There is an abundance of love in my life. . . .

I communicate clearly and comfortably. . . .

I am honest with myself and others. . . .

I take time to tune into myself and others, responding to all situations with clarity. . . .

I am sensitive to the needs of others. . . .

I take responsibility for my side of everything. . . .

I am assertive and respectful. . . .

My negative feelings guide me to changing their sources. . . .

I express all my feelings in constructive ways. . . .

My increasing personal power is for making this world a more harmonious place to live for everyone. . . .

I maintain balance amidst change. . . .

I trust the future. . . .

Know that in focusing on affirmations you have created patterns of energy that will manifest in your life both within and around you. You will find yourself acting in accord with the affirmations. . . .

Now imagine yourself being in a place, a mountainous place, a meadow in the mountains with a lake in the center of the meadow. Imagine being by a mountain lake in a very peaceful meadow. You can see the sky reflected in the lake, the trees, the mountains reflected in this lake. A very peaceful crystal clear mountain lake. . . .

Creating the scenery around you . . . experiencing it, sights, sounds, colors, smells, textures, the atmosphere . . . the silence, the movement, the freshness of this place, all the plants that grow here, the animals and insects that live here—all a part of this place

. . . aware of the water, the mountains around you, as though the meadow were cradling you. And you can see the lake is so still and so quiet, and crystal clear. . . .

You can look down into the lake and see the bottom of the lake. . . . This is a very magical lake, you can use it to help yourself be peaceful, to clear yourself and to refresh your life. Now the first thing you can do with this mountain lake is to gather up all of those things that have been going on in your day-to-day activities— that make you spin your wheels. . . . Imagine throwing all those things into the water and then the lake will transform them, they will all disappear into the lake to be transformed. . . . All the different things that stress you out and make you spin, keep throwing them into the lake. . . .

Symbolize them and throw them into the lake. Responsibilities that you have . . . feelings that you have . . . relations with friends, family . . . things that you have done . . . things that you haven't yet done . . . throw it all into the lake to be cleansed, transformed, and each time you throw something into the lake, you'll find yourself feeling lighter and becoming more and more present. . . . You can watch them—watch the splatter as they hit the surface of the water . . . watch the ripples of the water rolling out over the surface of the lake . . . watch all that you throw in dissolve and disappear into the depths of the lake.

◆

After there is no more to throw in, watch the surface slowly come to a very quiet state once again. Know that as the lake becomes calm, at the same time, the whole of your inner dimension becomes calm and quiet and as clear as the water of the mountain lake. . . . You'll be able to see into the depths of yourself, of beingness itself, as clearly as you're able to see into the depths of the lake. Let this calming process occur.

◆

In tune with the clarity and peacefulness of this mountain lake, imagine the same quality of peacefulness and receptive reflection residing inside of you . . . so peaceful you reflect clearly. Feel that peace within you. . . . Know that as you feel this peace within you, you're able to be fully receptive and perceive clearly whatever is going on around you. Just as the mountain lake reflects clearly, you can listen, see clearly . . . a very accurate reflection of what's going on around you is created in your consciousness. Notice the quality within yourself as you are able to listen receptively, and your reflections are clear and acute, true reflections.

When you're able to be quiet in yourself, quiet as a mountain lake, you can be aware of the needs of those around you . . . of the needs of the environment around you . . . you can hear them . . . and be aware of your own needs.

Integrity of Life

This mountain meadow is a very quiet and peaceful place yet full of life, thriving, teeming with life . . . the meadow is full of life, the lake is full of life, even the air is full of life. . . . Imagine all the life in this place, the pulse of life, all the different plants and animals. . . . All the different kinds of life forming a webwork of relationships, all relating to one another. Feel the quality of energy that vibrates out of the different forms of life here, each unique, each with an integrity of their own, each life, each being distinct in and of itself, yet part of the whole.

◆

Now, draw your focus into yourself. Let your awareness move deeper and deeper inside yourself. Become aware of the quality of energy that emanates from your center, the very essence of who you are, the tone of your personality whatever that means to you, just as other people seem to have a tone, imagine yours . . . be very receptive and listen to the tone of your being. The essence of who it is that you are, however you imagine that, listen. Feel, be aware, sense, see, experience the essence of your being . . . your character. . . . It may be color, it may be sound, it may be qualities, vibrations, whatever you imagine it to be. . . . Experience the very essence of your being. The center out of which all your life force energies spring.

◆

Experience the integrity of this quality. Acknowledge the dignity of your being, just as every form of life has an integrity of its own, so too, your being has an integrity of its own. Honor your integrity, appreciate yourself, believe in who you are. Love yourself as you love life itself. . . . Know that the person you are is fully complete, whole, you are enough being who you are. You are so uniquely who you are, the tone of your being is so *you* that it can't be compared with anything else. To compare it is fully irrelevant, it simply is what it is. Acknowledge the dignity of your own unique way of expressing life in the world. Not another form, not another person, nothing expresses life as you do. Just as a flower does not question its self-worth, you need not either. You simply are, only you have this particular tone, this particular quality . . . only you express life in this way. Feel the integrity of your energy. . . . Feel

the integrity of life being expressed through you, as you give it
form, as you give it shape in your own characteristic way. Honor
yourself.

◆   ◆   ◆

Trust yourself, knowing that you are a complete, full being, you are
enough. . . . Nurture yourself with this sense of fullness. Let this
sense of fullness—your full essence—form waves and roll through
your whole being, returning you to yourself.

◆

Let it roll through all those areas in your life where you felt you
were not good enough, where you felt inadequate. . . . Fill up
those areas, letting yourself feel whole. Let the waves of your
essence roll through you however you imagine that, let them fill
any holes within you, and fill any holes in your life, returning you
to your sense of wholeness.

◆   ◆   ◆

Now extend your awareness to include the other people in your
life. Focus in on one person at a time and be aware that they, too,
have a tone to themselves that is uniquely theirs. . . . Each person
has a quality that is uniquely theirs just as you do. Life is being
expressed through them in their own way. . . . Each person has
integrity of their own. Each person is different. To compare one
tone to another is fully irrelevant, like comparing one particular
musical note to another. Some you may like better than another,
but nonetheless each has integrity. . . . Acknowledge the integrity
of all the different people in your life.

◆   ◆   ◆

Now extend your awareness to include all the different life forms.
All the diversity in life on the earth . . . each form of life has an
integrity of its own. Each entity by the very fact that it's *alive* has
an integrity of its own . . . giving shape to the life flowing through

it, giving shape to life itself. The very fact that it's alive means it deserves respect, it deserves its place in the world, it has a space in the world. Know that just as each form of life, each entity invites respect by the very fact that it *is*, so too do you. Acknowledge your integrity. You needn't question your value, the very fact that you are alive gives you value . . . .

Bathe in the knowingness that your life deserves the space that you have on the earth. By affirming your integrity, you affirm the integrity of all life, of each form of life, of each entity alive . . . as you deserve the space you occupy, your life deserves to be respected for the integrity of life itself. Let yourself fully *occupy* the space that is yours. . . . Don't occupy more space than is yours, crowding others, but don't shrink from the space that is yours either. . . . Protect yourself from manipulation and let yourself fully occupy your life, in this time in this place, honoring the integrity of who are you. . . . And as you honor the integrity of your life, honor your intelligence, let yourself be confident of your life, taking up the space that is yours, expressing yourself clearly and fully. Know that the integrity of your life in and of itself is justification for the expression for who you are. You needn't be a particular way, your life justifies your expression. Your life *is* expression. . . . Residing in the dignity of who you are, you defy manipulation. As you honor life itself, you honor the integrity of your life, of all life, of life itself. . . . Feel yourself doing this as you move through the activities of your life filling up the space that's yours and expressing life through your own unique tone and quality, different than everything that has ever been or shall be, your life has integrity of its own. . . .

Just as the sun radiates out light, heat, warmth, let your center radiate who it is that you are, creating your space in the world, unique for yourself to fill, the space that only you can fill.

◆　◆　◆

Know that there is a space for everyone to fill, for everyone has a unique quality. Honor the integrity of all those with whom you come in contact . . . each person, each form of life. And so the real creativity of life continues. Feel yourself, see yourself moving through your activities with respect for others, fully respecting yourself as you respect others. Manipulation ceases to exist in this atmosphere for no one is ever more important, nor less important than another . . . integrity has no value, it simply is. Bathe yourself in this knowingness. . . . Nurture yourself with this knowingness.

Equalizing and Enriching Relations

Residing in your reflective, receptive power. Feel your power, feel your openness. Let yourself be open and powerful at the same time. . . . Breathing in power, and as you exhale, feel yourself opening up. . . .

From this place of receptivity, of reflection I now want you to imagine being in a room with lots of people, some kind of gathering, meeting or event, with lots and lots of people present.

◆

Now be aware of the people who are in this room, and whatever seems to be missing in terms of the elements of humanity, then bring in the people who are part of the missing elements. . . . Let the people in the room be as diverse as all of humanity . . . all different ages, all different races, different cultures. Let the room be full, enriched with the vibrance and diversity of humanity. Different cultures, different sexes, different sexual orientations, different classes. . . . Now imagine beginning to interact with everybody.

◆   ◆   ◆

Notice as you relate to different people, those in the room and those in your life, when you feel better than others, more important than others . . . maybe because you know more, or because you feel more capable . . . or because you have more money or power . . . or friends and connections . . . for whatever reason . . . because you're bigger or prettier or younger or older . . . for whatever reason. . . . Notice when in your life or when in relation to the people in this imaginary room you feel better than others.

◆   ◆   ◆

Notice when you don't feel as good as some people . . . if you think they are better than you are, because they may have more . . . know more . . . have more connections . . . are prettier . . . friendlier . . . whatever it may be . . . notice these feelings in your awareness.

◆   ◆   ◆

Now, notice who feels better than you. . . . Is someone not taking you seriously?. . . Does anyone belittle you, trivialize you?

◆

Notice if any people admire you at the expense of their own self-respect, taking you more seriously than themselves.

◆

Now symbolically put all of this competitive energy into your mental housecleaning device, or let it soak into the ground . . . and bring into your awareness the qualities of dignity and integrity. . . . Notice how, with the presence of dignity and integrity, everyone is equal to everyone else, there is no one better than

another . . . people simply are. . . . Infuse all the situations you've
become aware of with respect; the value of life percolates through
everyone. . . . Go over each of the relations you discovered earlier
in which you felt you were one-up or one-down and change your
feeling to one of mutual support and respect. . . . Notice which
attitudes you need to change.

◆

Feel yourself able to respect your own integrity, being of equal
value to all of those around you, believing in your own experience
and able to respect others' integrity . . . believing in their experience, knowing they are equal to yourself. . . . No one has to prove
anything. Everyone has something to offer. . . . We are all intelligent, feeling, spiritual beings. . . . Infuse all of your relationships
with the quality of integrity, of mutual respect, of common dignity.

◆   ◆   ◆

When this is here you create a basis of trust, moving from separateness to connection. Feel trust. . . . Create an atmosphere in which
hearing is as important as expressing. Feel how this creates a basis
of trust. . . .

We can appreciate what we have to offer to those around us and
what they have to offer us . . . having relationships of equality and
cooperation . . . relationships that help us move through our
activities . . . relationships that enable us to tap our creativity . . .
relationships that enable us to experience very deep levels of
ourselves, of each other. . . . Very intimate relationships that
inspire our creativity, inspire our experience of life itself.

◆   ◆   ◆

Now, imagine the sun shining down upon us, shining within us,
the vibrance of the sun, the radiance of the sun. As though there
was a tiny sun inside each of us, radiating out, warming ourselves
and those around us, feel that soft, warm place within you . . . the

place that smiles at the warm spots inside others. And from that center of radiance imagine residing in that quiet, warm, soft center. Smiling inside your glowing center. As you reside in your center, you can open your center and allow yourself to connect with others with warmth, moving below the surface and sharing your core . . . having the courage to reveal yourself. Everyone connecting to warmth, sharing our hearts, our souls, our knowingness . . . expressing what is felt. . . . Imagining yourself in different life situations, sensing what you need to do in order to come from your center, to be real . . . to be vulnerable, powerfully vulnerable.

◆ ◆ ◆

When you come from your center, feel yourself easily connecting to others, sinking into realness, richness . . . our connections vivid, rich and real. Each inspiring warmth in the other . . . expressing appreciation of one another. . . . Acknowledging the richness, the value, the integrity of yourself and each person who you connect with . . . the depth of our humanity.

◆ ◆ ◆

Feel life expand as the meaning of human connection penetrates through your life. Life is enriched with meaning, with love . . . we care for one another, feel the care we share. . . . When we care, we take care of one another . . . sharing our good times and our hard times . . . we work and play together. The emotional climate of our lives is rich. . . . Notice how in this climate our commitments are born. . . . It is when we connect that we feel mutual responsibility. Let yourself appreciate your community, its diversity . . . let yourself receive the support of those around you and share your own commitment, giving them support.

◆

Now, be aware of how you can move forward with this collectivity, what ways you can join in, and what ways collectively we can move forward, spreading the sense of trust, and overcoming and dissolving whatever stands in the way of it. . . .

Become aware of anything you may need to communicate to particular people in your life so that you can enrich each other's lives with mutual respect and support.

Choice Patterns

Bring to mind your life of late . . . the situations at home, with your family, with friends, what's been happening at work, what's happening in your community . . . let the whole of your life be present with you now, as you reside in this peaceful reflective space . . . let your life parade through your awareness.

◆   ◆   ◆

Now, remember decisions you have made at home . . . with friends . . . at work and in the community . . . choices you've made about what to do . . . or not do . . . or things to change . . . or let be . . . choices on how you spend your time . . . what you share with others . . . what you don't share. . . . Bring to awareness different choices you've made in the arenas of your life . . . simply be aware of them.

◆   ◆   ◆

With each of the choices you've brought to mind, with each one now, ask yourself how you came to choose the particular course you did . . . why you did what you did. . . .

Without judgment, notice what you believe in each of the different scenes. . . . What policy were you operating out of? What were your intentions?

◆

Were you sensitive to the needs of others? Did you remember your own needs? Did you include others in your process?. . . Did you move into connection or isolation?. . . Reflect on these questions as you review the choices you have made.

◆   ◆   ◆

Notice all that makes up the basis of your choices. . . . What quality of energy is present?. . . open or shut down?. . . hot or cold? . . . trusting or anxious?. . . connected or alienated?. . . Which aspect of yourself makes the different choices?

◆

Now look at the choices other people in your life make. . . . How come they do as they do?. . . Notice the patterns. . . . Is there anything that regularly gets disregarded?. . . Anything that is always taken into account?. . . What kind of social fabric do all of you weave together?

◆   ◆   ◆

Is it strong, supportive?. . . Is it brittle or soft?. . . Is it cohesive or moving every which way?. . . Are there frayed edges?. . . Can you count on each other?. . . Are some areas weak or rotting while others may be reliable and durable?. . . What kind of ties do you share? What bonds you?. . . Reflect on the social fabric of your home life, and your community life and the life of your workplace.

◆   ◆   ◆

Ask yourself how it could be better . . . more cooperative . . . energy flowing easily? Now make any adjustments or repairs that might be needed to create strong, nurturing fabric that supports everybody's needs. Everyone supported, yet doing their part in keeping the fabric from tearing, doing their part to help keep it all together . . . everyone being able to count on one another. . . . Make the basis of your choices be loyal yet open and flexible. . . . Imagine creating an atmosphere so everybody can be both reliable and open.

◆   ◆   ◆

Notice how you will act on what you have become in tune with. . . . Notice if there is anything you need to communicate with someone in particular. . . . Decide what you are willing to do.

♦

Tell yourself upon what basis you'll make various choices in the future.

Crystal Clear Communication

Know that this reflective mountain lake is like a crystal ball—you can watch whole scenarios unfold within it. The lake reflects whatever you like, you can observe scenarios unfold before you, and they will become crystal clear. Just as water reveals the true colors of a stone you can now discover the true color of any relationship. Now choose one particular relationship you would like to work on, a relationship that is troubling you, that bothers you, something that is going on between you and another person that concerns you. . . .

Replay particularly significant scenes that took place between you . . . let the lake reflect them back to you . . . just watch the interactions replay before you, do not become involved in them, simply watch them as though you were watching a movie of somebody else's drama. . . . Notice the atmosphere between you, all the details of the scene, as though you have control of the film and you can rewind it. Go back and freeze the frames in which the particular things that happened bothered you. Just make note of those things . . . exactly what took place that bothered you.

♦

Once you've watched them fully, notice what feeling surfaced in you, just notice the feeling . . . the energy present in you, just notice the feeling—open, closed, fearful, angry—the basic raw emotion. . . . Now ask yourself why you feel that way. What is it that you believe about the situation that makes you feel that way?. . . What is it that you think in general that makes you feel that way?. . . How are you making the situation worse?. . . Knowing all this, residing in your knowingness of what happened . . . how you felt .. and what you think . . . now imagine what you want in order to feel better? What would you like to have occur?

♦   ♦   ♦

Imagine putting aside your experience for a moment; put it all on an imaginary mental shelf for the time being.

Clear yourself, recenter yourself . . . so you can see the depths of the lake clearly—crystal clear. . . . Again focus on the magic of the reflective lake and let it reflect what you imagine to be the perspective of the other person in the interaction. . . . Rerun these same scenes and watch the interaction from the other person's point of view, whatever you imagine that to be, and guess what happened that bothered the other person. . . . Put yourself in the other person's shoes, watch the scenes through his/her eyes. . . . Just play it back and notice the frames that bothered the other person, experience it all from his/her perspective. Notice the other's feeling, the quality of emotion, the raw feeling present in response to these occurrences. What basic feeling is present? And what idea did this person have that brought the feeling about? What thoughts, interpretations, does the person make to bring this feeling about? Guess.

♦   ♦   ♦

What is going on inside your friend that makes it all that much worse?. . . Knowing all this, imagine what the person would like in order to feel better.

◆

Now clear the scene, clear yourself, putting the information about this person's response to the events on an imaginary mental shelf. . . . Clear yourself by looking to the bottom of the lake, crystal clear lake . . . see the bottom of it. Now imagine each of you replaying the scene with a very clear awareness of each other. Being very clear how each of you played into the problems, how each of you would be different . . . how you would communicate differently, how you would listen, how you would respond, knowing what you know now. Watch it all unfold.

◆

If you hit a snare in communication keep centered and imagine what the other person feels, and what you can do to enable the person to understand how you're feeling. Just watch it all unfold.

◆

When you see it unfold in a way that feels good to each of you, imagine entering into the scene, imagine you being the person you've been watching yourself be. . . . Fill the scene with respectful clear communication. . . . See how it feels to be in it, to experience it, when you're able to keep communication open and respect each other. Cooperating, each of you having room for your choices and respecting the other. See if compromises need to be made. How does it unfold? Feel what it's like.

◆

Notice what you need to do to bring this vision into the interactions with your friend in your everyday life. Take note of what you need to remember, to communicate and act on to carry this harmony out into your relationship.

Anger Yields Justice

In this peaceful reflective space become aware of whatever you sense to be your own greater purpose, if you have a symbol for this bring it to mind. Reflect on your sense of purpose, maybe specific activities, it may be living out a sense of yourself, an exploration of life itself. . . . Sense the greater purpose of your life now. . . . Your purpose may change from time to time. Be aware of your purpose in this particular chapter of your life. . . .

Take the quality of this purpose, this sense of yourself, of your life, of your dignity, take it into your activities and see the little things that you do, day in, day out enlarged by your purpose. . . . Feel yourself, continue to be in accord with your purpose as you move through your activities, day in, day out.

◆   ◆   ◆

Imagine you have an umbilical cord continually attached to your greater purpose as you move through the affairs of your life from moment to moment . . . day to day . . . situation to situation . . . continually aware of the greater purpose of your life, life itself. Make the cord that attaches you to your purpose very flexible, so that energy can freely flow from your greater purpose into your situation wherever you are, whatever you're doing, whatever is going on around you.

◆

Notice when you, your sense of purpose, your dignity, your integrity is violated, whether you personally, or your deep sense of the integrity of life itself, of social justice is violated . . . be aware of the different situations in life that cause you to feel violated, to feel angry, to feel rage.

◆

When you find yourself angry be sure you keep the cord to your greater purpose clear and open, energy moving back and forth between you and your purpose, continually resourcing each other as your purpose grows, as you become stronger.

◆

Pick one particular situation in which you're angry . . . feel if the anger creates any knots inside . . . let them loosen up . . . drain the hardened energy into the ground . . . let yourself be flexible and strong instead.

◆

Let the anger fuel your convictions, opening the cord to your greater purpose, giving you strength. . . . Notice the opposite of the injustice and imagine how your angry energy can fuel its creation. Give yourself a vision to strive for. . . . Notice what the anger wants you to do. . . . Decide if you want to do that with your anger . . . or if you want to take it elsewhere. . . . Scan your life and notice where you can take this anger. Scan the community, notice where you can take this anger, and let it work *for* you . . . *for* the community. . . . Create a positive channel for it to move out . . . to bring justice about.

◆ ◆ ◆

Reflect on what within you exacerbated the situation. What was your side?. . . Were you keeping your power? What were you doing that made this possible? Let the whole situation teach you.

◆

Transform your own energy . . . moving yourself into a new context of circumstances. . . . Let yourself be both assertive and respectful. Ask for what you want and leave room for others to choose. . . . Honor your purpose, the purpose of life itself.

◆

Now you can explore your greater purpose in other situations where negative feelings are present. . . . Scan your life and notice where you may harbor anger, or bitterness, or cynicism . . . or hostility . . . or hatred or depression. . . . Choose any situations, feelings you would like to work on, working in one area at a time.

◆

Bring your sense of greater purpose to awareness and imagine attaching the cord of your purpose to the negative feeling. Let your purposeful energy transform it into lessons, wisdom. . . . Give yourself a vision to strive for.

◆

Notice what needs to change within you so you can express your feelings creatively, furthering your purpose, furthering the purpose of life itself. Expressing what is so for you . . . let yourself ask for what you want. . . . Exploring what needs to change both within and around you.

◆ ◆ ◆

Finishing what you are doing . . . reviewing all that you discovered in this meditation. . . . Noticing what you need to do to act on your discoveries. Imagining doing what you choose. . . . Always in tune with your greater purpose in all the different circumstances in your life. . . . All your feelings being creative forces in your life.

Family: Past and Future

You are now at a very receptive, reflective place where you can receive insights and create realities that are in accord with the greater rhythms of life. With this sense of quiet, take time now to recreate your childhood home. Remember where you grew up . . .

and bring your family into the scene, exploring your childhood family . . . re-experience your relationships with your family, parents, siblings, extended family . . . watching yourself interact in your family, separating a part of yourself and watching the interactions between you and your family.

◆　◆　◆

Take time to explore each of the relationships that you had, just watch them, and as you watch them from this perspective, you can see your own perspective and you can also see the perspective of each of the members of your family. . . . How they experience the family, your family. What bonds you? What binds you? Take time to simply explore this.

◆　◆　◆

After you explore, work with it, to bring it into greater harmony, wherever changes may be needed—as though it happened differently . . . imagine the patterns of the family unfolding in such a way that everyone's needs are met, everyone is cared for, everyone is respected, everyone shares, everyone is responsible. . . . Imagine this occurring, imagine patterns being set up that are nurturing and freeing at the same time.

◆　◆　◆

Notice what you need to do to feel good about your family; maybe you need to communicate something in particular. . . . When you discover what you need to do, imagine doing what you're willing to.

◆　◆　◆

You may wish to create a symbol of this loving supportive family which you have now experienced. Know that you can use this symbol whenever you are with your childhood family to help you bring these energies into the scene. The fact that you can imagine it makes it possible. . . . When you are ready, acknowledge your

mutual love and say goodbye to your childhood family . . . let
them leave the scene.

◆   ◆   ◆

If you have a new family, bring this family in, if not, you may wish
to create an imaginary family. . . . Explore the patterns of interaction—what bonds you . . . what binds you . . . notice the quality
of sharing . . . notice if there are any residual patterns left over
from childhood that are no longer appropriate. . . . Now notice
how it is to be an adult with children this time around.

◆   ◆   ◆

Take time to create the quality family you'd like to have now and in
the future. Work with your current family, and if you have no
family now, create one from your community, with people you
know or maybe with people you would like to know. Feel family in
your life now . . . the sharing of support, love, laughter. . . .
Imagine everyone being able to express both negative and positive
feelings in this atmosphere of support. . . . Experience how your
family lives . . . how they connect, with you, with each other,
where you're intimate, what ways you share support, what struggles
you share, good times, bad times . . . your commitment to one
other . . . the community your family is within. . . . Notice what
the others are doing, notice all of you affecting each other. Notice
each of your perspectives. . . . Notice your responsibilities to each
other. . . . Notice how you enjoy and play with one another,
festivities you share.

◆   ◆   ◆

As you experience this new family, notice what needs to be done
to bring this energy into your life, notice if there is anything that
needs to be communicated. . . . Imagine yourself doing whatever
you're willing to do, to bring this quality of family into your
life. . . .

Acknowledge yourself and each of the members of your family; thank your family members for all these energies you've connected with, acknowledging all of you for the support and love you share.

Countout

Finishing what you are doing, make yourself ready to come out to outer conscious levels.

◆

Acknowledge the fact that the very process of your being able to imagine all that you have makes it possible . . . makes it probable . . . makes it so . . . Let yourself believe in the goodness of people.

◆

Go over any choices you have made . . . energies you have become attuned to. . . . Project this energy into your life. . . . Tell yourself you will intuitively, naturally act in accordance with these energies.

◆

In a moment I am going to count from one to five . . . at the count of five you will open your eyes feeling revitalized, refreshed and relaxed . . . remembering all that you experienced . . . ready and able to act on the energies you've evoked.

ONE—coming up slowly now. . . .

TWO—becoming more aware of the room around you. . . .

THREE—at the count of five you'll open your eyes, revitalized, refreshed and relaxed. . . .

FOUR—coming up now. . . .

FIVE!—Eyes open feeling revitalized, refreshed and relaxed, remembering all that you have experienced, ready and able to act on the energies you have evoked.

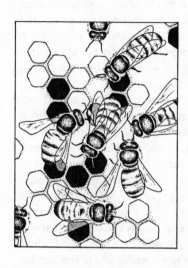

Chapter Ten

The World We Live In

"Above all, where there is no vision we lose the sense of our great power to transcend history and create a new future for ourselves with others, . . . Therefore the quest is not a luxury; life itself demands it of us!"[1]

A VISION

If we can imagine it, we can create it. Trust is to society what oil is to machinery. Imagine a world that ran on trust rather than oil. Imagine a world where we've learned how to be honest with ourselves, and to each other . . . where the only safe way of being is to be honest. Imagine a world where respect was sacred, where intuitions, spirituality, and emotions were all as valued as the intellect.

Imagine a society that was in synchrony with the cycles of nature, where human life was sustained on renewable sources of energy as is the rest of nature, where the earth is cherished, and whatever is taken out is returned. Imagine knowing that there would always be a place for you, your family, your community, your descendents, and your species—a place on earth. Imagine how it feels to always belong—belong in a diversified community, for it is the diversity in nature that gives the web of life its strength and cohesion. Imagine a time where everyone welcomes diversity in people because they know that is what gives community its richness, its strength, its cohesion. Imagine being able to relax into our connectedness—into a web of mutually supportive relations with each other and with nature.

Imagine a world where responsibilities were of equal importance to rights, where it was understood that enough was good, and that more than enough wasn't, where there was a deep understanding of the difference between wants and needs, a world where greed, opportunism, coercion and manipulation were all social crimes, a world where unaccountable power-over was arrested. Imagine a world where there was collective support in the overcoming of individual limitations, where mistakes weren't hidden but welcomed as opportunities to learn, where there was no reason to withold information, where honesty was a given. Imagine a world where what is valued most is not power but nurturance, where the aim has changed from being in control to caring and being cared for, where the expression of love is commonplace. Imagine a society that reveres patience rather than efficiency. Within patience there is respect, a deep trust—a knowing that in its own time the rosebud will bloom.

Imagine a world where bureaucracy, like the dinosaur, is extinct. Imagine a world on a human scale where work has regained its dignity, where work has regained its creativity, where you are part of the decisions that make a real difference.

People feel healthier when they take pride in keeping their homes clean and beautiful. Imagine everyone taking that same pride in making their communities beautiful. Imagine the whole of humanity honoring the same sense of responsibility for maintaining the earth.

Imagine a world where trust and honesty are the oil that makes society thrive and evolve—not power and deception, but cooperation and connection. The very fact that you can imagine these things makes them real, makes them possible.

It is impossible, ultimately, to preserve ourselves apart from our willingness to preserve other creatures, or to respect and care for

ourselves except as we respect and care for other creatures; and
. . . it is impossible to care for each other more or differently than
we care for the earth.[2]

Is it possible to heal the wounds of the people, of whatever sort,
caused by the process of separating them from the land, while
keeping them separated by virtue of a process which literally con-
sumes the land itself?[3]

You *can* choose respect, trust and mutual aid. You *can* choose life.
   We live in the belly of the beast, but we can emerge, slay it, and
heal our earth. If we can imagine these things we can create them.
We can let this vision give us the strength and patience for the
struggle that lies before us. If we can imagine it, it is possible—if we
can imagine it, we can begin to make it so.

THE TRUTH

We have mocked primitive humans for imagining themselves to be
one with nature. We "know" that we are separate from the environment. We have mastered it. Indeed, we have declared war on
it, and we have won. We have defeated the air, crushed the sea,
slaughtered the land, and stand alone in glorious victory, sick and
gasping, like an infant who has triumped over its mother.[4]

   For the first time in history, we cannot be secure that the next
generation will inherit the earth. Why? Because man has created
conditions that threaten the very cradle of life itself. Each species
is important to the ecological balance of the environment (although at this point, I think the rest of the planet would benefit
from the elimination of homo sapiens). "In over a little more than
two decades, 15 - 20 percent of the earth's total species of plants
and animals will have become extinct—a loss of at least 500,000
species."[5] Think of each species as being an intersection point in
the web of life. Now imagine how weak a spider web would be if
one-fifth of all its connecting points were broken. Species have
always become extinct on this planet, but in the past new forms of
life developed and filled in the spaces. Now when a species disap-

pears from the scene, it leaves only a gaping hole behind. If this trend continues, eventually the web will collapse. In our humanoid arrogance, we forget that our welfare is interdependent with the welfare of others. And now our country is in the hands of a man who has said, "If you've seen one redwood tree, you've seen them all." Playing God is a dangerous game. Maybe it would be good to let go of the arrogant idea that man was created in the image of God, and replace it with the idea that Nature was created in the image of God.

These days the great goal is to have human-like machines; we neglect to notice that in the production of such machines, we've transformed humans into machines and even gone so far as to replace people with robots. Eventually we'll have machines making machines and people will be obsolete, as indicated by *Time* magazine making a computer the "Machine of the Year" in 1983, supplanting their traditional "Man of the Year."

In today's over-specialized world, the centralization of capital has created huge-scale operations we all depend on: supermarket chains, gigantic hospitals, high-rise apartment buildings. If you file a complaint, the bureaucracy takes a year to process it, with no guarantee that the result will resolve the problem. It is no wonder that we have become cynical.

The meaning of life has escaped us—an understanding of how individual acts relate to the whole. When was the last time you thought of a cow when you drank a glass of milk? Our experience doesn't show us that each act is in fact a part of the whole (the web). If you don't *feel* a part of the whole, whatever happens simply "makes no difference anyway" (alienation). It is no wonder the crime rate is so high: the offender cynically justifies his actions by saying to himself, "What difference does it make?" There is a direct relationship between crime and the context in which it occurs. If there weren't, the crime rate would be the same in every society. Much as we would like to think otherwise, the rise in crime is in direct correlation to the decay in our society. One of the main reasons why meditation is so important is because it returns us to our sense of wholeness.

Our country has been looked upon as the most advanced in the world. At a closer look, you can't avoid drawing the conclusion that, in fact, our society is in a decline. All you need do is walk downtown and let your heart know the faces of the people in the streets. Now we have come to the point of being afraid to walk in the streets, much less use the city parks in broad daylight. Over the last ten years according to the FBI violent crime has increased 47 percent (that's only the reported crimes).[6] The solution is not just to find and lock up the "sick" people running around. When twenty-six people can witness a murder and not even pick up a phone to call the police—much less try to stop it—it is clear we're *all* in trouble.[7] Now we build ten-foot fences or put bars on our windows to protect us from our neighbors; and we sit back in solitary "security." Morals simply don't exist if we don't act on them.

> Can we justify secrecy, lying, and burglary in our so-called intelligence organizations and yet preserve openness, honesty, and devotion to principle in the rest of our government? Can we subsidize mayhem in the military establishment and yet have peace, order, and respect for human life in the city streets?[8]

Society, by definition, should be what holds people together, yet ours does the opposite. It tears people apart. Witness the fall of the extended family, the rise in the number of institutionalized people: the disabled, the old, the retarded, the "different." And yet our society hypocritically prides itself on honoring the individual—individuality is held sacred.

In the old days, everyone was a member of the community and the fabric of society was kept strong and healthy by passing on tradition in humanly meaningful ways such as songs, rituals, and storytelling by the elders. These methods were qualitatively different from those of today, where there is no interaction and information is received from newsprint, TV, sanitized school books and computer programs—all absorbed noncritically—swallowed in the name of "this is the way the world is." We don't know how to think for ourselves; schools sit us down in rows to memorize the facts, and regurgitate them when given the signal. In the old days, we sat in a circle to hear a story and then could talk about it with the teller. Where there is interaction there is substance—we share our feelings and ideas and learn to think for ourselves. Now "progress" has replaced our storytellers with bank tellers, and our elders are relegated to rest homes—no longer considered useful in a society whose highest value is production and consumption.

With no participation on our part in choosing the values we live by, we've become passive receptacles carrying on the needs of our society. We've become automatons trying to live up to Madison Avenue's image of a fulfilling life, something we can never ultimately attain (there's always someone looking better and owning more). We've become storefront mannequins; we do put on a good show, but interactions of depth and honesty have become a rarity. We don't even know what honesty is any more, much less why it's important to the fabric of society. If we can't count on one another, where do we turn?

Alas, the old days are gone, and we must work to change things before all of us go with them. When we act out of immorality, no longer can we look at ourselves in the mirror, much less look one another in the eye. We've forfeited our humanity and have become blind to each other, which only paves the road to more atrocities.

In this country, we're prone to toss around the word "freedom." In essence, freedom means having choice, and, in essence, having choice means taking responsibility for where you are, and choosing where you want to go. Therefore, *freedom means taking responsibility for the future.* Not being prey to whatever befalls you is the difference between humans and other species of life—the difference between acting and reacting. The former has a vision of the desired future, whereas the latter has no concept of the future at all. What's the point of saving money for our children's future if there is none? To sit back as if we were powerless is to be lemmings jumping into the sea.

IGNORANCE = FEAR
UNDERSTANDING = CHALLENGE

Political understanding has expanded my external horizons, for it enables me to know how all the pieces fit together into the whole so that what appeared to me as chaos has come into focus. Now I can understand the dynamics at play, choosing how I want to relate to them, so I can act rather than react. I remember the revelation it was for me to understand that change comes out of conflict. So conflict was not to be avoided but to be understood and worked with. When people came to understand that the earth was round, all of a sudden the threat of falling off the edge was transformed into the invitation to explore.

This country seems to do everything possible to keep us from thinking for ourselves. Without independent thinking there is no fundamental understanding. Everything I've learned that helps me make sense out of our world did not come from school or from the prevailing ideology.

I'm not talking about the kind of understanding whereby you memorize facts, figures, or dogma, whether it be from the Bible, the Koran, Ghandi, Freud or Marx (which isn't to say they have nothing to offer). I'm not talking about how to relate to new situations by repeating some formula or learning by rote. A fundamental understanding of mathematics enables you to apply the proper procedures to new situations so you can reach a conclusion and explain how you got there. When you understand *why* $2 + 2 = 4$, not just that the arithmetic book tells you it does, you will always know on your own that $3 + 1 = 4$ (and $2 + 2$ will never equal 5, even if Big Brother tells you it does). I am talking about learning/knowing, which enables you to decide for yourself where you stand and how to move forward.

You know when you've been working on a problem and you finally understand it, something clicks—the "Aha!" experience—and all of a sudden the pieces fall into place, fitting into the whole. The whole itself becomes a part of your life, within your own grasp and no longer a mystery. You've mastered the problem so now you can *choose* how you want to relate to it. You know how to take it apart and put it together again.

I don't mean to say that independent thought occurs in a vacuum. The point is not to become a dogmatic fundamentalist, but to know how to reach a fundamental understanding. What you want is methods that enable you to understand—bring things into focus—in the same way as arithmetic does for numbers.

Meditation is a tool for understanding the subjective; dialectical materialism/dialectical humanism is a tool for understanding the objective.[9] The tenets of this philosophy run through this book: problems come from the material conditions of our lives; change is constant, coming out of the contradiction between what is and what could be better; it is never either/or, but always both/and;

one-sided, circular, static thinking is fallacious.

Dialectics teaches that everything contains its own opposite—as there is death within life, there is life within death. Duality is within everything, giving rise to conflict which, in turn, leads to change. Change is constant. What is a solution today becomes a problem tomorrow. Materialsm teaches that everything is potentially knowable and that all ideas come out of a particular historical context. Humanism teaches that people have a spiritual aspect that transcends economic self-interest and can choose how to respond to any given situation. In other words, there is no permanent truth; what is true today is never true forever. There is no fate, no predetermination. Change primarily comes out of the dynamics *within* things. It is constant; it is not mechanical but dynamic, born out of contradiction. We are not faceless masses determined by our environment. Each of us chooses how to respond to our conditions. Within each individual, there is both baseness and nobility—a duality out of which each of us chooses to act.

With knowledge comes the gift of moving out of the dark. All of a sudden you know where you stand, and you can choose which way you want to go without fear of falling off the edge.

This philosophy brings me closer to a political understanding which enables me to know the context of our lives—of our problems. Blame is no longer a response of mine, nor is guilt. It is the same feeling that you get when you understand what's wrong when trying to fix something, and the urge to kick it, or kick yourself, evaporates because you have discovered what limitations currently exist as well as what is needed to overcome them. Ignorance equals fear, frustration and powerlessness; knowledge equals power, choice and challenge.

Through experience, each of us has learned that when we come to understand a problem we can, at that point, take steps to resolve the situation. When a baby cries out of hunger you feed her, i.e., you understand that she is hungry and conclude that you must feed her, thereby changing her condition to one of being fed and comfortable. Result: actions changed conditions and solved the problem—she stopped crying and felt okay. If your understanding is wrong, if you think the baby is cold, when in fact she is hungry, her crying will continue until you correctly figure out what is going on. That's what much of education is supposed to be all about—

learning problem-solving skills. Contemporary problems are not the result of some evil force which, by definition, is beyond our understanding and control. There are no mysteries outside of our potential understanding. When we come to understand the source of social problems, just like understanding why a baby cries, we can work to change the conditions that gave rise to them, and thereby begin to resolve them. People make history, whether consciously or unconsciously. Our future is shaped by *all* of us. The real question is whether or not we're going to begin to do so with foresight.

Democracy is meaningless without participants. Not to think for ourselves is to usher in a new Hitler. In order to exercise *real freedom* we are obliged to learn to be responsible decision-makers— *1984* is here, Big Brother is here, and only if we stand up and make our voices heard loud and clear will we keep him from consolidating his power. Sins of omission can be as destructive as sins of commission.

> When the Nazis came for the Communists, I said nothing—I was not a Communist. When they came for the Social Democrats, I said nothing—I was not a Social Democrat. When they came for the Jews, I said nothing—I was not a Jew. When they came for me there was no one left who would protest. [10]

The fact is that you are a part of society; taking a position of being apart from it only perpetuates what's wrong. Not only is the personal political, but the political is personal. As with our personal problems, we each know that complaining doesn't change a thing, for it focuses only on the past (static thinking), whereas the future is the issue. When you find yourself complaining, thereby giving energy to the problem, instead ask yourself, "What could be the ideal? What is good in life? What can be good in society?" Here meditation is invaluable, for it enables you to have a vision toward which to aspire. This also reveals the conditions holding back the change illuminating *where* the struggle needs to take place (the contradiction between what is, and what would be better).

ILLUMINATION THROUGH INVESTIGATION

There has been life on this planet for millions of years. What has happened to us that we can continue to sit back and simply leave it up to "those politicians" whom we're always complaining about—when the possibility of annihilation is so near. This is rank reaction—taking no responsibility. It has been said by members of our Government that we can win a limited atomic war. There is *no* winner in an atomic war, but the very fact that they think there could be makes them liable to try it. Our leaders fully distort what life is all about.

> Our recent secretary of agriculture remarked that "Food is a weapon." This was given a fearful symmetry indeed when, in discussing the possible use of nuclear weapons, a secretary of defense spoke of "palatable" levels of devastation. Consider the associations that have since ancient times clustered around the idea of food—associations of mutual care, generosity, neighborliness, festivity, communal joy, religious ceremony—and you will see that these two secretaries represent a cultural catastrophe. [11]

We need to stop taking the words of our country's leaders at face value and investigate to see whose interest they're really serving. If you hear an ad on TV, do you automatically believe it? Of course not. You investigate because you are aware that the advertisers are more concerned with profits than truth. Our leaders are more concerned with votes than truth.

> The conventions of the two parties are media events in which we, the people, are reduced to passive spectators just as we are at the annual superbowls. Once a candidate is chosen, the party platform disappears and we are left with the same choice between personalities as between Coca Cola and Un-Cola ... our political party system produces politicians whose only interest is in being elected and re-elected, and who cannot provide the kind of political leadership which we now need to confront and resolve the mounting contradictions of our society. [12]

If you took the time you would discover that our country's leaders are serving the interests of big business—their campaign financiers who pay for the ads which get the votes. If they were serving the interests of most of us, as they continually claim, why do things keep getting worse and worse? Or are they simply incompetent? Either way, a change is called for. To do nothing is to leave our society in the hands of "those politicians."

Confidence comes from understanding. Just as we have confidence in being able to care for a baby, we can build confidence in our ability to care for society. Together we can take responsibility and not allow our future to cease to exist, moving from reaction into action, creating a future for our children.

Our country is being run by men who believe we can win an atomic war; their fantasies are *real* and no longer do we have the privilege of dismissing fantasy. "We'll be wiped out in twenty minutes, and within thirty days after a nuclear exchange 90 percent of Americans will be dead."[13] Maybe 100 percent of the Russians will be dead—should we call this winning? We have enough arms to kill life on earth twenty times over, and we need *more*? Yet our government plans to spend 294 billion dollars in 1985 for the military, and on top of that another 137 billion is necessary to pay for past military costs. This adds up to 63 cents of every one of our tax dollars being eaten up by the military.[14] "Two men are sitting in a large pool of gasoline. One has seven matches, and the other has only five."[15] It is ludicrous. The arms race is simply a question of who gets to the finish first.

"The Soviet Union has frequently sought a joint promise with the United States not to be the first to use nuclear weapons, but Washington has always rebuffed the idea."[16] If our country were attacked we could still do in our enemy with the submarines we have in the ocean. Yet we continue to spend billions more on this so-called defense. If defending ourselves is the issue, why is it that we design first-strike bombs? The real issue is that military spending means big profits to the corporations in the business. It also means we can continue being the bully on the block saying to other countries, "If you don't fall in line, then we'll drop it on you." Since Hiroshima we've threatened to use nuclear warheads at least twelve times.[17] Most of us shake our heads when the big kid in the neighborhood is mean and bossy to the smaller ones. Let's stop being duped. Do we want to be participants in this kind of behavior? Our country has become the bully of the international neighborhood.

Hasn't humanity evolved beyond the "might makes right" attitude? Our leaders are always referring to "our" backyard. (Backyards for everyone else stop at their property line.) We arrogantly invade Grenada so it runs as we think fit, or support the Contras' invasion of Nicaragua because we don't like what the vast majority of their own patriots want. Maybe we should stop spending all our energy worrying about what our neighbors are doing and clean up the garbage that is truly in *our* backyard.

CONTROLLING INTEREST

The American mentality: in getting more, more, more, you'll find happiness—the bigger, the better. Fulfillment is equated with money and money is equated with power. The scarcity mentality in the midst of abundance—"The more money you have, the more you need."—certainly puts into question the idea that wealth holds the key to happiness. Wherever this philosophy prevails it breeds death and destruction to nature and to the heart and soul of humanity.

We live in a system where money is endowed with the qualities of life. Protect it so it may grow and develop! The epitome of this ideology is the designing of the neutron bomb, created to kill people and preserve property.

Under capitalism the only goal is to make a profit which you go out and reinvest, otherwise it is a waste of time to have made it in the first place, for it will just dribble away and you will have nothing to show for it later. Profits never occur by simply making ends meet—breaking even. By definition, profits leave you with *more* than you had before, so to survive under capitalism one must constantly reinvest one's profits which means getting bigger, bigger, and BIGGER. The process of getting bigger inside a finite space necessitates pushing everyone and/or everything aside in order to make room—or simply gobbling them up. *Laissez-faire economics has become a process of elimination* with bankruptcy on the one hand and corporate mergers on the other.

Farmers are driven off their land at a rate of 1,900 per week;[18] they can't afford to keep up, nor can the corner store undercut the supermarket. Now only those who have made it into the big time have survived to compete. This process centralizes money and has brought about the age of the multi-national corporations which also live in a dog-eat-dog world, consuming one another in ever-proliferating corporate mergers. They have an insatiable appetite, and the rest of us are being eaten alive just to keep their profits from becoming superfluous.

> Multinational corporations have no loyalty to the United States or to any American community. They have no commitment to the reforms that Americans have won through hard struggle. Instead of giving us more each year, they demand that we accept less—or else. They give robots who are nobodies the jobs of workers who are parents, neighbors, consumers, taxpayers. If any American city or the American government is not willing to give them the same tax breaks, labor peace and environmental deregulation as they can extract from other governments, if American workers do not accept wages and benefits competitive with those of Japanese or Mexican or Filipino workers, they do not hesitate to shut down a plant that has been the heart of the economic life of a city or region. With each plant closing, the domino theory begins to operate. City workers and school teachers find that they are no longer needed; small businesses go bankrupt. So millions of workers, skilled and unskilled, blue collar and white collar, have already been laid off and other millions live in fear, knowing that it is only a matter of time before the axe falls on them.[19]

Clearly this very process makes the rich richer and the rest of us poorer. The American dream has turned out to be a lie. Paul Samuelson, Nobel Laureate in economics, graphically illustrates the reality of the income structure in our country: If a pyramid were made out of childrens' blocks with each layer representing a thousand dollars of income, the top would be far higher than the Eiffel Tower whereas the vast majority of us would be within three feet of the ground.[20] Despite our hopes, our work, our patriotism, now in 1984 the American dream has become a nightmare. Every day more and more join the 15 percent of us who live in poverty.[21] The very economic survival of great numbers of Americans is teetering on the verge of collapse.

There are over one-hundred drugs sold by United States firms in Central America that are banned for sale internally by the Food and Drug Administration.[22] These drugs are not sold down there in the name of the people's health, but in the name of profit, and the corporations get away with it because they receive total license from U.S. backed totalitarian regimes. Whether it's sales or production the corporations receive U.S. military protection for their securities (not people's) so they can continue reaping profits which are no longer available inside the U.S. borders.

> There is, in short, a huge tacit conspiracy between the U.S. government, its agencies and its multinational corporations, on the one hand, and local business and military cliques in the Third World, on the other, to assume complete control of these countries and "develop" them on a joint venture basis. The military leaders of the Third World were carefully nurtured by the U.S. security establishment to serve as the "enforcers" of this joint venture partnership, and they have been duly supplied with machine guns and the latest data on methods of interrogation of subversives. . . . The "rich" include a great many U.S. companies and individuals, which is why the United States has provided the guns, and much more. Labor costs have been kept low under this system. The "side effects" in the form of widespread hunger, malnutrition, diseases of poverty and social neglect, millions of stunted children, and a huge reserve army of structurally unemployed and uncared for people are the regrettable but necessary costs of "growth" and "development." These side effects have not been heavily featured in the western mass media.[23]

And do we benefit from their profits? They are certainly not trickling down, instead unemployment itself is moving up the social strata. As everything contains its opposite, the free-enterprise system has ripped off our freedom and made us all hostages of the corporations. It's time to take back the word "free"—tear it off of "enterprise"—what kind of freedom is there in unemployment? The benefits of capitalism for the people in the United States are in an irreversible decline, which means that unemployment will continue to rise while the earth's resources will continue to decrease at an alarming rate, devoured by the multi-nationals in the name of keeping their capital well employed and, as always, the land continues to bleed its wealth into the pockets of the rich.[24]

In fact, it is extremely rare to find a large fortune that wasn't founded in part on illegal or at least unethical practices. In saying this I don't mean to be cynical. Great fortunes can almost never be acquired ethically for a very simple reason: *money is an instrument of trade and in an ethical trade everyone would come out at the end relatively equal.* If, then, at the end of a lifetime of exchange, one man comes out rich and the other poor, the poor man has been cheated and the rich man is a cheat. This is made explicit in the first rule of success in business: "buy cheap and sell dear," or, in other words, "cheat those with whom you deal." If our entire economic system is based on the exhortation to cheat, we can hardly be surprised or indignant to find that the biggest rewards go to those who are the biggest cheaters. The real question we need to ask ourselves is this: are these the people we want to reward?[25]

Everyone wants to own their own home, which is a virtual impossibility these days. The bank owns my home. Last year, only 2 1/2 percent of the total we paid to the "savings" company went to increase our equity in the house—maybe enough to buy us the doorjamb. By the time the mortgage is paid—a day I might not live to see—how many times over will we have paid for the house? If I want an alternative to the mortgage system I have to settle for being a renter, which is even worse. Everybody but the bankers gets the raw end of the deal. Somebody's getting rich from my work, which is therefore paying for somebody else's leisure. I don't want to support the bankers' vacations; I have enough trouble buying my own food. I can't afford to have my hard-earned money go to make the rich richer. Meanwhile, the banker smugly sits back, thinking he is fully self-reliant and a good guy for "helping me out." Instead of patronizing, he should give *us* credit for paying for his vacation— the interest system is pure usury. And Americans entertain the same pretentious attitude toward the "underdeveloped" world— "giving them aid." People in these countries want to support our standard of living about as much as I want to pay for the bankers' vacations. They starve because their country's land produces food for our tables. The people of El Salvador go hungry so we can drink coffee in the morning. I know it's uncomfortable to look at the facts, and that this is hard to believe, but if you investigate you'll discover that it's true.

There is no such thing as self-reliance, it's all a matter of power and trade, and the deals are not based on fairness. (Our work is as valuable as theirs.) When the United States uses one third of the world's total mineral resources and consists of only 4.8 percent of the population, something is askew.[26] Or do we believe we are better, and therefore deserve it (the height of arrogance)? To maintain this one-up position military might is dispersed throughout the world in the name of protecting "freedom."

This game is nothing new. Witness Marine General Smedley D. Butler's testimony before a congressional committee in 1935:

> I spent 33 years and four months in active service as a member of our country's most agile military force—the Marine Corps. . . . And during that period I spent most of my time being a high-class muscle man for big business, for Wall Street and for the bankers. In short, I was a racketeer for capitalism.
>
> I suspected I was just part of a racket at the time. Now I am sure of it.
>
> Like all members of the military profession I never had an original thought until I left the service. My mental faculties remained in suspended animation while I obeyed the orders of the higher-ups. This is typical of everyone in the military service.
>
> I helped make Mexico and especially Tampico safe for American oil interests in 1914. I helped make Haiti and Cuba a decent place for the National City Bank boys to collect revenues in. I helped in the raping of half a dozen Central American republics for the benefit of Wall Street.
>
> The record of racketeering is long. I helped purify Nicaragua for the international banking house of Brown Brothers in 1909 to '12. I brought light to the Dominican Republic for American sugar interests in 1916. I helped get Honduras "right" for American fruit companies in 1903. In China in 1927 I helped see to it that Standard Oil went its way unmolested.
>
> During those years I had, as the boys in the back room always say, a swell racket. I was rewarded with honors, medals, promotions.
>
> Looking back on it, I feel I might have given Al Capone a few hints. The best he could do was to operate his racket in three city districts. We Marines operated on three continents.[27]

The readier the Pentagon and CIA were to bring down or raise up governments in underdeveloped countries, the better the investment climate for U.S. corporations. U.S. military power was used to establish the ground rules within which American business could operate. The U.S. Government acted as consultant for rightist coups in Bolivia, Brazil, Chile, Greece, and Indonesia, and their generals opened their countries to U.S. investment on the most favorable terms. Wherever the flag has been planted around the world, in some 500 major military and naval bases and in the command posts of over a dozen military interventions, U.S. corporations have moved in. The construction of a worldwide military empire has been good business. [28]

Because I expose the limitations of capitalism do not assume I am advocating communism. We have reached a time in history when we must break with dualistic, either/or thinking. Communism has its problems too. We must reconceptualize the order of society altogether.

THE PARTY'S OVER

The party's over. . . . We were entertained by three great magicians, illusionists. One was the illusion that somehow, against all laws of nature, infinite growth in a finite environment is possible. . . . The second entertainer said that by some strange law of nature there is an unlimited supply of people who are prepared to do mindless repetitive work for quite modest remuneration. . . . The third illusion, which is still rampant, is that science can solve all problems. I have no doubt that science can solve any individual problem when it's clearly defined. But my experience is that as it solves problem A it creates a whole host of new problems. . . . At the height of success, with technological competence unequaled in all human history, we read nothing but questions of survival. . . . These entertainers turn out to be illusions, but we still talk to each other as if these entertainers would return. They won't. They can't. [29]

In the old days things were made to last; they were made to use, not to sell. Today they are made to break so that more and more can be sold. And this is the kind of thing we're using up the earth's resources for? It is an insult to our integrity. Whatever happened to the values of durability and pride in workmanship?

What is going to happen if we go too far and there are no more resources? If we continue to choose to ignore the depletion rate there'll be nothing left. We've got to let go of the idea that somehow in the future we'll invent something that will overcome our difficulties. Anything one makes uses raw materials and energy and there are always wastes in the modern productive process. By definition, if it is material there is a limited weight and volume, so by the time there is a product one ends up with *less* than what one started with. Producing is not the answer, rather it's the problem—the pervasive myth that we always need to *increase* the Gross National Product. If we learn to slow down maybe the planet will last. Wendell Berry makes vital distinctions:

> We cannot create biological energy anymore than we can create atomic or fossil fuel energy. But we *can* preserve it in use. . . . We cannot do that with machine-derived energy. This is an extremely important difference. . . .
>
> The moral order by which we use machine-derived energy is comparatively simple. Whatever uses this sort of energy works simply as a conduit that carries it beyond use; the energy goes in as "fuel" and comes out as "waste." This principle sustains a highly simplified economy having only two functions: production and consumption.
>
> The moral order appropriate to the use of biological energy, on the other hand, requires the addition of a third term: production and consumption, *and return*. It is the principle of return that complicates matters, for it requires responsibility, care, of a different and higher order than that required by production and consumption alone, and it calls for methods and economies of a different kind. In an energy economy appropriate to the use of biological energy, all bodies, plant and animal and human, are joined in a kind of energy community. . . . They are indissolubly linked in complex patterns of energy exchange. They die into each other's life, live into each other's death. They do not consume in the sense of using up. They do not produce waste. What they take in they change, but they change it always into a form necessary for its use by a living body of another kind. And this exchange goes on and on, round and round, the Wheel of Life rising out of the soil, descending into it, through the bodies of creatures.[30]

Our society has reached the point of diminishing returns. We must pull ourselves out of our fascination with quantity—thinking *more* of everything will solve our problems—and begin to look at the quality of life. (Stop being worried about how many matches we have and realize we're sitting in a pool of gasoline.) We need to endeavor to begin to believe in our neighbors, not our possessions, always focusing on quality not quantity. If we don't create values that cherish life itself as sacred, instead of private property, then our children will inherit only an uninhabitable wasteland—they may own it, if they are alive at all, but it won't be worth a damn if it can't support life.

FROM "I" TO "WE" CONSCIOUSNESS

The "free enterprise" system is essentially a "me first" system, a fearful race for "my" place in the economic sunlight, and to hell with everybody else. . . . Yet the irony of today is that the "me first" system is coming to mean more and more an "all last" system. . . .

Modern industrial society under these conditions forces millions of men and women to devote their life's energies to work that is routine, individually meaningless and soul destroying. The system, it is true, produces commodities in immense quantities, but for the vast majority of people it suffocates every vestige of their creativity.

And how, underneath it all, we *hate* it, hate the pressures that are applied by endless commercial demands! How we hate a system which makes the buying and selling of *everything*—our products, our labor and time, even our thoughts—central to our lives! For we know that we have within us capacities for a wholly different kind of life—much warmer, much closer to our real nature, much nearer to our fundamental human needs.[31]

We need to try to believe that it is possible to lead better quality lives. As we begin to believe it we will begin to know how to create it. That's what this book is all about. Cultivate a belief, and you'll find that your intuition will follow suit with insights that are in alignment. No longer can we afford to remain cynical. Do we want to assume nothing can be done when literally *everything* is at stake?

The American story: strive, compete well, be enterprising, and you'll make it. True, maybe, up to the twentieth century for white men, and women attached to them. But times have changed, and the conditions that gave rise to competitive behavior having real survival value are long gone. Now who can compete with the corporations? Do you think you could successfully start your own electric company? Competition is the acid that is eating away at all our stability.

As Americans, we seem to have our own special definition of freedom, which is freedom to *ignore* all the repercussions of individual acts—a freedom to pursue your own personal hustle.[32] What better ideology could be developed to support the gluttonous behavior of the multi-nationals? This brand of freedom as freedom *from* responsibility has a boomerang effect. We all pay the price ecologically by creating a carcinogenic environment. Slater hits the nail on the head:

> The kind of growth Western culture has experienced over the past three hundred years would be considered a sign of gross malfunction in any other context. Healthy growth is paced differently—it does not absorb or destroy everything living around it. It is cancerous cells that grow and reproduce rapidly in total disregard of their connection with surrounding cells. From this viewpoint technology would have to be regarded as a cancer on human culture, Western culture as a cancer on the human species, and the human species as a cancer on terrestrial life—a cancer that may in the end be treated by radiation and radical surgery at the same time.
>
> Let us hope another cure can be found. . . . The only conceivable outcome of the present philosophy of constant economic growth is ecological catastrophe. . . .
>
> We are used to hearing pathological growth figures cited with pride and awe, only recently tinged with alarm: that scientific knowledge doubles every ten years, that half of all the energy consumed in the past two millennia has been consumed in the past century, that the tempo of human evolution is 100,000 times as rapid as that of prehuman evolution, that the earth's urban population will double in eleven years, that a civilized teenager is surrounded by twice as many newly manufactured goods as she was as an infant, that 90% of all the scientists who ever lived are now alive, and so on.

"It has been demonstrated that when normal tissues are grown on a glass surface the cells stop growing when they touch each other. But cancer cells similarly grown on a glass surface continue to grow, unimpeded by cellular contact." (David Bakan) Studies of cancer cells seem to suggest that some kind of mutually limiting communication present between normal cells is weak or absent between cancer cells. It is as if cancer cells had been heavily indoctrinated with the ideology of individualism and personal achievement.

Imagine a mass of cancerous tissue, the cells of which enjoyed consciousness. Would they not be full of self-congratulatory sentiments at their independence, their more advanced level of development, their rapid rate of growth? Would they not sneer at their more primitive cousins who were bound into a static and unfree existence, with limited aspiration, subject to heavy group constraint, and obviously "going nowhere?" Would they not rejoice in their control over their own destiny, and cheer the conversion of more and more normal cells as convincing proof of the validity of their own way of life? Would they not, in fact, feel increasingly triumphant right up to the time the organism on which they fed expired?[33]

And isn't it karmic that more than any other disease, the idea of being eaten away by cancer haunts us all? Like attracts like; everything is in sync.

This way of viewing the world has poisoned the subjective landscape of every inhabitant of Western culture. Like cancer, individualism must be eliminated or eventually it will eliminate us. We each have to inspect every nook and cranny of our consciousness and exorcise all "me-first" attitudes. This is a difficult task; the meditations will be of great help. We need not get down on ourselves for having these feelings; they're what we've been taught from the get-go, but once we understand how destructive this kind of thinking is, there is no excuse for avoiding doing something about it. Simply admitting that you're wrong doesn't make you right. Feeling guilty is simply self-indulgence, change is what is called for.

My process of overcoming my individualism continues to evolve—remember my symbol to overcome impatience in groups—the sailboat which utilizes the natural forces to get to her destination? In a meditation recently—more layers of the onion peeled away—I looked at the fact that the sailboat represented me alone getting to *my* chosen destination—not a very collective frame of mind, though an improvement at the time. A new symbol came to me; I'd seen a jelly fish in an aquarium a while back which moved in the most graceful way—all the different parts of it dancing in the water—what was so awesome about it was that it actually was not one organism, but a community of them.

A common deception rooted in individualism: if everyone becomes self-aware and self-responsible, then society will no longer be askew. Again the focus is on "me." The banker taking responsibility for society by seeing a therapist is full of self-deception. There is no such thing as true self-awareness without social awareness; nothing is devoid of an economic and cultural context—nothing exists in a vacuum. The idea that it is even possible to fix oneself in the midst of a sick society is fully erroneous, to say nothing of the arrogance of such a notion. Even if it were possible, the solution is short-lived—the earth is sinking, and salvation can only be achieved collectively. We as individuals don't create our problems any more than we can individually solve them. I don't trust a corporation to be able to clean up its act by being "self-aware"—which boils down to being more efficient—any more than I trust the individual to clean up his act without taking society into account. Cleaning up one's act in isolation boils down to suave insensitivity—the kind of behavior acted out by those people in the human potential movement who believe that "You create your own reality." The issue is not self-awareness, personal potential, or self-responsibility. The crucial issue is collective awareness, cultural potential, and social responsibility. An idea whose time has come: the declaration of *inter*dependence.

Making major decisions on the basis of anything other than self-interest is foreign to our consciousness. Collectivity is seen as standing in the way of the individual ("I'll make it despite the group.") rather than the very thing that holds one up. In consequence one doesn't experience social solidarity but rather isolation. And from lack of mutual support one gets burnt out. This leads to cynicism and self-hatred which further compounds the isolation and burn-out—the vicious cycle has begun.

We don't live in isolation, we only *feel* isolated or, more precisely, alienated—an understandable consequence of our self-reliance mentality. We forfeit the experience of the inherent relatedness of everything. We're not a part of everything, instead we're apart from everything. There's much chatter on the surface, but deeper inside there's a hole that cries out to be filled. That gnawing feeling inside each of us—"I'm just not good enough!"—an emptiness that yearns to be filled by being accepted back into the whole. This is why we have fantasies of glory, dreaming of shining out above the crowd; alas, we each crave to be fulfilled by being more than enough. The catch-22 is that stars are the ones who have more than enough alienation. Being Number One is the loneliest place of all. Trying more, striving more, is a vicious cycle; despite our drives we can only fill the hole by rejoining the *whole*—relaxing and remembering our connection to one another.

Our society is riddled with stress-caused diseases. *Stress comes from a lack of mutual support—muscular tension is caused by holding onto your own private position.* We feel we're out there all alone fending for ourselves, and God save us if we lose what little footing we've gained. I don't believe chronic tension is a problem in societies that haven't been contaminated by competitive ideology. In such cultures people trusted their fellow citizens to be there when the going got rough. In the West it's the opposite: "never show your weakness," for others will use it to their own advantage, pulling out from under you what little you've managed to build up. The irony of our culture is that *individualism fully stifles individuality.* Out there, alone, fending for ourselves, we cannot afford to be disapproved of, to be exposed. So we squelch anything we think, feel, or want that is out of line. Our values imprison us, our fear of disapproval is the guard that keeps us in jail.

Our creativity never gets a chance. Our creativity never gets expressed. Uniformity creates rigidity—when monoculture is practiced (the growing of only select strains) crops are much more vulnerable to disease epidemics or plagues of pests.[34] We are no different. Diversity on the other hand creates flexibility and survives the unpredictable. We've got what we fear most—uniformity, and we've lost what we need most—community. Community is the antithesis of uniformity.

We have traded in subjective autonomy for the American myth of objective autonomy. We need to turn it on its head: be subjectively autonomous and objectively participating with consciousness in the relationships that already exist. If we don't, then we're creating a fertile soil for fascism to root and grow.

Without a flow of energy anything withers away and dies. Western cultural taboos inflict upon us the damming up of the flow of
life-giving, warm, nurturing energies: the emotional, the spiritual,
the intuitive. These energies are traditionally associated with "sec-
ond-class citizens"—women, who, as we know, aren't taken seriously. These taboos court subjective death, allowing enough energy
through to survive physically; keeping the heart of society pumping.
Beta consciousness, the only level allowed in the driver's seat, is
promoted. Cold, calculating beta thinking survives to discover all
the more efficient means of controlling/conquering nature. Being
objective is the only "legitimate" approach and it necessitates separating oneself, observing, calculating, and then acting in the name
of control—a one-up arrogant position. To be subjective—thought
of as fully suspect, never to be trusted—is to care, to feel, to be
involved, to be a participant in the whole—to have "lost control."
What has life come to that we are obliged to leave our feelings out
of it? Arid, hard, cold ground is the worst condition for life. Dead
on the inside, there is no reason to restrain oneself from inflicting
death on the outside, for life has lost all value. *It is time to be
suspicious of the objective and legitimize the subjective.*

The very basis of conservative values and politics is "hold on to
what you've got"—"keep striving," "get more," "don't relax"—result-
ing in muscular tension, national stress, international problems.

> The exploitative system is now tearing apart the whole fabric of
> civilization. The will to "success," the will to outsell, outwit,
> outdo and if necessary outgun others kills the intuitive, instinctive
> sympathy and relatedness which we would otherwise feel towards
> each other, and it is these that form the invisible, essential bonds
> which hold societies together. As individuals, a "me first" system
> makes us hard, calculating and lonely. It makes the policies of
> nations implacable. [35]

Holding on and grabbing is the antithesis of life; life is fluid, it
moves. To hold on is to kill all energy flow and to kill life itself. The
affirmation of life, the trust of life means forward motion that
enables life itself to flourish; it doesn't pave the way for private
property to grow, suffocating everything in its path. We are all

suffering from a deep psychic starvation. Who wouldn't welcome back the days of the barn raising? We can replace alienation—feed our souls by honoring our connections instead of continually pretending our independence, honoring our deeper human experiences—living *amidst* life rather than continually trying to control it from above.

Envy and greed are an insult to integrity for in each one the center of consciousness is no longer in the beholder but in the object of desire. A person's center of consciousness is outside herself if she is worrying about what someone else has got and how she can get it. This is when people are fully capable of committing atrocities. With their center outside themselves they become vacant shells—rationalization becomes unnecessary. With both greed and envy people are much more occupied with what they're wanting than with who they are. Not feeling good about their own life, not trusting those around them, they separate themselves out, withdraw and manipulate. Energetically this results in becoming denser, blocking energy flow and becoming hardened and brittle—easily breakable. Greed holds on and shuts down. Howard Hughes suffered from constipation, "He once sat on the toilet for 72 straight hours—without enemas he would go as long as 28 days without a movement."[36]

To relax into the webwork of life, one opens, one becomes flexible, making the web strong. Trust and generosity open up making the community strong. We can regain our humanity before it's too late by beginning to relate to one another in nurturing ways. Although it may feel contrived to begin with—remember developing new habits always does—smile at people in the streets, share with your neighbors, stop and help someone who's having car trouble. Dig new channels for your energies to move down.

We only have so much energy; we can choose to spend it welcoming life, change, and newness, or spend it holding onto what we have, trying to get what we want. Conservative values necessitate protecting what was. If we choose to spend our energy protecting the values that are no longer appropriate, we are shielding ourselves from the truth of what life has become. As with muscular tension, in holding onto your own private position you block the flow of life-giving blood. Conservative values do the same for the community. We can see it on one another's faces; after years of holding on the body becomes stiff and disjointed. We all prefer to be around warm, openhearted, relaxed people. To be openhearted is to have courage to face the truth, to face change, to face conflict.

RESPONSE-ABILITY

To do nothing is impossible; none of us lives in a vacuum. The lack of confrontation is an act of compliance with the status quo and as such does nothing but strengthen it.

> It is important to be aware that every act of self-restraint in relation to an inhumane structure constitutes positive feedback for that structure—a vote of confidence. Our definitions of "responsibility" have always placed a heavy emphasis on self-control, but "response-ability" means responsivity or it means nothing at all.[37]

Look at it this way: imagine a situation in which you are being unduly blamed for something and your friends don't speak up on your behalf. Their opinion may as well not exist if they don't put it out there to be counted when you need it. You're left alone to fend for yourself. It's at times like this that you know who your friends *really* are. The same is true for society—it's about time that we begin to stick our necks out and stop pretending the ship's not sinking, which is the equivalent of deserting the ship. Where can we go? We can't swim in space, but we can get back onto an even keel.

To remain silent amidst destructive ideas and actions in the name of keeping the peace only sets up a protective coating which fosters further decay because the cover-up enables us to deceive ourselves into thinking all's well. With no intervention things are degenerating at a continually accelerating rate. But now the buffer zone itself is beginning to decay. Your silence puts your interest in comfort above that of life itself—a trade-off you no longer have the privilege to make if you are committed to life on earth.

> People are the nerve endings of social systems. If they are stupid enough socially to bear the pain such a system inflicts upon them,

the system will go right on inflicting it. Social mechanisms are mindless, undirected. Insofar as they are deprived of information about human needs and responses, they will be inhumane.

Most Western societies are like people with no sense of pain— they blunder into horrible injuries because they have lost access to vital information from their peripheries. We are the numbed and atrophied nerve endings of our societies. We have been trained to smile politely when some social situation tramples upon us, and every time we do so we give it a lesson in inhumanity.[38]

When we express our differences to one another we awaken each other's numb spots. We need to put our views out there publicly, to be grappled with and talked about. Disseminating life-affirming views makes them visible and exposes the rest for what they really are (life-denying). The more it's all exposed, the more people there will be to unite with, the more people there are united, the more powerful our work for change becomes.

All my writing will be in vain if you use it *solely* to improve your own personal lot. We'd better get it out of our minds that it's up to the individual; that idea courts catastrophe. It's time we move out of our own personal niches and act collectively to save the planet. You may feel the individual risk you take to do something about the world is too great—but it can't be compared to the risk we all take if we choose to remain complacent—that's inviting doom.

If you're not busy working to save the planet—which can be done only by collective action—you are busy *adding* to the nearly insurmountable problems. In other words, if you're not part of the solution you *are* part of the problem. People whose exclusive preoccupation is their own personal growth and development have the same mentality as the drug firms which kill in other countries in the name of company growth and development, or the rapist who attacks for personal satisfaction and power. None looks beyond personal wants. And to exonerate themselves they blame the victim—the equivalent of telling the rape victim she asked for it because she shouldn't have been out alone, or saying that by wearing jewelry you tempt the innocent bystander and turn him into a thief.[39] This kind of thinking misses the boat altogether and invites the eventual drowning of everyone alike.

"That hope sways on an edge so delicate that it is possible that the choices anyone of us makes could tip the balance."[40] Life takes on meaning when one dedicates oneself to issues that are bigger than one's own individual concerns; it's enobling when the greater issues take precedence. Going beyond the self is true transcendence—that's *real* heroism. Even if our vision is unlikely to materialize we'll find ourselves feeling better, for we've moved out of our individual negativity/cynicism into a positive position of belief and solidarity—from powerless reaction to powerful action. We act differently when we have a vision—we have something to strive for, we have a direction to move, a reason to live. And if we are not successful, at least we go out with the dignity of having tried. No one is a victim when they stand up and fight for a vision of a better world. We all know that harder times are coming, but to hoard private stashes and hole up with them is only a temporary solution and perpetuates the very mentality that got the world into this mess in the first place. In fact it is when we are divided that we get overwhelmed with the devastation—taking a one-down, isolated "I" position. Instead you can remember the strength of our collective commitment. Let that feed your confidence to strive for justice. It is through being in it together that we move from despair to inspiration.

What are you willing to give up for the sake of humanity? That's real social responsibility. No longer is it "get mine" despite everybody else. We need to realize that if we are to commit ourselves to saving civilization a drastic change is needed within each of us. We have to change our subjective landscape as well as our objective course of action completely. We must face the truth and stop practicing knowing what isn't so, an ability we Westerners are particularly agile at. Despite our attempts to ignore it, the truth is that we must curb our own selfish appetites in order to guarantee that humanity won't be one of those 500,000 species extinct by the year 2000. Ultimately that boils down to the fact that the standard of living for most of us must go down to enable the starving to eat and to keep us from polluting our environment. I think we'll survive with one or two kinds of breakfast cereal instead of one-hundred and three.[41] If something is material, it is by definition limited—there is only so much to go around. There are no easy answers, but one thing is for sure: our consumer lifestyle pollutes the earth and, as much as we would like to think otherwise, it is an installment plan for planetary suicide.

We need to scrutinize and simplify our needs, distinguishing them from our wants, ceasing to allow luxuries the status of needs. If we don't give energy to the consumer mentality inside us it will die for lack of support. When you're wanting something notice the energy behind it. If you let yourself you will discover whether it's your eyes or your belly speaking—you know how it feels when your eyes are bigger than your belly.

If we develop local self-reliance we won't need to consume one-third of the world's resources; we won't need to practice neocolonialism to protect our "way of life," to protect our "freedom" at the expense of others. We won't be at the mercy of huge scale operations if we organize things on a human scale. Local self-reliance is the antithesis of neocolonialism.

> The responsible consumer must also be in some way a producer. Out of his own resources and skills, he must be equal to some of his own needs. The household that prepares its own meals in its own kitchen with some intelligent regard for nutritional value, and thus depends on the grocer only for selected raw materials, exercises an influence on the food industry that reaches from the store all the way back to the seedsman. The household that produces some or all of its own food will have a proportionately greater influence. The household that can provide some of its own pleasures will not be helplessly dependent on the entertainment industry.[42]

Would you give up fancy cold remedies, your electric dishwasher or R.V., if it meant your children's children would be guaranteed a full life? Look at the positive side: if we give up central heating we'll reconnect with nature. We'll be unable to ignore the elements of nature. We won't eat up all the sheep because we'll remember that their wool provides us with sweaters for our warmth We won't cut down all the trees because we will want to protect the soil for our crops. In short, we will have re-entered life on earth; we'll once again *belong* and therefore be able to relax into our natural position in the ecosystem, the only stable economic system, where the natural order is *supporting* us.

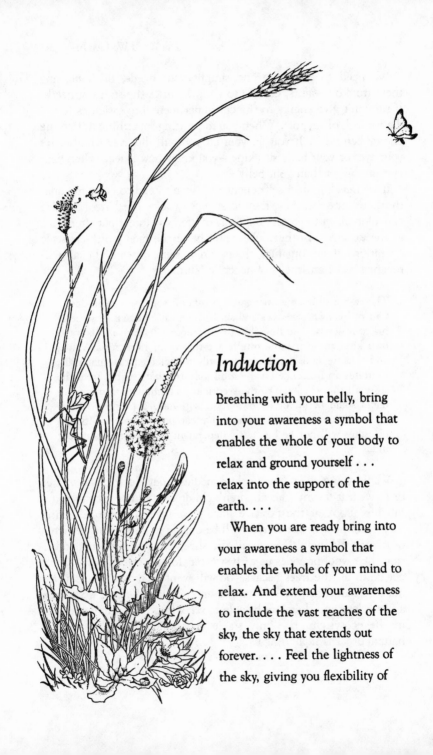

Induction

Breathing with your belly, bring
into your awareness a symbol that
enables the whole of your body to
relax and ground yourself . . .
relax into the support of the
earth. . . .

When you are ready bring into
your awareness a symbol that
enables the whole of your mind to
relax. And extend your awareness
to include the vast reaches of the
sky, the sky that extends out
forever. . . . Feel the lightness of
the sky, giving you flexibility of

thought, relaxing your mind. . . .

Now bring in your symbol for emotional relaxation, nurture yourself with a feeling of connectedness. Feeling supported by all the life around you, supported by life itself. Just as you can relax into the support of the earth, you can relax into the support of the community. . . . Relaxing into the webwork of life, the net of relationships of which you are a part, supporting your life. As you emotionally relax you can be receptive to the nurturance all around you. . . . Feel how, as you emotionally relax, energy flows and your needs are met, nurturance soaks into your whole being, you become open. . . .

And entering, experiencing, your creative self-restoring center, where your expanding awareness flows. Here you are receptive to energy and information beyond the ordinary limits of space and time. Here your knowingness grows, here your knowingness gives you the gift of vision, vision of the ideal. . . . Here your knowingness reveals what is in need of transformation to make the ideal real. Here you discover the energies, the information that you need to create change in the world around you.

I am going to suggest several affirmations, if you wish to affirm them repeat them to yourself after me, feeling as though they are fully true.

I believe in myself, I believe in my family and friends; we believe in our community; there is a free flow of support among us in creating change. . . .

I am honest with myself and others. . . .

I am aware of the impact of all of my actions on others and I act responsibly. . . .

I am open and generous. . . .

I help my community come together. . . .

I trust the support of others. . . .

I am of the people; I trust our process and feel our collective power. . . .

We maintain balance amidst change. . . .

We gain strength from our connection to the peoples of the world. . . .

We have confidence in our ability to care for the world. . . .

A spring of creativity continually flows through us and out into the world. . . .

We believe in life, we are dedicated to protecting life. . . .

We trust the future, we work to bring about a positive future. . . .

Know that in focusing on affirmations you evoke powers from the depths of beingness itself, powers that manifest both within and around you. In focusing on affirmations you cause yourself to align your energies with them and you will discover yourself acting out of these very powers you have evoked. . . .

Listen very carefully to all that is said letting the words draw up your deepest knowingness, knowingness from the depths of life itself.

From Holding On into Openness

Feel that as you are relaxed you are open . . . your body opens . . . your mind opens . . . your feelings open. . . . Let yourself enjoy this open state. . . . Find that place within you where you feel very wise, very strong and yet open . . . fully receptive in your strength

. . . receptivity being your strength. Feel openness. Experience this openness. . . . Imagine yourself being a little seed, all enclosed . . . you're planted and you're watered. . . . Slowly you develop . . . then you burst out from your shell, you grow up towards the sun . . . you reach out towards the sky . . . you get bigger and bigger. . . . And then you create blossoms that start out being enclosed buds just as you used to be an enclosed seed. . . . Then they open up. . . . Feel that the process of growth is a process of opening.

◆

Feel how openness allows movement through you, fluid motion moving through you, welcoming newness. . . . It's that very fluidity that gives you strength. Feel the strength that you have in this receptivity . . . and know that it's as soon as you shut down and become rigid and brittle that you become vulnerable to being broken. As long as you're supple and open, movement carries you. Let yourself spread this openness throughout your being, making your whole life fluid. . . . Massaging all that's been rigid into an open, supple, fluid state of being. . . .

Experience how life itself is fluid, constantly moving, moving all the time. . . . Observe the life in your body and let it be open, notice if there are any areas that you hold onto, any private positions you hold onto.

◆

What do you have to do to avail yourself of the support of life itself . . . to avail yourself of the support of community, of collectivity that we live in? Imagine letting go into the webwork of community. . . . Massage the areas of hardness, of tension with the fluid openness of life itself . . . reassure the areas, let your body know it can trust the energies, that it can be open to the energies of life. . . . Feel your body softening , letting go of your private position of holding on, and relaxing into the support of community. Feel yourself getting stronger and stronger as you relax into the receptivity of community.

◆　◆　◆

Become aware of your mind. Explore your attitudes, your ideas, your beliefs. Notice if you have any beliefs that are hard, that are dogmatic, beliefs you hold on to rather than beliefs that help you move, expand and grow. . . . Notice if you have cynical ideas that say nothing will change anyway. . . . Notice any beliefs that tell you you have to fend for yourself, you have to defend yourself.

◆

If you find any old beliefs that keep you from receiving the collective energy around you, transform the belief. Put the belief through your mental housecleaning device or let it soak into the ground. Insert the opposite: one of openness and trust in your community. Allowing yourself to be a part of the network of relationships. Let yourself trust the fluidity of life itself.

◆　◆　◆

Send your mind softening energy. Let your ideas be supple, not stiff and stubborn but resilient and strong. . . . Let your beliefs welcome newness, welcome learning. Let the climate of your mind be open and relaxed, resilient and strong. . . . Know that in so doing your mind is very clear and your perception brings you true understanding grounded in the present. . . . Let your mind be open, let your beliefs be supple, let your ideas grow and reach up into the sky. Imagine that each of your beliefs is like a flower that blooms.

◆

Become aware of your feelings, the emotional climate of your life. Notice any feelings in your emotional life that are tight, constricted, alienated . . . feelings of separation or loneliness, areas in your emotional life that have become parched and dry . . . or brittle and bitter . . . or cold and icy. Scan your life and notice feelings that no longer receive the nurturance of others, of life itself, feelings that close you off and move you into further isolation, feelings that are dense, dark, hard.

◆   ◆   ◆

Remember the flower that bursts out of its bud, opens in the warmth and light of the sun. . . . Find a warm soft spot inside you somewhere and let it come to the fore and spread like the sap that carries life through a tree, reaching up to the sky. Let your feeling reach to the openness of the sky. . . . Let the light of the sun in, let the warmth in. Give yourself permission to be warm-hearted, to be light-hearted. . . . If any beliefs crop up that stop you from warming up, lightening up, transform them as you did the others earlier.

◆

Everyone has warm spots inside them. Give yourself permission to touch the warmth of others, to receive the warmth of others. . . . Feel yourself soften, relax into the simple meaning of human connection. . . . Fill the hardness with softness . . . fill the darkness with light . . . moisten the dry spots with the love of life itself . . . fill the separations with human connection . . . let yourself be emotionally open to life, to others. . . . As you open you move into a feeling of wholeness, know that as you open emotionally your feelings become fluid, ever changing as life changes, enriching your life . . . filling your life with color, with meaning, welcoming the gift of the future.

◆

As you open, your spirit lightens. Feel the spirit of life percolating through. Let your spirit be open too. . . .

Let the openness extend to include all the people in your life. Let yourself be supported, flexible, a part of the life of the

community you live in. Just as your heart pulses with life, feel the
heart of your community pulsing with life. . . . And know that in
being a part of community you are supported and also share the
support you offer . . . . Feel yourself softening, flexible, connected.
Each of those dense spots you found earlier, flood them with the
energy of trust and connection, a sense of community. . . . Flood
yourself with the good feelings of community life. . . . Letting go of
separation, replacing it with the strength of connection. Feel the
resiliency inherent in all of the connections of life itself.

◆   ◆   ◆

Now look out into this coming week, watch yourself move through
the week, notice when you find yourself tightening up, holding on,
alienating yourself, separating yourself. . . . Then remember
openness and bring through the support and connection you have
with your community and with the fluidity of life itself. . . . Notice
the ways in which you can let go into the support that exists for
you. . . . Notice how in so doing you find yourself with extra
energy, no longer expending it to hold on, you now have the
energy you need to support others in a constant mutual exchange
of community support. No longer burnt out but revitalized by the
exchange of energy. Notice how this can occur in the coming week.

◆   ◆   ◆

Notice how it is you can remember to allow this to occur,
remember to get your strength from your community, no longer
using up your energy in separation, instead feeling openness and
connection. . . . The spirit of life is everywhere.

Regaining Honesty And Trust

It feels good to simply be with yourself, present with your body . . . with your mind . . . with your feelings . . . with your spirit . . . present with the whole of your self. Moving deeper and deeper into yourself, relaxed and aware. Aware and relaxed, deeper and deeper. Feeling the deepest tones of your being, the qualities of energies always present deep within you. Feel them move through you, deep inside of yourself. Let them carry you deeper into your self, discovering yourself again as you return down into yourself, relaxing into who it is that you are. . . .

Now imagine rounding energy, the energy of wholeness, whatever that means to you . . . maybe sound, maybe feelings, vibrations, calming energy, the softness of velvet. . . . Imagine yourself surrounded by this rounding energy, soothing energy. Let the energy of wholeness soak into your body . . . your mind . . . your feelings . . . your spirit. . . . Uniting the whole of your being . . . returning you to yourself, to your wholeness. Enabling you to simply be receptive to yourself, to be comfortably present with yourself . . . as though the soothing energy opens up within you very soft and soothing music, the softness of beingness itself. And let the music soothe you, return you to your wholeness. Surrounded by soothing energy. From this place, give yourself permission to be fully receptive, take care of yourself however you need to, so that you can allow yourself to be fully soothed and fully receptive. Quiet in yourself, receptive and whole.

◆

As you're being receptive, residing in yourself, be aware of the word honesty, *honesty*. . . . Fully experience the word *honesty*, what it means, the quality inherent in the word *honesty*. Simply meditate on the quality of honesty in this receptive state, whatever it may mean to you. . . .

Imagine as though the quality moves through you just as round-ness, as wholeness moved through you. . . . Let it be above your head and all around you. Breathe it in, let it be inside you. . . . Bring it through the sky of your mind. . . . Bring through all the associations you have with honesty.

◆

Notice what aspects in yourself and in your life harmonize with the quality of honesty. Scan your life and notice how the quality of honesty resonates . . . if it comfortably resides within the different aspects of your life. Notice if honesty is wholly present as you think about yourself . . . about others . . . about work . . . about leisure . . . about the world, if the quality of honesty, resonates with these different areas of your life, if it lives with these areas or if it doesn't fit in somewhere. . . . Notice if you are true to your principles. Is it your principles that guide your choices in the different aspects of your life?. . . Notice the qualities of sincerity, loyalty, openness, notice if these qualities are present in your relationship with yourself.

◆

Let yourself know what is so in the different aspects of your life. Shine the light of awareness into the dark areas of avoidance. Allow the light of truth to illuminate your whole life . . . letting your life be whole again. . . . Let the divisions of yourself be mended. . . . Scan your relationships and notice if they are true to principle. . . . Is there anything you are avoiding?. . . Anything

you are hiding?. . . Is there anything you don't want to acknowledge?. . . Do you ever say one thing and do another?. . . Have you
any secrets?

♦

Give yourself permission to see the parts of you that you may prefer
to avoid . . . the parts of you you deny—but they are there
nonetheless. . . . Know that in so doing you heal yourself, you
become whole once again. . . . Be compassionate with yourself,
honor yourself, love yourself and be honest with yourself.

♦

In the privacy of your own awareness expose yourself, witness who
you are, become aware if you ever find yourself subordinating what
you know, what you believe, just to keep the peace . . . or do you
ever subordinate principle to take advantage of opportunity?

♦

What can you do to be true to principle?. . . to be honest?. . . to
be genuine?. . . to once again stand on firm ground?. . . Are you
willing to do this?. . . If so, imagine doing so and feel your
integrity getting stronger and stronger . . . whole again . . . your
whole self residing in the light of truth. . . . Your humanity is
animated. . . . Feel yourself returning to your sense of wholeness.
The whole of yourself unified, fully present with who you are. . . .
Bring in the quality of honesty and let it heal the divisions within
you, heal the pain of being divided, heal yourself with wholeness. . . .

Now let honesty heal the divisions in your relations. Let the
energy give you strength to keep your resolve. . . . Let yourself be
open and receive the energy of honesty.

♦ ♦ ♦

Know that where the quality of honesty is present it creates ground
for *trust* to grow. . . . As you are whole you relate to the humanity

of others, you inspire their return to wholeness. Truth is magnetic, feel it now, as honesty spreads, trust grows. . . . Notice the quality of trust, notice the places in yourself, in your thoughts, in your life where the quality of trust resonates, where it flows through you, whether it flows through the people in your life. . . . Notice if the different people in your life are honest with themselves, with others.

◆

Make any adjustments that you need in yourself, in your thoughts, in your life, so that trust can flow . . . or protect yourself when it does not flow through others in your life.

◆ ◆ ◆

As you are trustworthy, as you are honest, you create trusting relations with your family, your friends and with your community. As trust grows let it flow . . . let it be like a river carrying you. . . . Feel the support that you receive when trust is fully present . . . feel the support that you give others. . . . Imagine the whole community carried in the current of mutual support . . . feel the energy flow, carrying you, carrying others, supporting all of you, trusting energy. . . . Uniting you with yourself, uniting you with your friends, uniting you with your family, with all who are around you. This energy is food for the soul. . . . As the energy flows, notice how you can fully trust the process, letting it flow . . . letting the energy flow. . . . Feel the energy flow through you, flow around you, yourself a part of it all. Feel yourself able to merge with your humanity . . . with humanity itself. . . . Feel yourself open and strong at the same time. . . . Feel the community open, flexible and strong at the same time. . . . Honest, trusting, flowing, strong energy united with the whole. Wholeness . . . as the energy flows, let it flow into the whole of yourself, your body, your mind, your feelings, your spirit, the whole of yourself.

◆

Let it move out into the activities of your life, inspiring all to be honest and trustworthy. . . . Everyone has an underground spring of humanity, imagine everyone's spring drawn up into the mighty river of trust, honesty, support . . . the river of humanity, it carries us all. . . . As this energy spreads, it exposes deceit and clears the ground for only trust to grow. . . . You may want to create a symbol for this honesty, this trust, this flow of supportive energy within and around you, the humanity of us all. Whenever you bring this symbol to awareness, it will tap the great power of humanity that supports us all, it will enable you to be fully honest with yourself and your friends, fully trusting, and know that it will also reveal deceit, for you will clearly feel the discordance when your symbol is present.

◆

If you have any concerns, you may want to imagine talking to the symbol, for in talking to it you will come to know what you need so as to be true to your integrity. Or you may want to shine the light of the symbol into situations to discover what is discordant.

◆   ◆   ◆

Choose what you're going to do with this information you've come to know. Whatever you resolve to do with it and whatever you have decided to take upon yourself in this meditation, imagine carrying through and doing it. Heal yourself with wholeness.

Is It a Want or a Need?

Let yourself enter a very quiet place inside of yourself. Let yourself simply be present with yourself. With each inhalation draw all your energies into yourself and simply be present with all of yourself. Be in your own presence. Reside in your own energy, simply be present with the whole of yourself, acknowledging yourself . . . being present with yourself. . . .

Acknowledge the full range of your feelings . . . all of the feelings—some say one thing, some say another—they may contradict one another. . . . Let yourself acknowledge and be present with all the feelings that flow through you, giving yourself permission, thorough permission to feel your feelings. Be aware of all your feelings of desire and all your feelings of satisfaction. . . . Let your feelings flow through you, all of them flow through.

Notice what you're wanting in your life. . . . Notice if you crave anything . . . if part of you wants something and part of you doesn't. . . . Look out over the landscape of your life, over the terrain of your relations, of your work life, of your home life, of your habits, of your aspirations, how you maintain your health and nurture yourself . . . what you do or want to do to enjoy yourself. Look out over the landscape of your life and notice the things that you like to do or want to do. . . . Notice things you want to acquire, note what your wishes are.

◆ ◆ ◆

Now let the desires, shoulds, coulds, all of them, soak into the ground. . . . And simply let yourself relax into the life that percolates through you, become aware of the resilience of life, the

continual renewal of life, transforming energies constantly, the old
energies fertilizing the ground for new energies, the resilience, the
renewal, the transformation. Let yourself relax into the trust of life
itself. . . . Experiencing the intrinsic knowingness of life, the
self-clearing, self-healing capacities intrinsic to all life. Reside in
this knowingness of life, enabling yourself to be as clear as the
wisdom inherent in life itself. . . . Let your consciousness take on
this clarity, this self-clearing knowingness of life itself . . . feel this
self-healing knowingness reside inside of you . . . trust it, trust
yourself, reside in the knowingness of life.

♦

Now bring back to your awareness those things you discovered as
you scanned the landscape of your life. You are now going to use
the knowingness of life itself to distinguish between your wants and
your needs. With this knowingness you'll discover what is good for
your life, for life itself, and what is not. Bring to mind one thing
you desire, be it a food, a thing, a type of relationship or activity—
choose one desire or habit to explore. . . . Now notice what kinds
of feelings resonate with it. Notice where your center is. . . .
Notice if this resonates with your integrity or with Madison
Avenue?. . . With knowingness notice the rhythm of the feelings
involved. . . . Do they clamor or are they soft? . . . Notice their
shape, are they round or sharply edged?. . . Does it simplify your
life while at the same time connect you with nature?. . . Or does it
simplify your life by disconnecting you with nature?

♦   ♦   ♦

If the rhythm is smooth, if it resonates with your integrity and the
integrity of nature, imagine how it is you can satisfy it and how
your need for it enables you to live in health and harmony. . . . If
you discover that in fact it is a want or a craving, imagine cracking

off the shell, for inside of the craving you'll discover a true need. . . . Within each want is a true need of a higher, clearer order that may be completely different than the original want, but can be satisfied in a healthful manner.

◆

Imagine harmonious ways to meet your need. Give yourself permission to nourish yourself. . . . If you discover greed, nurture the place out of which it springs, massage the hardness, let it soften . . . feel yourself relax, let the greed soak down into the ground . . . If you discover envy let it be healed with the richness of life itself. . . . Imagine satisfying only your needs.

◆

Now look out over the rest of the landscape of your life, notice the difference between your wants and your needs. Clear out the wants, honor the needs. . . . Notice what part of yourself is desiring things. If it resonates with life itself, if it is a need that feeds your life or if it is a want that is a compensation for disconnection, a craving, and if it is, let it be transformed by peeling off the surface like an onion and discover what true need is underneath the want. . . . Honor your true needs. Let go of the cravings. Let the bad habits be transformed, put them through your mental housecleaning device. . . . Know that in so doing you are creating space for you to be even more attuned to what is healthful for yourself and others, for life itself.

◆   ◆   ◆

Honor your needs, and notice how as you honor your needs, you feel more connected to all the life within and around you. . . . You can relax into the support of the webwork of life itself. . . . Become aware of the choices that you can make to honor your true needs, to honor your life, relax in the webwork of life and to let go of the alienated wants; let the cravings soak down into the ground, let the greed, the envy, let it all soak down into the earth to be transformed.

◆

You deserve to have your needs fulfilled . . . notice the choices you can make to honor your needs, imagine a daily routine based on these choices. How does it feel?

◆ ◆ ◆

Now notice the support in the community, in the webwork of life, to enable you to honor these needs. . . . Allow yourself to receive the support around you, giving yourself the strength to honor yourself, to honor your true needs, to honor life itself, to honor the earth. . . . Know that in honoring only your needs you create room for others' true needs to be met, for you have taken only your fair share.

Caring Acts Heal The Future*

Become aware of the web of life. Life regenerates itself. Life reproduces itself. Experience the resilience of life itself. . . . All forms of life give life to life of another form. All life belongs to the great web of life. . . .

Focus in on your own life now, the home that gives you shelter, the clothing that gives you warmth, the foods that give you sustenance. . . . Acknowledge the earth for providing for your

---

*At the end of this meditation, before returning to waking consciousness, you may want to read parts of "A Vision" in the text. Feel free to embellish on it.

life. . . . Acknowledge the work of others who produced your
shelter, your clothing, your food—all the people involved from
gathering, to transporting, to creating, to exchanging, all the
people involved in every aspect of providing for your life . . . the
webwork of society, people producing for each other . . . the work
you do to pay for these things, what your work provides for others.
Each act is part of the whole, the whole of society.

◆

Now notice in the constant exchange of energy among people and
between people and the earth, notice where there is balance, a
give and take that is fair and equal, where there is as much giving
as receiving. . . . Just as your body gets sick, when it expends more
energy than it receives or receives more than it expends, so too,
with society . . . so too, with the earth. . . . Scan your home life,
your work life, your community life, and notice how balanced the
exchanges of energy are. . . . Notice how every act of everyone
relates to the whole, which actions give it strength and which
deplete it.

◆   ◆   ◆

Notice the repercussions of your own personal life style. Notice
how your actions affect others . . . notice how your actions affect
the whole of the web of life.

◆   ◆   ◆

As you discover the imbalances, as there are likely to be many in
the way our society is now organized, send them healing energy.
Just as you can send energy to the ailments of your body, so too,
you can send healing energy to the ailments of society, of the
earth. . . . The earth cries in some places and so does our society—
give yourself permission to care. . . . From that place of care send
healing energy.

◆

Scan your community now and notice who else cares, who among the people you know care?. . . Imagine awakening the depth of caring we all share. . . . Sense our caring, awakening all the numb spots. . . . Imagine gaining confidence and courage out of the connection of mutual care we share. . . . Notice what this caring, healing, shared energy wants you to do. . . . What can you do to make space for life to regenerate itself, to heal itself?. . . What can you do to bring the quality of generosity into your life?. . . Is there anything you are willing to give up?. . . How can you revere life?

◆ ◆ ◆

Let yourself be empowered by the care we share, let yourself be uplifted by the celebration of life. . . . As we care for life, life makes us strong. Imagine that together we care for one another, no one is left out; instead all sharing the caring for each of our lives, for life itself. Together, life makes us strong and resilient . . . together, we can make each other strong. . . . Freedom means taking responsibility for the future. Feel how our strength, the strength of life itself makes us equal to the challenge. . . . Feel ourselves rising to the occasion, uplifted by life, by one another, to secure the future of life itself . . . to secure the future of our children . . . to secure the future of our children's children . . . to secure the future of the earth. Let yourself move beyond your individual concerns and in so doing you transcend your separateness and join with others in caring, in healing, in securing life itself.

◆

Rooted in the collective strength we share . . . strength flowing through us like sap through trees, imagine being able to challenge any action you come across that is destructive to life. . . . Imagine being able to transform yourself and inspire others to transform themselves so that all that is done is done in accord with the

balance of life. . . . All the imbalances that you discovered earlier
. . . imagine what is to be done to regain balance. . . . If you come
across cynicism, complaining, powerlessness, envy, greed or any
other energies that block the flow, that constrict life in yourself or
in others, transform the energy, send it softening life-giving
healing energy and imagine openness being created . . . and the
openness being filled with generosity and care.

◆ ◆ ◆

Imagine how it feels to do what is needed . . . imagine others doing
what is needed to regain the balance of life itself. Imagine everyone
speaking up and acting on behalf of life itself.

◆

Imagine everyone having the confidence to care for the earth and
each other . . . know that we can do it. . . . We can secure the
future of life. . . . Feel everyone returned to the wholeness of life
itself. A time when fences and bars have fallen away, a time when
generosity and care flows between everyone . . . everyone returned
to the wholeness of life itself.

Countout

Begin to finish what you are doing and go over all the insights and
feelings you have had in this meditation . . . energies you've
become attuned to . . . choices, agreements you've made. . . .
Project these visions into your life, set the stage for action.

◆ ◆ ◆

Know that the very fact that you have imagined these visions
makes them possible, makes them probable, makes them *real*. . . .

Tell yourself this now. . . . Acknowledge the collective power we share. . . .

Make yourself ready to come out to outer conscious levels. . . .

In a moment I'm going to count from one to five. . . . At the count of five, you'll open your eyes, remembering all that you've experienced . . . feeling refreshed, revitalized and relaxed . . . having brought with you the energies you became attuned to, ready and able to act on them.

ONE—becoming more aware of the room around you. . . .

TWO—coming up slowly now. . . .

THREE—at the count of five you'll open your eyes feeling relaxed, revitalized, and refreshed, remembering all that you've experienced. . . .

FOUR—coming up now bringing with you what you've experienced. . . .

FIVE!—Eyes open, feeling refreshed, revitalized and relaxed, remembering all that you've experienced, feeling a sense of well-being, ready and able to act on the energies you've attuned yourself to.

Chapter Eleven

Creating
the Future

You are needed. We are all needed. Let us ignite our moral outrage and collectivize our commitment to life—moving from cynicism to an impassioned force standing up for our humanity and the rights of the many generations to come. "United we stand, divided we fall," has become cliché because of its deep truth. Divided, we are prey to manipulation and domination. Political organizing and replacement of the old values we've been living by will keep us alive, will pass on the planet to the next generation.

We respect those who stick up for themselves when insulted. The integrity of the whole of humanity and the earth is now under constant assault. When we stop complaining and commiserating—keeping ourselves powerless and the problem "out there"—only then can we ask, *"What are we going to do about it?"*

FROM VICTIMS TO VISIONARIES

When we only focus on the injustices of the past we get stuck there and don't see ourselves as creators of the future. Remember it's the struggle between the real and the ideal in which development is born. Change is not born out of simply venting frustration toward what is, but by replacing it. We need to see ourselves as powerful, sharing visions, not just rejections. This will awaken our inspiration, empowering us to struggle to create our future. If we are going to pull this one off we must move beyond rebellion. We can transform our fears into our challenges, moving from being victims to being visionaries, moving from being reactionaries to being revolutionaries.

> We hold these truths to be self-evident; that all men are created equal; that they are endowed by their Creator with certain inalienable Rights, that among these are Life, Liberty, and the Pursuit of Happiness—That to secure these Rights, governments are instituted among Men, deriving their just Powers from the Consent of the Governed; that whenever any Form of Government becomes destructive of these Ends, it is the Right of the People to alter or to abolish it, and to institute new Government, laying its Foundation on such Principles, and organizing its Powers in such Form, as to them shall seem most likely to effect their Safety and Happiness. [1]

Two-hundred years after these words were written Vincent Harding sheds new light on these old truths:

> We can now understand that the first constitutional creation of the American nation was more like a poorly attended dress rehearsal, with most of the rightful and necessary performers and creators barred from the stage. Women were locked in homes, black people held in thrall in both South and North, Native Americans harassed, destroyed, and driven from their land, and poor people of every hue taught to let their propertied "betters" make the crucial public decisions for them. Now, nearly two hundred years later, all the hidden, driven, enslaved improvisers are thronging toward the stage, walking on it, creating the drama, reshaping the sets, reflecting the realities of the modern world. Of course many of the

old-line actors think that the show is still theirs, that they are at least in charge of saying which of the "newcomers" will be allowed to participate and how; they believe that their access to the levers of destruction gives them ultimate power to deny new creation. But I am certain that they are wrong. The making of the United States—like the making of the modern world—is beginning again:
O, let America be America again—
The land that never has been yet—
And yet must be—[2]

FRIENDS AND ENEMIES

Well, if you're still with me, hopefully convinced that you are responsible for your part in fixing the mess we live in, I'd like to emphasize that you concentrate on working both on the outside and the inside. Know that you are now ready to move your reawakened inside out. To change the institutions that dictate our lives, the question becomes, "How?" and the answer is that you exorcize the values that support and justify these institutions, and at the same time undermine the structures that hold them up. In other words, rearrange the values you live by and organize politically—tear down the old structures and replace them with new ones, based on new values.

To organize, the questions come up: With whom do you unite? And where do you work so that it makes a difference? In addition, how do you recognize the socially-defeating attitudes that need to change, and then, ridding yourself of them, what new attitudes do you replace them with?

Again, ask the questions: Does it primarily affirm life, or does it constrict it? Is it respectful or arrogant? Is it hot or cold? Is it flexible or rigid? Does it trust life or kill it? Does it focus on quality or quantity? Who does it serve? Who benefits? Whatever action, situation, feeling you're dealing with, answer the questions above and you will begin to know what to do about the situation.

We need to change our criterion to one that protects life, not power/profit. Are the intentions for money (power and profit) or for people (life and justice)? We have reached the point on this planet where these two are absolutely antithetical. We unite with those who believe in the whole of humanity and struggle *against* those who believe in money, power and superiority, acting out of the cancerous "get mine" mentality.

Let's say you want to clean up the river. First you investigate to discover what's messing it up. Maybe you find that up-river there's a factory which is using it for the disposal of wastes. Who benefits? Clearly you don't, but the factory does; therefore, going up to have a friendly talk with the owner will be a waste of time. He may be a nice guy, telling you he'll look into it—you won't hear from him again. His priority is a sound business, which means profits which come from keeping costs down. His actions are killing life; his needs are antithetical to yours. So with whom do you unite? Obviously, you realize the chances are the community also wants a clean river. Your neighbor, whom you may not get along with, will be of much greater help—your interests are the same: you both want a clean river. So figure out what side of the fence people are on in any given issue—where their interests fall. Then organize accordingly.

We must get it out of our heads and stop judging by how it *feels* personally rather than what it *does* socially. *We meet nice guys all over the place who do atrocious things.* We must look deeper into where people's interests lie, not how congenial they are. Anger or a headache are not by nature wrong just because they feel bad. Similarly, just because something feels good it does not necessarily follow that it is right.

We must be on guard against these nice reasonable men. They have learned that a quiet and passionless manner carries an extraordinary credibility. . . . But with a creeping sense of horror one realizes that it is these reasonable men, for all their plausibility, who have made the world what it is. . . . They have fooled us too long, these reasonable men. They don't deliver the goods they promise. These men who sound so knowledgable, so informed, are certainly not providing the answers we are looking for, and for us to expect them to do so and to get angry because they don't is as foolish as to get angry with water when it refuses to flow uphill. *They believe in money and power; and we believe in people.* And as long as we remain in awe of them we will always be led in the wrong direction. They will go on telling us that of course they are taking us south towards the sun and we will continue to find ourselves further and further towards the cold north. We must get rid of these false navigators; we must begin to distrust utterly everything they say.[3]

It's crucial that we know who our allies are and what our enemy is capable of. If our "reasonable" government can "morally" justify the training of foreign military in torture techniques to protect their interests abroad, there is no reason to believe they won't resort to such tactics at home when necessary. What reason do we have to tell us that the military coup in Chile cannot happen here?

John Stockwell, who resigned from the CIA after a thirteen-year career, wrote, "through the CIA, the United States government has run in the last three-and-a-half decades 10,000, 15,000 to 20,000 covert actions. In these . . . there have been more than one million killed—direct victims of the United States' harsh policies . . . this organization ranks literally on par with the Gestapo."[4]

We need to turn to *one another* for we are the ones with the wider view; the experts are usually focused only on their own interests. No one can do it alone—no one has to; each of us is surrounded by others who care. If we just look, we'll see.

WORKING ON THE OUTSIDE

The problems are big, the solutions aren't fully known yet, and there are no easy answers. But that doesn't mean we should give up before we even begin. Authentic change for big problems takes time. Patience is a very important attribute we each need to develop, otherwise we drive ourselves nuts. The plot can't be presented, acted out, and resolved in the neat packaging of a half-hour show with munchie breaks every ten minutes. We need to struggle against the instant-gratification mentality which TV has bestowed upon us. Just as raising a child to be responsible isn't something that can be accomplished by sitting her down and presenting an impassioned speech on the meaning of life, social problems can't be solved in one dramatic gesture—it takes years of painstaking, patient struggle to realize our visions. We need to support each other for the long haul.

Cleaning up the river may seem a bit remote particularly since the owner is probably nowhere to be found because, in all likelihood, the factory is part of a huge conglomerate and it will take more than community organizing to effect change. So, as a responsible person, you ask yourself, "What can I do for social change?" Notice in what way your humanity is assaulted daily. If it hasn't gotten that bad for you yet, I suggest you tune into your reawakened inside to discover what *you* believe in. What's most important to you? Listen to your instincts, what are your convictions? What cries out to you? You have something to offer and if you work out of where your heart is you'll be most effective. Believe with such passion that you go out and tell others about it. That's when politics *move*.

We are social beings, so you are not the only one who feels this conviction. There are others, in fact others are probably already organized. Don't start an organization. Join one. (You don't need to reinvent the wheel.) I won't say which organization to join, but it is my belief that it must be one that struggles with the causes of the problems as opposed to treating the results. We know that just treating the symptoms is ineffectual (performing skin grafts rather than turning off the heat), therefore we need to replace institutions, not just ameliorate their abuses.

If a voice comes up in you saying, "I hate groups, I'm not a joiner," all I can say to that is the ancient wisdom of the *I Ching*, "perseverance furthers," and the greater issues take precedence over your distaste for groups. You don't have a big choice in the matter anyway if you are committed to do something, for alone you are ineffectual. Remember that all of us have been afflicted by our society; we've each received expert training in the art of being competitive, i.e., non-cooperative. When you have trouble in groups, struggle is what's called for—not despair or dropping out (you're not in it for yourself). As Americans we've been well trained in maintaining unprincipled peace and either/or thinking, leading us to believe that in all struggle there is a winner and a loser. To the contrary, only through struggle do *all* the issues get put on the table so that people can see all the implications and decide what is best. If we remain silent so we don't rock the boat we invite mistakes. But struggle must take place not in the context of who's right and who's wrong, but in the context of mutual respect for differing points of view. The following sections will help you deal with the troubles that arise in working together.

Some feel they can't join a group because they don't know enough. This attitude usually comes from the feeling, "I'm not good enough," in comparing themselves to the ones who seem to be the experts. They are so intimidated they feel they have to have it all together before they join up. We're not in it to compete with one another. The ones who seem to be experts haven't always been so, but got that way through having been *engaged* with the struggle, and are usually overjoyed when anyone decides to join—the more the merrier.

I don't mean to imply that political work is solely a somber affair. It is the greatest of human joys to move out of isolation and into collectivity. But however it feels the fact is that political work works, it's our only legitimate insurance policy. If the peasantry in a little country like Vietnam can win against the richest, biggest, most technologically advanced country in the world, I think we've got a chance—the challenge is before us.

WORKING ON THE INSIDE

You've heard the phrase, "You are what you eat." Well, you are also what you think, so if you transform your thinking you transform yourself. If you internalize life-affirming values on a deep level it will be those values you act out of. As I have said before, none of us is lucky enough to remain unaffected by the destructive attributes of our society (the outside world has moved in on us all). As we transform our thinking it will empower us to transform our society more effectively. Conversely, as we engage in political work—behavior based on new values—we will find these new values rooted further into our consciousness. Action is the lifeblood of beliefs.

This whole book is about our being able to reposses the innate capabilities of our consciousness. Consciousness is, by definition, awareness. We experience the present, we define it in terms of our past experience, and then we project possibilities for the future. Our consciousness is a mirror of the external world. Whatever limitations exist objectively also exist subjectively, and vice versa. We need to become masters of our own thoughts, extricating those which empower the very institutions that are undermining our lives. This is a necessary part of becoming truly independent so that we can use our *full* intelligence to change the objective conditions around us.

You might ask, "How do I *discover* which of my attitudes are socially detrimental if I can't judge by how they feel?" Another myth rooted in individualism is that you can always discover the truth from your deeper experience. When you relax, as this book teaches, you do become open to universal knowingness, but you are still stuck because you can only interpret it through your own limited experience. So, looking within will not teach you which particular beliefs are anti-social. Although once you know which beliefs you want to change, working within will be of great benefit. We learn about these beliefs from each other. I have yet to meet a man who discovered sexism by looking within. The problem with exploring only within oneself is that inside is simply the tapestry of belief structures woven from your own individual past experiences, and, needless to say you have not experienced everything. The only way you can perceive knowledge you receive directly into your awareness (psychically, not through the five senses) is for it to be clothed by the thought forms *already* in your mind.

Even if we were receiving true knowledge, by the time we perceive it, it has been distorted by our own limited personal world views. This was brought home to me very clearly in a session I taught a while back. One of the participants was a very well-intentioned white man in a high-ranking executive position. We did a meditation wherein everyone created/got in touch with spirit guides. He described his guides as a black man who took care of the grounds and a woman who took care of his sanctuary. His past experience had never exposed him to the idea that some people would take offense at his perception of these guides as being in subservient roles. This was normal for him—that it was either racist or sexist never *occurred* to him, which doesn't negate the fact that he did have a profound and moving experience with his guides.

When I tell this story people often respond by saying "Good, his guides will teach him about racism and sexism." That would be nice, but even if they wanted to they would have great difficulty finding the appropriate thought forms in his mind with which to clothe the information. It would be like trying to teach someone about color when you only have a vocabulary relating to shape. Remember, if you have no flour in the pantry it places severe limitations on the bread you bake. This dynamic operates both in the projection and the reception of information. A man of privilege has little or no experience of what it feels like to be oppressed.

We each take our own thoughts for granted because they come from our own limited experience. We need each other to point out individual limitations, for *collectively we are not limited*. We each come to understand situations with a new perspective when we listen to people describe experiences different from our own. We learn from social practice, not meditation practice, although meditating on where and when you are feeling one-up or one-down will be of great help in discovering what needs to be changed. Once you discover beliefs that are more respectful, meditate—get them down on the right level so you can *act* out of them.

If you find yourself in a dominant group it is your responsibility to turn to the dominated and learn from them what attitudes you continue to carry that are patronizing, offensive, and perpetuate these power relationships. Men learn from women, whites from people of color, straights from gays, rich from poor. . . . This does not mean they have to teach you directly—they have enough problems to deal with, but you can read their works, go to cultural events, or talk to friends who have more experience with the oppressed group, and most important, inform yourself of their historical struggle.

> As we become separate, and are manipulated as objects, we lose our own sense of self-worth, our belief in our own content, and acquiesce in our own exploitation. When we women, for example, see men as embodying the *content* of the culture, and ourselves as not possessing inherent value, we submit to the rule of men and devote our energies and talents to furthering men's desires instead of our own.[5]

If you are in a dominated group you owe it to *yourself* to identify with your own group and not with your oppressor. For slaves to identify with the master is not the key to their freedom. Instead it fully mystifies the true source of their problems, and thus removes them further from resolution, which can only come from a *struggle* for their freedom. Women's liberation isn't to be male identified; blacks' liberation is not to be white identified; workers' liberation is not to be owner identified; liberation for the disabled is not to be able-bodied identified, or homosexuals, straight identified. . . . When we stop identifying with the oppressor and allowing him to define us, we can discover our own identity within our own group. Just as each individual is the expert on herself, knowing what's best for herself because she knows her experience better than anyone else, so too social groups are the experts on themselves. Women, not men, must define the values we want to live up to—we are the only ones who know our *own* experience. The same is true for every group, and no group is inherently superior with the God-given right to define and dominate any other group.

This is what the separatist phase of political movements was all about—with space to look for themselves people became clear about what they wanted to shed and what they wanted to embrace. But it is necessary for *all* of us to work together for we're *all* in it together. We need separate caucuses, not separate movements. Together we can develop our cultural autonomy and give up the privileges we maintain at other people's expense. We can work together to get off each other's backs.

We must look and see who it is we are identifying with and if it serves our collective interest. We can help each other do this; that's what consciousness-raising groups are all about: for people to discover their own power. That's what criticism in political groups is all about: to discover and correct mistakes.

Often people say that those who are oppressed are so because they chose it—karma is the old blame-the-victim mentality. Victims of injustice perpetuate their positions because they have not been allowed to think that life could possibly be different. Because of enforced ignorance and economic deprivation they have never had the space to question their beliefs and therefore, through no fault of their own, have become supporters of their own oppression. It is in the interest of the elite to keep us from questioning, for when we come to understand the true source of our problems then we will take steps to change the conditions which cause them. It is not in the interest of those who eat five-course meals to allow those who starve to contemplate the possibility that life could be different. No wonder it was illegal to teach slaves to read.

You don't have a boss just at work; inside of you resides another boss who continually regurgitates the rules and regulations for the maintenance of the status quo—keeping you in line. You do have to answer to the boss at work—you'd lose your job otherwise, but your subjective boss has no such power. If you question that authority you won't lose your job, but instead you will regain the liberation of your soul. You will free yourself to have clear relationships, and allow yourself to move from mechanical, programmed roles to creative and independent action. Subjectively we all live in a police state as long as we don't investigate our beliefs and rid ourselves of the ones we discover to be detrimental.

To maintain the social order the elites have injected us with all kinds of myths: Women are naturally fickle and therefore not dependable; you can get whatever you want if you work hard enough; the higher up in the social strata you are the more smarts you have; without the people at the top "caring" for the people at the bottom, the bottom folk would sink into barbarism; if you're poor you're lazy. . . .

If you really committed yourself to investigate just one of these statements, the deception would quickly be revealed. Investigating it means looking into the conditions that gave rise to the different points of view involved. When I look into my own experience, I know that I am dependable; I know the fact that I am not rich and don't have many material things I want is not a reflection of either laziness or lack of intelligence. And I know that without law and order imposed upon me I would not regress into barbaric behavior. Would you? You need to look into *who* the different beliefs are serving.

It is fully understandable that we identify with these myths. They are what we're taught and we have learned them well. They are seductive; the more you accept them and live by them the more goodies you get. But the system is limited in how many goodies it can and will dole out. There is a part of me that wants to make myself fully "feminine" as defined by Madison Avenue, but most of me knows it is not in our interest to let that voice have the upper hand. The less I respond to those thoughts the more they become echoes in the back of my mind and eventually fade all together, for I have not kept them alive by my behavior.

WORKING TOGETHER

Just as we need each other's support in pointing out self-defeating attitudes such as saying "can't," "never," "always," . . . we need each other to point out when our thinking is socially defeating. We each have different experiences and if we welcome feedback from one another then we can remove the shackles from our minds, leading to the removal of the shackles from humanity. This is why collectivity is so important. Together we can discover the real potential of society. Feedback is always in a context of our common goals—not an end in itself—just as you only work on obstructive beliefs when they hinder forward motion. As Hinton describes the transformation in a Chinese village:

> What made self-revelation possible for the work team members that day was the deep commitment everyone of them had to the success of the land reform movement. They freely examined themselves and their comrades, not for partisan advantage, not for the sake of exposure, not as an exercise in *mea culpa*, but in order to remove obstacles in the way of more effective work. This was the objective framework around which the unfolding of the subjective attitudes revolved. And this, not coercion, not curiosity, not some narcissistic self-torture made self-and-mutual criticism viable and grounded in necessity.[6]

We learn through social practice. Because everything is constantly changing, and because we've all been socialized by various systems of oppression it is always necessary to use criticism to correct and learn from mistaken attitudes and actions. As with all work, criticism must always be done in the spirit of unity.

Because we each take our own attitudes for granted, we need each other to point out what needs to be changed for our collective well being. We must begin to give each other feedback, criticizing what we notice in one another that we think has become detrimental to our common interests. It is not to point a finger at the bad guy and isolate her from the group. We are not supporting each other by blaming; we are supporting each other in *changing*. It is a given that we all continually make mistakes—the only way to avoid that is to do nothing.

Pretending we are perfect and hiding mistakes is a behavior inflicted on us by that deadly individualism. If everyone is fully autonomous it makes sense to hide mistakes because if they are admitted, one is treated as a bad guy and it will interfere with individual advancement. We are not autonomous; we all make mistakes for understandable reasons. Because we are so programmed to hide them, we need to create a nurturing, open environment for us to admit to them. We can create an atmosphere of genuine trust, always moving into "we" consciousness. This takes naked honest courage, and caring in all of us.

Watch yourself, be sure you aren't criticising to make yourself shine out compared to your mistaken friend. Be sure your motivation is one of unity, not to isolate one another, that your intention is to strengthen the group not yourself. If it is the latter, self-criticism is needed. Conversely, be aware if you're remaining silent for the sake of "peace," not wanting to be a "troublemaker," or are you afraid you may be exposed as wrong? Silence is just as bad as blaming; we have to *support* each other in changing. We are in relationship with one another and criticism must *always* be given in the spirit of *unity*, of collectivity, of common interests. When we work through conflict it *always* strengthens us; we find ourselves feeling a stronger unity with one another. We are intelligent human beings, if we trust each other we will arrive at attitudes and actions that serve our common good.

Giving one another feedback strengthens our abilities to attain what we're working towards. When giving a criticism point out the unity you each have with one another. What is your common task? (Giving feedback on an issue that has nothing to do with your expressed unity is none of your business.) If there is agreement, express how you think the specific action or attitude that has been going on weakens your common interest and what change would strengthen it, further it. Criticism must always be directed at the attitude and the act, while supporting the person receiving the feedback. Be concrete, avoid value judgments and name-calling. The purpose is change, not blame. Use "I" statements, not "you" statements. And don't assume you're right until collective investigation. Be dialectical—nothing is 100 percent bad, there is duality in everything. Look at both sides. Try and look for the reasons the person is doing it—what conditions gave rise to it? This will help you understand the feelings involved. Be self-critical; since you are in relationship with this person be conscious of what you may be doing to collude with what is going on. Ask yourself what can be done to support change occurring, and express that.

We are so conditioned not to make waves that criticism is something most of us find very difficult; even acknowledging what we appreciate in one another is hard to do. This too is important to express because it feels good to know we are not being taken for granted, so we each are less likely to burn out. Because none of this is easy it's very important to structure feedback into the ongoing activities of the group.

We are trying to heal ourselves; to reawaken our societal nerve endings to get back on an even keel, so we can become a functional society, meeting fundamental human needs. No longer can we remain silent, nor isolate one another by pointing the blaming finger. We are supporting one another in overcoming each of our shortcomings thus strengthening our collective power. *To remain silent is to treat enemy ideas as friends. To blame is to treat friends as enemies.* These two patterns have become the norm in the United States, and, in consequence, we fully incapacitate ourselves for creating a better world. We must never forget we unite with those who have common interests; they are our friends. We must also never forget that just as social conditions change, so too do people—everything changes. Always, change is the one given. The crux of it is: let us have change with consciousness, so we can choose the change we want.

THE FUTURE IS BORN OUT OF HISTORY

Every step along the way of creating the great wealth of our nation, those of us who have stolen the riches have given up our humanity—lost it in the blood of the American Indians and the sweat of the African slaves.

> It is a terrible, an inexorable, law that one cannot deny the humanity of another without diminishing one's own: in the face of one's victim, one sees oneself. Walk through the streets of Harlem and see what we, this nation have become.[7]

American culture has reached its present pre-eminent development and high reputation on the forked tongue of the white man. Our country is not so full of illiteracy or ignorance as it is of sophisticated *ignoring*. We have created a decultured, homogenized, polished atmosphere of denial.

Each step toward "development" is also a step away from nature, destroying both ourselves and all that is around us. And now our "great" nation views itself as the protector of "freedom" for the world (not the earth) — in reality a protector of the interests of our own greed.

Amassing and protecting wealth, power and privilege distorts the soul of people, divorcing them from the whole. Remember, no great fortunes are born out of fair deals. With the privilege wealth pays for we have become the ugly Americans viewing the "underdeveloped" world as primitive, exotic, and behind the times thus justifying our "helpful" intervention. Men, to maintain their supremacy, view women as stupid, weak, and sentimental. If we are really so helpless why did they find the witch burnings necessary to get rid of millions of us to consolidate their power? Whites, to justify keeping the best jobs and the best homes, view people of color as incompetent, unmotivated, and potential criminals — the height of hypocrisy, when it was whites who not only stole the land but the people too. Having separated themselves from the rest of us, the privileged, in the name of protection, have cast themselves into roles of managing directors, lest everyone else get out of control.

I don't mean to picture everyone as being humane except the privileged white men. They have always had their opportunist collaborators in some women and people of color. And conversely some white men have refused to play by the rules of the game. One may be born poor or rich but where one stands is not carved in stone; people change, and the crucial question is whose interest do you promote and defend, i.e., who are you loyal to? If people of color and women manage, despite adversity, to clamber into the affluent American Dream, they, along with everyone else who makes it in must of necessity create a plastic protective coating so they can sleep at night. This is not a difficult task, for all Americans are already insulated from the cold facts of reality by prime time; the mass media creates the frenzied atmosphere of consumerism. It's a full time job for those of us who don't buy the game to break through the layers of lies and see the light of reality. It is not in the interest of the affluent of our society to see life as it is, instead they stereotype, trivialize, devalue and dehumanize the exploited; hence there is no call for them to be concerned. They have to become callous because open, caring people cannot be at peace if they know their position is being paid for by the suffering of others. The poor develop callouses on their hands, the rich develop them on their hearts, and consequently all are better protected from pain. Remember it is in the the denial of conflict that compulsive behavior is born, so the richer one gets the more rigid, hardened and neurotic one becomes and the further he or she has opted out of the human community.

Those who are creating the problem are *not* those who can solve it. Insulated, they don't even know they're in a burning house.[8] To bring balance back into the world we ought to look for spiritual leadership to those who have *not* been born into patriarchal/white/ capitalist privilege and therefore *cannot* take its values for granted. Everything contains within itself its own opposite, every form of dehumanizing oppression gives birth to the great humanizing struggle for emancipation; those who at every turn have been negated, their integrity insulted, their lives trampled on, who despite all the humiliation courageously maintain a sense of dignity for who they are; those who, in breaking out of their roles have created a legacy of struggle. Rather than begging for permission to assimilate, they have always pointed out the American lie while upholding the American vision of a country governed by the people themselves. Historically in America, Blacks have always been in the forefront of exposing hypocrisy on the one hand, while igniting inspiration on the other. The Civil Rights movement profoundly shook the conscience of America, exposing the hypocrisy of institutionalized racism in the Land of the Free. Aroused Americans of all kinds joined in, then stirred into movement: women, Latinos, Native Americans, lesbians and gays, disabled . . . also began to organize, struggling for their dignity to be respected.

I am sickened by what my country is built on and its culture of denial; I am sickened by what it has become. But I am healed by a vision of our country with its enormous potential for truly embracing human diversity—in that, my patriotism is born. I don't blame myself for my country's history. I am not guilty, although I *am* responsible for my country's future. My American identity is built not on denial, nor guilt, but on embracing the humanity of everyone.

It is not a question of your birthright but of where you stand, what you believe in and strive for. I'm not suggesting that those who have access to privilege and are morally outraged at the state of decay should cower in the dark, riddled with guilt, and wait for others to fix it. (Feeling guilty simply takes a victim position; what is in question is not the past but the future.) To regain our humanity those of us with privilege are called to stand up against the tide and join in collectively struggling for a world that runs on trust rather than oil, creating a culture rich in diversity, humanity and respect, not wealth. Arrogance needs to be transformed into humility. It is in the legacy of struggle that the well of sustenance, courage, faith, and vision can be found. All people can gain strength in drinking from that well. Rising to the occasion, together we create the future. Freedom means taking responsibility for the future.

> Now, as we dare to take responsibility for our own future as individuals and peoples, as we give up the fantasy that presidents or the best charismatic leaders can solve the most basic problems of our society, the moment of great possibility opens before us. . . . Keeping the faith, creating new faith, we may enter the terrible and magnificent struggle for the re-creation of America.[9]

History has delivered us to the point of choice between death and destruction or life and re-creation. As no one wants the former, we must take a stand for the latter and be on the side of life. There is no room for complacency for that is choosing to usher in the end. The biggest mystery of life, the one thing we can count on, is the fact that it is regenerative. In the end it is always on the winning side of the struggle. Despite seemingly overwhelming adversity, grass grows up through concrete. In the end the blades of grass crack the concrete and stretch towards the sky. Let's be sure that humanity comes through too, and is not one of the species extinct by the year 2000. We need to give ourselves credit for the strength of our incredible resilience. If circumstances were the sole determining factor none of us would view things as we do, we would have become automatons long ago. We have great life-giving power within us. As the world within us has come alive, by trusting our own nature, we can protect nature—inside, outside—working inside out to create a world that runs on trust, in which everyone is both cared for and cares for, where we cherish the earth as our mother—for nature itself is the giver of life. We must take a stand and be on the side of life. The choice is ours.

Notes on the Following Meditations

The meditations on sexism and racism more than any of the others were born out of a collective process. It all began when I was developing visualization tapes for gay men with AIDS. In my investigation of the needs it became quite clear that addressing internalized homophobia was imperative, given the level of self-blame that many men were putting themselves through. To do this a client of mine agreed to gather some friends together to talk about their experience. The idea was for me to be able to tune into their experience—as I have been doing in my support groups for years—and lead a meditation off of their discussion. These men were from a community of gay men which often calls itself The Færie Circle; they have not simply come to terms with being gay, but out of their collective strength have come to the place of embracing it as a gift.

The process we went through was extremely moving to me. I was entrusted with the heartfelt experiences of these men as they gave me a glimpse into what it was like to grow up gay in a homophobic society. I was humbled to witness their struggle to reclaim their dignity, to love themselves and other men, and to rid themselves of the ignorant condemnations of the dominant society. Needless to say, the meditation that came out of it was just what was needed for the project.

We had discovered a powerful process together and I came to the conclusion that I needed to do the same thing with different groups of people for the book.

The book was in the last stages of production and there was neither the time nor the space to include meditations on all the myriad oppressions our culture perpetuates. So I settled for what in my opinion are the two biggies: racism and sexism, consoling myself that the rest would have to constitute another book. If it is any consolation to the reader, it is my belief that every kind of oppression follows the same patterns. That is, the dominant group trivializes the oppressed whether Jewish people, "mental patients," people with physical disabilities, . . . and proceeds to define them, their circumstances and their choices. Consequently, the meditations designed for people of color and women can easily be adapted by replacing the specifics and keeping the generalities.

All the meditations in this chapter except the first two could also be used as a basis for discussion in groups endeavoring to deepen their understanding and ability to deal with the issues each meditation addresses.

I have no illusion that these meditations, particularly the ones that address racism and sexism, are the last word on the subject. But if anyone finds them helpful in reclaiming their personal power and humanity, then my work will have been worthwhile. The more personally powerful and humane each of us is, the more effective all of our work becomes in dismantling the institutionalization of racism and sexism.

Many of the meditations in this chapter are particularly long; feel free to pick them apart and use them a piece at a time. There are also lots of affirmations; use the ones you like.

(Please see the acknowledgements for appreciation of those who supported the creation of the "ism" meditations.)

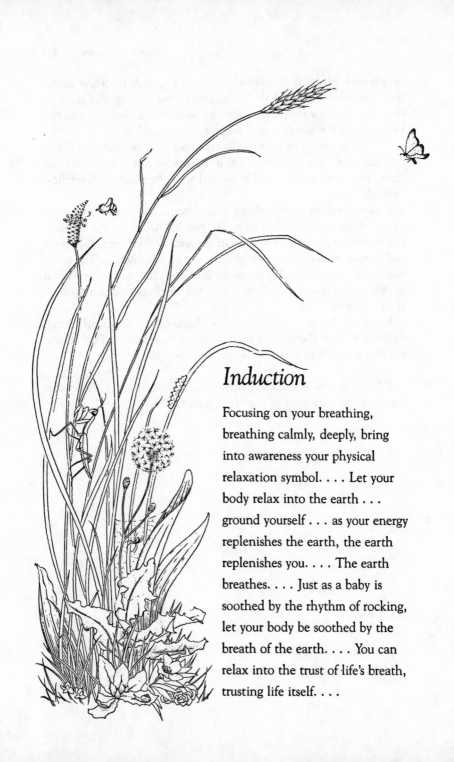

Induction

Focusing on your breathing,
breathing calmly, deeply, bring
into awareness your physical
relaxation symbol. . . . Let your
body relax into the earth . . .
ground yourself . . . as your energy
replenishes the earth, the earth
replenishes you. . . . The earth
breathes. . . . Just as a baby is
soothed by the rhythm of rocking,
let your body be soothed by the
breath of the earth. . . . You can
relax into the trust of life's breath,
trusting life itself. . . .

Bring into awareness your symbol for mental relaxation. . . .
Breathe in the sky, let the sky relax your mind . . . let the sky open
your mind, your mind is as vast as the sky. In the quiet of your
mind you are fully receptive. In the quiet of your mind you are
fully intelligent and creative. . . . Let your mind relax into the
universality of knowingness itself. . . . Your mind is as open and
vast as the sky. . . .

Bring into awareness your symbol for emotional relaxation.
Become aware of the emotional climate present in you now. . . .
Take care of your feelings. Give your feelings permission to relax
into the support of life itself. . . . Let the "shoulds" soak into the
ground making space to receive the nurturance from life, from
those in your life. . . . Appreciate yourself, appreciate others
appreciating you, let yourself emotionally relax, opening to the
appreciation of life itself. . . .

Bring into awareness your symbol for your level, your creative
self-restoring center. . . . Feel the universal life force energy that
flows through everything, flow through you. Let it replenish you,
let it return you to yourself, to life itself. . . . Let yourself be
strengthened by the knowingness of collectivity. . . . Let yourself
be healed by the goodness of people. . . . Let yourself be empowered by your kinship with all the peoples of the world . . .
keeping the faith, together we heal one another, together we heal
the earth. . . . It is here, in this space of receptive quiet that all
people coalesce. . . . Here vision is born, here creativity is born,
here we come to know, intimately know, the reverence of life
itself. . . . Out of this receptive knowingness we gain the strength
to struggle for a just world. With this knowingness let yourself
deepen your inner experience. With your breath go deeper into

knowingness itself. With your breath go deeper and deeper into communion with life itself. Let yourself breathe in the power of the goodness of people, of humanity, of life. . . . Enrich your knowingness now, drink of the well of life. When you next hear these words you will be at an even deeper level of knowingness, very receptive, very creative and in tune with all that is; full of faith, full of strength, full of vision, empowered to heal.

◆　◆　◆

Finishing what you're doing . . . feeling the power of life surging up into you, giving you faith, giving you strength, giving you vision . . . energy you can bring into the world around you, healing energy. . . .

I am going to suggest several affirmations. If you wish to affirm them to yourself repeat them to yourself after me; feeling their power, evoking their power, attuning yourself to their power. . . .

I believe in life. . . .

I believe in myself, I believe in my family and friends; we believe in our community, there is a free flow of support among us in creating change. . . .

We gain strength from our connection to the peoples of the world. . . .

I am of the people, I trust our process and feel our collective power. . . .

My personal power is born out of collective life. . . .

I live in the spirit of unity. . . .

Only what is good for everyone is good for me. . . .

I take only my fair share. . . .

I am trustworthy. . . .

I am open and generous. . . .

I am competent and humble. . . .

I honor the dignity of all people. . . .

I get to know each person I meet for who they truly are. . . .

I am enriched by everyone striving for excellence. . . .

I am enriched by cultural diversity. . . .

I observe the impact of all actions on our collective well-being. . . .

I am honest with myself and others, I am true to principle. . . .

I am courageous, I always put my convictions into practice. . . .

I honestly and lovingly give criticisms that strengthen our collective power. . . .

I openly receive criticisms that strengthen our collective power. . . .

I welcome learning from mistakes. . . .

I stand on the side of justice. . . .

I respect the differences among everyone dedicated to justice. . . .

Our differences strengthen our collective power. . . .

Principled struggle brings clarity, empowering our forward motion. . . .

I learn from the past, I welcome the future. . . .

I am dedicated to creating a safe future for all the children. . . .

I stand on the side of life. . . .

We have the power to create a future in which all life thrives. . . .

Know that in focusing on affirmations you evoke powers from the depths of beingness itself, powers that manifest both within and around you. In focusing on affirmations you cause yourself to align your energies with them and you'll discover yourself acting out of these very powers you have evoked. Know that this is so.

Keeping the Faith

As you hear the sounds of these words you'll go deeper and deeper into the universal realms out of which all life springs, you'll feel yourself relaxing into the resilient support of the web of life. With each word you hear you'll become increasingly attuned to the connectedness of life, the mutuality of life. With the sounds of these words moving through your awareness your consciousness will expand from your usual individual awareness into cosmic consciousness. Give yourself permission to enter into your natural state of fluid connectedness, supported, supporting life, supported, supporting humanity. . . .

Feeling the rhythms of life percolating through you . . . the pulse of life, the breath of life, the hum of life. . . . Knowing life percolates through all creatures, through all people. . . .

Sense the universal breath—what we breathe out the plants breathe in, what the plants breathe out we breathe in. Energy constantly supporting, transforming, moving—universal breath interweaves all that lives upon the earth. . . .

Feel the great synchrony of the universe. The movement of electrons, the movement of planets, all in synchrony. . . . Let your tensions be washed away by waves of universality; feel yourself sinking deeper into the support of life itself. . . .

Experience the fluidity of life . . . everything moving, carried by time . . . day into night, season to season, year to year. History is alive. . . . Each generation gives life to the next, generation to generation to generation, each generation dreams and struggles for a better life for the next, history in the making. . . .

Remember those who passed before who cared, living, breathing beings devoted to life, dedicated their lives to the struggle for humanity, they live on in the spirit of humanity. . . . Summon up the courage of those who passed before, empowering ourselves, the spirit of humanity lives and breathes in us now. Let our ancestors rejoice in our rising to the times. . . . Aroused, together we take up the call, make history, create the future. . . . Feel life percolate through everyone; life regenerates itself. Life endowed us with life; now we are called upon to preserve life itself. . . .

Give yourself permission to experience the fullness of your devotion to life, feel it in the depths of your heart, your soul, your whole being . . . allow yourself to care. . . . Remember the special moments in your life, times where your heart was warmed . . . celebrations . . . shared joys . . . shared love . . . majestic landscapes . . . the wonder of life itself. Feel your passion for life.

◆ ◆ ◆

Let your feelings merge with the feelings of others who have a passion for life . . . passion ignites passion . . . ever widening passion for the protection of life, everyone caring . . . forming a great wave of humanity to change the course of history; history is alive within us . . . together we have great healing powers, together we transform ourselves and heal the earth.

◆ ◆ ◆

When we listen we hear cries. . . . species die out, whales give up, rain is poisoned and people starve as the greedy keep taking more and more and more, spilling a path of carcinogens in their wake . . . babies are born deformed, great forests are leveled, oceans polluted . . . and the earth quakes and spits fire and storms more than ever before. . . . Listen.

◆

Remembering the powers, the power of people united, the power of life itself . . . healing powers are all around and within us. Life is about transformation. . . . Let all the pain, the rage of yours, of the earth's, let it transform itself into a great healing force, a force as fierce as a mother protecting her young.

◆

Let the power of life surge through you, empowering you, uplifting you, arousing you . . . aroused, humanity forms a great moving wave; passion for life carries us, empowers us to emancipate life itself . . . to create a future where the dignity of all life is respected . . . where the life of every single baby of every kind is honored. . . . Our ancestors rejoice as we answer the call of history protecting the claim of life itself. . . .

You have your life to offer, you can make a difference. The passion, the power of life lives within you too . . . feel yourself a part of the great struggle, healing powers move through you. Listen to your convictions, listen to your instincts, what do you believe in? What cries out to you?

◆   ◆   ◆

Give yourself permission to struggle for what you believe in. . . . Remember who your allies are . . . joining together, feel how much *more* powerful you are, everyone is, as we're joined together . . . with community strength we *can* make a difference. . . . Give yourself permission to believe that together we can make a difference . . . that we will make a difference. . . . Life always wins in the end, grass grows up through concrete and reaches for the sky. . . . Life regenerates itself, life always wins in the end. . . .

As we take a stand on the side of life, humanity pulls through, the spirit of humanity lives on and each generation will continue to dream and to struggle for the next generation . . . trusting the future, keeping the faith. . . . Let yourself be empowered by life itself. . . . Let yourself be inspired by life itself and we'll heal the future.

Patience, Endurance, Courage

Create a place that seems and feels infinitely peaceful. Whatever that may mean to you, infinitely peaceful, a place that radiates tranquility, serenity, maybe a place in the desert, in the mountains, the plains, wherever you imagine it. Create a place, an infinitely peaceful place. . . . Peaceful energy that seems to be primordial. Serenity that transcends space and time as though tranquility were in this place always. . . . Peaceful energy, that's all around you and soaks into you. So peaceful it's almost piercing. Quiet that is so acutely quiet in the peacefulness you can hear it. Peace . . . tranquility . . . breathe it into your whole being.

♦

Somewhere nearby, imagine finding a tree, there is a special tree, a tree that is very old. . . . Let yourself be in front of this tree, see it from all dimensions, feel it, sense it, imagine the bark, imagine the branches stretching up into the sky, the roots stretching down into the ground. . . . This tree, notice how it fully belongs in this place, as though it's merged with this place, with this landscape and yet autonomous and strong. . . .

Now imagine that as you breathe you draw into yourself more and more of the sensations of this tree, almost as though you merge with the tree, as the tree merges with the landscape. Let yourself merge with the tree, let your breath enable you to be in communion with the tree, as though your body were the tree and you had roots that stretch deep into the earth and branches that reach up into the sky. . . . Breezes blow through you and the ground always is below you, all around your roots, enabling you to stand. To stand firm, with the wind and all the weather, through all the seasons. . . . Your roots bring up rich nutrients and water from the depths of the earth, letting it feed the whole of your body as you grow up towards the sky . . . bask in the sun . . . cleansed by the rain . . . birds occasionally land on your branches, and animals walk around your trunk. . . . Feel the sense of seasons, yet a sense of timelessness in time. Feel the endurance you possess, let yourself be this tree, enduring through time, enduring through storms, discover the world as a tree knows it. . . . Basking in the calmness of this peaceful place in which this tree lives, growing out of the calm quietness, living fully in each moment and yet living in timelessness.

◆   ◆   ◆

Now take this sense of rootedness, of reaching to the sky, of calm emanating from the whole of your being, the endurance, the timelessness, take these qualities into your life. . . . Imagine taking these qualities, this peacefulness, and transform them, transmute them into *patience*. . . . Patience, patience that transcends time and space, a well of energy that is strength . . . present for you always. Patience . . . primordial patience that enables you to blend with the currents of the moment, carrying you through all times as you move from activity to activity. . . . Move the qualities of how it is to live as a tree into your life, enabling you to be calm, to transcend time as you move through life, moment to moment, season to season, fully present wherever you are. Feel yourself taking your life moment by moment, a step at a time, grounded

and open. Standing firm yet reaching to the sky. . . . Embrace
these qualities in your life and they will enable you to be healthy,
basking in the sun, being cleansed by the rain, being enriched by
the earth, fully patient with life, letting creativity flow through
you—just as water flows through the tree enabling it to grow.

◆   ◆   ◆

Patience gives you a well of strength. While you live in the present,
the peaceful present, you are fully receptive to the voices around
you and within you. Being fully present, the present moment has
expanded, making room for all that is so . . . you can hear the
whispers of the universe . . . you experience what is so in the
moment, and know that this patience also gives you a vision of the
future . . . illuminates what *can* be so. When you are patient your
receptive knowingness is fully present. As you're patient, wherever
you choose to focus your awareness you hear, you sense the subtle
messages that tell you what is so, what can be so. You merge with
your life as the tree merges with the landscape. . . . Being patient,
being peaceful, you can focus your awareness wherever you choose,
discovering wisdom in the present moment. As you reside in
tranquility you hear messages, you are fully sensitive, fully receptive
and come to know what is so, wherever you look, wherever you
feel, wherever you direct your awareness, you discover subtlety. . . .

Sensitize yourself to this knowingness, moving forward calmly,
knowingly. Carried by patience, you have the strength of the past
united with the vision of the future. . . . Living in the present
moment, carried by patience, you have strength, wisdom and
vision. Just as the tree endures thousands of storms, know that you
have the endurance to make the best possible future a reality.

◆

Now let this patience create an openness, create a channel, for courage. Patience gives you the receptivity of knowingness and the strength of endurance. . . . Courage carries you forward. . . . Courage enables you to act on what you know to be true. Courage enables you to put into practice your convictions . . . just as the tree's roots bring up water, sustenance from the depths of the earth so that the tree may grow and reach for the sky. As you inhale, imagine drawing up courage from the depths of collective knowingness, draw up courage from the depths of humanity's wisdom. . . . In so doing you are empowered to reach into the world and bring about goodness.

Let the legacy of humanity's struggle provide you with heroism. . . . Now having the courage to act on the messages of universal knowingness. Let courage empower you.

◆

Rooted in courage, give yourself permission to be bold; Rooted in courage, give yourself permission to stick your neck out, to speak up, to act on your knowingness. . . . Know that you can endure storms. . . . Know the world grows as you bring in your truth, your vision of what is right. . . . Imagine filling your body with the strength of courage and let it spread through all your feelings . . . and immerse your mind with courage . . . and your spirit, let your whole self fill with courage which is the fullest expression of humanity itself.

◆

Create a situation in your awareness now where in the past you may have let things slide, knowing that what was going down could have been better, clearer, true to principle. . . . Maybe with someone who operates out of assumptions you disagree with . . . maybe at a conference you can speak from the floor. Choose a situation. . . . Create it in your mind's eye. . . . Feeling the scene, now, imagine courage giving you the nerve to speak your piece, to go against the tide, to struggle with respect and belief in your convictions. . . . Imagine what someone you look up to would say.

◆

Living out your fullest potential, what would you say?. . . Rooted in courage, believing in yourself, believing in your experience, having confidence to express what you think. . . . With courage you can truly honor what you believe. Imagine courage coming right up into your feet, and up your backbone . . . and let confidence emanate out of you; express yourself. . . . Give your convictions the eloquence they deserve, let your convictions come alive. . . . Imagine this now, imagine speaking up.

◆   ◆   ◆

You may want to create a symbol for all that you are experiencing now. Talk to the symbol, decide how you are going to bring these qualities out into your life, how you are going to act on this knowingness. Honor your convictions. . . . Notice if there is anything you have to give up to manifest this energy.

◆   ◆   ◆

Imagine doing what you've chosen . . . notice how you'll remember to do so. Feel it all occurring, know that you can dip into the courage of humanity whenever you choose. Know that you are fully capable of always giving life to your convictions. Know that others support you in so doing. . . . We gain strength from one another. Together we have patience, endurance and courage to heal the world with giving life to our convictions, giving life to our vision.

◆

Know that these qualities are always present. Knowingness . . . Patience . . . Endurance . . . Courage . . . present with you whatever you do, wherever you go, whomever you're with.

Who Benefits?

Life regenerates itself, life pulsates through you and around you all
the time. Life is the wisest of all teachers, when we listen to the
spirit of life we learn, we discover what is so, we come to know
what is needed to heal our own body, our community, our society
and even the earth itself. . . . Life is intrinsically intelligent.
Letting life be your teacher, you can tap into all knowingness. . . .
With life flowing through you, with life's brilliant light you can
penetrate into the essence of any concern and discover what is so.
Trust nature, trust your own nature, with life as your teacher you
are intelligent. . . . By simply focusing your awareness you can
come to know what is needed to heal, for life is a creative regenerative force. Sense the intelligence of the life that percolates through
your whole being, through beingness itself.

◆

Bring into the light of life any concern you may have that you
would like to gain clarity about. . . . It could be a project you're
involved with, a development in the community, some decision at
work, a person who has come into your life, an event taking place
in the world . . . choose a particular concern that you would like to
gain clarity about.

◆

Like a film, play back scenes that are relevant to your concern,
simply play them back and watch them in your mind's eye . . .
remember them vividly, the whole atmosphere surrounding what is
taking place, the quality of energy present. Bring the whole of the
situation into your awareness now, feel it, sense it, color it in.

◆   ◆   ◆

Keep the situation in mind and now notice each of the people
involved. . . . Intuitively sense each person . . . how open and
flexible they each are . . . their motivations . . . their trust . . .
their sensitivity to others . . . what directions people are moving in
. . . where they each have been. . . . Sense all these things.

◆ ◆ ◆

Is quality or quantity focused on?. . . How does each person feel
about power, profit, property?. . . How do they feel about people,
life, justice, mutual respect?. . . Who do they trust?. . . Who are
they loyal to?

◆

Are people aspiring to the same ideal?. . . Are they moving in
unison?. . . What's the quality of exchange between the different
people involved?. . . How do people feel about one another?. . .
Is everyone equally respected?. . . Is anyone manipulating?. . .
How do people feel about others who are not involved?. . . Are
people exclusive or inclusive?

◆

Replay the scenes and trust your sense, feel out the situation, is it
warm in some spots and cold in others? Is it flexible in some places
and rigid in others?. . . Is the atmosphere open to change, to
learning?. . . Is respect for life itself present?

◆ ◆ ◆

Is the quality of the process being attended to, or only the product?. . . Are people acting out of the same information?. . . Is
information shared freely or hoarded anywhere?. . . Is there
anything hidden?. . . Is power concentrated anywhere?. . .
What's the source of information? Does it spring from direct
experience? Is it solid or superficial?. . . What assumptions are
present?. . . What roles are people playing?. . . Are there any
stereotypes being taken as reality?. . . Are people open to feed-

back? With knowingness sense the impact of different people's actions. . . . Is there accountability?

◆ ◆ ◆

Notice the different perspectives present, see it through other people's eyes. . . . Notice where the support lies for the different points of view. . . . Notice how people align. . . . Sense what direction everything is moving . . . is it likely to change? Are any other tendencies gaining momentum? Allow all of this to be revealed in your awareness.

◆ ◆ ◆

Notice the impact of the whole situation on others . . . and on the earth. . . . Who and what pays?. . . Who benefits?. . . Let the spirit of life be your teacher. . . . What kind of responses will the situation evoke?

◆

Review what you discovered to be discordant with the spirit of life. . . . Now notice what inside of you personally resonates with the discordance.

◆ ◆ ◆

With the regenerative healing powers of life itself, transform all the energy into an affirmation of life. . . . Feel it becoming open and flexible, amenable to change.

◆

Knowing what is so inside of you and around you, become aware of your allies and sense what can be done so that all that transpires serves life itself . . . how can whatever constricts the flow of life-giving energy be stopped? How can transformation take place?. . . Imagine being able to work together in unity, respect and a celebration of life itself . . . how can you support one another? What do you need from one another?

◆

Notice how you can act on all the insights you have discovered . . .

what needs to be communicated to whom. . . . Choose what you
are willing to do and imagine doing it.

◆   ◆   ◆

Acknowledge life as your teacher. . . . With the intelligence of life
you can always penetrate any situation and intuit the intentions,
the benefits or detriments . . . you can come to know what is so.

Empowerment (for People of Color)

Create now, your own place of power, a very special place . . .
create it now, with your imagination, a place where you feel your
personal power; it may be deep down in the ground or high up in
the sky. It may be a place you've once been or a place you've often
been, or maybe your place of power is solely a creation of your
imagination—wherever it is, imagine being there. . . . Create it,
feel it, be there . . . experience this place charged with power,
power that springs from the source of life itself, this space is
potent. . . . Imagine as though this were the home of your spirit
. . . feel the magnetic core of your being vibrating with the spirit of
this space. . . . However you create it, feel it, know it, this is your
place of power. This is the germinating ground of your creativity
. . . the creativity unique to you. . . . The power deep within you
resonates with this place you create. As you hear these words you'll
find yourself more and more in tune with your own individuality. . . . The sounds of these words will carry you deeper and
deeper into yourself, into the power of life itself. . . . Feel yourself
moving down into the depths of beingness itself . . . feel yourself
going deeper, and deeper into yourself, into your source of power,

your source of knowingness . . . where you are attuned with the
universal energy that moves through you, that always moves
through you. . . . Relaxing into yourself now, returning to yourself. . . . However you imagine it, feel the essence of your being,
the deepest qualities of who it is that you are . . . feeling your own
energy, your own personality, your own qualities . . . it feels good
to simply be present with yourself . . . to reside in the presence of
who you are . . . it's a good feeling to acknowledge yourself, your
center, the source of your strength, the source of your creativity
. . . feeling the essence of your individuality, the essence of your
being, the particular person that you are. Affirm the unique
character of yourself. A being that is different from anyone who
ever has been, or anyone who ever will be. This is your
essence. . . . Bathe yourself in the healing energies of this essence.

◆

Your experience is clear, your knowingness is always right there,
responsive to whatever is happening right then, fully responsive in
the moment, alert to what is so, feel your dynamism . . . fully
possessing yourself, your integrity, knowing yourself, defining
yourself, knowing you are okay, you are beautiful, fully possessing
the space that is yours. . . . Feel that, claim your space, yourself,
your integrity, your ability to create your reality as you choose it to
be. . . . Experience the power you have, the power inherent in
being human, claim your personal power. . . . You can respond
however you wish, the choice is yours . . . feel that, acknowledge
your own knowingness, your own clarity, your own character,
acknowledge that your first response is right, for you know what is
so for you . . . you are the *only* one who knows what is so for you.

◆

Let yourself feel your full intelligence, beauty, power. . . . Give

yourself permission to be fully you, to embody your fullest potential. Fill up your entire self with your power. . . . Love your self . . .
your body, love your body . . . your mind, love your mind . . . your
emotional and spiritual self . . . love your whole self.

♦

Love your expression of life itself . . . expressing what it means to
be human in your own particular way, trusting your own intelligence, claiming your own power, claiming your own space whatever
you do, wherever you go. . . .

Feel yourself moving through the world, fully possessing yourself,
claiming your space, interchanging with whomever you see, with
integrity, with power from within, power that resides deep inside
always. . . . Always responding the way *you* choose, knowing
what's right to do to preserve, to express, to assert your humanity,
putting forward what is true for you . . . knowing what's right to do
to create the reality you choose, to express your truth . . . acknowledge your confidence, you are a powerful being, you can determine
your choices. . . .

You have fully claimed your personal power . . . so much so that
the energy that emanates from you is so vibrant that it simply
wouldn't occur to anyone to tell you what they think "your place"
is, what they think you can or can't do, how far you can or can't
go. . . . You know you determine your choice for yourself. You
define your situation.

♦

If anything comes into your awareness that sabotages your power,
that cuts short your choices, that insults your integrity, if anything
comes in that keeps you from fully possessing your space, look at
the scene. . . . Your knowingness is fully responsive and will tell
you what needs to be done to fully repossess your space, to reclaim

your power. . . . Talk to the characters in the scene, transform the constricting energy and create an atmosphere of mutual respect. . . . If it is times past, rewrite the scenes. . . . If it is in your current life and as you imagine talking to the people, if that still doesn't change the scene, then with agility and knowingness notice how to maneuver around it, maneuver through it, changing your position. . . . Transform the negativity and redefine the situation maintaining your integrity, your boundaries, your choices. . . . You choose it, *you* define it.

◆ ◆ ◆

Make room for your power, for your personal power to grow, for you to become even more fully who you are, begin to purge yourself of the ancient anger. . . . Let it soak down into the ground and fill the holes it leaves in its wake with the love you have for yourself, for life itself. . . . Healing the bruised child that may reside inside you, softening the scars from all the dehumanizing experiences you never asked for. . . . Be kind to yourself . . . quiet your frenzy toward perfection, you are already more than good enough. Love yourself. . . . Transform the energies of the past, re-create your life.

◆ ◆ ◆

Replay your past, remember those times when you've been degraded, remember those experiences you never asked for. . . . Times you've been dismissed, your feelings disregarded, your humanity ignored. . . . Times when assumptions were made and taken as facts, sometimes spoken, sometimes not. . . . Times you've been taunted . . . remember those times, transform the energy, let it all soak into the ground, re-create your life, heal yourself, love yourself.

◆

Remember times you were looked at with disgust, seen as somehow less than human. . . . Ground it all, let it soak into the earth to be transformed, and fill yourself with gentleness, with kindness, with love for yourself. . . . Remember the times where your abilities were doubted . . . times your honesty was questioned. . . . Times you were distrusted . . . remember those times you never asked for . . . clear them all out, re-create your life, heal yourself, love yourself.

◆ ◆ ◆

Ground all of those negative pictures of the past . . . anything that kept you down. . . . Imagine it all going right down into the ground, healed by the earth, leaving you clear, powerful, defining your space, for *you* are the one who knows who you are.

◆

If there are any people, in your present or your past, that keep giving you messages to keep you in what they think of as "your place," that keep you down . . . notice what you're inclined to do . . . you may want to send them compassion, you may want to simply avoid them, or move them out of your space. . . . Notice what you need to do to re-create the scenes. . . . Some of these messages may be from your own people, your own family, or community, where you've been told what "your place" was supposed to be. . . . Re-create the scenes so that everybody is respected; everybody defines themselves, and discovers one another, no one molds themselves into imposed roles. . . . Re-create the scenes so everyone has choice. . . . As you re-create the scenes you heal yourself with the fullness of life itself.

◆ ◆ ◆

If there are any voices inside you that tell you who you ought to be, what you should and shouldn't do, ground it, let it all soak down into the ground, healed by the earth.

◆

And in so doing you empower yourself, you heal yourself with the fullness of life itself. . . . Now imagine healing yourself with the essence of who you are. . . . Cleanse yourself with your essence. . . . Massage the scars with the affirmation of your life, of your power . . . so clear, so cleansed that nowhere inside do you see yourself through their eyes, *they* are the ones who don't understand, they are the ones with the limitations. . . . Heal yourself and feel your horizons expand. . . . Heal yourself and feel yourself become more fully who you are, embodying your potential . . . stretch the limits, break the limits and still reach further . . . grow into yourself.

❖   ❖   ❖

If there were any scenes you couldn't recreate, with your strength now, with your power, project a protective shield, like a mirror, a shiny silver mirror . . . and bounce back all the dehumanizing energy. Bounce back their definitions of who you are and let those who want to keep you down see how hollow their stereotypes really are. . . . Bounce back the energy to anyone who wants to keep you down, bounce it back, bounce back all their projections, all their limited expectations, so they can see what is so and come face to face with themselves, and learn from their own limitations. They can experience their energy for what it is.

❖

Know that with your knowingness, with your agility you can move around these people with ease and maintain your own boundaries, maintain your own integrity. Acknowledge your ability to live a life with fullness, to live fully, amidst all the contradictions. . . . Acknowledge your power . . . honor yourself.

❖

Acknowledge all those in your life who have supported you to be who you truly are. . . . Acknowledge the love you share.

❖   ❖   ❖

Feel the connection that you have with others who are defining their own space . . . creating a collective strength, feel community, as each individual defines their space . . . everyone strives to live up to their fullest potential . . . feel the strength of our differences united . . . creating cohesiveness. . . . It is the diversity in nature that gives the web of life its strength and cohesion. . . . Each of us a different individual, defines our own space, who we are, what we want, what our choices are, where we're going . . . we take it for granted that we each define our own space . . . collectively, respecting one another. . . . True freedom emerges out of respect for one another. . . . Create a time in your mind's eye where we live in a culture of mutual respect . . . a time that celebrates cultural diversity. . . . A time where we no longer need our guards, no longer need our shields . . . a time where you can take yourself for granted and relax into an atmosphere of mutual respect . . . a time where power springs from within.

❖ ❖ ❖

Let this vision spread a sense of relaxed security through yourself . . . through your community . . . through the world.

❖

If we can envision it we can create it. Know that this is so.

From Racism to Respect (for White People)

Feel the spirit of humanity flowing through you . . . extend your awareness to include the great diversity of peoples and cultures of the world. . . . Just as the earth is magnificent in all its variety . . . mountains, plains, tropics, deserts—all having a character and

beauty of their own, yet each particular place is different, there are
no two places upon the earth that are the same. . . . So too,
humanity is magnificent in its variety of cultures . . . each with
different language . . . different traditions . . . different dress . . .
each with different homes, different rituals, different festivals . . .
diversity in custom as rich as the variety of flowers, diversity as rich
as life itself. . . . Life is about expression. . . . Just as all places are
of the earth, each with soil, and plants and animals and weather
. . . all peoples of the world are *of* humanity . . . no two persons
the same, yet each person and all peoples celebrate with the food
they eat . . . everyone laughs, dreams and struggles . . . everyone
appreciates relaxing after hard work. . . . Everyone is warmed by
the growing of children. . . . Everyone loves to play . . . everyone
mourns their dead. . . . Everyone has the spirit of humanity flowing
through them. . . . Take time to appreciate the depth and breadth
of humanity, all we have in common with people everywhere in
what it means to be human, and yet all the ways that we are
different, appreciate the depth and breadth of humanity.

◆

Now notice your attitude when you bring to mind other cultures.
Do you feel they are somehow deficient, primitive, not quite as
good as our culture? Are they exotic, backwards, not fully
understanding what is so?. . . Take time to wash away the
arrogance you've been taught, remember it's the culture of white
people that has brought the world to the brink of destruction. . . .
Imagine the arrogance being transformed into humility and respect.
Let yourself be open to what other cultures have to offer . . . what
we can learn from them.

◆　◆　◆

Don't blame yourself for your attitudes, they have been implanted by our society which regards property with reverence while disregarding people, disregarding humanity. And so our society has painfully severed us from other peoples, severed us from our own humanity. . . . We can *heal* our wounds, we can make genuine humanizing connections with peoples of other cultures. To heal we must search out and uproot the lies, uproot the arrogance, and as we weed out all the attitudes that separate and alienate us, we make room for our humanity to rise up and flourish in an atmosphere rich in diversity and full of sharing what it means to be human—sharing our passions, sharing our dreams, sharing our struggles. . . . To make connections we must look within and discover what separates us, transform it, and in so doing we create the climate within ourselves that makes room for true trusting relationships, each of us becoming fuller human beings—our lives enriched.

Now look at the area, the town or city in which you live. . . . The richer the neighborhood the less people of color are likely to be around; but the homes have views and the horizons are wide. . . . In the poorer parts of town, there are fewer and fewer white people around, and there is hardly a horizon to be found. . . . How do you feel in these different parts of town?. . . If you feel safer in the richer part of town remember their crimes go on behind boardroom doors. . . . Are you scared in the poorer parts of town?. . . Remember here even the innocent are policed to death. . . . Pay attention to all that passes through your mind as you bring all of this into the light of your awareness. . . . Now notice as you look around town what kinds of work people do.

❖ ❖ ❖

Is there any kind of work you consider below your dignity?. . . Does somebody have to do it? Do you feel someone else is more

suited for it?. . . Why?. . . Do the rich deserve the interesting
well-paying jobs while the poor are left with the monotonous
low-paying jobs—if they are lucky enough to be hired at all?
Whose labor made the rich rich? Whose labor keeps their homes
and streets clean?. . . As you explore all this notice any beliefs you
have that justify the state of things—that say somehow whites
deserve more.

◆

You needn't feel guilty—you didn't create the situation but any
beliefs you have that justify it perpetuate it. . . . Your consciousness
is fluid, transform your beliefs into respect for the dignity and
capability of all people. . . . Allow yourself to feel moral outrage
and know that in the long run, together, we can change the way it
is.

◆   ◆   ◆

Now, like watching a replay of your past, from the very beginning
of your life bring back memories involving people of color, early
memories . . . beginning to understand or misunderstand who
people of color were . . . how they lived, what they did, how the
rest of society treated them. . . . What you were told . . . and if the
people you knew fit the picture you were told. . . . Reflect on how
you felt about it all . . . watch your development as you grew older.
Give yourself permission to remember, *vividly* remember.

◆

Occasional times that were rich with meaningful connection,
however momentary . . . remember the many times you've been in
a position of more power. . . . And remember the hundreds of
constrained and uncomfortable incidents where the energy simply
didn't flow, and if it did, it was only because the roles were not
equal. . . . Remember times at school . . . in the streets . . . on the
buses . . . in the stores . . . in people's homes . . . at big events . . .

hundreds of constrained uncomfortable incidents . . . and still some that broke the barriers and made genuine connection . . . and others that may have knocked right up against the unspoken barriers. . . . Replay your life and remember, *vividly* remember times leading all the way up to the present . . . let them parade right through your mind's eye. . . . Re-experience them, how did they feel?

◆   ◆   ◆

Re-create significant events, remember people's expressions, comments, how they treated one another. . . . Re-create the particular events that somehow stick out. Pay attention to all that ran through your mind in these times.

◆   ◆   ◆

Now focus your awareness on the particular situations that stand out . . . especially re-create the uncomfortable ones . . . and bring to mind different situations in your life now in which people of color are involved. . . . Notice the atmosphere of each of the different scenes. Notice the quality of interactions.

◆   ◆   ◆

Now, choose one that has a number of people involved . . . remember the details of the scene.

◆

I'm going to ask several questions . . . let reflections of these questions shed light on the situation . . . these questions may uncover more beliefs that are in need of transformation.

Are your responses to each of the people of color based on who you've come to know each person is, or are your responses based on what you think the person is and what you think that means?. . . Are you responding any differently than you would if they were white?. . . Is there anything you would usually do that you feel you can't in the presence of these individuals?. . . Can you trust them?. . . If not, why not?. . . What do you assume to be so about any of these people?. . . Notice how each situation would be different if only white people were present. . . . Are people pretending to act natural?. . . Is the energy constrained?

◆　◆　◆

Now notice who defines the parameters . . . who speaks the most . . . who's taken seriously. . . . Are the people of color there to loan legitimacy to the group or because of who they are, not what they are?. . . Are they seen as representing all the people of their own race?. . . When they speak are they taken just as seriously as anyone else?. . . If people disagree do they express it as they would with a white person, or smile politely and move on?. . . Is information withheld from them?. . . Is their participation peripheral to the functioning of the group?. . . Is their competency or honesty in question?. . . When you are finished reflecting on this situation you may want to reflect on others.

◆　◆　◆

Now once again bring back into your awareness the depth and breadth of humanity. . . . Remember even though we may feel separated we are each an expression of life, we are all human, distinct, yet within each of us resides the dignity of life itself. . . . We are all human, we each have pains and pleasures, problems and passions.

◆

Remember times when you've made human connections with someone, sometimes maybe in small momentary ways, sometimes maybe in rich, important ways. . . . Remember times where you've made a human connection with people of another culture, of another race . . . times in which you each broke out of the separation that we're usually put in, and made a connection that enriched your lives. . . . Remember times where you're on equal

footing with a person of color—each of you respected. . . .
Remember the different times that this has happened. . . . If no
times come to mind then imagine what it would be like if you *did*
feel human connection.

◆

Appreciate the generosity of people. . . . Let yourself be enriched
by a different cultural experience . . . let yourself laugh, share, care
together . . . enriched by your differences, comfortable with your
differences . . . enriched by your common humanity.

◆   ◆   ◆

Now extend your awareness through time and envision the future
in which this sense of connection that you've had, that you're
imagining now, with people of other cultures, with people of other
races, is commonplace. . . . Just as humanity flows through us all
. . . imagine a time where there is easy fluid rapport flowing
between you and individuals of another race, where this is
commonplace. . . . Imagine there being strong cultural pride in
everyone. . . . Imagine everyone acknowledging the heritage and
legacy of different peoples. Envision a time in which there is strong
cultural identity and connection, the sharing of human identity
across cultures. . . . Feel what this would be like . . . create this
time.

◆   ◆   ◆

If you can imagine it, it makes it real, makes it possible, together
we can bring it about . . . a great humanizing time.

◆

Create a symbol that represents this kind of society, something that
embodies this future, a time that we've been able to struggle to
create together, where cultural differences enrich one another's
lives, and all individuals are experienced as *individuals*—individuals
with a heritage. . . . And bring this symbol into your present, into

the presence of the world now, a world that separates us all the time, a world where wherever we go we find ourselves among people, sometimes we're scared, sometimes we can't feel connected, we don't know one another, and instead our ignorance fills in the gaps. Now, let the gaps be filled with the quality of your symbol instead. . . .

Now let the energy of the symbol spill out into each of the uncomfortable scenes you were focusing on earlier. . . . Ground out the constrained, dehumanizing atmosphere and fill the scene with the energy of your symbol. . . . Let the scenes be filled with laughter, sharing, caring. . . . Let the scenes be filled with respect, trust and appreciation of everyone's differences.

◆   ◆   ◆

Now imagine what you could have done differently in these situations. . . . Imagine how an atmosphere of genuine sharing could have been created. . . . Imagine what you'll do next time.

◆   ◆   ◆

With your symbol in your awareness, let it fill you with confidence to take risks, for it is only in taking risks that you learn . . . and making mistakes is vastly better than being constrained, always afraid you're going to say something wrong. Let your symbol fill you with knowingness, remembering everyone's humanity . . . let it give you the courage to take risks, to move out, to move from separation into a sense of connection and respect . . . the stereotypes crack as you act differently than you have been taught. . . . Celebrate the life that all of us have, the humanness, the laughter. . . . Let your symbol empower you to do that; let go of the discomfort, and let yourself be filled with courage and openness to gain strength from connection, gain strength from an affirmation of differences. Let the energy heal all the old wounds.

◆

Take time to transform all the dehumanizing, hollow ideas you've been taught, and all the fears and anxieties, let it all soak into the earth and the earth heals it. Let it all be replaced with a commitment, a moral commitment to making a human world, a just world . . . to struggle for this time together. . . . Feel yourself enriched by the struggle. Feel our humanity rising up and flourishing in an atmosphere rich in diversity, sharing what it means to be human . . . struggling for a human world together.

◆   ◆   ◆

Imagine moving through the activities of your life, and whenever you find yourself feeling separate, fearful, guilty, or any other feelings that keep you from moving forward into an affirmation of connection, with your symbol in mind become aware of how you can recognize the separations and move into connection. . . . Keep your symbol in awareness and you'll come to know what is needed. . . . Notice the support you have in your community to help you move into connection; the support there is in other communities to help you move into connection, having the confidence to take risks, to make mistakes, to learn, to connect.

◆   ◆   ◆

Know that your symbol creates the climate within you to be able to stand up against mistreatment whenever you come across it. . . . Your symbol will enable you to help others move into connection. . . . Imagine it.

◆   ◆   ◆

Tell yourself you'll remember your symbol whenever you need it. . . . Know that the spirit of humanity flows through all of us. . . . We can create a world that is full of trust, sharing and caring; a world where the integrity of everyone is respected, the integrity of life itself is respected, a world where respect and sharing of differences is commonplace. . . . How good it will feel to feel connected all the time.

Reclaiming the Self (for Women)

Create a place that supports you. You know well how to support
others, how to care for others, how to encourage others, how to
nourish others. . . . You know well how to reassure others, how to
understand others, how to support others. . . . Bring all these
qualities into your place of support, for you deserve to be supported
too, you are important. . . . Create a special place in your imagination where you can now receive support. . . . You may want to
bring in other women who believe in you, who care about you,
who take you seriously. Invite any others from your past and
present who will stand by you. . . . Create your own very special
supportive space.

◆

Now you are on the receiving end. Fill up this space with warm,
caring, loving energy. . . . As you breathe, breathe in all these
nourishing qualities, fill yourself with care for your own self. . . .
You may want to create imaginary spirits who also support you and
invite them into this place, your place of empowerment. . . .
Imagine them telling you how *wonderful* you are. . . . Imagine
hearing about all the good qualities you have, how smart you are
. . . how strong and resourceful you are . . . how dynamic and
creative you are . . . how sensitive and interesting you are. . . .
Imagine hearing all this and more from those who stand by
you. . . . Breathe it all in. Give to yourself as you have given to
others. . . . Give yourself permission to take yourself seriously, to
believe in yourself. . . . Let yourself be empowered by remembering

who you truly are. Fill yourself up with this knowingness, replenish yourself, honor yourself . . . you deserve it.

♦   ♦   ♦

It feels good to be cared for. . . . Just as nurtured children grow strong and hardy, feel yourself grow strong and hardy, confident and competent as you receive the nourishment you deserve.

♦

Nurture your personal power and it will grow even stronger; to do this travel back into the past, take those who stand by you with you, if you wish; you are now going to remember, *vividly* remember all those times you've been robbed of experiencing the fullness of yourself. As you hear these words they will bring back into your awareness now times in your childhood when you were told what nice girls *don't* do. . . . "Nice girls don't play rough." . . . "Nice girls don't climb trees." . . . "Nice girls don't get so dirty.". . . Remember, *vividly* remember all those times you had to constrain yourself, restrain yourself. . . . "Don't make waves." . . . "Act ladylike." . . . "Don't be smart; be sweet.". . . All those times you were told to curb yourself and be a Nice Girl. . . . Remember them now, re-create them now.

♦   ♦   ♦

Rewrite the scenes, break the constraints so you get to do what you always wanted to. . . . Imagine being able to push to the limits of your capacities. . . . Discover the fullness of life. Feel yourself growing into the fullness of who you are.

♦   ♦   ♦

With the fullness of yourself love who you have become. . . . Women are givers of life, let yourself be supported, be encouraged by those who stand by you. . . . Affirm your own character, your own life, breathe life into your creative capacities, give life to your ideas   let your own interests be animated. . . . Take yourself seriously, let yourself be assured, trust yourself to pursue your own creativity, your own interests. . . . Feel yourself as dynamic, capable, competent, you are a creative being. Give yourself permission to pursue what interests you. Imagine doing what you would like to do. . . . With the fullness of yourself, stretch the limits, break the limits, live up to your potential. . . . Feel yourself in command of all your capacities, independent and able . . . know that you *can* do it, let yourself receive support to do it. . . . Believe in yourself, you deserve it. . . . Encourage yourself as you encourage others, receive support for yourself as others have received support from you. . . . Feel yourself empowered to express the fullness of who you are. Imagine how you can be more fully who you are.

◆   ◆   ◆

Feel strong in yourself, in command of yourself, empowered by who it is that you are, scan the situations in your life now, scan the relationships you have, scan the activities of your life and notice if ever you find yourself shrinking from your fullness, shrinking back and making room for another. . . . If ever you say to yourself that what you think, what you feel are not as important . . . whenever you put your concerns aside and care for another . . . transform all that devalues who you are.

◆   ◆   ◆

Change the situations so everyone cares for one another. Assure yourself that you are just as important and notice what needs to be done to equalize the scenes, so everyone only takes and gives their fair share. . . . Make the relations equal, be loyal to yourself. . . . Others will be okay, give yourself permission to be devoted to yourself too.

◆

Scan your life and notice when you complain and remember that you can initiate change. Things don't have to stay the same. . . .

Notice what needs to change to create balance, imagine it all occurring. . . . If you find yourself getting stuck, imagine what friends and guides would say.

❖   ❖   ❖

Believe in yourself, in who it is that you are, take time to love your body, to reclaim your body. . . . You needn't try to make it what it's not. . . . This is *your* body, and the beauty of life resides in your body, no matter how tall or how small, how big or how old your body is, the beauty of life, the beauty of you resides in your body. . . . You are a person like none other, like no one who ever has been or ever will be, there is no need to gauge yourself against a model. The integrity of your body deserves respect. . . . Take time to let all the judgments, all the dissatisfactions soak down into the ground and be healed by the earth. . . . Your body is yours, no one else's, there is no place for others' judgments. Ground all of it. . . . Reclaim your body, love your body, possess yourself. . . . Let go of any feelings that tell you you have to fashion yourself . . . dress yourself . . . paint yourself to catch the eyes of others. .   . Your body is already fine the way it is . . . occupy it, reclaim it, honor your body and love yourself.

❖   ❖   ❖

Reside fully in your power, notice what you need to do to maintain your integrity, to remain in command of yourself as you move through the world. . . . Particularly notice how you can maintain your dignity among men. . . . Give yourself permission to keep your integrity and assert your power. . . . Imagine sharing support among women, all of us empowering one another . . . a strong community of women, empowered women. . . . Notice what you need to do to maintain your dignity among men—to protect the dignity of all women.

❖   ❖   ❖

Create a vision of the world in which everyone is cared for . . . imagine a world in which everyone is supported in discovering their fullest potential . . . where there is no such thing as "women's work," as "a man's job" . . . instead we all do what needs to be done together . . . a time where everyone's bodies and everyone's capacities are respected . . . a time when we live together in mutual care.

◆   ◆   ◆

Acknowledge the support others have for you . . . the support you have for yourself . . . the support you have for other women. . . . Go over what needs to be said, what needs to be done to honor who you are . . . who women are.

Nourishing Yourself (for Men)

Imagine a very quiet and tranquil place to be, imagine a warm and comfortable place to be. Create your own place of comfort, a place where you can relax and let all the concerns of your life drain away . . . create your own place of comfort . . . imagine soothing colors . . . a gentle breeze . . . the warmth of the sun . . . soft music . . . create your place of comfort. . . . Be there now. . . . Feel this place, quiet and sensuous place, here you can just be with yourself and relax. . . . Imagine all the details of this scene, relax into the tranquility, security, comfort of this place. . . . Here you can let go and be replenished with the gentle, peaceful energies of this place; let yourself be nourished by this warm and gentle place. . . . Feel the edges inside being soothed. . . . Feel the hard spots softening.

◆

However you imagine all of this, however you experience comforting qualities, quieted by it all . . . breathe in the qualities and let them massage you into feeling very quiet inside . . . breathe in these qualities and let them awaken the gentle and nurturing parts of you, for you are a sensitive being . . . find the quiet place inside . . . be receptive to the quiet inside . . . feel how it resonates with this comforting place you have created. This tranquil and gentle quality that you feel within and around you is very healing, it can make you whole again. . . . Feel the warm, tender, loving qualities beginning to stir inside you, let them fill you, let them heal you. . . . Let them grow inside you.

◆

All those parts of you that you left behind as you grew into being a man, you can reclaim them now, make yourself whole again, heal yourself, feel yourself. . . .

As you hear these words move back through your awareness, let these words carry you back into the past, way back into your past, into your childhood. . . . Beginning to remember, *vividly* remember, times in your childhood where you were told to be a man—"Don't cry, be a man." . . . "Don't show your pain, be a man." . . . "Don't be scared, be a man." . . . "Don't be soft, be a man.". . . Be a Real Man. Remember all those times you were expected to be a Real Man, remember them, re-create them now.

◆ ˙ ◆ ◆

Now with your loving, healing, comforting energies give your boyhood self what he really needed . . . change the demands . . . let the fears and the hurts be felt and soothed . . . transform the expectations into sympathetic, tender understanding . . . soften each of the scenes . . . reclaim all that you really felt, make yourself whole again. . . . Transform the constrictions and re-create the scenes so you are free to be who you truly are, feeling the fullness of what it is to be human. . . . Change the energy of the scenes, make them fully human.

◆   ◆   ◆

Now go back to those times where you were afraid but had to pretend to be brave . . . remember times you were bullied. . . . Rough times, tough times . . . times you bullied others . . . hard times, cold times. . . . Remember times you *had* to prove something. . . . Times *you* had something to prove . . . remember these times . . . times with friends, times with foes . . . fights you had . . . remember, *vividly* remember, re-create these times in your awareness now.

◆   ◆   ◆

Now imagine the warmth of the sun, the warmth of your healing self, the kindness of the others, let the warmth melt away the hostility, thaw the icy rivalry, let all the antagonisms drain down into the ground. . . . Imagine a gentle rain clearing the air, draining away the pain, the competition, the fear of shame . . . as the ground softens with the gentle rain feel the whole scene soften. . . . Imagine everyone letting down their guard. . . . As the rain nourishes the grass and it grows greener, taller, kindness and caring nourishes people and we grow fuller . . . fill the scenes, heal the scenes with kindhearted energy . . . light-hearted energy.

◆   ◆   ◆

Remember all those times you had to measure up . . . remember those times you had to be smarter . . . be stronger . . . be faster . . . be bigger . . . all those times you had to prove yourself . . . all those times you had to measure up . . . you had to perform to be accepted, to be recognized you had to be better than the next guy . . . remember all those times . . . bring them back to awareness now. . . . Remember them, *vividly* remember them . . . re-create them now.

◆   ◆   ◆

Bring in the warm, tender, kindhearted healing qualities . . .
reassure your past self that he is already good enough, reassure him
that he's fine the way he is. . . . Change the atmosphere of the
scenes . . . ground out all the frenzied striving . . . create a climate
of affirmation of everyone, appreciating differences. Imagine
everyone encouraging, supporting, cooperating with one another.
You aren't expected to know it all already, instead everyone teaches
one another, feeling that it's safe to make mistakes. . . . Drain away
the fear of shame . . . heal the scenes . . . fill the scenes with
kindness, encouragement and respect.

◆   ◆   ◆

Feel the quality of energy change within you as you heal the past.
Feel yourself becoming more flexible and caring. . . . As you relax,
your feelings flow through you with ease. . . . As you ease up you
become a fuller being . . . feel this. . . . As you let go you become
extremely sensitive to those around you, you are enriched by your
sensitivity, for it is in sensitivity that you truly discover others.

Now scan your present life, bring to awareness your relationships
with your family . . . your friends . . . your co-workers. . . . Bring
to awareness different things you're involved in. . . . Notice the
emotional climate in the different spheres of your life. . . . Notice
if that boy who had to be so hard and invincible, notice if he's
active in any of your relationships now. . . . Look within and find
that part of yourself that still feels he needs to prove himself, he
needs to perform, to shine out, to dominate . . . he needs to know
it all, to be in control of everything. . . . That part of yourself that
thinks he knows what's best for everyone. . . . Find that part of
yourself. The boss inside, the commander-and-chief within, the
domineering one who thinks he knows it all. . . . Find him inside,
for he is uptight, cold and lonely.

◆   ◆   ◆

Imagine taking care of him, imagine being compassionate with him
. . . be gentle, be kind . . . do what you need to do to take care of
him, so he too can relax . . . let go of having to know and loosen
up . . . let him heal so he can be tender and trusting . . . so he can
be sensitive and emotional. As he relaxes you can truly join with
others, share with others, care with others . . . be human
together. . . . Feel these qualities beginning to spread out into all
your relationships now, so these are the qualities that are active. In
so doing you can truly connect with meaningful depth.

◆   ◆   ◆

Imagine being able to express yourself fully, passionately, while
remaining within your own space, express yourself fully while
respecting others. . . .

Now transform any ideas you have of women and what they're
all suited for . . . the work they are supposed to do . . . what you
expect them to do for you. . . . Any views you have of them as
objects of desire to be conquered, possessed and controlled. . . .
Let it all soak into the ground, healed by the earth.

◆   ◆   ◆

Feel yourself respecting the integrity, the intelligence, the strength
of all women. . . . Imagine welcoming women to express themselves
fully . . . imagine everyone sharing—discovering who we each
truly are . . . shedding the prescribed roles, free to get to know who
we really are. . . . As we do we are all healed. . . . We are whole
human beings again. . . . Celebrate the kindness of men, the
competence and strength of women. Share in equality, imagine
it. . . . Imagine the humanizing experience, the creative, humanizing experience of discovering our fullest potential, men being soft
and strong, women being soft and strong. . . . All of us supporting
one another in discovering our true selves. Imagine the whole

society full of creative and receptive people, powerful, yet supportive of each other. . . . Imagine this time, all the "shoulds" of who
one is "supposed" to be, all the shells that imprison us are broken
and no one has to perform anymore. . . . No more expectations of
who we're "supposed" to be . . . feel us joining together . . .
everyone providing room for others to express themselves with
passion yet within their own space. Everyone connected, everyone
respected. . . . Acknowledge your commitment for creating this
time when we can be human beings together, living in a climate of
mutual respect and support.

◆   ◆   ◆

Imagine being open to hearing feedback whenever you fall back
into dehumanizing ways of being. . . . Be gentle with yourself, so
you can learn new ways. Be patient with yourself so you can
change.

◆

Imagine sharing with and caring for other men, creating a community of men. . . . Imagine being able to share with other men, so
they too can relax and join with others. . . . Imagine all kindhearted men being able to bring other men around, so that all the
pin-ups come down and the patriarchy begins to disintegrate. . . .
With your humanity, with your healing strength you are all part of
healing our culture, creating a time when everyone is safe to
express their humanity. . . . A time of sharing, of caring, of trust.

Healing the Organization

Bring to mind the group, the organization you work with. Imagine a place you often meet . . . imagine everyone meeting in this place. Re-create the details of the scene, each of the people, what they're wearing, where they're sitting, the atmosphere of the scene.

◆

Feel the spirit that unites you, the convictions that you share. . . . What you all believe in, what you aspire to . . . the visions that you share. . . . Feel all of this flowing between you. Give yourself a moment to believe in what you're doing together; why you're doing what you're doing . . . know that together you can make a difference, you will make a difference. . . . Feel the spirit that unites you.

◆

Alone you cannot do it; together you can; together you can make a difference; you *need* one another. . . . Acknowledge the qualities that each person brings.

◆

Joined together you are a powerful force. . . . Building on one another, learning from one another, feel the dynamism . . . experience the vast intelligence of the collective mind you create with each of your qualities joined together.

◆

Let yourself trust it, know that together you can come up with the best course of action, together you're extremely resourceful. Let yourself reside in the collective mind of which you are a part; trust it. . . . As everyone opens to trusting the whole, great power is unleashed. . . . Imagine working in concert, in harmony, dynamic and powerful. . . . Imagine being able to depend on one another, count on each other, rely on the group mind. Feel how it is to work in unison, all of you joined together in effective work, each person appreciated, each person adding to the whole, everyone building on the others and the whole becoming much greater than the sum of its parts. . . . Great power is unleashed.

◆

Change is constant, new situations emerge, people learn, people change, nothing is permanent but change itself. . . . Imagine the group mind, the collective intelligence being so fluid, so cohesive, that it can effectively respond to whatever new situations arise, like a chameleon that changes color whenever need be, yet moves in the direction it chooses. . . . Feel the agility of the group, responsive and open while staying on course. . . . To do this within your unity, diversity is needed for different strengths are needed at different times. And people have different capabilities. . . .

To make the ideal real, to manifest your vision, what is real *now* must be fully grasped, and worked with, and so again, within your unity diversity is needed. All the different perspectives dance together bringing all the angles into clear view; all the complexities, all the subtleties are brought into focus. . . . As you struggle over your different perspectives understanding becomes much sharper, much deeper, and together you come to a greater understanding. Feel how this is so. . . . If you all thought the same you would become dense, brittle, dogmatic—unable to fully grasp the situation, unable to rise to the occasion. Take time to rejoice in your differences. It is out of differences that learning grows, it is out of differences that creativity is evoked. Rejoice in your differences. . . . It is diversity within unity that creates flexibility and your collective mind becomes brilliant . . . concentrating your energies, together you can always come up with the best course of action. Grounded in your unity, embracing your diversity, great creativity is unleashed. . . . Feel the spirit of your collectivity, united in purpose, strong, powerful and effective. . . . Trust it.

◆   ◆   ◆

To fully embody the potential of your work, to deepen your unity, to advance your purpose, you must discover and amend whatever impedes the flow of energy between you. . . . For without easy flow of energy rigidity or decay sets in. . . . To keep your group dynamic and vital you need to discover what impedes the collective intelligence, what obstructs the activity. There is always something that hinders the progress of the work. If you watch for these things, you can learn from them, you can amend them and in so doing you empower yourselves to be much more effective. You maintain your flexibility, you maintain vital collective health, you keep the group alive and well. Just as you need to care for the health of your body, you need to care for the health of your organization, keep the energy flowing. . . .

As you hear the questions that follow let them illuminate the terrain the group works in, let your awareness discover the atmosphere of the work, the current character of the group. Allow these questions to bring into light the workings of the work. In so doing you discover the weak links *before* they break. . . . While keeping in the forefront of your awareness your unity and diversity, bring sharply into focus each of the members and all the activities in the life of the group.

◆

Reflect, discover, notice: Where the energy is hot or cold, where it is fluid or dense . . . how does the energy flow?. . . Does it stand still anywhere? Is it too concentrated in one place and lacking in another? . . What is the quality of exchange between people?. . .

What are different people engaged in?. . . Are each person's talents fully exercised?. . . What roles do people play?. . . Any stereotypes being perpetuated?. . . Is everyone equally respected?. . . Is anyone taking a one-up or one-down position?. . . Does anyone expect special treatment?. . . Are some consistently taken more seriously while others are consistently discounted?. . . Is anyone becoming increasingly isolated?. . . Is there much said *about* someone and little said to them?. . . In the name of peace do things slide by that should be rectified?. . . Do you let them go because they don't affect you personally?. . . Are mistakes touched on lightly, not given the attention they really deserve?. . . Are you aware of your own weaknesses yet remain complacent?. . . Do you take exception to yourself?. . .

What do people complain about?. . . Is any one person blamed?. . . What's demoralizing?. . . What's stressful?. . . What is going on inside of you, inside of others that feeds the problem? What's going on in society that feeds it?. . . In what atmosphere does it thrive?. . .

Is each person reliable?. . . accountable?. . . honest and sincere?. . . What are people's intentions?. . . What aspect of themselves are they acting out of?. . . Is everyone caring?. . . Principled?. . . Are people supported in their personal lives?. . . Is there room for feelings . . . for fun, for humor, for acknowledging appreciation of one another?

◆   ◆   ◆

Where is the *main* source of tension?. . . What are the different sides?. . . Does the tension grow out of differing points of view?. . . Is there an atmosphere of safety and respect in which to fully express and struggle over different approaches so everyone learns, so understanding is heightened?. . . Or does tension grow

out of different styles of work?. . . Or lack of communication?
Reflect, review all that has come into focus.

◆

What's holding back forward motion?. . . Where are the weakest
links that are calling for immediate attention? Isolate them so they
can be mended before they cause serious trouble.

◆　◆　◆

What particular acts are a reflection of this weakness?. . . What
specifically happened?. . . Who?. . . When?. . . Where?. . .
How does the greater society come into play?. . . What in the
histories of the group and individuals gave rise to this limita-
tion?. . . How do you collude with it?. . . Answer each of these
questions in your reflection

◆　◆　◆

For the particular weak links you have been focusing on, notice
what is needed to remedy the situation, make the links strong
again. . . . What new actions are called for?. . . What new
attitudes are called for?. . . What can you do to support it coming
about?. . . What kind of atmosphere will nurture the change, so it
takes root?

◆　◆　◆

Remember, people change; remember, change is constant; people
learn, people do change. . . . Reside in the collective power of
your group mind. Notice what needs to be done to create a trusting
atmosphere in which anyone can acknowledge their individual
limitations, in which everyone can acknowledge the collective
limitations. . . . Create a nurturing atmosphere in which true
learning can take place . . . an atmosphere grounded in mutual
commitment to your shared conviction, an atmosphere of care, of
trust, of openly learning from mistakes . . . an atmosphere that
remembers everyone has been afflicted by our society . . . imagine

everyone supported by the collective intelligence. Imagine everyone discovering where patience is needed and where a push is
needed. . . . Together you can investigate and discover what needs
to be done. . . . It is out of learning from mistakes that true
development takes place. Imagine everyone welcoming criticism. . . . Imagine everyone taking responsibility for their side of
what has been done . . . and what needs to be done.

◆　◆　◆

Imagine expressing all that has been made clear for you in this
meditation, especially what in yourself and others needs to be
criticised. Give yourself the confidence you need to express
yourself. Know that in so doing you empower the work.

◆

Trust the strength of your collectivity, of which you are all a part.
Trust the intelligence of your group mind, the agility of your
activities, trust the progress of the work. . . . To fully allow yourself
to commit yourself to the work, notice if you have any personal
anxieties that hold you back, that are calling for attention. . . . Is
there anything you need to ask for personally?. . . Imagine
expressing your concern . . . imagine being cared for and supported
by the collective resources.

◆　◆　◆

Take time to appreciate each of the people in your group. . . .
Imagine everyone expressing their appreciation of each other . . .
sense the group becoming light-hearted amidst all the important
concerns.

◆

Reside in the power you create together . . . power you can use to
affect the world . . . power you can each use to move through the
world more effectively. . . . Notice how your ability to deal with
people who promote what you struggle against is greatly

enhanced. . . . Imagine the progress of the work becoming increasingly effective. . . . Honor your shared work. . . . Trust each other
. . . trust life, the flexibility, the resilience, the self-healing power
intrinsic to life. . . . Feel the life of your organization always
growing, always changing, always making progress. . . . Celebrate
it. Trust the future.

Countout

Go over all that you have experienced in this meditation . . .
insights you've gained . . . any choices you've made.

◆

Know that the very fact that you can imagine all these things
makes them real—makes them possible. The energy already exists.

Imagine a time that reveres patience . . . care is shared . . .
respect is commonplace . . . trust is everywhere . . . a time where
everyone taps great life-giving powers . . . power surges up from
deep within each of us. And the power outside all of us is equally
distributed among us . . . everyone has power inside . . . outside
. . . inside out.

In a moment I'm going to cou. ι from one to five, at the count of
five, you'll open your eyes remembering all that you've experienced
. . . feeling refreshed, revitalized and relaxed. . . .

ONE—becoming more aware of the room around you. . . .

TWO—coming up slowly now. . . .

THREE—at the count of five you'll open your eyes feeling relaxed, revitalized, and refreshed, remembering all that you've experienced. . . .

FOUR—coming up now, bringing with you your sense of well-being. . . .

FIVE!—eyes open, feeling refreshed, revitalized, and relaxed, remembering all that you've experienced, feeling a sense of well-being. Ready and able to express the visions you have evoked.

Annotated References

Chapter Three

1. Meditating on a quality is a therapeutic technique from psychosynthesis. See *The Act of Will* by Roberto Assagioli, M.D., Viking, New York, 1974.

Chapter Five

1. Capra, Fritjof, *The Turning Point*, Simon & Schuster, New York, 1982. This book describes, in easily understandable terms, the findings and political implications of physics, and the limitations of the classic scientific paradigm. Carolyn Merchant's *The Death of Nature*, Harper & Row, San Francisco, 1980, is a comprehensive book detailing the history of science. See also *Women and Nature* by Susan Griffin, Harper & Row, New York, 1978, and Appendix A of *Dreaming the Dark*, by Starhawk (cited later). And most of all, keep your eyes open for David Kubrin's forthcoming *Marxism and Witchcraft*.
2. Mander, Jerry, *Four Arguments for the Elimination of Television*, William Morrow, New York, 1978. This book is very important in fully exposing the impact of television as hazardous to the health of society.
3. Capra, op. cit.
4. Zukav, Gary, *The Dancing Wu Li Masters*, William Morrow, New York, 1980.
5. Capra, op. cit.
6. Ostrander, Sheila, and Schroeder, Lynn, *Psychic Discoveries Behind the Iron Curtain*, Prentice-Hall, Englewood Cliffs, New Jersey, 1970.

7. Mitchell, Edgar D., *Psychic Exploration*, Putnam, New York, 1974.
8. Koestler, Arthur, *The Roots of Coincidence*, Random House, New York, 1972.
9. Ibid.
10. Mander, op. cit.
11. Ibid.
12. Pogrebin, Letty Cottin, *Grow Up Free, Raising Your Child in the 80's*, William Morrow, New York, 1978.
13. Mander, op. cit.
14. Ibid.
15. Pogrebin, op. cit.
16. Ibid.
17. Ibid.

Chapter Seven

1. *Fatal Accident Reporting System 1981*, National Highway Traffic Safety Administration, 1982.
2. Stellman, Jeanne M., and Daum, Susan M., *Work Is Dangerous to Your Health*, Vintage Books, New York, 1973.
3. Pelletier, Kenneth R., *Mind as Healer, Mind as Slayer*, Delta, New York, 1977.
4. Capra, op. cit.
5. Hughes, Richard and Brewin, Robert, *Tranquilizing of America*, Warner Books, New York, 1979.
6. Castleman, Michael, "On Staying Alive," *Source Book on Health and Survival*, ed., Amanda Spake, Foundation for National Progress, San Francisco, 1981.
7. Illich, Ivan, *Medical Nemesis*, Bantam, New York, 1976. This is an extremely well-researched and thorough exposé of modern medicine.
8. Ibid.
9. Gorz, André, *Ecology as Politics*, South End Press, Boston, 1980. The chapter on health care in this book is the best political analysis of medicine I have come across.
10. Illich, op. cit.
11. Drummond, Hugh, *Spirited Guide to Health Care in a Dying Empire*, Grove Press, New York, 1980.
12. Ibid.
13. Ibid.
14. Gorz, op. cit.
15. Capra, op. cit.

16. Ibid.
17. Ibid.
18. Ibid.
19. Drummond, op. cit.
20. Capra, op. cit.
21. Gorz, op. cit.
22. Ibid.
23. Simonton, O. Carl, M.D., Mathews-Simonton, Stephanie, and Creighton, James L., *Getting Well Again*, Bantam, New York, 1978. This book is a must if you are struggling with any death-threatening disease.
24. Mander, op. cit.
25. Gorz, op. cit.

Chapter Eight

1. Roberts, Jane, *The Nature of Personal Reality, a Seth Book*, Prentice-Hall, Englewood Cliffs, New Jersey, 1974. All of Jane Roberts' books are good, but this one is required reading for anyone who wants to understand the dynamic relationship between consciousness and reality, experience and beliefs.

Chapter Nine

1. Mitford, Jessica, *Kind and Unusual Punishment, the Prison Business*, Random House, New York, 1974.
2. Lyons, Gracie, *Constructive Criticism*, Issues in Radical Therapy, Oakland, 1976. This is Lyons' apt description and an important contribution to the resources for keeping any group alive and well. She clearly delineates the detrimental influences of society on our thinking and behavior, as well as providing easy communication guidelines.
3. Freire, Paulo, *Pedagogy of the Oppressed*, Seabury Press, New York, 1970. Freire's work analyzes in depth the difference between education that thinks with people as opposed to for people, i.e., teaching how to think—not what to think.
4. Rosenberg, Marshall, *From Now On*, New Society Publishers, 1984 (4722 Baltimore Ave., Philadelphia, 19143). This section is an adaptation of a communication process developed by Rosenberg. His book is extremely good for facilitating supportive relationships.

Chapter Ten

1. Harding, Vincent, *There Is a River, The Black Struggle for Freedom in America*, Vintage Books, Random House, New York, 1983. This book details the struggle of African Americans from the beginning of the slave trade through Reconstruction. Harding has a deep feel for the role of spirituality in political struggle. It is a sobering book because it so clearly depicts how ingrained racism is in our country, but it is also inspiring to grasp the depth of the legacy of Black struggle.

2. Berry Wendell, *Unsettling of America*, Avon Books, New York, 1977. This book is very important in gaining what I would call a spiritual understanding of our relationship to the land and the devastating effects of agribusiness. See also his book, *The Gift of Good Land*, North Point Press, San Francisco, 1981.

3. Churchill, Ward, ed., *Marxism and Native Americans*, South End Press, 1983. Preface, Winona Laduke. This book is an important contribution to grappling with the philosophical implications of Marxism.

4. Slater, Philip, *Earthwalk*, Bantam, Doubleday, New York, 1975. Slater has an amazing knack for summing up Western cultural limitations.

5. *The Global 2000 Report to the President*, prepared by the Council on Environmental Quality and the State Department, U.S. Government Printing Office, Washington, D.C. (Carter Administration).

6. *Statistical Abstract of the United States*, U.S. Department of Commerce, Bureau of the Census, Washington, D.C., 1984.

7. *Encyclopedia of American Crime*, Sifakis, Carl, Facts on File Inc., New York, 1982 (Murder of Kitty Genovese).

8. Berry, op.cit.

9. Adding "dialectical humanism" to dialectical materialism was first put forward by James Boggs in *Racism and the Class Struggle*, Monthly Review Press, 1970. This book is a must for understanding the role racism has played in the development of our country; particularly see the chapter "Uprooting Racism and Racists in the United States." In getting a handle on the Marxist dialectical materialist method of thinking see *Elementary Principles of Philosophy* by Georges Politzer, International Publishers, 1976, and *Four Essays on Philosophy* by Mao Tse-Tung, Foreign Languages Press, Peking, 1968, especially the section "On Contradiction." Both of these books are good but do not include dialectical humanism and therefore neglect the central role choice plays in development.

10. Attributed to Martin Niemoeller, a German clergyman.

11. Berry, op. cit.

12. *Manifesto for an American Revolution*, National Organization for an American Revolution, 1982 (National Center, Box 2617, Philadephia, 19121). This book is both pragmatic and visionary at the same time. It realistically and nondogmatically assesses our nation's problems and what is necessary to overcome them while at the same time it puts forward a vision of a nation based on decentralized forms of power and a new sense of social responsibility.

13. Dr. Helen Caldicott, interview in the *Sierra Yodeler*, Jan., 1980.

14. Derived from *Your Income Tax Dollars at Work*, War Resisters League, 1984 (339 Lafayette St., New York, 10012).

15. Barbara Boxer, U.S. Congresswoman, quoted by Herb Caen, *San Francisco Chronicle*, May 27, 1982.

16. Article on the Pledge, by Leonid Brezhnev, read by Andrei A. Gromyko at U.N. Special Disarmament Session, *N.Y. Times*, June 16, 1982. Also see Speech by K.V. Chernenko at a meeting in Moscow, March 2, 1984, called *Safeguard Peace and Ensure the People's Well-being*, Novosti Press Agency Publishing House, Moscow, 1984.

17. Ellsberg, Daniel, *Protest and Survive*, eds. E.P. Thompson and Dan Smith, Monthly Review Press, New York, 1981. An important book in deepening one's understanding of the nuclear issue.

18. Lappé, Frances Moore, Collins, Joseph, and Kinley, David, *Aid as Obstacle, Twenty Questions about Foreign Aid and the Hungry*, Institute for Food and Development Policy, 1980, 1981. (1885 Mission St. San Francisco, 94103). If you want to understand the real impact of our "aid" it is clearly delineated in this work.

19. *Manifesto*, op. cit.

20. Samuelson, Paul A., *Economics: An Introductory Analysis*, 7th ed., New York, 1967.

21. *San Francisco Chronicle*, August 3, 1984.

22. Chris Hedges, *Christian Science Monitor*, May 14, 1981.

23. Herman, Edward S., *The Real Terror Network*, South End Press, Boston, 1982. This is a frightening exposé of our government's role in "protecting freedom" world-wide. A well-researched documentation of the hypocritical U.S. policies in a string of harrowing tales, including the use of torture to maintain "freedom."

24. I am indebted to Winona Laduke, op. cit., for this graphic metaphor.

25. Slater, Philip, *Wealth Addiction*, E.P Dutton, Inc., New York, 1983. An insightful depiction of the psychology of capitalism and greed,

and like all of Slater's writing, it is very entertaining reading.

26. *Statistical Yearbook*, United Nations, New York, 1981.

27. Pete Hamill, *San Francisco Chronicle*, Nov. 11, 1983.

28. Barnet, Richard J. and Müller, Ronald E., *Global Reach*, Simon & Schuster, New York, 1974. This book is an in-depth analysis of the power of the multi-national corporations, something which is indispensable for all of us to understand if we are going to bring about a just society.

29. Schumacher, E.F., *Good Work*, Harper & Row, New York, 1979. For a more comprehensive description of Schumacher's perspective see also *Small is Beautiful, Economics as if People Mattered*, Harper & Row, New York, 1973. This book fully elaborates on the difference between quality and quantity. Ernest Callenbach's novel, *Ecotopia*, Doubleday, New York, 1975, graphically illustrates what a decentralized, steady state, ecologically sound economy would be like.

30. Berry, op. cit.

31. Greene, Felix, *The Enemy*, Random House, 1971. This book is very readable and clearly depicts the contradictions of capitalism that unavoidably lead to imperialism.

32. "Pursuing your own hustle" is a description to be found in Boggs, James and Grace Lee, Paine, Freddy and Lyman, *Conversations in Maine, Exploring Our Nation's Future*, South End Press, Boston, 1978. This book is full of profound insight into the nature of American culture. Although it doesn't directly name spirituality, I think it is invaluable in deepening one's understanding of the relationship between spirituality and politics. See also the Boggses' book *Revolution and Evolution in the Twentieth Century*, Monthly Review Press, 1974, which clearly transforms the common view that revolution is simply a dramatic rebellion—"shooting it out in the streets"—into an understanding of the historical role revolution has played in the advancement and development of what it means to be human.

33. Slater, *Earthwalk*, op. cit.

34. *The Global 2000 Report*, op. cit.

35. Greene, op. cit.

36. Slater, *Wealth Addiction*, op. cit.

37. Slater, *Earthwalk*, op. cit.

38. Ibid.

39. I am indebted for this analogy to Letty Cottin Pogrebin, op. cit.

40. Starhawk, *Dreaming the Dark, Magic, Sex and Politics*, Beacon Press, Boston, 1982. Starhawk's work is central in healing the separations between politics and spirituality.

41. Counted in local supermarket, September, 1984.
42. Berry, op. cit.

Chapter Eleven

1. *Declaration of Independence*, 1776.
2. Harding, op. cit.
3. Greene, op. cit.
4. *San Francisco Chronicle*, April 21, 1984. See also *Inside the Company: CIA Diary* by Philip Agee, Doubleday, New York, 1975. (He also resigned from the CIA.)
5. Starhawk, op. cit.
6. Hinton, William', *Fanshen, A Documentary of Revolution in a Chinese Village*, Random House, New York, 1966. This is a wonderful account of the concrete differences the revolution made in a village in China. For added insights into the importance and impact of criticism, see *Prisoners of Liberation* by Allyn and Adele Rickett, China Books, San Francisco, 1981.
7. Baldwin, James, "Fifth Avenue Uptown," in *Man Alone*, Dell, New York, 1962.
8. Metaphor attributed to Malcolm X.
9. Harding, op. cit.

Intuitive Problem-Solving Resources

Iglehart, Hallie, *Woman Spirit, A Guide to Women's Wisdom*, Harper & Row, San Francisco, 1983.

Gawain, Shakti, *Creative Visualization*, Bantam, New York, 1982.

Mariechild, Diane, *Mother Wit: A Feminist Guide to Psychic Development*, Crossing Press, Trumansburg, New York, 1981.

Wallace, Amy and Henkin, Bill, *The Psychic Healing Book*, Wingbow Press, Berkeley, 1978.

Acknowledgements

The book was born one night six years ago when I was driving home on the Bay Bridge from one of my weekly support groups. I realized that the meditations I led in the group were universally applicable, for I simply led them in response to the concerns of the members each week, the same kinds of concerns that come up for all of us in our day-to-day lives. So I began to get them transcribed and took a pile of transcripts to my mother, Casey Adair, who is an editor by profession, to see what she thought about them. She volunteered to edit this book but said I needed something to tie together all the meditations. That sounded fine to me—the only problem was that I was a teacher, not a writer.

I went to my friend Lynn Johnson, who was a writer, and who about a year earlier, out of frustration, had offered to help me update the handouts I used in my theta workshops. (There was a lag of about three years between what I was teaching and the scripts I gave people to work with.) Lynn was excited about the idea of collaborating on a book. Without Lynn's support, this book would never have become a reality—I am profoundly indebted to him. For the following two years I would go over to his house in the mornings, we would do an energy circle and I'd pace and back and forth dictating the information I taught in the workshops while Lynn typed, occasionally interrupting with a suggestion for improvement. Then Lynn's life took a major turn: he got involved with a business that left him with no time to work with me. There I was, half-way through the book and unable to either type or write; I was forced to become a writer (I have yet to learn to type). I developed a third ear to listen to what I said in my head and then wrote it down.

Above all I want to express appreciation to my mother and editor, Casey, who gave me enormous moral support and was willing to deal with my writing. Her editing was miraculous to me. The original draft of the last half of the book was written in a series of unrelated paragraphs. Imagine a hundred pages of that. The only order to work with was which chapter each bit belonged in. Casey indeed has been a miracle worker! And a dedicated one at that, she has devoted hours upon hours every week for four years.

Thank heaven for the barter system! This book would not have been possible without it. Over the years participants in my groups and workshops have bartered with me. They offered their skills in lieu of payment for groups, workshops or individual sessions. This book was truly a community effort.

Julia Cato has also played an indispensible role. She has been part of every stage in the development of the book: She transcribed over a hundred meditations which provide the backbone for all the meditations in the book; she wrote large portions of the energy circle chapter; she typed all the rough draft; she helped edit and proofread all the meditations.

I am grateful to Peni Hall who, through the years, kept my workshops in order by being sure the word got out. And thanks to many others who traded with me, helping to transcribe, type and proof over the years. Special appreciation to those who dedicated heaps of time: Gidalia, Judith O'Connor, Kathleen Defendorf, Colette Andrews, Barbara Johnson, and Autumn Riddle. And to others who helped out: John Adair, Peter Adair, Tina Ann, Kathy Bowden, Wendy Cutler, Ginger Gilcrease, Judith Fischer, Virginia Harris, Ann Hershey, Trisha Joel, Hilary Johnson, Diana Lion, Meridian, Nance Massarella, Kirie Pederson, France Montpas, Margaret Smullin, Ellen Trabilcy, Emily Warn, Alison Warner, Batya Weibaum, and Beth Youhn.

Thanks to Maurya Godchaux for doing the research I needed for Chapter Ten. And thanks to Jane Lev, Murray Edelman, Janet Bogardus, Janet Greyson, Marjory Nelson and Roma Guy for taking the time to be interviewed about the impact of energy circles in their lives.

Then there are the folks at Wingbow who agreed to co-publish with me, especially Randy Fingland, who is the antithesis of the ruthless editor stereotype—he spent hours explaining this or that process to me and he was both encouraging and agreeable to all the changes I suggested.

Special credit goes to Sasha Rosen, who spent over a hundred hours coordinating and getting the whole thousand-page manuscript keyed into her word processor and coded for the typesetter. I will always remember her for the time she stayed up all night getting all the dots spaced right in six hundred pages of meditations.

It has been a pleasure working on the production with David Blake, Bob Steiner and Christina Kelly and all the others at Turn-around Typesetting, and an honor to work with the designer, Janet Wood, and the illustrator, Joan Carol, both of whom have superb talent and were enormously patient with me.

My grateful thanks to all those who read the manuscript at various stages of its development and gave me both encouragement and insightful criticisms: Zelda Barnett, Joan Carol, Janet Cole, Vince Dijanich, Hugh Drummond, Linda Farthing, Donnie Gold-macher, Suzie Goldmacher, Paul Kival, Julia Lasage, Tom Mosmil-ler, Torie Osborne, Freddy Paine, Will Roscoe, Brad Rose, Philip Slater, and Marlene Willis. And to those who both read it and additionally helped me navigate through the publishing world: John Boonstra, David Charlsen, Ruth Gottstein, Roland Dickey, and Sherry Thomas. Special thanks to Roland, who later patiently explained what picas, m spaces, leading and running heads were.

I have heartfelt appreciation for my comrades, whose support is particularly important to me (having spent years being viewed by political activists as being a little off my rocker), Grace Lee Boggs, Jimmy Boggs, James McFadden, Bill Aal, Rick Whaley, Ellen Smith, and James Jackson, and special thanks to Grace, Jimmy, and Bill, who each spent hours pouring over the manuscript and gave extremely helpful and detailed feedback.

Special thanks to those who organized workshops for me in their home towns. I'm also very grateful to the SPIRiT collective who supported my work in myriad ways. I am appreciative of my house-mates and comrades who were willing to relieve me of my respon-sibilities and do a little extra for the last six months. Special thanks to my partner, Vince Dijanich, who has shown incredible patience. Thanks to Penny Doran and Sally Davis who provided their homes when I needed to get away to work.

On the spiritual side I want to express my warm appreciation to everyone in my women's groups who, week after week, year after year, sent energy to the book. I especially want to thank those who have been in it for the long haul: Roma Guy, Virginia Harris, Julia Cato, Peni Hall, and Diane Jones.

There are a few people whose work has had an enormous impact on my internal development. On the spiritual side there are José Silva and Jane Roberts. On the political side, Ann Tompkins, who taught me dialectical thinking; David Kubrin, a historian of science who gave me a class analysis of the historical role of rationalism; and most of all, my comrades who, in an atmosphere of mutual respect and dedication, created a context for me to deepen my political understanding by leaps and bounds.

It was a special honor to be entrusted with the experiences of those who came together to talk about the impact sexism and racism had on their lives. These meetings were extremely moving and were a great help in the creation of the meditations. My comrades Rosie Goldsmith, Bill Aal, Melissa Young, and David Marcial were the ones behind the one for white people. Helen Stewart, Virginia Harris, and Lee Woodward immensely deepened my understanding of the impact of racism on people of color. Additional insight for this one was gained from Audre Lorde's essay "Eye to Eye: Black Women, Hatred and Anger" (to be found in Sister Outsider, Crossing Press). Tom Mosmiller, Bill Aal and Gil Lopez helped with the one for men. Women in my support groups helped with the women's meditation: Mickie Spencer, Virginia Harris, Roma Guy, Carol Fusco, Tina Ann, Maurya Godchaux and Gail Kimmel. Special thanks to Virginia and Tom, who went over every word of the final drafts with me. And then to finish it off, Colette Andrews, in typing, made a few insightful improvements.

Thank you all—and those whose names somehow slipped through the cracks.

Most of all, thanks to all those who have participated in my workshops and groups over the years. Your support has not only been objective (providing me with a livelihood), but subjective as well, for it has provided me with the opportunity to learn—and feel a part of a community of people. My development came not through my attending any training but by your doing so—thanks for taking me seriously.

Last week when I was driving the other way on the Bay Bridge, I thought of all the support I've received for the book and it quite literally made me cry. . . . Thanks.

ABOUT THE AUTHOR

Born in 1950, Margo Adair lives in San Francisco and, for the past ten years, has maintained a practice which includes teaching Applied Meditation, Tools for Political Analysis, leading support groups, working with individuals and consulting. She has conducted workshops in Los Angeles, Minneapolis, Seattle, Hawaii, Albuquerque and Vancouver, British Columbia, and she has also worked with people in half-way houses, drug-treatment programs and jails. Margo is a founding member of both the SPIRiT Collective and the Bay Area Chapter of NOAR. Margo is not constrained by academic tradition because she never finished high school. Her process of self-education includes experience in Silva Mind Control techniques, self-hypnosis, brief therapy, biofeedback, Psychic Institute training, psychosynthesis, holistic health, psychedelics, flipping out, radical psychiatry, non-violent persuasion, criticism/self-criticism, and both feminist and Marxist theory. Her perspectives have primarily evolved through continual work with people.

Working Inside Out Meditation Tapes:

All of the meditations in this book are recorded on a series of twenty sixty-minute cassette tapes. They include music specially composed by Stefan Dasho. These recordings are studio-produced with stereo sound and Dolby noise reduction. These are designed to use in conjunction with the book or independently.

Tapes are available *only* in quantities of one, two, three, five, ten, fifteen and the full set of twenty. (The wholesale price of $4.95 each is available for any purchase of twenty or more tapes.)

To order tapes, cut out the form included on page 420 and send it with a cashier's check.

PRICE LIST (Available *only* in the following quantities.)		Shipping & Handling* 4th Class Mail	1st Class Mail	U.P.S.
One Tape @	$10.95	$1.69	$1.90	$2.74
Two Tapes @	$ 9.95 = $19.90	$1.69	$1.90	$2.74
Three Tapes @	$ 8.95 = $26.85	$1.69	$2.25	$2.74
Five Tapes @	$ 7.95 = $39.75	$1.69	$2.53	$2.74
Ten Tapes @	$ 6.95 = $69.50	$1.94	$3.20	$3.16
Fifteen Tapes @	$ 5.95 = $89.25	$2.44	$4.73	$3.57
Full Set or 20 Tapes	$ 4.95 = $99.00	$2.44	$6.33	$3.99

Add 6% or 6½% Sales Tax if inside California

*Prices based upon January 1, 1986 rates. Please check with the United States Postal Service, or United Parcel Service, to ascertain the correct rates if you believe there's been a change.

Working Inside Out tape series:

Tape 1 Side A:	Relaxing
	B:	Symboling/Internalizing a Quality
Tape 2 Side A:	Ocean Breath: Stress Reduction
	B:	Affirmations] [Centering for the Day
Tape 3 Side A:	Rehearsing the Future
	B:	Creativity Flowing
Tape 4 Side A:	Mental House Cleaning] [Self Protection
	B:	Stretching the Imagination] [Running Universal Energy
Tape 5 Side A:	Fear as Challenge
	B:	Stretching Your Confidence into a New Area
Tape 6 Side A:	Vitality of Life/Rapport with Body/Healing
	B:	Healing Attitudes/Food, Rest, Exercise
Tape 7 Side A:	Wise Self
	B:	Respite: Enlighten the Heart and Relieve Pain
Tape 8 Side A:	Sexuality: The Dance of Life
	B:	Enjoyment] [Evoking the Quality Needed
Tape 9A Side A:	Meeting Your Potential Self (uses female pronoun)
	B:	Exploring the Terrain of Your Life
Tape 9B Side A:	Meeting Your Potential Self (uses male pronoun)
	B:	Exploring the Terrain of Your Life
Tape 10 Side A:	Transforming Defeating Messages
	B:	Transforming Trauma into Wisdom
Tape 11 Side A:	Purpose, Choice, Habits
	B:	From Impasse to Insight
Tape 12 Side A:	Integrity of Life
	B:	Equalizing and Enriching Relations
Tape 13 Side A:	Choice Patterns
	B:	Anger Yields Justice
Tape 14 Side A:	Crystal Clear Communications
	B:	Family: Past and Future
Tape 15 Side A:	From Holding On into Openness
	B:	Regaining Honesty and Trust
Tape 16 Side A:	Is It a Want or a Need?
	B:	Caring Acts Heal the Future/Vision
Tape 17 Side A:	Keeping the Faith/Vision
	B:	Empowerment (for People of Color)
Tape 18 Side A:	Healing Organization
	B:	From Racism to Respect (for White People)
Tape 19 Side A:	Who Benefits?
	B:	Nourishing Yourself (for Men)
Tape 20 Side A:	Patience, Endurance, Courage
	B:	Reclaiming the Self (for Women)

] [denotes separate meditations; / denotes combined meditations

TOOLS FOR CHANGE

Sampling of Workshop and Lecture Descriptions

SPIRITUALITY AND POLITICS: Healing the Spirit

For the first time in history we cannot be secure that the next generation will inherit the Earth. Do we secure our future and create a just world with spiritual transformation or political organizing? What is the source of our problems and where is the source of power to bring about solutions? Addressing the limits of both sides, and striving for a synthesis by bringing the human element into politics and political awareness into spiritual practice. It is when we heal the split that we can return to our sense of connectedness, wholeness and have the power to change the way it is.

APPLIED MEDITATION: Intuitive Problem Solving

This workshop takes the hocus-pocus out of spirituality. It teaches how to create a language to speak to one's deeper experience and tap intuitive knowingness. Techniques will be presented to relax, reduce stress and avoid burnout, recognize and avoid defeatist thinking, release creativity and maintain health. Learn how to collectivize consciousness with energy cycles, use the imagination as the medium of psychic awareness, channel healing energy, cultivate faith to energize probabilities, and create positive visions with which to work.

EFFECTIVENESS TRAINING FOR:
Leaders, Practitioners and Organizers

Learn how to establish trust and empower people for their own self-improvement and independence instead of their relinquishing their personal power and empowering you. Conversely, learn how to keep your own energy clear and not take on someone else's problems, thus keeping your relationships on equal terms and avoiding burnout. Come to understand and learn how to transform what commonly divides us. Learn to cultivate and nurture what unites us. Also included: how to design and lead meditations on any issue, and how to insure accessibility through workable sliding scales.

CRITICAL THINKING: Political Analysis Without Dogma

Learn how to make your *own* analysis in an atmosphere of safety, respect and permission to disagree. We will explore the dynamics of power—personal power, collective power, economic power and political power, the differences between a personal and political approach, individual freedom versus social responsibility, the potentials and limits of Spirituality, Feminism, Marxism, and New Age politics—finding ways to take the best and leave the rest.

ADDITIONAL COURSE TITLES

Political:

Keeping the Faith: Healing Self & Organization
Visionary Thinking: Spirituality with No Hocus Pocus
The Enemy Inside: How We Keep One Another Powerless
Criticism/Self-Criticism: Making Conflict Deepen Unity

Relational:

Conflicts: How They Arise, How to Transform Them
I to We Consciousness: Alienation into Collectivity
Energy Circles to Collectivize Consciousness for Insight
Combatting Internalized Sexism, Racism, Homophobia
Equalizing Relationships

Personal:

One-to-One Deep Trance, Problem Solving and Faciliation
Health Through the Power of the Mind

Readings from *Working Inside Out*

Organizational Consulting

For schedules and/or information on organizing a workshop in your area write:

Tools for Change
P.O. Box 14141
San Francisco, CA 94114

Enclosed is a cashier's check for: $ _____

$ _____ for sending me _____ tapes of the numbers
listed below.   (quantity)

$ _____ for shipping (specify shipping method(s),
see page 414).

$ _____ 6 or 6½% tax for California residents.

$ _____ total amount enclosed.

Send me Tape Numbers: _____

Name _____

Address _____

City_____ State _____ Zip _____

Phone_____
(to serve you better if we need to contact you regarding a problem with your order)
Send cashier's check to: Tools for Change
P.O. Box 14141
San Francisco, CA 94114

Please also send me information on:
☐ Workshop schedules
☐ Arranging workshops
☐ Visualization & AIDS cassette series (co-produced by
S.F. Shanti Project)
☐ Personalized meditations that can be recorded for my specific
concerns
☐ Additional *Working Inside Out* tape series order forms
☐ Ordering information for this book